Corporate Value of Enterprise Risk Management

Corporate Value of Enterprise Risk Management

The Next Step in Business Management

SIM SEGAL

WILEY

John Wiley & Sons, Inc.

Published by John Wiley & Sons, Inc., Hoboken, New Jersey.

Published simultaneously in Canada.

For general information on our other products and services or for technical support, please contact our Customer Care Department within the United States at (800) 762-2974, outside the United States at (317) 572-3993 or fax (317) 572-4002.

Wiley also publishes its books in a variety of electronic formats. Some content that appears in print may not be available in electronic books. For more information about Wiley products, visit our web site at www.wiley.com.

Library of Congress Cataloging-in-Publication Data:
Segal, Sim, 1964—
  Corporate value of enterprise risk management : the next step in business management / Sim Segal.
    p. cm.
  Includes index.
  ISBN 978-0-470-88254-2 (cloth); ISBN 978-1-118-02328-0 (ebk);
ISBN 978-1-118-02329-7 (ebk); ISBN 978-1-118-02330-3 (ebk)
  1. Risk management. I. Title.
  HD61.S364 2011
  658.15'5—dc22   2010045243

Printed in the United States of America

10 9 8 7 6 5 4

Contents

PART III: RISK GOVERNANCE AND OTHER TOPICS

Foreword

I N MY FORMER ROLE leading Standard & Poor's ERM evaluations, I visited with hundreds of executives from companies all over the world and in all types of businesses, and discussed their ERM programs. I watched these ERM programs evolve, and witnessed their successes, and sometimes their colossal failures. Much more often than not, firms struggled both with having a clear objective for their ERM efforts and with the day-to-day problems of implementation. This perspective tells me that there is a tremendous need for clear thinking and clear exposition of the actions needed to practice ERM. The value-based approach that Segal developed, and introduces for the first time in this important book, definitely provides that clarity. Many other ERM books merely outline the problem and leave the readers to figure out how to implement a solution on their own. Here you will find each and every step of ERM implementation clearly laid out for the practitioner to follow along. In addition, Segal's approach to ERM:

- Is robust, yet highly practical
- Is able to quantify strategic and operational risks (this alone makes this book a worthwhile read)
- Takes the mystery out of risk appetite, one of the most elusive ERM topics (two-thirds of those believing that defining risk appetite is critical to their ERM programs have not yet done so)
- Supports better decision making

This book is also highly accessible to every business leader. Segal's writing style is smooth and in plain language. He offers crisp insights that can benefit everyone interested in ERM, from the ERM-savvy to the ERM novice.

Finally, this book offers a very credible business case for adopting ERM. I have read nearly every book related to this topic, and I heartily recommend this one. This could well be the only ERM book you will ever need.

—Dave Ingram, CERA
Senior Vice President, Willis Re
Former leader of Standard & Poor's insurance ERM evaluations

Preface

 PURPOSE OF THE BOOK

Adoption of enterprise risk management (ERM) programs is a strong and growing global trend. However, while ERM programs have a lot of potential, traditional approaches to ERM often struggle to generate sufficient buy-in from internal stakeholders, such as business decision-makers. The primary reason for this is that traditional ERM approaches lack a business case for their adoption. In response to this difficulty, I developed the value-based ERM approach, and this book is its first in-depth presentation.

The value-based ERM approach is designed to have a built-in business case for its adoption. At its core, it is a synthesis of ERM and value-based management. This synthesis provides the missing link between risk and return. It is this connection that transforms ERM into a strategic management approach that enhances strategic planning and other business decision making. As a result, the value-based ERM approach is seen by internal stakeholders—business segment leaders, senior management, and the board—as a way to help them achieve their goals of profitably growing the business and increasing company value.

The value-based ERM approach has several other advantages as well. It works equally well in all industry sectors. I have used this approach to help implement ERM programs for corporate entities in a wide range of sectors, such as manufacturing, energy, entertainment, technology, services, telecommunications, banking, and insurance, as well as for non-corporate entities, such as professional associations. The value-based ERM approach also works equally well regardless of geography or accounting system. In addition, the value-based ERM approach is an advanced yet practical approach to ERM. I have used this approach exclusively in my work as an ERM consultant, helping organizations to quickly, fully, and successfully implement their ERM programs.

Finally, the value-based ERM approach also overcomes the three core challenges that prevent traditional ERM programs from achieving their full potential:

1. An inability to quantify strategic and operational risks
2. An unclear definition of risk appetite
3. A lack of integration into business decision making

The value-based approach quantifies all types of risk: strategic, operational, and financial. This is often referred to as the "holy grail" of ERM. I am unaware of any other ERM approach that can fully quantify strategic and operational risks. In addition, the value-based ERM approach provides a clear, quantitative definition of risk appetite that can be used in the risk governance process. Finally, the value-based ERM approach, due to its linkage between risk and return as well as its sheer practicality, fully integrates ERM information into decision making at all levels, from strategic planning to tactical decision making to transactions.

I often am encouraged when I read introductions to allegedly new ERM information in articles, books, and seminars that tout an ERM approach that "adds value" to the business, only to end up disappointed when I find the same old traditional ERM approaches, which have no direct connection to value. In sharp contrast, this book presents an ERM approach that is centrally focused on measuring, protecting, and increasing company value.

 ## INTENDED AUDIENCE

The primary audience for this book is corporate stakeholders, including:

- Heads of ERM programs, such as chief risk officers (CROs) and their staff
- Heads of internal audit
- Heads of compliance
- Senior executives, such as CEOs and CFOs
- Management, such as business segment leaders
- Heads of strategic planning
- Heads of human resources
- Boards of directors, including chairs of audit committees and chairs of risk committees
- Shareholders

- Rating agencies
- Regulators

Other audiences for this book include the following:

- Stakeholders of non-profit organizations, such as charitable organizations and professional associations
- Heads of government bodies
- Financial planners and their customers
- Professors of MBA/EMBA programs in Finance, and their students

Corporate Audiences

Heads of ERM programs, such as chief risk officers (CROs) and their staff, will learn an advanced yet practical approach for either implementing an ERM program for the first time, or for enhancing an existing ERM program. They will learn an ERM approach that offers several advantages, such as:

- Builds buy-in among the business segments, senior management, and the board
- Satisfies all 10 key ERM criteria (which also serve as benchmarking criteria for any ERM program)
- Avoids the five common mistakes of risk identification
- Overcomes the three core challenges of traditional ERM programs by:
    - Quantifying strategic and operational risks in a consistent manner with financial risks
    - Clearly defining risk appetite in a way that it can be used in the risk governance process
    - Integrating ERM into key decision-making processes, including strategic planning, strategic and tactical decisions, and transactions
- Satisfies rating agency ERM requirements
- Satisfies regulatory risk disclosure requirements

Heads of internal audit and heads of compliance will learn how to quantify the value that they bring to the company, in terms of its direct impact on company value. They will also learn their ERM roles and responsibilities.

Senior executives, such as CEOs and CFOs, will learn an ERM approach that can offer them the following advantages:

- Improves the company's shock resistance, making it more likely to achieve the strategic plan goals
- Potentially leads to a higher stock price, resulting from a more effective set of tools for communicating with stock analysts
- Potentially leads to a better rating by satisfying rating agency ERM requirements

Management, such as business segment leaders, as well as heads of strategic planning and heads of human resources, will learn an ERM approach that can offer them the following advantages:

- Well-defined methodology to manage risk exposures to within risk appetite, and quantitative information that supports decisions on risk mitigation alternatives
- Better prioritization of limited resources, by focusing efforts on the most important risks and the most impactful component drivers of the key risk scenarios
- Enhanced strategic planning process, with a more sophisticated and dynamic ability to project results for the baseline scenario as well as key risk scenarios, including upside and downside ranges of outcomes
- Decision-making tool for selecting projects with the best risk–return profile for all types of routine decisions, including strategic planning, strategic and tactical decisions, and transactions
- Enhanced business performance analysis, with metrics that reflect the entire contribution to company value during the past period, and that correct a serious flaw in balanced scorecards
- Improved incentive compensation plan, by (a) providing a firm basis for asserting that it is not a risky compensation plan subject to new SEC disclosure requirements; and (b) better aligning management and shareholder interests through correction of two suboptimal aspects of common compensation schemes

Boards of directors, including chairs of audit committees and chairs of risk committees, will learn the following:

- What questions they should be asking management about risk management practices
- How to gain comfort that the key risks of the organization are well understood and effectively managed

- What their roles and responsibilities are regarding risk governance
- How to satisfy SEC disclosure requirements on risk governance

Shareholders will learn what they should expect from companies in which they invest, in terms of a robust ERM program to protect and grow company value. In addition, they will learn how to identify companies with superior abilities to manage risks, through an enhanced ability to interpret their risk disclosures.

Rating agencies will learn what they should be including in their ERM evaluation criteria. In addition, they will learn an ERM approach that offers them enhanced *prospective* information about a company, including the likelihood that the company will properly execute its strategic plan.

Regulators will learn what they should be requiring from companies to better protect against bankruptcies, as well as shareholder losses generally.

Other Audiences

Stakeholders of non-profit organizations, such as charitable organizations and professional associations, in analogous roles to their corporate counterparts listed earlier, will learn analogous lessons. Using a generalized version of the value-based ERM approach, these stakeholders will learn how to improve the chances of achieving their (usually multiple) goals.

Heads of government bodies will learn how to apply the value-based ERM approach to their entities, and how this can better leverage their limited resources and help them achieve their strategic objectives.

Financial planners and their customers will learn how the value-based ERM concepts can be applied to help individuals identify their key risks, robustly define their risk appetite, and better allocate their assets among a range of financial products (such as investments and insurance), on an integrated basis, to increase the chances of achieving their personal goals.

Professors of MBA/EMBA programs in Finance and their students will learn a full range of ERM concepts and how they are practically applied. This book is currently serving as the basis for an MBA/EMBA course I am teaching at Columbia Business School. Any professor wishing to use this book as a required text for a similar course will be provided with supplementary teaching materials, including the syllabus, lecture materials, exercises and solutions, and exams and solutions.

SUMMARY OF THE CONTENTS

The book is divided into three sections:

Part I: Basic ERM Infrastructure (Chapters 1–3)
Part II: ERM Process Cycle (Chapters 4–7)
Part III: Risk Governance and Other Topics (Chapters 8–10)

Part I: Basic ERM Infrastructure (Chapters 1–3)

Chapter 1, Introduction, highlights the major events over the past 10 years that contributed to the growing popularity of ERM. This provides the context for a better understanding of traditional ERM approaches and their short-comings, which are discussed in the following two chapters. The chapter concludes by discussing two major challenges to the ERM movement.

It is important to clearly define ERM before delving into the heart of our discussions. ERM is a complex and wide-ranging topic. In addition, there is a lot of confusion in the market regarding what ERM is, and, as a result, there are many disparate definitions. Finally, even the concept of risk itself is often understood in differing ways, because it is so common a term as to be taken for granted. We therefore devote the entirety of Chapter 2, Defining ERM, to first defining risk and then defining ERM in four ways: by a basic definition; in terms of the 10 key ERM criteria; by the four steps in the ERM process cycle; and by its fundamental benefits. The 10 key ERM criteria introduced in this chapter are a foundational element for this book, and are revisited frequently throughout. In addition, the 10 key ERM criteria can be used to benchmark any ERM program to determine its level of robustness.

Chapter 3, ERM Framework, begins by discussing the failure of traditional ERM approaches to satisfy the 10 key ERM criteria and the three core challenges to these programs. The chapter then introduces the value-based ERM framework and discusses how it satisfies all 10 key ERM criteria, and how it resolves the three core challenges of traditional ERM programs. The value-based ERM framework is central to all discussions that follow.

Part II: ERM Process Cycle (Chapters 4–7)

Chapter 4, Risk Identification, discusses the first step in the ERM process cycle. The three components of risk identification include risk categorization and definition; qualitative risk assessment; and emerging risk identification. Although risk identification is the first step in the ERM process cycle, traditional approaches are still suboptimal. This chapter discusses the five keys to success-ful risk identification. One of the five keys to success is defining risks by their source, a crucial building block that most organizations fail to construct properly, leading to several difficulties with their ERM programs. In addition, several applications of the risk categorization and definition (RCD) tool are discussed. This chapter concludes with a discussion of two "killer risks."

Chapter 5, Risk Quantification, discusses the second step in the ERM process cycle. This chapter begins by stressing the importance of practical modeling, a critical characteristic of the value-based ERM approach. Next, this chapter discusses how to calculate the baseline company value—an internal calculation of company value consistent with the strategic plan. This is a key element of the value-based approach, which quantifies risks in terms of their potential impact on baseline company value. The chapter then discusses how to quantify individual risk exposures, revealing the secrets of how to quantify all types of risks, including strategic, operational, and financial. This is illustrated with several case studies. The chapter closes with a discussion on how to quantify enterprise risk exposure, the aggregate measure of risk exposure at the enterprise level. This represents the distribution of possible outcomes, capturing combinations of multiple key risk scenarios occurring simultaneously, includ-ing their interactivity.

Chapter 6, Risk Decision Making, discusses the third step in the ERM process cycle. The first decisions involve defining risk appetite (enterprise level tolerance limits) and risk limits (tolerance limits below enterprise level). The discussion reveals how to develop a clear, quantitative definition of risk appetite that can be used in the risk governance process. The chapter then discusses how to integrate ERM information into decision-making processes. This includes enhancing the strategic planning process and providing a universal protocol for all decision making, whether related to risk mitigation or to routine business, such as strategic planning, strategic and tactical decisions, or transactions. In the discussions of mitigation decisions, this chapter reveals how to quantify the value of mitigation in place, which can be used to illustrate the value of internal audit or the compliance department.

Chapter 7, Risk Messaging, discusses the fourth and final step in the ERM process cycle. The first part of this chapter addresses internal risk messaging, which includes integration of ERM into business performance analysis and incentive compensation. One notable element of the business performance analysis discussion is how the value-based ERM approach can correct a fundamental flaw in balanced scorecards. The second part of this chapter discusses external risk messaging, which is about using ERM information for communications with external stakeholders, including shareholders, stock analysts, rating agencies, and regulators.

Part III: Risk Governance and Other Topics (Chapters 8–10)

Chapter 8, Risk Governance, addresses three aspects of risk governance: roles and responsibilities; organizational structure; and policies and procedures. The roles and responsibilities are discussed for internal ERM stakeholders including corporate ERM; the ERM committee; risk experts; business segments; the board of directors; and internal audit. In the discussion of the roles and responsibilities of corporate ERM, an entire section is devoted to listing all the ways in which the value-based ERM approach helps achieve one of their most challenging responsibilities: building buy-in for the ERM program.

Chapter 9, Financial Crisis Case Study, answers the question, "Because banks massively failed, causing the global financial crisis that began in the United States in 2007, and they claim to have been using ERM, can ERM be any good?" The chapter begins with a summary of the financial crisis, and then proceeds to evaluate bank risk management practices against the 10 key ERM criteria to determine whether banks were actually practicing ERM.

Chapter 10, ERM for Non-Corporate Entities, reveals how to generalize the value-based ERM approach for application to non-corporate entities, including non-profit organizations, such as charitable organizations and professional associations; government bodies; and individuals.

The book concludes with a glossary of ERM terms.

Web Site

The following Web page provides additional resources for this book: www.simergy.com/ermbookresources.

The following Web site provides additional resources on ERM: www.simergy.com.

Acknowledgments

I WOULD FIRST LIKE to thank those who reviewed the draft manuscript and provided feedback that improved the quality of this book. I would especially like to recognize those whose contributions of time and effort were unusually generous, and to whom I am deeply indebted: Rich Lauria, Leslie Bauer, Adam Litke, Dale Hall, Michel Rochette, Hugo Rodrigues, and David Romoff provided numerous corrections and insights that enhanced both the content and readability of the text.

In addition, I would like to thank Barbara Minto, inventor of the Minto Pyramid Principle and the author of *The Minto Pyramid Principle: Logic in Writing, Thinking, & Problem Solving*. The ease with which this book flows for the reader is due to the Minto technique, which helps writers clarify their thinking and express concepts logically and smoothly.

Finally, I would like to thank my publisher, John Wiley & Sons, and the outstanding editors with whom I have had the pleasure of working: Sheck Cho, Stacey Rivera, and Chris Gage. I would also like to thank Rachel Rabinowitz for introducing me to Wiley.

Corporate Value
of Enterprise
Risk Management

PART ONE

Basic ERM Infrastructure

1

Introduction

History is the sum total of the things that could have been avoided.

Konrad Adenauer

ENTERPRISE RISK MANAGEMENT, or ERM, is generally defined as follows:

The process by which companies identify, measure, manage, and disclose all key risks to increase value to stakeholders.

One of the challenges with ERM lies in understanding what this definition means. There are many interpretations, and some would say misinterpretations, of this short definition. In the next chapter, we will fully and properly define ERM. For now, consider ERM simply as an approach to treat risk holistically in an organization.

EVOLUTION OF ERM

ERM has been gaining significant momentum in recent years. We will discuss the following eight most important factors driving this trend, which are as follows:

1. Basel Accords
2. September 11th
3. Corporate accounting fraud
4. Hurricane Katrina
5. Rating agency scrutiny
6. Financial crisis
7. Rare events
8. Long-term trends

The first seven factors involve significant discrete events and are listed in chronological order, while the remaining factor includes trends that have developed gradually over time. Some of the discrete events originate from, or relate primarily to, the financial services sector. However, it is helpful for those in all sectors to understand these events because they are commonly known in ERM circles and their impacts on ERM are felt in all industry sectors. In addition, it is helpful to understand the chronology because the order of events has played a role in ERM development. The cumulative impact of events, and the regulatory and corporate responses to them, has led to the current environment for ERM.

 ## BASEL ACCORDS

Basel II,[1] an international guideline for risk management, influenced the advancement of ERM practices in the financial services sector. The Basel Accords are guidelines developed by a group of global banking regulators in an attempt to improve risk management practices. Basel II, the second of two accords developed by the Basel Committee on Banking Supervision, was published in 2001.

There are three pillars in Basel II:

- Pillar 1: Minimum capital requirements
- Pillar 2: Supervisory review
- Pillar 3: Market discipline

Pillar 1 specifies methods to calculate capital requirements, offering standardized options based on industry averages and advanced options for more sophisticated banks based on their own internal models, customized to account for the specifics of the company, its businesses, and its risks, and largely using management's own estimates for most parameters.

Pillar 2 allows for supervisors to review the bank's risk management practices and risk exposures and, if necessary, apply a multiplier to increase the amount of minimum required capital calculated in Pillar 1.

Pillar 3 addresses appropriate risk disclosures.

The most important advancement since Basel I was the expansion of scope to include operational risks, moving banks in the direction of a holistic treatment of risk (although many other risks, including all strategic risks, are still excluded).

In retrospect, it is easy to criticize and say that the Basel Committee failed in their goal, as evidenced by the global financial crisis that began in the United States in 2007. However, these accords were widely adopted and did represent an improvement from prior practices. Even if the Basel Accords fell short of their goal to develop a standard benchmark for stellar risk management practices, they did however result in an enhanced focus on risk in the banking sector and beyond, as others held up the banking sector as a model for managing risk. Solvency II, a set of risk management standards for European Union (EU) insurance companies scheduled to take effect in November 2012, is clearly influenced by Basel II, and is largely analogous to it.

 ## SEPTEMBER 11TH

The terrorist attacks on the United States on September 11, 2001, advanced our thinking in the area of ERM by raising awareness of four major aspects of risk:

1. Terrorism risk
2. Concentration risk
3. Risk complexity
4. Need for an integrated approach

Terrorism Risk

Virtually all organizations are more aware of the possibility of a terrorist attack as a result of September 11th. Many of these organizations, particularly those operating in or near major cities or potential terrorist targets, have also thought through various terrorism scenarios. They have examined the potential impacts of an attack impacting their physical assets, employees, customers, stakeholders, suppliers, and/or the economies in which they operate. These exercises have led to some preventive mitigation (such as decentralizing offices) as well as enhanced business continuity plans. An additional benefit is the general raising of awareness of the possibility of the previously unthinkable. This is helpful, since ERM requires management to keep an open mind to a more complete range of future scenarios.

Concentration Risk

Even before September 11th, companies were aware of the danger of concentrations of risk. For example, companies try to avoid depending too much on a single large customer or supplier; investing too much of their assets in any one sector; or having too much knowledge, power, or access concentrated with one employee. However, September 11th dramatically changed the way companies, and governments, thought about concentration risk.

The result was a complete rethinking of where and how resources are, or might become, exposed in a concentrated way to terrorism or other types of risk. Where are our most critical employees located? Where do we gather our most critical employees together? Where are the bulk of our invested assets geographically? Are any of our key customers or suppliers or other credit counterparties exposed to significant concentration risk? One manifestation of this was many employers decentralizing their locations out of major landmark buildings and also out of major cities.

Risk Complexity

September 11th raised awareness of the complexity of risk. A complex set of interdependencies, which remains beneath the surface until a significant disruption reveals it, became apparent in the aftermath of the attacks. There were numerous secondary impacts that were unexpected, or at least had not been examined until then.

Though it may appear obvious now, few would have predicted how severely the airline business would be impacted. After all, statistically, even with a moderate increase in terrorism, flying is still far safer than other modes of travel. According to a study by Sivak and Flannigan published in the January–February issue of *American Scientist*, even if a terrorist event equivalent to September 11th occurred every month, flying would still be safer than driving.[2] However, the human factor is a significant component of risk complexity. It is more difficult to account for fear and other irrational human tendencies, which often direct actions that are counter to our collective best interests. A Cornell University study found that an additional 725 people lost their lives in just the three months following September 11th as a result of a shift from flying to driving.[3]

Another type of risk complexity that was highlighted as a result of September 11th was that while there are mostly downside impacts from a horrible event, there are often upside impacts as well. For example, anyone in the security business can tell you how much opportunities increased after the attacks. In addition, companies providing teleconferencing benefited as well, as business travel decreased dramatically. While this is not a new concept, again, the sheer scale of September 11th increased awareness that in considering a risk scenario, it is important to factor in the potentially offsetting upside impacts as well.

Need for an Integrated Approach

September 11th highlighted the need for an integrated approach to risk management. It moved the U.S. government closer to managing risks on a basis more consistent with ERM principles. The government reorganization in response to September 11th is analogous to the beginnings of an ERM program. They established the Department of Homeland Security, later organized under the ODNI (Office of the Department of National Intelligence), which centralizes efforts regarding most risks facing the country. One of the key recognitions was that the government was in possession of intelligence which should have, or could have, prevented the attacks, but due to a lack of coordination, sharing, and prioritization of information, a disaster occurred. It is the same within companies. Many companies possess excellent information, but fail to realize their potential—both in terms of averting disasters as well as capitalizing on opportunities—due to a lack of integration between separate business segments.

 ## CORPORATE ACCOUNTING FRAUD

In 2001 and 2002, a wave of accounting scandals rocked the business world. Enron, Tyco, and WorldCom were just three of the most prominent examples. These firms suffered dramatic financial collapses and had executives convicted and sentenced to prison. The names of these executives—Jeff Skilling, Ken Lay, Andrew Fastow, Dennis Kozlowski, and Bernie Ebbers—still send shudders down the spines of executives everywhere, nearly a decade later. In addition, Arthur Andersen, the audit firm for both Enron and WorldCom, went out of business as a result of the scandals. The fallout from all the accounting scandals included two significant events that led many companies to improve their risk management processes.

The first event involved litigation, and increased the accountability of members of the board of directors and, more important, their personal financial liability, in the event of undetected corporate accounting fraud. In a WorldCom lawsuit, a settlement was reported that involved 10 outside directors paying damages out of their personal assets amounting to approximately 20 percent of their net worth, and which were not allowed to be reimbursed by their directors and officers (D&O) liability insurance coverage. An Enron lawsuit settlement involved similar personal payments from directors.

These settlements were significant in that they led to two major trends. First, serving on a board of directors became less attractive due to the increased liability. Many companies saw directors retiring from the board, and found it more difficult to recruit directors. The second, and more important trend for ERM, is that the remaining directors became more diligent about risk, and began asking management what was being done to protect the company against key risks. In many instances where companies have adopted ERM, it was precipitated by pressure on management from a member of the board of directors.

The second event involved legislation and enhanced the risk management practices of companies and their auditors in relation to ensuring the accuracy of external financial reports. In 2002, the U.S. Congress passed the Sarbanes-Oxley Act, also commonly referred to as SOX. Similar legislation was later adopted elsewhere, including Japan (J-SOX), France, Italy, and some other countries. This legislation required companies to establish a highly detailed and expensive process for identifying risks to, and establishing, documenting, and testing the effectiveness of risk controls for, the financial reporting process, and to have company executives formally attest to the accuracy of the financial reports. In an effort to comply with SOX, many companies adopted a modified version of the COSO Internal Control framework developed in the early 1990s.[4]

Though SOX has been widely criticized as onerous and ineffective, it did raise corporate awareness of risk regarding financial reporting accuracy as well as more generally. Many companies used process maps to help identify vulnerable areas (e.g., regarding the handoffs and access to data) in the reporting process, and some began to expand the use of process maps to identify risks and inefficiencies in other company processes as well. SOX also empowered employees to identify and address some new risks, as well as to raise, and get funding to resolve, some known issues.

 ## HURRICANE KATRINA

The August 2005 hurricane that devastated the city of New Orleans taught us many lessons regarding risk management, but two of them in particular have helped advance ERM practices in a way that is both lasting and significant. These lessons relate to:

- Worst-case scenarios
- Natural disasters

Worst-Case Scenarios

Like September 11th, Hurricane Katrina opened the imagination up to worst-case scenarios, even though they may be remote in likelihood. According to the U.S. Army Corps of Engineers, Hurricane Katrina was a 1-in-396-year event. The lesson here is to put more emphasis on the impact of risk scenarios, rather than on the likelihood. The likelihood may be very small, but it is more a matter of not exposing yourself to anything that can wipe you out completely.

Natural Disasters

Up until relatively modern times, people have been largely exposed to the elements of nature. For example, before Benjamin Franklin invented the lightning rod in 1747, every city faced the very real possibility of entire neighborhoods burning down with each new lightning storm. Each new technological advance over the years has brought with it more power over our environment, as well as a growing sense of invulnerability.

Katrina reminded us of our vulnerability to natural disasters and the fallibility of our best attempts to prevent or mitigate them. This was dramatically underscored in the wake of the powerful hurricane and the ensuing flooding, which showed the most powerful nation in the world unable to stem the virtual loss of a major city to nature. After Katrina, many companies began to incorporate more natural disaster scenarios in their ERM programs, and that practice continues today.

RATING AGENCY SCRUTINY

In October 2005, rating agency scrutiny of company ERM programs took a great leap forward. Standard & Poor's (S&P) added ERM as an additional distinct ratings category for their credit ratings of insurance companies, globally. Though the other major rating agencies did not follow their approach precisely, they did begin to highlight how they were addressing ERM, in response to questions raised as a result of S&P's move. S&P's ERM review advanced the global practices of ERM in four ways:

1. Rapid advancement
2. Continual evolution
3. Growth beyond requirements
4. Expansion to all sectors

Rapid Advancement

Insurance companies moved, and moved quickly, to begin implementing an ERM program or enhance their existing ERM programs. S&P's move was bold and brilliant from a marketing perspective. As a separate and distinct component of the overall rating, the ERM "grade" a company received would be publicly available. As a result, companies were highly motivated to get a good grade. S&P published their ERM ratings criteria in some detail, and companies used this as a guide for enhancing their ERM programs. Companies needed to be prepared in time for their next meeting with S&P, and since implementing ERM has a long lead time, many scrambled to prepare for the S&P ERM review.

Continual Evolution

Insurance companies began to enhance their ERM programs each year. S&P made a strategic decision to raise the bar on the level of sophistication that would be required to maintain the ERM rating, and did so each year since the introduction of its initial ERM review criteria. Once companies achieved the ERM rating they desired, they quickly became even more concerned about the possibility of losing that rating, and what that might signal to bondholders and shareholders alike. As a result, S&P helped encourage a continual evolution of ERM programs at these companies.

Growth beyond Requirements

Insurance companies began to take ERM programs even further than S&P requirements. Once companies began to develop robust ERM programs, some of them began to tout how their ERM programs afforded them a competitive advantage. Spurred on by a certain level of competition, others began to investigate how they too could use ERM for competitive purposes.

Expansion to All Sectors

Other sectors became, and continue to become, more aware of the need to advance their ERM programs. S&P enjoyed much success with their insurance ERM reviews, not only in terms of their moving the sector forward in ERM sophistication but also in terms of attention. S&P received a phenomenal level of press coverage for their innovative approach. This led to S&P announcing in May 2008 that they would enhance their ERM reviews as part of their credit ratings of non-financial companies. This is an important and much-needed development, because most non-financial sectors have been lagging in risk management practices as compared to the financial services sector. Although the non-financial sector ERM review is not treated as a distinct ratings category like that in the insurance sector, even before its formal incorporation into the ratings process, these companies are becoming more aware of S&P's ERM criteria, and are acknowledging the need to improve their risk management practices.

 ## FINANCIAL CRISIS

The global financial crisis that began in the United States in 2007 has shaken up the status quo in the world of risk management and has opened the door for all companies to look at how to improve their ERM programs. First, the crisis has clearly laid false the claim by the banking sector that they had best-in-class risk management practices. This is important, because others in the financial services sector had been enamored with the banking approach and were of the opinion that all they had to do was mimic it. In Chapter 9 we describe what banks were and were not doing in terms of ERM practices.

In addition to witnessing the fall of the mighty in the banking sector, companies had their own direct experience in the crisis that, if they survived it (and many did not), served as a wake-up call. During the heart of the crisis, there was a lull in ERM advancement as individuals and companies were just scampering to survive. However, after the worst seemed to be over, companies in all sectors of the economy began to perform assessments of their ERM programs to determine priorities for enhancements. As before, the financial services sector is actively engaged. However, the non-financial services sector is also moving forward, some companies more quickly than others. In particular, Steve Dreyer, who leads S&P's global initiative to incorporate ERM into their credit ratings for non-financial services companies, indicates that "coming out of the financial crisis, many companies in the consumer products sector enhanced their ERM activities, in part due to their experience with the financial crisis and its impact on their supply chain. Likewise, energy companies exposed to recession-driven low natural gas prices have focused more intently than ever on proactively managing exposure to commodity price movements."

Another important consequence of the financial crisis is that it is no longer as difficult for those involved in the ERM process to get management to consider worst-case scenarios. Living "in the tail"—which refers to experiencing what was previously considered so unlikely an event that it would graphically reside in the extreme downside tail-end portion of the distribution curve illustrating the range of possible events—has opened management's imagination of what else can go badly, and how badly it can go.

In addition, it is expected that fallout from the financial crisis in the forms of legislation, regulation, and litigation could have significant positive impacts on the advancement of ERM globally. At the time of the writing of this book, it is too early to determine these impacts. However, there are two consequences that are worth mentioning that have the potential to accelerate adoption of ERM programs:

1. SEC disclosure regulation
2. Dodd-Frank legislation

SEC Disclosure Regulation

In February 2010, the SEC passed a regulation requiring the disclosure of risk governance as well as risky compensation programs. These are both discussed in Chapter 7. Adopting an ERM program would help companies comply with this regulation. The regulation may reveal the presence, or lack, of good risk governance at companies. In addition, the regulation requires an ability to determine whether the incentive compensation program is risky, and this cannot effectively be done without a proper ERM program in place.

Dodd-Frank Legislation

In July 2010, the Dodd-Frank legislation became effective. Much of the legislation was written to merely empower regulators to design and implement new requirements, which will take awhile to emerge. However, there is one aspect of the bill that has the potential to advance ERM practices. The bill created a new entity, the Financial Stability Oversight Council, and empowered it to make recommendations regarding new risk management requirements for financial institutions.

 RARE EVENTS

In 2009, two threats resurfaced related to risk events so rare that they had not been taken seriously in modern times. Although these threats did not result in significant impacts, they played a part in helping management keep an open mind about rare events, which is important in ERM. The two threats were:

1. H1N1 flu pandemic
2. Pirates

H1N1 Flu Pandemic

For many years, scientists have been saying that it is only a matter of when, not if, we will experience a pandemic disease of similar virulence as the 1918–1919 flu pandemic, or the Spanish Flu, when, according to the Center for Disease Control (CDC), more than 2.5 percent of the global population died. Though many companies did include such scenarios in their ERM programs, most approached it with a bit of skepticism. This is no longer the case. As the 2009 flu season approached, there were significant fears that the impending H1N1 flu pandemic might be as deadly as the 1918 flu. Although it turned out to only be about as deadly as a typical seasonal flu, this experience changed attitudes. Before H1N1, the fact that an "old" date (1918) was attached to the deadly event made it seem more unlikely or unreal to us.

Pirates

Though not a particularly important factor, piracy is worth mentioning because it is another example of something that previously seemed un-imaginable in modern times. However, in 2009, pirate attacks off the coast of Somalia received a lot of media attention and became a concern for the shipping industry and cruise lines. Before this occurred, if you raised this as a potential risk, the response would have been, "Pirates? Are you kidding?" Pirates evoke a far distant history of wooden ships and cannon. It had been over 100 years since the last attack on a U.S. ship by pirates. Yet, again, a remote (and ridiculous-sounding) risk event becoming reality is more fodder for ERM programs, which include exercises to identify emerging risks—risks currently not on the radar screen but that might become important in the future. Events such as this have made us more aware of the gap between our attitude before a remote event occurs and immediately afterwards, and how quickly our mind-set, and our reality, can change.

 ## LONG-TERM TRENDS

In addition to the events laid out chronologically earlier in the chapter, there are two other drivers of ERM adoption worth mentioning that have evolved over a long period of time. One is technological advancement. ERM requires a lot of computing power. Until recently, the run time for the required calcula-tions was prohibitively slow. However, the continued increase in processing speeds is now making ERM feasible, and companies are beginning to take advantage of this.

Another driver is increased risk savvy in the business world and even in the general population. Until fairly recently, consumers of information have been content to receive "best-estimate" projections, be they earnings fore-casts or weather forecasts. However, in recent years, consumers have become more comfortable with the concept of volatility (the best estimate does not always occur) and also more accustomed to receiving and process-ing multiple scenarios (ranges of possible results, either above or below best estimate). As a result, forecasts have taken a more sophisticated turn and commonly provide a range of possible or likely occurrences. For exam-ple, television weather forecasts of hurricanes routinely display a range of possible paths, often with color-coded probability ranges produced by so-phisticated weather models. Another example is media coverage of elections, where analysts now present consumers with numerous detailed scenarios that might influence different results.

 ## CHALLENGES TO ERM

As a result of all the factors driving awareness and adoption of ERM programs, ERM is currently a hot topic, and has been for a few years. Most companies have begun adopting ERM, are considering adopting ERM, or are curious to learn more about ERM. Boards of directors are asking about it, and their management is actively seeking knowledge about it. Even non-profit organizations and government entities have an interest in ERM and how they can adapt it for their use. At companies implementing ERM, many have a formal full-time position of chief risk officer (CRO) to lead the development, implementation, maintenance, and enhancement of the ERM program.

In response to this demand, providers of products and services have been rapidly investing in growth to serve the growing ERM market. Conferences are adding ERM as a topic to their agenda or offering entire events dedicated solely to ERM. Universities are building ERM curricula for executives as well as students, and are searching for both content and qualified professors. Consulting firms, audit firms, and technology providers are continually seeking to develop and expand their ERM products and services and are competing to hire ERM practitioners from the limited pool of qualified people.

With all this momentum, it may seem inevitable that ERM will become a large and sustaining movement in the corporate world and beyond. However, there are two major challenges that currently threaten to derail the ERM movement:

1. Confusion over ERM providers
2. ERM programs falling short of expectations

Confusion over ERM Providers

The first challenge is confusion in the market over just what ERM is and who is offering valid ERM services. The rapid proliferation of providers of ERM products and services has resulted in many ERM providers that narrowly define ERM in a way that plays to their limited set of products and services, which are usually risk management offerings that pre-date ERM. This confusion over what constitutes ERM may also lead to the tarnishing and eventual abandonment of the label *ERM*, although the valid underlying ERM concepts would live on under a new name. Chapter 2 addresses this by providing a robust definition of ERM, which can be used to evaluate whether a company's risk management program is, in fact, an ERM program. Another result of this confusion in the marketplace for ERM products and services is that it may dissuade some companies from adopting ERM.

ERM Programs Falling Short of Expectations

The second challenge is that the majority of ERM programs are falling short of expectations. There is no consensus yet on ERM best practices, and there are a variety of methods being employed. Most ERM frameworks and approaches currently in use, while producing some valuable benefits, are resulting in suboptimal ERM programs. Chapter 3 defines the ERM framework for an advanced yet practical approach that helps companies avoid these issues and successfully implement a robust ERM program. The majority of the book describes this framework and approach in more detail.

 ## SUMMARY

Due to a confluence of significant risk-related events, mostly over the past 10 years, as well as longer-term supporting trends, the time for ERM seems to have arrived. Some disastrous events, both man-made and natural, have raised management's awareness of specific sources of risks, the possibility of worst-case scenarios, and the need for an integrated approach to managing risk. Some actions, both proactive and reactive, by external stakeholders—rating agencies and government bodies—have improved risk management practices and disclosures, as well as raised management's awareness of the benefits of an ERM program. While poised to continue to grow as a business approach, ERM suffers from some confusion in the marketplace and a lack of leading practices. In the next chapter, we will begin to clear up some of this confusion by thoroughly and clearly defining ERM. The remainder of this book will then go on to delineate leading practices for ERM.

 ## NOTES

1. Basel II replaced the original Basel Accord. While there is now a Basel III emerging, it is not materially different, from the perspective of our discussion. The primary difference is higher capital requirements.

2. "Definitive Statistics Comparing Driving with Flying," available at www
   .fearofflying.com/about/research.shtml#driving. The study indicates that
   such an increase in terrorism would make flying about as risky as rural
   interstate driving, which is one of the least risky types of driving. Therefore,
   overall, driving would still be riskier.
3. "How We Calculate Risk: Fear of Flying After 9/11 Led to Increase in Auto
   Deaths," available at http://thestatsblog.wordpress.com/2008/01/16/fear-
   of-flying-after-911-led-to-increase-in-auto-deaths/.
4. The COSO Internal Control framework is intended as a process to help achieve
   effectiveness and efficiency of operations, reliability of financial reporting, and
   compliance.

CHAPTER TWO

2

Defining ERM

Security is mostly a superstition. It does not exist in nature, nor do the children of men as a whole experience it. Avoiding danger is no safer in the long run than outright exposure. Life is either a daring adventure or nothing.

Helen Keller

B EFORE WE CAN even begin to define ERM, we must define risk. While *risk* is a very common term, it has several connotations. We need a very clear and specific understanding of risk itself, in terms of how we will use it in the context of ERM.

 DEFINITION OF RISK

We will discuss the following three fundamental aspects of risk:

1. Risk is uncertainty.

2. Risk includes upside volatility.
3. Risk is deviation from expected.

Risk Is Uncertainty

A good way to think about risk is that it is present whenever there is less than 100 percent certainty that an event will occur precisely as expected. If that is our definition of risk, is there anything that does not involve risk? This may bring to mind the famous quote about uncertainty by Benjamin Franklin: "The only things certain in life are death and taxes."

Other than these two eventualities, is there anything else in your life that does not involve risk? Interestingly, even death and taxes involve uncertainty, regarding the timing of the former and the exact amount of the latter. So, it may be that absolutely everything involves uncertainty.

Risk Includes Upside Volatility

When you think of the risks in your life, you probably think of negative events, such as losing your job or losing your health. On a daily basis, risk may be as simple as the chance of not getting somewhere on time because of traffic or weather conditions. However, in an ERM context, we will define risk as *any* deviation from expected. Defined this way, risk includes both downside and upside volatility.[1] For example, you certainly would consider the possibility that your bonus will be lower than expected as being a risk; however, you are unlikely to think of the possibility of your bonus being *higher* than expected as being a risk. But that is exactly what our definition of risk asks you to do— consider risk as the possibility that results may not be exactly equal to expected, but rather are either lower or higher than expected. The "upside volatility" refers to the range of possible upside risk events, and the "downside volatility" refers to the range of possible downside risk events.

Including upside volatility in the definition of risk is important in ERM, because we need to appropriately reflect three characteristics of risk:

1. Offsets from other business segments
2. Offsets from other events
3. Cost of volatility

Offsets from Other Business Segments

A single event that is a downside risk event for one business segment might be an upside risk event for a second business segment. For example, consider a

BLESSING **IN DISGUISE**

In October 2007, a swimmer named Michael Phelps was training for the 2008 Beijng Olympics when he broke his wrist.[2] Having won six gold medals at the 2004 Athens Olympics, Phelps had hoped to beat the world record of seven Olympic gold medals set by Mark Spitz in 1972. Despite publicly denying it at the time, in a later interview, Phelps admitted that the moment he realized he broke his wrist, he knew that his dream of winning eight Olympic gold medals was in jeopardy. During rehabilitation therapy for his wrist, Phelps was limited to doing kicking exercises in the water. Once he was fully healed, it became apparent that the injury had been a blessing in disguise. The extensive leg workouts gave him a competitive advantage that propelled him to his goal of winning eight Olympic gold medals in Beijing. Stronger legs made him faster, allowing him to push harder off the walls when turning and to kick harder during his swimming strokes.[3]

tour company in the United States that markets national tours as well as tours to China to U.S. citizens. Assume a risk event occurs where the U.S. dollar becomes devalued against China's currency, renminbi (RMB). The tour company would expect a decrease in business for their tours to China, but they also might expect an increase in business for their national tours. In such cases, management must understand the *net* impact of the single event on the enterprise as a whole.

A related concept is that what appears to be a downside risk event can ultimately turn out to be an upside risk event for the entity. One example is a moderate external attack from a competitor, which strengthens the entity's defenses, allowing it to survive what would otherwise have been a fatal attack later on from a larger competitor. This is analogous to the famous quote by Friedrich Nietzsche: "Whatever does not kill us makes us stronger." For a related anecdote, see "Blessing in Disguise."

Offsets from Other Events

Multiple risk events can occur simultaneously, with some being downside risk events and others being upside risk events. In these cases, management needs to measure the net impact of all risk events combined. For example, during one period, everything goes precisely as planned, except for two things:

1. A *downside* risk event occurs, such as a cost savings program not being executed as expected, resulting in fixed costs being $10 million *higher* than expected.
2. An *upside* risk event occurs, such as an unexpected decrease in the cost of raw materials used in production, resulting in variable costs being $10 million *lower* than expected

The net effect of these risk events—one upside and one downside—is zero. In an ERM context, had we applied an approach that only captured the downside risk event, we would have ignored the offsetting upside risk event.

Cost of Volatility

An excess of volatility, even where the upside is more impactful than the downside, can lower value by increasing the cost of capital. In other words, not all upside volatility is necessarily good news, because it is accompanied by additional downside volatility as well. Consider a simplified example of two companies: StableCo and WildCo, both with one million shares outstanding. Both companies are in the same industry sector being valued by the same equity analyst. The analyst projects the cash flows (in millions) for the coming 10-year period for each company. The cash flows are shown in Table 2.1.

Assume that the equity analyst values each company as the present value of their 10-year projected cash flows (see "Present Value"). If the discount rate used to value both StableCo and WildCo were the same 6 percent rate, StableCo would be valued at $80.10 per share and WildCo would be valued at $91.22 per share, or $11.12 per share more than StableCo. However, it is unlikely that the same discount rate would be used to value both companies.

WildCo does have more total projected cash flow over the 10-year period. The upside volatility is expected to generate more additional dollars of cash flow than are lost by the accompanying additional downside volatility, as

TABLE 2.1 Cash Flow Projection: StableCo and WildCo

Cash Flows (in millions)	Year 1	Year 2	Year 3	Year 4	Year 5	Year 6	Year 7	Year 8	Year 9	Year 10	Total
StableCo	10	10	10	11	11	11	12	11	12	12	110
WildCo	10	5	25	−2	18	10	28	2	24	6	126

PRESENT **VALUE**

resent value is a calculation that reduces a series of future cash flows to a single equivalent value at the present time, adjusting for the time value of money. For example, assume that, for you, the time value of money is a 6 percent interest rate, in terms of your business dealings with your local bank. In other words, you are indifferent between the bank offering you $106 one year from now or offering you $100 today. Now, assume the bank offers you $100 one year from now and $150 two years from now. What is the present value, i.e., what is the single value today which you would accept in place of these future cash flows? The present value is calculated as:

$$Present\ value = \frac{\$100}{(1.06)^1} + \frac{\$150}{(1.06)^2} = \$227.84$$

The future cash flows are said to be *discounted* to the present time.

compared to StableCo. However, WildCo also has higher overall volatility than StableCo. This is illustrated in Figure 2.1, which graphs the values from Table 2.1. Investors require a higher rate of return when there is higher volatility or uncertainty. Higher risk goes with higher required returns.

Assume that the additional volatility of WildCo translates to the equity analyst adding 300 basis points to the discount rate. The equity analyst will now value WildCo using a 9 percent (6 percent + 3 percent) discount rate,

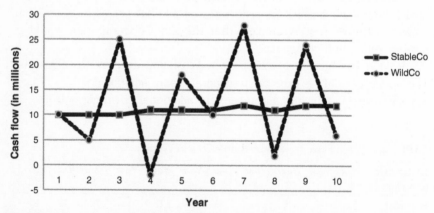

FIGURE 2.1 WildCo Is More Volatile Than StableCo

reflecting the higher level of risk in the stock. This produces a valuation for WildCo equal to $78.84 per share, which is $1.27 *lower* than StableCo's valuation. In this case, the additional volatility (which reflects all volatility—upside and downside) of WildCo outweighed the additional cash flows, resulting in a lower valuation than the less volatile (and lower total cash flow) StableCo.

Risk Is Deviation from Expected

Risk is generally thought of as the possibility of a loss. This is the most common reference used, even by many ERM practitioners. However, loss is an incomplete concept because, as discussed earlier, it excludes upside volatility, which is the possibility of an unexpected gain. But loss has an even more insidious shortcoming. It often inadvertently causes people to overestimate the severity, or magnitude, of a risk. This is because when considering a negative (downside) risk event, or scenario, it is natural to visualize, for example, the loss as the total outflow of cash. Unfortunately, this results in double-counting some expected losses, which should be excluded.

Consider the following example. A Fortune 500 company is considering litigation risk. Several risk scenarios are developed, including one worst-case scenario where the company could have a total of $100 million in after-tax litigation costs. In this example, the loss from this risk event might be thought to be $100 million. But that would be incorrect. This large company experiences litigation costs each year, and a certain amount is normal and expected. Because our definition of risk is deviation from expected, the risk severity, or impact, should only include the excess over the amount expected. The annual expected litigation cost is likely to be included in the company's strategic plan baseline financial projection. Assume that it is, and that the annual expected litigation cost is estimated at $35 million in the baseline projection. The risk severity of the worst-case litigation risk scenario would then be:

(Litigation costs in worst-case scenario)
− (Litigation costs in baseline scenario)
= ($100 million) − ($35 million) = $65 million

While this may seem like a straightforward distinction, it is one that is often overlooked. It is easy to forget to deduct the amount expected. In some cases, those individuals involved with developing the risk scenario may not be familiar with the strategic plan baseline financial projection and what items it incorporates. In other cases, the strategic plan baseline projection should have accounted for an item, but omitted it. In the latter cases, the risk scenario development exercise offers an opportunity to enhance the baseline projection.

The strategic plan projection is usually developed with primary focus on value drivers, and this influences which items are included and their accounting. The ERM process, in this case specifically the risk scenario development process, brings in another perspective—the risk drivers. Bringing both aspects of business—both risk and return—into the strategic planning process improves its robustness.

Now that we have clarified the three fundamental aspects of the definition of risk, we will move on to the definition of ERM itself. However, we will further expand on the definition of risk in Chapter 4, in the section "Risk Categorization and Definition."

 DEFINITION OF ERM

ERM is a complex process. To help provide a solid understanding of ERM, with its key nuances, we will spend the remainder of this chapter defining ERM from the following perspectives:

- Basic definition
- Key criteria
- The ERM process cycle
- Fundamental benefits

Basic Definition

In Chapter 1, we provided a short definition of ERM:

> The process by which companies identify, measure, manage, and disclose all key risks to increase value to stakeholders.

In the next section, we describe the key criteria implied by this basic definition, and that comprise the defining characteristics of an ERM program.

Key Criteria

There are 10 criteria that are the critical defining elements of an ERM program. These can serve as a useful benchmark against which to evaluate whether a company truly has a robust ERM program. Currently, most ERM programs are relatively immature, as measured against these criteria, and are slowly evolving toward a robust program. These criteria are:

1. Enterprise-wide scope
2. All risk categories included
3. Key risk focus
4. Integrated across risk types
5. Aggregated metrics
6. Includes decision making
7. Balances risk and return management
8. Appropriate risk disclosures
9. Measures value impacts
10. Primary stakeholder focus

Criterion 1: Enterprise-wide Scope

Enterprise is the first word in ERM. This means that ERM must apply to every area of the company. One never knows where a significant risk event will occur. In fact, it often occurs precisely where management is not looking. Unfortunately, most ERM programs do not have a comprehensive enterprise-wide scope. In such companies, one or more of the following situations exist:

- A "golden boy" unit
- An area deemed insignificant
- A limiting approach
- Differing cultures
- Incomplete implementation

A "Golden Boy" Unit The most noteworthy, and troubling, situation is the presence of a "golden boy" unit. This is a business unit that enjoys special rules because it has been generating large revenue growth and/or profits. The special rules usually take the form of exempting the business unit from scrutiny or even routine oversight processes, such as corporate reporting criteria, risk management activities, or internal audits. This can be the result of a misalignment of incentives (e.g., management is paid for revenue or earnings growth and is not held accountable for increasing the firm's risk exposure). Whatever the cause, the result is either a lack of understanding of the risks involved in the business, or worse, willful ignorance.

One example of this was AIG Financial Products (AIGFP). AIGFP caused the collapse of AIG during the global financial crisis that began in the United States in 2007. They exposed AIG to enormous risk exposure in credit default swaps (CDSs). Before these exposures exploded into drowning losses, AIGFP was a growing source of large profits for AIG, and this led to their being exempt from corporate risk management scrutiny.

An Area Deemed Insignificant   Another situation is a business unit that is deemed minor enough to omit from the ERM process. This often happens as a result of rolling out an ERM implementation in stages, where priority order is based on size of the business segment. In considering whether or not to extend the ERM program further, management decides to omit a small business area. This is potentially dangerous. Large losses often arise from small or obscure parts of the firm believed to have very little risk. However, risk exposure is not always in proportion to the visible size of the business; it is therefore critical to consider risks that may arise from anywhere in the company.

Nassim Taleb, author of *The Black Swan: The Impact of the Highly Improbable* and other books on large loss events, points out that large losses will eventually appear in business areas with certain qualities that generate routine, and relatively minor, income for a long period of time.[4] Companies that ignore this warning, and deem apparently minor areas of their organization too small to include in their ERM program, may be unknowingly exposed to a ticking time bomb of risk exposure with a fuse of unknown length.

A Limiting Approach   A common reason that many corporations cannot roll out their ERM program to all of their operations is because the approach they are using only works with their primary business segment. This is especially true for financial services companies with a holding company structure containing many different types of businesses. In these cases, the ERM approach commonly used for the banking or insurance operations is based on capital requirements and cannot be applied to other businesses that do not have any capital requirements.[5]

Differing Cultures   In some organizations, two (or more) cultures exist, causing some business processes not to be adopted uniformly. In these cases, ERM may have been adopted, and even successfully implemented, by one part of the enterprise while another part, operating under a different culture, remains uninterested or unaware of ERM. This is more likely to occur in companies where business segments are more independent, as opposed to those with a more authoritative corporate department. Competing cultures can be caused by a variety of differences that separate them, including, but not limited to, the following:

- Office location
- Time zone
- Local culture
- Language
- Types of business
- Origins (e.g., a merger of two companies)

Incomplete Implementation   In many situations, it is simply the case that ERM is in an earlier stage of development and has not yet been extended fully to all business segments. Eventually, the ERM program may become truly enterprise-wide. Most ERM programs are currently in this situation. Until the ERM program covers all areas, the company remains vulnerable. An ERM program that does not fully extend across the entire enterprise is similar to the watertight bulkheads (walls) that were not extended high enough above the waterline on the infamous *Titanic*, resulting in its rapid sinking and massive loss of lives on April 15, 1912.

Criterion 2: All Risk Categories Included

The word *all* in the basic ERM definition means that all risk categories must be included. In Chapter 4, we will improve on the standard industry terminology for risk categories, but for now, we will use the common industry terms. Risk categories, for most companies, include financial risk, strategic risk, and operational risk. The definitions of these risk categories are as follows:

- **Financial risk.** Unexpected changes in external markets, prices, rates, and liquidity supply and demand. This includes market risk, credit risk, and liquidity risk.
- **Strategic risk.** Unexpected changes in key elements of strategy formulation or execution.
- **Operational risk.** Unexpected changes in elements related to operations, such as human resources, technology, processes, and disasters.

There is one additional risk category—insurance risk, which generally applies only to insurance companies. Insurance risk involves poor performance of the pricing, underwriting, reserving, or setting of required capital for insurance products.

Including all risk categories is critical for the validity of an ERM program. Key risks can reside in any of the risk categories. Ignoring a risk category, or not having a balanced focus among all risk categories, can expose the company to excessive risk and result in focusing limited risk mitigation resources on the wrong priorities.

Surprisingly, the vast majority of ERM programs focus all, or most, of their attention only on financial risks. The primary evidence of this imbalance is the lack of a sufficiently robust approach to quantifying strategic and operational risks. There are three main causes of this neglect:

1. Inability to quantify strategic and operational risks
2. Myth regarding importance of financial risks
3. Financial analyst bias

Inability to Quantify Strategic and Operational Risks One basis for this imbalance is an inability to quantify strategic and operational risks. For financial risks, there is a large amount of objective market data to use in developing risk scenarios, which include quantitative impacts on financial results. However, for strategic and operational risks, which are heavily dependent on the specific makeup of the organization impacted, there is far less data available. In addition, popular quantification methods do not adequately support strategic and operational risks. The quantification methods either do not provide any quantification, or worse, they dramatically understate the severity of the risk. In Chapter 3, we explore this issue in more detail and describe an emerging approach that resolves this, and other, issues.

Myth Regarding Importance of Financial Risks A second source of the disproportional focus on financial risks is the belief that financial risks are the most important risks—that they are the majority of the risks that most threaten the organization. This is not supported by experience, and in fact, quite the opposite is true. Research studies consistently show that strategic and operational risks represent the majority of the key risks for a company and also comprise the biggest threats.

A research study published in December 2009, which I directed and co-authored, examined the distribution of risks by risk category.[6] The analysis was

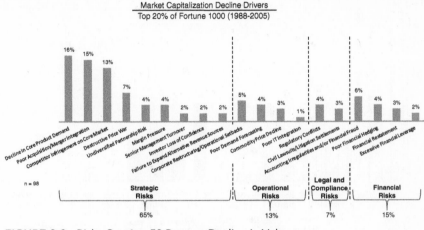

FIGURE 2.2 Risks Causing 50 Percent Decline in Value

© 2009, Audit Director Roundtable, Corporate Executive Board.

based on the occurrence of negative events, related to public companies, appearing on the front page of the *Wall Street Journal* in 2006. Only 1 percent of such front-page news were financial risks, while approximately two-thirds (64 percent) were strategic risks and approximately one-third (35 percent) were operational risks.

Similar results are found in other industry research, confirming that the source of significant risk events for companies is, in decreasing order: strategic risk, operational risk, and financial risk. In Figure 2.2, an 18-year study by the Corporate Executive Board Company shows the root causes for one-year market capitalization declines of 50 percent or more, involving the top 20 percent of the Fortune 1000. Approximately two-thirds (65 percent) were strategic, 20 percent were operational (including legal and compliance risks categorized as operational), and only 15 percent were financial. However, even the 15 percent may be overstated, because many if not all of the risks categorized as financial appear to be operational, specifically human resources-related (such as performance risk, which is management or staff not performing their function as expected).[7]

Figure 2.3 shows a six-year study by Mercer Management Consulting examining the triggering events for the 100 largest one-month value declines among the Fortune 1000 between 1993 and 1998. The vast majority of the risks were strategic (61 percent), one-third (33 percent) were operational, and only 6 percent were financial.

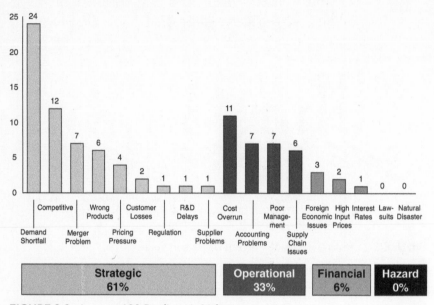

FIGURE 2.3 Largest 100 Declines in Value

Another research study shows that the vast majority of members of boards of directors believe that the biggest threats for their organizations are strategic risks rather than financial risks. Figure 2.4 shows the results of a 2006 survey of directors by The Conference Board, which asked directors about the biggest threats facing their organizations. The research reveals that, across all sectors,

FIGURE 2.4 Directors' Ranking of Biggest Threats

Source: The Conference Board, *The Role of U.S. Corporate Boards in Enterprise Risk Management,* 2006.

directors believing that strategic risks are the biggest threats outnumber those believing the threats to be financial risks by more than 3 to 1 (53 percent versus 16 percent). Even within the financial services sector, directors voting strategic risks as most important outnumbered those voting for financial risks by almost 2 to 1 (48 percent versus 26 percent).

Part of the myth that financial risks are the most important is based on an incorrect approach to risk categorization and definition; in confusing the source of a risk with its outcome, risks that are either in whole or in part strategic or operational risks are frequently miscategorized as exclusively financial risks. One example is the global financial crisis that began in the United States in 2007. There were multiple sources of risk that led to the financial crisis, many of which were not financial risks. See "Criterion 2: All Risk Categories Included" in Chapter 9 for the case study analysis.

Financial Analyst Bias   A third cause of the lack of appropriate focus on non-financial risks is financial analyst bias. Most of those doing the modeling share a financial-centric mind-set. Their education is focused on financial risk. Their training and certification is in financial risk. Their experience is only with financial risk. Even the name and purview of their department may limit them to financial risk. In addition, their techniques cannot readily handle strategic and operational risks; their methods work best when there is a wealth of objective quantitative data available, which is not the case with strategic and operational risks.

The lack of sufficient inclusion of non-financial risks may be the result of one or a combination of the previously mentioned factors. Whatever the reason, this represents a dangerous flaw in most ERM programs. The importance of this cannot be overstated. These partially quantitative ERM programs fail to quantify the vast majority of the key risks in terms of their individual and collective contribution to the overall volatility of the organization, in terms of the key metrics.

These partially quantitative ERM programs give the strong impression that they are not incomplete, causing management to erroneously rely on, and misinterpret, the information. This false impression is given by the level of precision implied by the data handed to management by the financial modelers (also known as *financial analysts* or simply *modelers*) of these flawed ERM programs. The modelers routinely provide outputs from their models showing the volatility of key metrics, presented in a way that implies a high degree of accuracy; one example is showing the figure out to a large number of significant digits.

This problem is rampant in the financial services sector, where it is even more common to find this imbalance in the quantification of key risks. One example, from the banking sector, is the "Value-at-Risk" (VaR) metric. VaR is often defined as the maximum amount of capital that can be lost in a single day, within a given small predefined likelihood. Another example, at insurance companies, is the "economic capital" metric, which is the amount of capital needed on hand today to limit the probability of ruin, over a given time horizon, to within a given small predefined likelihood. In both of these examples, these numbers are commonly provided to management in number form that includes a large number of significant digits, implying a high level of accuracy (e.g., a number is shown as $35,455,809, rather than $35 million). In addition, these numbers are often provided without the proper disclaimers of incompleteness regarding overall firm volatility. This offers an incorrect representation to management, despite being quite unintentional, that this (financial-only) volatility represents the bulk, or even the totality, of the risk exposures about which management needs to be concerned.

This is alarming because of the dangerous nature of ignoring the majority of the key risks in the metrics, and particularly so because this is often occurring under the guise of an enterprise risk management program . . . yet the word *enterprise* seems ignored. However, what is even more shocking is that what the (usually) math-savvy modelers are doing violates a basic mathematical concept we all learned in elementary school—the rule of significant digits. See "Significant Digits."

SIGNIFICANT **DIGITS**

The rule of significant digits can best be illustrated through a simple example. Assume we have two numbers. The first number is 2. What do we know about the level of accuracy of this number? It might be rounded up from 1.50 or it might be rounded down from 2.49. Now, we have a second number, which is 2.04. This number is presented to us out to two decimal places. What do we know? Well, we know it has far more implied accuracy than the first number. However, the second number similarly may be rounded up from 2.0350 or rounded down from 2.0449. The significant digits rule indicates that where two numbers have different levels of significant digits, we must report the sum of those two numbers with the same number of significant digits as the less accurate of the two numbers. In this case, we must report the sum of the two numbers out to only zero decimals.

$$2 + 2.04 = 4$$

Alternatively, as a business matter, we could merely report each number separately, without summing them, and indicate the differing levels of accuracy of each number, if there is a desire not to lose the additional information that one of the numbers has more significant digits. This would maintain the integrity of the information and not mislead.

The significant digits rule also states that we *cannot* report the summation of the two numbers as follows:

$$2 + 2.04 = 4.04$$

This would be misleading, giving the false impression that we have confidence in the sum of the two numbers out to two decimal places. But this is not true. Claiming that the sum is 4.04 would mask the poor level of confidence in the accuracy of the sum, whose true value, expressed out to two decimals, ranges anywhere from 3.54 to 4.53, as shown:

$$(\text{Minimum}, \text{Maximum}) = (1.50 + 2.04, 2.49 + 2.04) = (3.54, 4.53)$$

Modelers in partially quantitative ERM programs are violating the rule of significant digits. They are omitting the impacts of strategic and operational risks from the ERM metrics, which purport to be holistic or all-inclusive, and then presenting these metrics with only the financial sources of risks included, and out to a high degree of significant digits. From the available research data, it seems clear that financial risks are certainly not the totality of the key risk exposure, and they are not even the majority of it. The research suggests that, on average, financial risks are likely to represent only a small percentage (at most, 15 percent) of the total volatility of the enterprise and that the strategic and operational risks account for the majority of the volatility. Therefore, if modelers are providing ERM metrics to management representing the total firm risk exposure but the metrics only include financial risk exposure, it is as if they are presenting the sum of two numbers to management:

Total enterprise risk exposure = (Risk exposure from financial risks)
+ (Risk exposure from non-financial risks)

where:

a) The risk exposure from financial risks is calculated out to a large number of significant digits, and
b) The risk exposure from non-financial risks is estimated as zero (and worse yet, not even shown as a zero, but merely omitted from the page)

For example:

$$\begin{aligned}
\text{Total enterprise risk exposure} \\
= (\text{Risk exposure from financial risks}) \\
+ (\text{Risk exposure from non-financial risks}) \\
= (\$35,455,809) + (0) = \$35,455,809
\end{aligned}$$

If we assume, perhaps generously, that the financial risks represent a full 15 percent of overall firm risk exposure, then the total enterprise risk exposure, rather than $35,455,809, is actually closer to the neighborhood of a quarter of a billion dollars (number of significant digits intentionally minimized). This gives some perspective on how much of a disservice is done by omitting quantification of strategic and operational risks.

In some financial services companies, rather than use zero, they estimate the non-financial risk exposure as an arbitrary percentage (e.g., 15 percent) of the financial risk exposure. This is almost as bad a practice, and certainly still violates the significant digits rule, because the large number of significant digits in the financial risk exposure number is masquerading as a highly accurate number worthy of our respect and attention. In fact, it is not that useful a number and should be afforded the level of disrespect that it deserves.

The only defense offered by these modelers as to why they do not attempt to quantify strategic and operational risks is related to the first reason stated earlier—an inability to quantify. However, they verbalize their argument a bit differently, saying that "you can't quantify strategic and operational risks with accuracy." What they mean, of course, is that it is not possible to quantify these risks with the same level of accuracy as financial risks. And that may be true, but that doesn't justify not estimating them at all, considering they represent the larger component, which, as shown earlier, is an egregious alternative that violates the business purpose of the ERM metric in question.

Criterion 3: Key Risk Focus

The word *key* in the basic definition indicates that ERM should only include the major risks to the company's value. ERM is not intended to include a comprehensive list of potential risks, which could range in the hundreds or thousands. ERM is strategic in nature and is focused on a relatively small list of risks that have the largest potential impact to the firm. For a company's first time through the ERM process cycle, a reasonable number of key risks may be in the range of 10 to 30. Approximately 10 risks might be appropriate for a pilot exercise, if management wants to build buy-in before implementation. However, 20 to 30 risks are needed to produce a robust set of results to rely on for decision making. The specific number of key risks that is appropriate for the enterprise depends on a proper categorization and definition of risks and also on finding an appropriate cut-off point during the qualitative risk assessment process.

However, the number of key risks does *not* depend on the size of the organization. In other words, just because one company is 10 times the size of another does not imply that it has 10 times the number of key risks. If the two companies are otherwise identical, they will have approximately the same number of key risks (the number of key risks may not be exactly the same, because, for example, the larger company may have more key risks related to reputational issues). This is because the number of key risks is merely a reasonable number of risks on which senior management can focus, at a given time, in a priority manner. It is based on people and their reasonable limits of focus. There is only one CEO, one board of directors, and one senior management team. The magnitude of the impact of the key risks will vary significantly by company size, but the number of key risks should not vary that much.

This is in stark contrast to the way many companies try to approach ERM. Many companies mistakenly believe that ERM is merely an extension of a Sarbanes-Oxley (SOX) exercise. The Sarbanes-Oxley Act passed in response to a wave of financial reporting scandals. In trying to comply with SOX, most companies created lists of every possible risk to financial reporting accuracy. The list of risks often numbered in the hundreds or even thousands for the larger companies. Each risk was tracked against information on its mitigation, including assignment of a risk owner. SOX compliance became a quarterly routine of verification that the risks were adequately mitigated. When ERM came along, many companies wrongly assumed it was similar to SOX, with which they were familiar, with the only difference being that ERM applied to all risks rather than just inaccurate financial reporting. Compounding this issue, some technology vendors reinforce this false notion by capitalizing on the software needs of maintaining an exhaustive list of every potential risk for every company process. Similarly, some audit firms further this misunderstanding by relabeling an expanded version of a SOX exercise as ERM and claiming that it is part of a governance, risk, and compliance (GRC) program.

Criterion 4: Integrated across Risk Types

Virtually all companies have been managing risk since their inception in some fashion. However, companies have traditionally managed each type of risk in isolation, rather than on an integrated basis: The information technology (IT) department deals with technology-related risks; the human resources (HR) department manages people-related risks; the investment department covers market and credit risk; and so on. Unfortunately, this "silo" approach to risk management has three disadvantages. Silo risk management is:

1. Incomplete
2. Inefficient
3. Internally inconsistent

Incomplete The most dangerous weakness of silo risk management is that it provides an incomplete representation of the risk profile. Silo risk management does capture the most basic type of risk event—where one risk scenario occurs at a time. This provides the most fundamental picture of a given risk and how it can impact the enterprise. However, it is important to also measure the impact of multiple risks occurring at the same time. There are three reasons why limiting risk measurement to silo risk scenarios is incomplete:

1. **Ignores real-world complexity.** It is unrealistic for only one risk event to occur at a time. This may be true for worst-case scenarios, where each one is so unlikely to occur. However, many risks considered in an ERM program are of moderate likelihood. For only a single moderate risk scenario to occur at a time is like having everything happen precisely as you expect for every aspect of your business, except one. For example, your product strategy, your distribution strategy, your marketing strategy, your human resources plan, and so forth all go perfectly . . . except your technology update program is a little behind schedule. Reality involves far more uncertainty than that.
2. **Omits the largest threats.** Multiple risk events occurring simultaneously can result in some of the largest threats to a company's survival. After the first event, the enterprise is in a weakened state, increasing the

likelihood of some secondary events occurring. In addition, risks can interact to exacerbate each other. A research study performed by Deloitte Research called "Disarming the Value Killers: A Risk Management Study" revealed that over 80 percent of the 100 largest losses in shareholder value (over the 10-year study period, 1994–2003) were the result of two or more risks interacting.

This is also intuitive. Consider competitive boxers in the heavyweight division. They are often said to be able to "take a punch," which means a competitor can land a single solid blow to their chin and yet they can stay on their feet. But what can result in a knockout? It's usually a combination punch. This is a barrage of multiple blows occurring in rapid succession. Also consider people you may have known or heard about whose lives suddenly went into a downward spiral. Often it is not just one unlucky event that caused their downfall, but rather two or more shocks to the system that sends them reeling. It's the same for organizations. So, if you are not capturing multiple simultaneous risk events, then you may be missing something that could potentially ruin the firm.

3. **Does not capture offsetting risks.** Multiple risk events can offset each other. Our definition of risk includes both downside and upside risk events, so one event can offset the financial impact of another. For example, consider that one downside risk event lowers sales growth by some amount, but another upside risk event occurs that increases sales growth by an equal, and offsetting, amount. This seems fairly straightforward. What may be surprising is that even two *downside* risk events can offset each other, to some degree. For an example, see "Downside Risk Events Can Partially Offset Each Other."

DOWNSIDE **RISK EVENTS CAN PARTIALLY OFFSET EACH OTHER**

To illustrate how two downside risk events can partially offset each other, we will use a hypothetical global manufacturing company, called GlobalCo, as an example. Table 2.2 shows the GlobalCo strategic plan baseline scenario financial projection for the coming year. For illustrative purposes, in this example, we make the following simplifying assumptions:

(continued)

(continued)

TABLE 2.2 GlobalCo: Baseline Scenario

Baseline Scenario (in $ millions)	Year 1
Revenues	1,000
Expenses	900
Net Income (Revenues less Expenses)	100
Change from Baseline	N/A

■ GlobalCo is only in business for one year.
■ Expenses are 90 percent of revenues.
■ Income tax rate is zero.

Consistent with our definition of risk as deviation from what is expected, risk is measured by the shock to, or change in, the strategic plan baseline scenario financial projection. In this example, we will use the net income metric to represent the baseline, and risk will be defined as deviations from net income. Consider two different risk scenarios, each from a different source of risk:

Risk Scenario A: A new regulation is passed increasing GlobalCo's expense ratio from 90 percent of revenues to 95 percent of revenues.

Risk Scenario B: A new competitor enters GlobalCo's markets reducing their market share from 5 percent to 4 percent.

First, let's consider the financial impact of each risk scenario occurring by itself. If Risk Scenario A occurs by itself, the change in net income is a decrease of $50 million (shock scenario net income of $50 million minus baseline scenario net income of $100 million), as shown in Table 2.3.

TABLE 2.3 GlobalCo: Risk Scenario A

Risk Scenario A (in $ millions)	Year 1
Revenues	1,000
Expenses	950
Net Income (Revenues less Expenses)	50
Change from Baseline	−50

If Risk Scenario B occurs by itself, the change in net income is a decrease of $20 million (shock scenario net income of $80 million minus baseline scenario net income of $100 million), as shown in Table 2.4.

TABLE 2.4   GlobalCo: Risk Scenario B

Risk Scenario B (in $ millions)	Year 1
Revenues	800
Expenses	720
Net Income (Revenues less Expenses)	80
Change from Baseline	−20

Now, let's consider the financial impact of both risk scenarios occurring simultaneously. If Risk Scenario A and Risk Scenario B both occur together, the change in net income is a decrease of $60 million (shock scenario net income of $40 million minus baseline scenario net income of $100 million), as shown in Table 2.5.

TABLE 2.5   GlobalCo: Risk Scenario A and Risk Scenario B

Risk Scenario A and Risk Scenario B (in $ millions)	Year 1
Revenues	800
Expenses	760
Net Income (Revenues less Expenses)	40
Change from Baseline	−60

The $60 million decrease in net income from the combination of both risk events is lower than the sum of the two risks occurring separately, which is $70 million ($50 million + $20 million). So, in this case, the financial impact of the risks is not additive. The difference, an interactivity benefit of $10 million ($70 million −$60 million), is the amount that the risks offset each other. This is attributable to the additional 5 percent expense ratio (due to Risk Scenario A) that is operating on a revenue base that is $200 million lower (due to Risk Scenario B), which results in the offset of $10 million ($200 million multiplied by 5 percent).

In Chapter 3, we describe how a robust ERM framework addresses this issue by capturing multiple risk events and their interaction, including exacerbation or offsetting of financial impacts.

Inefficient   Silo risk management results in various inefficiencies. The most important of these inefficiencies are:

- **Overpaying.** The lack of awareness and coordination often present in silo risk management can result in the separate purchasing of hedges for related risk exposures in multiple parts of the company. This can increase the overall cost of mitigation, as opposed to that which could be achieved by buying in bulk.

- ▪ **Under-communicating.** The absence of a centralized approach and appropriately structured risk governance impedes information sharing. This inhibits the development of best practices in risk management. In particular, and most costly, is the inability to effectively share lessons learned from costly mistakes, potentially dooming other departments to repeat the same error.

In contrast, a robust ERM program is integrated, removes these inefficiencies, and results in appropriate bulk purchasing of hedges and sharing of information enterprise-wide.

Internally Inconsistent   A third disadvantage of silo risk management is that the organization may be making internally inconsistent projections regarding the market. Different business segments, developing explicit or implicit risk scenarios independently, may be making different assumptions, for example, about the direction of the economy or sector growth. As a result, different areas may unknowingly be making bets that are at cross-purposes. In contrast, an integrated approach would facilitate a single set of internally consistent market projections, and reconcile all bets on market direction, enterprise-wide.

Criterion 5: Aggregated Metrics

Another implication of the word *enterprise* in ERM is the ability to aggregate exposure metrics and risk decision making to the enterprise level. There are two main aggregate pieces of ERM information at the enterprise level. One is a calculated metric of aggregate risk exposure and the other is a management decision defining the target level of aggregate risk exposure.

The first is a calculated metric, or set of metrics, that aggregates the risk exposures to the enterprise level. This is called enterprise risk exposure. Assume that *company value* is one of the ERM metrics. This will be defined later in this chapter (see "Company Value"), but for now consider it simply as an internal valuation, performed by management, to calculate the value of the company to its primary stakeholder. The enterprise risk exposure may be expressed, for example, as "We currently have a 10 percent chance of losing 15 percent or more of our company value." This is just one example.

There are usually multiple metrics, each with multiple thresholds, and corresponding likelihoods. This is a calculated metric, or set of numbers, at one point in time.

The second aggregate element—the counterpart to enterprise risk exposure—is a quantitative definition, set by management, of the amount of enterprise risk exposure that is acceptable. This is called risk appetite. Another term for this is risk tolerance, which is used by Standard & Poor's. Risk appetite is the target level of enterprise risk exposure. Risk appetite is what management wants enterprise risk exposure to be, at the limit. Continuing our company value metric example, management may define risk appetite as "We want no more than a 7 percent chance of losing 15 percent or more of our company value." Again, this example involves just one data point, whereas, mirroring enterprise risk exposure, risk appetite is a set of defined targets for a set of metrics.

In this example, management defines risk appetite below the current enterprise risk exposure level, indicating a desire to reduce the level of risk. Because likelihood and severity go hand in hand, even our single data point definition of risk appetite can be expressed in two ways. In our example, management expressed a desire to reduce the likelihood, from 10 percent to 7 percent, of suffering a loss of 15 percent or more in company value. They focused on a specific level of severity—a loss of 15 percent or more—and wanted this to be less likely. This is the most common choice, because management focus is on the severity of events more than the likelihood. Management is well aware of the outcomes they would like to avoid. Nevertheless, management can express the desire for a reduction in risk by fixing the likelihood and targeting a lower corresponding severity. For example, management can define risk appetite as "We want a 10 percent chance to correspond to, at the maximum, losing 12 percent or more of our company value." This is equally valid.

Most companies still use silo risk management and do not yet have either of these aggregate elements. However, they are such a fundamental part of ERM that without these two elements, the ERM program cannot perform its primary function, which is to manage enterprise risk exposure to within risk appetite. In our example, management is indicating that they wish to *lower* enterprise risk exposure from its current 10 percent likelihood to within a 7 percent likelihood of crossing a threshold of a loss of 15 percent or more of company value.

The ability to produce aggregate information at the enterprise level—and particularly enterprise risk exposure and risk appetite—is not critical only because it supports the primary function of ERM. It is also of vital importance because this should be the first step, chronologically, in the risk decision-making process. Information on risk exposures and risk appetite should first be produced at the enterprise level, and then cascaded downward through the organization, in a type of allocation or budgeting process. For example, risk appetite is allocated or budgeted downward to determine risk limits. The type of risk limits set varies by organization, and can include geographic areas, business segments, and/or individual risks.

When this is implemented in the correct chronological order, it turns the risk management process upside-down, or more accurately, right-side-up, for the first time. Traditional risk management assesses risks at the local business unit or risk level, and decides on mitigation based on local business management's judgment, instinct, or, even worse, arbitrary rules of thumb established long ago for other purposes. Using a traditional risk management approach can result in under-mitigating some risks, which can be disastrous if such a risk event occurs and the company is not adequately protected. However, a more common and immediate consequence of the traditional risk management bottom-up approach is the converse—many risks are *over*-mitigated. This results in waste, as resources are unwittingly spent on excess mitigation which management would have vetoed, if the proper information had been available.

In contrast, ERM introduces a logical approach based on the overall volatility of the enterprise and the desired level of enterprise stability, or shock resistance, desired by management. This is more sensible, because this is how the shareholders and other key stakeholders perceive the volatility: in the way that it expresses itself at the enterprise level. Once the two essential aggregate counterparts of information—enterprise risk exposure and risk appetite—are determined, lower-level decisions can be made at the business segment, business unit, or risk level, depending on the specific risk culture of the organization, and how they choose to allocate their aggregate enterprise "risk budget" down through the organization.

Criterion 6: Includes Decision Making

The word *manage* in the ERM basic definition indicates the main purpose of ERM: responding to the risk, managing it, making decisions. Many risk management programs identify and quantify the risks, but then merely report them to management and the Board with little or no action built directly into the ERM process. For example, many companies conduct qualitative risk assessments with the primary goal of developing a simple risk status report to senior management or the board of directors.

	Status		
Key Risk	**Prior Period**	**Current Period**	**Projected Period**
Currency risk	E	N	W
Supplier risk	W	N	W
Regulatory risk	N	E	N
Compliance risk	W	W	W
M&A execution risk	N	W	W
IT failure	W	W	W
⋮	⋮	⋮	⋮

(W) = Within Limits
(N) = Near Limits
(E) = Exceeding Limits

FIGURE 2.5 Sample Heat Map

This report usually takes the form of a "heat map"—a simple chart listing key risks and scoring them with stop-light color coding: red (danger), yellow (warning), and green (okay). Some color codings refer to the overall scoring of likelihood or severity, while others refer to the level of exposure versus the risk limit. An example of the latter heat map is shown in Figure 2.5.

This focus on reporting seems to skip the most important step—actually *doing* something about the risk exposures. In a vigorous ERM program, the main purpose is making decisions and addressing the risk exposures, bringing them within the company's risk appetite. This primary activity is central to the ERM process and is repeated in each process cycle (see "The ERM Process Cycle" later in this chapter).

Criterion 7: Balances Risk and Return Management

Another aspect implied by the word *manage* in the basic ERM definition is that ERM is not just about risk mitigation. Prior to the introduction of ERM, risk management was exclusively about downside risk, employing mitigation to lower the exposure, and avoiding some risks altogether. The risk management function often manifested itself in the form of risk managers frequently saying no to projects, impeding the business segments from taking on more downside risk exposure. This sometimes frustrated business opportunities and business decision makers, because it was not always clear that the upside potential of the project was fairly weighed against the downside risk exposure. As a result, decision makers in the business segments often looked to minimize involvement by the risk management department.

However, ERM represents a quantum leap forward. Both upside and downside volatility are in scope. This means that the full range of business is recognized and addressed. Risk exposures from which the company does not benefit are considered for mitigation—a reduction in exposure. This was present in traditional risk management. But what is new with ERM is that risks for which the company is rewarded are considered for exploitation— an increase in exposure. This expanded approach allows for considering any business decision holistically: The upside risk-taking opportunity is considered alongside the downside risk exposures, for a full risk–return evaluation. Upside volatility is in scope and factored into the enterprise risk exposure calculations. As a result, ERM can identify where, and how much, additional risk may be taken, in the context of appropriate risk–return trade-offs. This involves a key linkage between risk and return, often missing in traditional risk management programs and even traditional business management approaches.

The importance of this cannot be overstated for risk management personnel. Rather than being the bearers of bad news whom business decision-makers avoid, they are now welcome at the strategy table. They are invited to decision-making conversations in the business segments and at the corporate level. The risk professionals now have a framework for bringing risk and return together, and can add value to important decision-making processes, including strategic planning.

Criterion 8: Appropriate Risk Disclosures

When first implementing an ERM program, the question often arises as to whether a new risk will be identified. The general answer is that the company already knows its key risks, and uncovering a completely new type of risk that management hadn't considered is unlikely. However, there is one risk that is frequently the single most overlooked risk, and that is the risk of improper risk disclosures.

The word *disclose* in the basic ERM definition implies offering external stakeholders real insights into the company's risks and ERM program. Unfortunately, risk disclosures are typically generic—they look very similar from company to company—and their risk lists are often exhaustive, appearing to list every major conceivable risk for their industry sector. Yet, there can be a vast range of ERM sophistication between companies in a given sector—some are quite advanced in their ERM process while others have not started theirs yet. This mismatch between what is disclosed to external stakeholders and what is the reality of the ERM program inside the company represents a significant risk.

Imagine a company that suddenly has its stock price fall 50 percent due to some risk event that did not occur for any of its competitors. Management is now under scrutiny. Many questions will be asked, some by shareholder litigation attorneys, including "What did management know, and when did they know it, regarding the potential impact of this risk on shareholder value?" Imagine further that the litigants are able to say, "This risk is listed as #35 in the risk disclosures, yet management should have known that based on the potential impact to shareholder value it should have been listed in or near the top five. Why didn't management list it as such?"

Now, imagine a second company that has its stock price collapse similarly. However, when asked similar questions by shareholders, management is able to respond as follows: "We cannot know what risk events will actually occur. However, we recently implemented an ERM program that measured the potential impact of all key risks on shareholder value, and used this to inform development of the risk disclosures. This resulted in a significant shift from the prior year's risk disclosures. We changed the order of the risks, the length of text, the tone, and the context of the information. We did our best to help shareholders understand the risks present, and the shareholders were as well informed as possible." The second company is in a much better position to defend the appropriateness of their risk disclosures.[8]

Virtually all companies are in the situation of the first company—they do not infuse their risk disclosures with information about the potential impact of key risks on shareholder value. For each such company, there are two possible explanations. One is that the company may be *unable* to do so because they do not measure the potential impact of risks on shareholder value. Most companies are in this situation. Another possibility is that the company may be *unwilling* to do so, because none of their competitors have yet disclosed this kind of information. It is just speculation, but we may be coming soon to a time when neither answer will be acceptable. At some point, either shareholder litigation may raise the stakes for external risk disclosures or regulations may require it. Chapter 7 discusses risk disclosures in more detail.

Criterion 9: Measures Value Impacts

The word *value* in the basic ERM definition indicates the importance of using holistic metrics in the risk quantification process—metrics that can fully capture the value of the company to the primary stakeholder. People often refer to the importance of *value-added*, yet few actually measure it. Management needs measures to inform their decision making. For public companies, the primary stakeholder is the shareholder. The market's measure of shareholder value is market capitalization, which is the stock price multiplied by the outstanding shares. We will define management's own measure of shareholder value as *company value*. Company value is a key metric that will be used throughout this book. It is management's internal valuation of what the company is worth to its primary stakeholders, which are the shareholders for public companies or owners for companies that are not publicly traded. See "Company Value."

COMPANY **VALUE**

We will define *company value* as an internal valuation, performed by management, that calculates the value of the company from the perspective of its primary stakeholder. For public companies, company value is the value of the company to shareholders. Unless otherwise specified, in this book, we will generally refer to public companies, although the concepts are analogous for non-publics as well. In addition, we define company value herein in one particular way, but this is often modified by management to conform to internal views on the definition of value.

We will define company value by defining each of the following three terms:

1. Distributable cash flow
2. Company value
3. Baseline company value

Distributable Cash Flow

Distributable cash flow is cash flow available to be distributed to shareholders. Distributable cash flow is generally calculated as:

Distributable cash flow$_{Non-financial\ services}$
$= Net\ income$
$+ Depreciation\ and\ amortization$
$- Increase\ in\ working\ capital$
$- Capital\ expenditures$

For financial services companies, distributable cash flow has an extra component and is calculated as:

Distributable cash flow$_{Financial\ services}$
$= Net\ income$
$+ Depreciation\ and\ amortization$
$- Increase\ in\ working\ capital$
$- Capital\ expenditures$
$- Increase\ in\ required\ capital$

Unless otherwise specified, in this book, we will use the formula for non-financial services companies.

Technically, distributable cash flow also includes changes in the level of debt, which includes repayment of principal to bondholders as well as issuance of new debt. To simplify our discussions and illustrations in this book, we will omit this.

Company Value

Company value is an internal valuation by management of the value of the company to shareholders, which is the present value of distributable cash flows:

$$Company\ value = \sum_{n=1}^{\infty} \frac{Distributable\ cash\ flow_n}{(1+d)^n}$$

Where:

- n = year of projection
- $Distributable\ cash\ flow_n$ = distributable cash flow, projection year n
- d = discount rate, which is management's estimate of the rate of return required by the shareholders for their investment; this is an estimate of the cost of equity capital

Technically, company value also includes distributable equity capital at time zero, which is calculated differently for different types of companies. For non-financial services companies, it is adjusted shareholder equity. For financial services companies, it is available capital (adjusted shareholder equity minus required capital). To simplify our discussions and illustrations in this book, we will omit this.

(continued)

(*continued*)
    There are many alternate ways to calculate company value. One example is to discount *distributed* cash flow, in the form of projected shareholder dividends, rather than *distributable* cash flow, which we will use in this book.

Baseline Company Value

The *baseline* company value is management's calculation of company value based on distributable cash flow projections consistent with the strategic plan baseline financial projection. Whereas market capitalization is the market's estimate of shareholder value, baseline company value is management's estimate, or "expectation," of shareholder value. The baseline company value is the value an investor would pay today, if they believed that management will be able to perfectly execute the strategic plan and that everything will go the way the company expects.

Surprisingly, very few companies have an internal valuation of the company for general management purposes, and even fewer use this metric in their ERM program. Traditionally, risk management programs quantify risk in terms of short-term period metrics; for example, the impact on today's balance sheet or the impact on next quarter's earnings. This is not adequate for capturing the full impact of all types of risks and is also inadequate for informing decision making. ERM must include more holistic metrics.

Criterion 10: Primary Stakeholder Focus

Many traditional risk management programs focus on maintaining their ratings as their central theme. In addition to a focus on ratings, financial service companies also focus heavily on maintaining regulatory capital requirements. This is understandable when you consider that traditional risk management is rooted in downside risk events and mitigation. However, ERM is more strategic, involves upside volatility as well as downside volatility, and begins with a focus on the primary metrics of the firm. So, while rating agencies and regulators are important, they are secondary to the primary stakeholder: shareholders. As such, rating agencies and regulators should not be maximally satisfied, because this often leads to less-than-maximal shareholder value.[9] For example, a financial services company that holds excessive capital may garner the top rating from rating agencies, but the fallow capital will lower future growth and returns and thereby lower company value.

Instead, ERM must focus on increasing value to shareholders. The level of satisfaction of secondary stakeholders is factored in, but only to the extent that it impacts shareholder value, or company value, which is management's estimate of shareholder value. For example, while searching for the risk-to-value trade-offs that might maximize company value, rating agency constraints must be taken into account because a lower rating might negatively impact value. But it might not. This is witnessed by the fact that most companies have long since migrated away from AAA ratings, deeming them too expensive and un-necessary in the quest to maximize company value, and the market has validated this shift. As another example, if regulators are not sufficiently satisfied, they may take action that will then result in a lower company value.

The ERM Process Cycle

ERM can also be defined in terms of its process cycle. We first clarify the definition of *process*. After that, we identify the components of the ERM process cycle.

Process

ERM is a process. It is not a periodic validation exercise, it cannot be completely delineated at the outset, and it is not an isolated stand-alone function. Rather, ERM is a continuous, evolving, and integrated process.

Continuous ERM is not a periodic validation exercise, like an annual car inspection. ERM is more like the continuing activities you do to protect yourself from risks involving your vehicle, such as routine car maintenance, safe driving practices, and auto insurance.

Evolving It is not possible to fully determine at the outset precisely what an ERM program will ultimately be for a particular organization. Though it is possible to lay out a high-level implementation plan, ERM evolves over time. It usually takes years for an ERM program to fully develop to maturity, and many things can change in that time. In addition, as the program develops, some aspects may gain more popularity and be expanded. The pace and scope of ERM adoption is a function of many variables, many of which are unique to each organization. The most common examples of these company-specific variables affecting ERM adoption are the following "10 Cs":

1. **Catalyst.** What or who initiated the desire to implement ERM?
2. **Commitment.** Is the Board focused on driving ERM adoption? Is senior management?

3. **Champion.** Is there a chief risk officer (CRO) to continually advance efforts?
4. **Culture.** Are they quick to adopt change?
5. **Centralization.** Does Corporate dictate requirements or are business segments independent?
6. **Climate.** Are there distractions slowing adoption? Conversely, has there been a recent risk event that has heightened risk awareness?
7. **Circumstances.** Is there an impending major threat or opportunity about which the ERM program has the opportunity to help evaluate decision alternatives?
8. **Contagion.** Can ERM concepts spread quickly across the enterprise via communication, training, inter-department interactions, and sharing of best practices?
9. **Cascade.** How long will it take for ERM applications, and supporting tools and techniques, to filter from the strategic level down to tactical and transactional levels?
10. **Confirmation.** Have rating agencies approved of the company's ERM program? What about regulators and shareholders?

Integrated In many companies, traditional risk management is a function housed in the corporate department, separate from the business segments. Risk management processes are considered an add-on that can be performed independently from other company processes. This is usually a sign that the company has a compliance-centric approach to risk management, concerned mainly with downside risk mitigation.

This is not the case with ERM, which is a more advanced approach that involves merging risk management and return management. ERM processes must be fully integrated with other key company processes, including:

- Governance
- Decision making
  - Strategic planning
  - Strategic and tactical decisions
  - Transactions (e.g., M&A)
- Business performance analysis
- Incentive compensation
- Communications with shareholders, rating agencies, and regulators

The ultimate goal, achieved in a mature ERM program, is to have ERM so integrated that it becomes part of the culture; ERM just becomes a better way of doing business.

Four Steps

There are four steps in the continuous ERM process cycle (see Figure 2.6). While there are other steps involved in establishing an ERM program (ERM framework discussed in Chapter 3 and risk governance discussed in Chapter 8), the four steps described here are the major steps that are routinely performed on a continuous basis, once the ERM program is up and running. The four steps in the ERM process cycle are:

1. **Risk identification.** Risk identification is the first step in the ERM process cycle. It involves determining the key risks, which represent the biggest potential threats to the enterprise. This entails narrowing down a very large list of potential risks to a small number of key risks. As stated earlier in this chapter, this is commonly in the range of 20 to 30 risks. This is primarily done using qualitative risk assessments, based on internal opinions as to the likelihood and severity of each potential risk. Risk identification is discussed in detail in Chapter 4.

FIGURE 2.6 ERM Process Cycle

2. **Risk quantification.** In the second step in the ERM process cycle, the key risks are quantified on both an individual and integrated basis. This involves using an ERM model to quantify the impact of individual risk scenarios, for each key risk, in terms of their potential impact on key metrics. Once this is completed, the impact of *integrated* risk scenarios— multiple risks occurring simultaneously—is quantified, leading to enterprise risk exposure metrics. Risk quantification is discussed in detail in Chapter 5.

3. **Risk decision making.** Risk decision making is the third step in the ERM process cycle. This consists of two categories of decision making. The first category includes decisions related to managing risk exposures to within risk appetite. The first step in this category is to define risk appetite. Once risk appetite is defined, decisions can be made to reduce risk exposures or to increase risk exposures. The second category includes embedding ERM into routine decision making, such as strategic planning, strategic and tactical decisions, and transactions. Risk decision making is discussed in detail in Chapter 6.

4. **Risk messaging.** The fourth step in the ERM process cycle is risk messaging. This consists of two distinct categories of messaging: internal risk messaging and external risk messaging. Internal risk messaging involves integrating ERM into business performance analysis and incentive compensation. This is a strong form of internal messaging; it is a powerful signal to management that risk and return must be considered together. Once risk exposures are tracked by the departments, the business segments, and the individuals generating them, and reflected in incentive compensation, it becomes clear that if one exposes the firm to more risk, more return is expected. The second category is external risk messaging, which involves integrating ERM into communications with shareholders, rating agencies, and regulators. Risk messaging is discussed in detail in Chapter 7.

Fundamental Benefits

Another useful way to define ERM is by its outcomes. In other words, "What are the reasons that a company should implement an ERM program? What do they get out of it?" We examine the benefits of ERM from the perspective of each major stakeholder:

▪ Shareholders
▪ Board of directors

- C-Suite
- Management
- Rating agencies
- Regulators

Shareholders

Shareholders—the primary stakeholders—benefit from ERM in two main ways:

1. Increased likelihood of achieving returns
2. Enhanced risk disclosures

Increased Likelihood of Achieving Returns   With an ERM program, the company has an increased likelihood of achieving returns—of executing its strategic plan as expected. This is a natural result of a more rigorous approach to identifying and responding to its most important threats, which are risks that can negatively impact its performance.

Figure 2.7 provides some unique evidence to support this claim, illustrating a correlation between ERM and resistance to declines in value. Standard & Poor's (S&P) has a separate component of its insurance ratings dedicated to ERM. S&P analysis reveals that North American insurers with better ERM scores tended to be more shock resistant through the heart of the global financial crisis (January 1, 2008–November 14, 2008) than their counterparts with lower ERM scores. Figure 2.7 also shows that, at the extreme, those with weak ERM programs suffered more than twice the value loss as those with excellent ERM programs.

Additional evidence that ERM helps companies deliver better performance is provided in Figure 2.8, which shows a correlation between ERM and the ability to stabilize volatility of results. This S&P study shows that better ERM was positively correlated with lower stock price volatility in 2009. At the extreme, those with weak ERM programs had more than twice the stock price volatility as those with excellent ERM programs.

Enhanced Risk Disclosures   ERM also provides shareholders, as well as potential investors, with a better sense of the risks and opportunities of owning the stock. This is due to the enhanced risk disclosures, which list the key risks prioritized from the perspective of the (current and future) shareholders: the potential impact to company value.

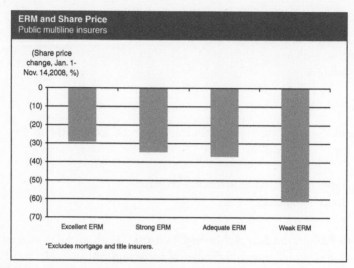

FIGURE 2.7   ERM Correlates with Shock Resistance

"Enterprise Risk Management Continues to Show Its Value for North American and Bermudan Insurers," Howard Rosen and Vladimir Uhmylenko, © 2010 by Standard and Poor's. Reproduced with permission of Standard & Poor's Financial Services LLC.

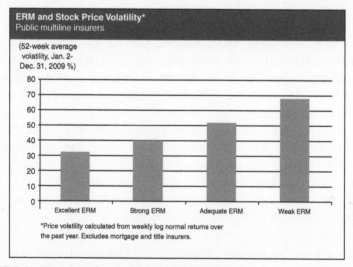

FIGURE 2.8   ERM Correlates with More Stable Results

"Enterprise Risk Management Continues to Show Its Value for North American and Bermudan Insurers," Howard Rosen and Vladimir Uhmylenko, © 2010 by Standard and Poor's. Reproduced with permission of Standard & Poor's Financial Services LLC.

Board of Directors

The members of the board of directors gain additional comfort that the key risks of the organization are well understood and effectively managed. This reassurance primarily comes from three aspects of the ERM program:

1. A disciplined approach to quantify enterprise risk exposure, based on all key risks
2. A clear definition of the firm's risk appetite
3. A formal process for managing exposures to within risk appetite, supported by a risk governance structure

ERM also places the board of directors in a comfortable position regarding the SEC disclosure requirements on the board's role in risk oversight.[10] In addition, ERM provides a solid basis for addressing the SEC disclosure requirements on risky incentive compensation programs.[11] A compensation program is considered "risky" if it creates risks that are "reasonably likely to have a material adverse effect" on the company. Each of these disclosure requirements is discussed further in Chapter 7 (see "Mandatory Risk Disclosures").

C-Suite

The C-Suite, and mainly the CEO and CFO, gain a more sophisticated risk management program, which provides better shock resistance. The company will experience less downside volatility and more strategic plan integrity—a higher potential to achieve strategic plan goals. Perhaps even more important for the CEO and CFO, ERM provides them with an advanced and more accessible set of tools for communicating these competitive advantages to key stakeholders, which can lead to a higher stock price and a better rating.

Higher Stock Price For communication with stock analysts, the CEO and CFO are better equipped to respond to, or proactively address, concerns about their ability to deliver results in the face of an impending risk or a developing risk event. This is because the ERM model quantifies the financial impact of key risk scenarios, in terms of the impact on company value (and other key metrics) and does so in a timely manner. For example, if analysts are overstating the impact an adverse market development will have on the company, the CEO and CFO are in a position to rebut this in a credible way because their information is bolstered by robust risk scenarios and an integrated quantitative ERM model. The CFO could respond:

> We have already thought through the eventuality now unfolding in the market. While it doesn't exactly match, it is fairly close to one of the risk scenarios that we considered for this risk event. You are overestimating the impact on one of our major business segments where we have the following mitigation in place . . . We also have a detailed contingency plan, which will involve the following management actions over the next period . . .

This kind of advanced ability to communicate quickly and in a credible manner effectively conveys management's superior abilities in risk management. Over time, similar communications can lead to a higher "management multiple" resulting in a higher stock price. The management multiple refers here to the factor that analysts take into account when valuing the company that to a large extent reflects their appraisal of the quality of management; a higher factor indicates a higher level of trust in management's ability to consistently and successfully execute their strategic plan. Essentially, the analysts are lowering the cost of equity capital for the company. A lower cost of equity capital, with all other things being equal, increases analysts' valuations and puts upward pressure on the stock price, to the extent that analysts influence the general market.

Better Rating   For communications with rating agencies, the CEO and CFO are able to satisfy the portion of the ratings review related to ERM. Over the past several years, rating agencies have increased their level of focus on ERM. S&P has led the way; as discussed earlier, they have a distinct component of their ratings dedicated to ERM, in the insurance sector.

While rating agencies have raised the bar on ERM requirements, forcing companies to advance their programs, their requirements are geared toward ERM from their limited perspective: protecting the interests of the bondholders. A truly robust ERM program has a broader focus—protecting the shareholder—which by its nature incorporates all secondary stakeholder interests to the appropriate degree. ERM helps determine the optimal level of satisfying secondary stakeholders—that which maximizes company value. Therefore, a complete ERM program will more than satisfy the ERM portion of rating agency reviews, and can lead to an improvement in, or strengthening of, the overall rating of the company, which means a lower cost of debt capital, which increases company value. Rating agencies tend to see the quality (or lack thereof) of a company's ERM program as a leading indicator of performance and credit-worthiness.

In addition, for financial services companies, the CFO may be able to persuade some rating agencies to lower their capital requirements for the company. While this is not the official position of the rating agencies, it may be possible to influence, at least implicitly, a downward adjustment to the capital requirements. At one point, S&P indicated that they would consider this in the insurance sector. Rating agencies have their own opinion of a sufficient capital level for a company, based largely on their industry perspective. In contrast, the ERM model estimates the impact of key risks on the company's capital position as one of its key metrics. This is a company-specific capital model, which offers the potential to be a far more accurate predictor of the company's true capital needs. The ERM model also reflects risk interactions, including offsets, resulting in a required capital level that is often lower than rating agency capital requirements. However, to succeed in having the rating agency consider the company's ERM model in setting the required capital level, the CFO must demonstrate the credibility of the ERM model calculations. To do this, the CFO must overcome the natural (and sometimes warranted) skepticism of the rating agency. After all, the ERM model, along with its data and assumptions, are a product of management which has a biased vested interest in lowering capital requirements.

Management

Management gains three significant enhancements to their decision-making abilities. They gain a well-defined methodology to manage risk exposures to within risk appetite, and quantitative information that supports decisions on risk mitigation alternatives. In addition, management gets a decision-making tool for selecting the projects with the best risk–return profile. The decision-making tool—the ERM model—supports all types of routine decisions, including strategic planning, strategic and tactical decisions, and transactions. Finally, management benefits from better prioritization of its limited resources. The ERM program allows focus on the most important risks.

Rating Agencies

Rating agencies enhance their ability to assess the credit-worthiness of the companies for which they provide credit ratings. Through the ERM lens, they see prospective information on the major threats to the company's strategic plan financial projections, which includes impacts to liquidity. The ERM program provides a complete shift in the kind of financial information typically provided to rating agencies, which is almost entirely retrospective. With the ERM program, rating agencies receive prospective insights into which risks are on management's radar, how the risks would impact the enterprise, the potential financial impacts, and management's estimates of the likelihood of each risk. They also receive data on enterprise risk exposure, which is essentially prospective information on the company's shock resistance. In addition, as more companies achieve a mature, robust ERM program, rating agencies will expand their sense of relative credit-worthiness between companies.

Regulators

For companies in the financial services sector, regulators are primarily concerned with preventing insolvencies. In the United States, there are financial costs to the government and political costs to regulators when financial services companies fail. When banks fail, the government FDIC guarantee covers depositors (up to a limit).[12] When securities firms suffer losses due to fraud, the government SIPC guarantee covers investors (up to a limit).[13] When insurance companies fail, although the government does not provide a guarantee, state regulators are held accountable politically, because they are responsible for protecting policyholder interests. In unusual times, like the global financial crisis that began in the United States in 2007, the government provides special funding to bail out companies deemed critical to maintaining the economic infrastructure.

Regulators benefit as more companies adopt ERM because it lowers systemic risk. For our purposes, we define systemic risk here simply as the risk that failures in one part of the economic system can spread contagiously to others, resulting in a cascading set of failures threatening to crash the entire system. ERM makes companies more shock resistant, lowering their risk of failure and making them more aware of their dependencies on other companies in the event those other companies fail.

 SUMMARY

Even with the most advanced risk practitioners, it is critical to clearly define both risk and ERM before delving into any discussion on ERM. These are concepts that are often defined in quite disparate ways. Risk is anything uncertain whose outcome can result in a deviation from expected results, up or down. ERM can be defined in four different ways: by its basic one-sentence definition; by its 10 key criteria; by its four-step process cycle; and by its fundamental benefits. The 10 key ERM criteria provide the most robust definition and can serve as a benchmark against which all ERM programs can be compared. These criteria will be referred to periodically throughout this book and will serve as a focal point of the next chapter, as we evaluate an advanced yet practical approach to ERM: the value-based approach.

 NOTES

1. Volatility is being used here in a general sense, as opposed to specific reference to the metric *standard deviation*.
2. "Phelps confirms right wrist is broken," available at www.baltimoresun.com/services/newspaper/bal-sp.phelps06nov06,0,3620926.story.
3. www.jockbio.com/Bios/Phelps/Phelps_bio.html.
4. *The Black Swan: The Impact of the Highly Improbable*, Nassim Nicholas Taleb, Random House, April 17, 2007.
5. Capital requirements are requirements by external stakeholders, such as regulators or rating agencies, to hold a certain amount of capital as a buffer against existing liabilities.
6. The research study is published in an article titled "IMPACT Study: focusing on risks that matter to you . . . and to the media," a Watson Wyatt Horizons publication.
7. Source: CFO Executive Board; Audit Director Roundtable research.
8. This does not constitute legal advice.
9. Throughout this text, we refer to stock analysts and rating agencies as stakeholders (the former being primary and the latter being secondary). Technically, stock analysts and rating agencies are largely acting as agents of the shareholders and bondholders, respectively, who are the true underlying stakeholders. For convenience, we use the term stakeholder interchangeably for the true underlying stakeholders and their agents.
10. Code of Federal Regulations, Title 17 (Commodity and Security Exchanges), Chapter II (Security and Exchange Commission), Part 229 (Regulation S-K), Item 407(h), effective February 28, 2010.
11. Code of Federal Regulations, Title 17 (Commodity and Security Exchanges), Chapter II (Security and Exchange Commission), Part 229 (Regulation S-K), Item 402(s), effective February 28, 2010.

12. At the time of the writing of this book, the FDIC guarantee covered up to $250,000 per individual bank account.
13. At the time of the writing of this book, the SIPC guarantee covered up to $500,000 per individual investment account and up to $100,000 per individual money market account.

3

ERM Framework

What you risk reveals what you value.

Jeanette Winterson, English author and journalist

HEN THE WORD *framework* is invoked, I become wary of what I am about to hear. It is a word that is adored by consultants. It is often accompanied by a visually appealing and complex chart with lots of boxes and arrows, or sometimes overlapping bubbles, which offers a feeling of reassurance and comfort when viewed up on an office wall. Unfortunately, these charts usually do not lead to anything actionable, or sometimes even discernable. I have seen many such framework charts on ERM. In sharp contrast, in this chapter, we will define the ERM framework in a specific, meaningful, and practical way. Our accompanying chart will facilitate our discussions, and will also be useful for ERM discussions within your organization, particularly with senior executives and the board.

In Chapter 2, we defined the ERM process cycle as having four steps which are repeated periodically—risk identification, risk quantification, risk decision making, and risk messaging. Equally important are two additional elements in an ERM program: ERM framework and risk governance. Consider each of these as ERM infrastructure or structural overlays within which the ERM process cycle operates. The ERM framework provides the functional structure and risk governance provides the hierarchical structure. Think of ERM framework as the "what (activities), how (they interact), and why (they are performed)," and risk governance as the "who (does what), when (they do it), and where (activities take place)."

Although ERM framework and risk governance are both elements of ERM infrastructure, we will discuss ERM framework in this chapter, move on to discuss the ERM process cycle (Part II, Chapters 4 through 7), and then discuss risk governance in Chapter 8. There are three reasons for this.

1. **Relative importance.** Good risk governance is a necessary condition for a robust ERM program, but it is not a sufficient condition. A company may have designed and implemented what appears to be a robust risk governance structure, but that alone cannot reveal much without knowing what activities are actually taking place. All the risk governance pieces might be in place around a hollow ERM program, much like an elaborate highway system with no vehicles traveling on it.

   However, the functional structure, or ERM framework, is more elemental, more closely linked to the quality of an ERM program. As a consultant, when I have initial discussions with a company about their ERM program, I often begin by asking about their ERM framework. That tells me virtually everything I need to know about the level of maturity of their ERM program. It is the ERM framework that reveals what activities are actually taking place and how many of the 10 key ERM criteria, discussed in Chapter 2, are present in their ERM program.

2. **Implementation sequence.** The order of our discussion more closely mirrors what companies experience when first implementing an ERM program. Initially, only the most basic risk governance structure is warranted before moving through the ERM process cycle at least one time. The way ERM evolves, is adopted, and becomes integrated into a company's key processes differs from company to company. Until it is clear what the ERM activities will actually look like, the comprehensive risk governance structure required to support them cannot easily be written.

3. **Context for understanding.** To understand risk governance it is important first to understand the ERM process steps. The roles and responsibilities of the different key players in ERM can only be discussed in the context of the ERM activities. The same is also true for the organizational structure, as well as policies and procedures, which, along with roles and

responsibilities, constitute risk governance. They can only be discussed once the entirety of the ERM process is well defined and understood. Finally, terms and concepts which will be needed to discuss risk governance are defined during discussions of the ERM process cycle (Chapters 4 through 7).

VALUE-BASED ERM FRAMEWORK

The ERM framework described in this chapter—the value-based ERM framework—is an advanced yet practical approach to ERM. This ERM framework represents an emerging approach toward which other frameworks in the industry may eventually evolve. A small but growing number of consulting firms and companies are employing this framework. It is the only framework of which I am aware that satisfies all 10 of the key ERM criteria. Other ERM frameworks will largely be a subset of the value-based ERM framework, which can be used to benchmark other ERM frameworks.

CHALLENGES OF TRADITIONAL ERM FRAMEWORKS

We will discuss the challenges of traditional ERM frameworks from two perspectives:

1. Inability to satisfy the 10 key ERM criteria
2. Three core challenges

Inability to Satisfy the 10 Key ERM Criteria

The 10 key criteria of an ERM program (discussed in Chapter 2) are:

1. Enterprise-wide scope
2. All risk categories included
3. Key risk focus
4. Integrated across risk types
5. Aggregated metrics
6. Includes decision making
7. Balances risk and return management
8. Appropriate risk disclosures

9. Measures value impacts
10. Primary stakeholder focus

These criteria must be in place for a risk management program to be considered a robust ERM program. Unfortunately, traditional ERM frameworks do not satisfy many of these 10 key criteria and often fail to achieve most of them. As a result, companies employing these traditional ERM frameworks discover that despite putting much good effort into development and implementation, their ERM program falls short of the bulk of their expectations.

Three Core Challenges

Years of research and client work in this area have revealed three core challenges to successful ERM implementation, which are like flags, or symptoms, identifying those companies that are using a suboptimal ERM framework and, as a result, are struggling to satisfy the 10 key criteria. These three core challenges are:

1. Inability to quantify strategic and operational risks (subset of Criterion 2)
2. Unclear definition of risk appetite (subset of Criterion 5)
3. Lack of integration of ERM into decision making (Criterion 6)

The first core challenge—an inability to quantify strategic and operational risks—is what I often refer to as the holy grail of ERM. The failure of traditional ERM approaches to deliver this elusive ability is the root cause of many other challenges in successfully implementing ERM.

The second core challenge is the most common question I am asked, which is, "What is risk appetite? How do you define it? How do you quantify it in a way that you can use it in risk governance?"

Finally, the third core challenge is the most prevalent one, and ultimately, the most important one: an inability to use ERM information for decision making. If ERM is not providing actionable information, not resulting in different decisions than would otherwise be made, then it has no purpose. Although some traditional ERM programs do provide some decision-making abilities, this is usually pretty limited. For example, most of the decisions resulting from traditional ERM programs involve financial risk (which, technically, makes this merely a glorified version of financial risk management rather than holistic enterprise risk management).

After we describe the value-based ERM approach, we will discuss how this emerging framework satisfies each of the 10 key criteria, including the three core challenges.

VALUE-BASED ERM FRAMEWORK

The value-based ERM framework is illustrated in Figure 3.1.

Figure 3.1 shows the major process flows for three of the four steps in the ERM process cycle:

1. Risk identification (highlighted in white)
2. Risk quantification (highlighted in grey)
3. Risk decision making (highlighted in black)
4. Risk messaging (discussed in Chapter 7)

Risk Identification

Starting on the extreme left side of Figure 3.1, we begin with all the risks in the universe, known or unknown, which can potentially impact a company's value. These correspond to all categories of risks, which for most companies are strategic, operational, and financial.[1] The flow of action, as indicated by the arrows, is to the right, as these risks attempt to impact the baseline company value, represented by the cube (in grey highlight) labeled "ERM Model." The ERM model calculates the baseline company value (see "Company Value" in Chapter 2 for the definition), as well as changes in the baseline company value resulting from simulating key risk scenarios.

However, not all risks in the universe will impact a particular company's value. Many of these potential risks are simply not relevant. The company's chosen strategy acts as a natural filter, eliminating risks that are irrelevant. In other words, the strategy will determine which risks will, and which will not, be important to the company. The strategy is composed of the company's choices that fundamentally define its businesses, including:

- What products or services to sell
- Which distribution channels to use
- Which customer markets to serve
- What value proposition to offer

For example, if the company does not do business in France, then sovereign risks related to France will likely not impact the company's value, are therefore not relevant, and may be screened out of consideration. Or, as another example, if the company is not manufacturing products using steel as a raw material, then it probably doesn't care if the price of steel rises

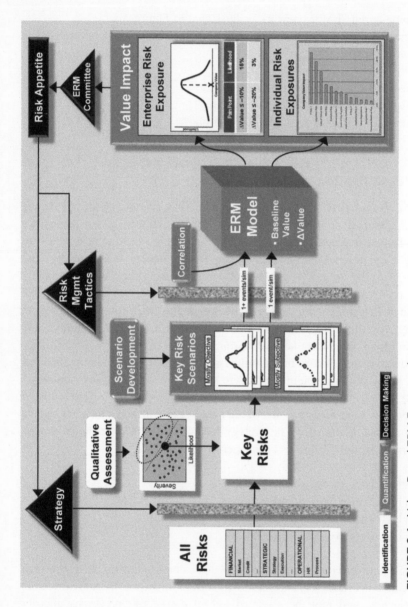

FIGURE 3.1 Value-Based ERM Framework

unexpectedly (all other things being equal). What remains, after considering the strategy as a filter to a comprehensive list of all potential risks, are just the relevant risks for the company.

However, the list of relevant risks is still too large of a list, from a practical standpoint. A qualitative risk assessment process must be conducted to further narrow down the list of relevant risks to a list of key risks, which are usually in the neighborhood of 20 to 30 risks. This process commonly consists of internal surveys asking management to first identify and then qualitatively assess the company's key risks by ranking them in terms of their frequency (how likely they are to occur) and severity (assuming they occur, how much they would impact financial results).

This is illustrated in Figure 3.1 by a likelihood-severity graph. Various methods may be used at this point to select a subset of the relevant risks based on their likelihood-severity ranking. In the graph, risks above and to the right of the line—those with higher likelihood and/or severity—are selected as this subset; this is just an example of one of these methods. This process prioritizes the list of relevant risks down to a smaller number of key risks. This determination of the key risks ends the risk identification process.

Risk Quantification

The key risks are those risks that will be quantified in the risk quantification stage of the ERM process.[2] In the value-based ERM approach, the quantification process begins with developing discrete deterministic risk scenarios for each key risk.[3] For example, a single key risk may have the following multiple risk scenarios:

- Very pessimistic
- Pessimistic
- Baseline—no risk event
- Optimistic
- Very optimistic

Not all risks have upside scenarios (the optimistic and very optimistic scenarios). However, one example of a risk that does have upside scenarios for many companies is stock market volatility. The market can move in a direction that increases the company's value, as well as in a direction that decreases its value.

Risk scenarios primarily consist of a description of the risk event, the likelihood of its occurrence, and the financial impacts. There are two types of key risks in terms of the level of difficulty, and therefore the type of approach used, in developing risk scenarios: "mostly objective" versus "mostly subjective."

Those key risks for which developing risk scenarios is mostly objective are those for which there exists a large set of objective external quantitative experience data. Most of the key risks in this category are financial risks. As an example, consider market risks. We have decades of experience with daily (and intra-day) data on the volatility of the major stock markets. As a result, we can construct a detailed, smooth, continuous distribution of historical risk scenarios for market risk.

For these types of risks, developing risk scenarios is mostly *objective*. The historical experience largely informs the understanding of the risk event, its likelihood, and its financial impacts. Management selects a set of deterministic risk scenarios from the continuous distribution, which introduces some subjective judgment. A number of risk scenarios—both upside and downside—is selected to adequately represent the shape of the distribution and capture its key inflection points. This is depicted by the set of upper graphs in Figure 3.1, where the continuous distribution is represented by the solid curve and the deterministic risk scenarios selected are represented by the dots.

In contrast, the key risks for which developing risk scenarios is mostly *subjective* are those for which no objective external quantitative experience data exist, or for which there is a very limited amount of such data readily available. Most of the key risks in this category are strategic and operational risks. Take, for example, the strategic risk related to execution of strategy. There certainly is no industry data available, because this is related to the particulars of the company's specific situation—strategy, competitive environment, capabilities of current management, and so on. For these types of risks, developing risk scenarios is mostly subjective. Management develops a set of deterministic risk scenarios using an adaptation of an approach from the manufacturing sector called Failure Modes and Effects Analysis (FMEA), which relies largely on input from internal subject matter experts. The FMEA process will be further discussed later in this chapter, as well as in Chapter 5. A number of risk scenarios, both upside and downside, are constructed and are intended to represent the shape of the unknown distribution. This is depicted by the set of lower graphs in Figure 3.1, where the lack of a known distribution is represented by the dotted-line curve, and the deterministic risk scenarios developed are again represented by the dots.

Even the "mostly objective" risk scenarios can benefit from the FMEA technique. Historical data is often insufficient. In addition, subject matter experts can contribute their knowledge and intuition, which can add significant value to the process. For these "mostly objective" risk scenarios, a combination of the two approaches is often best.

Once the risk scenarios are completed, we have all the risk-related inputs needed to quantify the individual risk exposures. We are now ready to quantify the impact on the baseline company value of a simulation involving only one event; that is, one risk scenario occurring at a time. This activity is represented in Figure 3.1 by the lower arrow labeled "one event per simulation" passing information to the ERM model for quantification.

We also must quantify the enterprise risk exposure. Enterprise risk exposure is the distribution of all potential impacts on the baseline company value from simulations involving one or more events; that is, one or more risk scenarios occurring at a time. This is a more realistic and complete representation of the firm's risk exposure, because in business, more than one variable deviates from the strategic plan during any given period. Enterprise risk exposure represents the overall aggregate volatility of company value.[4] This activity is represented in Figure 3.1 by the upper arrow labeled "one or more events per simulation" passing information to the ERM model for quantification. To perform this calculation, we need one additional risk-related input: the impact of risk interactivity, or correlation between risk scenarios. Some risks are more likely to occur together (positively correlated) than the multiplication of their probabilities would otherwise indicate, some are less likely to occur together (negatively correlated), and some are independent of each other (uncorrelated).

After risk correlation is determined, we are able to quantify the potential financial impact of individual risk events, as well as that of multiple simultaneous risk events, on company value and other key metrics. However, first we must consider another natural filter which dampens the financial impact of key risks: risk management tactics. Risk management tactics are implicit or explicit actions that mitigate the likelihood and/or severity of risk events.

One example of a risk management tactic is the purchasing of insurance. Consider an example of two companies—Company A and Company B—that are virtually identical and across the street from each other. Now imagine a disaster occurs whereby a hurricane totally destroys the headquarters of both companies, but thankfully results in no injuries or deaths. The gross financial impact on both companies is identical, amounting to the replacement cost of their buildings. Assume this is $100 million. Now assume that there is just one difference between the two companies: Company A had purchased $80 million of insurance coverage on their building, but Company B had purchased only $40 million. Although the gross risk exposure (also called inherent risk or pre-mitigation exposure) is identical for both companies, the net risk exposure (also called residual risk or post-mitigation exposure) is different:

Net risk exposure = (Gross risk exposure) − (Value of mitigation)
Company A: Net risk exposure = ($100 million) − ($80 million) = $20 million
Company B: Net risk exposure = ($100 million) − ($40 million) = $60 million

Risk culture is another example of effective risk mitigation that dampens the financial impact of risk events. Consider another example of two companies— Company A and Company B—which are again virtually identical. However, Company A has a risk culture of encouraging the early reporting of bad news, whereas Company B has a risk culture of "shooting the messenger" when bad news is delivered. Assume the same type of risk event occurs at both companies. At Company A, the risk event is identified and reported early on in the process. As a result, serious problems are averted long before the situation has an opportunity to get out of hand. However, the same risk event occurring at Company B might initially be hidden from management, causing it to grow and fester, until by the time it is identified it can jeopardize the company's very survival.

It is important to measure the potential impact of key risks on both a pre-mitigation (gross exposure) and a post-mitigation (net exposure) basis. There are two reasons for this:

1. Valuation of mitigation in place
2. Understanding the full potential impact of the risks

Valuation of Mitigation in Place

Measuring the potential impact of key risks on both a pre-mitigation (gross exposure) and post-mitigation (net exposure) basis offers unique insights into the value of the existing mitigation in place, which can highlight areas of under-mitigation or over-mitigation, or confirm appropriate levels of mitigation. These are significant insights.

As an example, consider the typical dilemma of those working in a risk mitigation area such as helping the company stay in compliance with laws and regulations. They often struggle to be fully appreciated within their organization. They are usually seen only as an expense, and whenever the company budget is under pressure, their department is often among the first to be considered for cost cutting. Even worse, the better they perform their job, the more unnecessary they can appear to be to upper management. Management tends not to react to this by saying, "We have not gotten fined much at all this year—great job!" Rather, more often, management will forget the potential exposure to fines and secretly think, if not openly verbalize:

Do we really need all those folks in Compliance? We pay almost nothing in fines anyway! Is this risk really that important that we need to mitigate it so heavily with all of this costly overhead?

However, quantifying risks on a pre-mitigation (gross exposure) as well as post-mitigation (net exposure) basis offers management a clear "before and after" picture of the impact on value (baseline company value) and value volatility (enterprise risk exposure) of the risk mitigation in question. This provides a rigorous quantitative approach to demonstrating the value added by the compliance department, or the value of specific risk mitigation. This is further discussed in Chapter 6, "Determining the Value of Mitigation in Place," where a formula for the "value of mitigation" metric is presented.

Understanding the Full Potential Impact of the Risks

A second reason that it is important to quantify risks on both a pre-mitigation (gross exposure) and post-mitigation (net exposure) basis is that it offers a deeper view of the full potential magnitude of the risk, because mitigation does not always work out as expected. For example, consider two risk events—Risk A and Risk B—each with identical potential financial impacts, on a post-mitigation basis, equal to $1 million. This is a relatively negligible impact for the company, which has annual profits of $1 billion. Informed by only the post-mitigation exposure information, management is likely to be equally indifferent to both Risk A and Risk B. Neither seems to deserve much attention. However, when examined on both a pre-mitigation (gross exposure) and post-mitigation (net exposure) basis, management is provided with the information shown in Table 3.1.

With this additional information, the difference between these risks is apparent. Management is now more likely to focus additional attention on Risk A. Risk A will only be the same minimal risk as that of Risk B if the $99 million mitigation in place operates as expected. However, there are situations in which this does not happen. For example, the $99 million mitigation may be an insurance contract, and the insurer may be unable or unwilling to pay the claim.

TABLE 3.1 Quantifying Risks A and B on Both a Pre-Mitigation (Gross Exposure) and Post-Mitigation (Net Exposure) Basis

	Pre-Mitigation (Gross Exposure)	Mitigation	Post-Mitigation (Net Exposure)
Risk A	$100 million	$99 million	$1 million
Risk B	$1 million	None	$1 million

Now we are ready to quantify the risks. Recall that risk is defined as any deviation from expected, and here *expected* is defined as the baseline company value. Baseline company value is the present value of discounted distributable cash flows consistent with the strategic plan's financial projection. The ERM model is constructed to project these distributable cash flows into the future, consistent with the strategic plan through the plan period (e.g., three years), out beyond the plan period, and then discount them back to the present time, with an appropriate discount rate. This is the same kind of fundamental calculation that an equity analyst would use if he or she had access to all the inside information that management does. This baseline company value is the amount investors would pay today if they believed that the company is going to perfectly execute its strategic plan and that everything will go precisely as management expects. See "Do Companies Measure Company Value?"

DO **COMPANIES MEASURE COMPANY VALUE?**

Most public companies are in business to make money, and their shareholders are their primary stakeholder. This means that distributable cash flow is king and that the primary metric should be company value, which is the present value of distributable cash flows. Because you can't manage what you don't measure, it is natural to assume that most public companies would measure company value, both for baseline financial projections as well as to test the value of alternate strategies and tactics.

Unfortunately, this natural assumption is incorrect. Relatively few companies measure company value and model it dynamically. Instead, most rely on market capitalization, which is a poor proxy. Market capitalization is a static, point-in-time estimate of the company's value, rather than a dynamic model which can be used to inform decision making. It is the market's opinion of the company's worth, rather than an internal management estimate, which would arguably be more accurate, because management has access to all the inside information. After all, why do rogue stock traders want inside information? Because it is valuable. Though nobody knows the future with certainty, local management can make the best guesses as to the expected distributable cash flows from their portion of the business, as well as reasonable ranges of volatility around that estimate. Capturing that information in a consistent manner around the entire enterprise and aggregating it to the enterprise level within a dynamic model produces a powerful tool for managing the firm.

Those companies that do build the capability to measure company value using such a dynamic model have a competitive advantage. They are able to strengthen their strategic planning process, because calculating the baseline company value in this way often identifies any areas of inconsistency in the strategic plan's financial projection. These companies also gain an enhanced value-based management capability—the ability to understand the drivers of value and manage it upwards. Finally, they develop a more sophisticated communications strategy for external stakeholders—primarily equity analysts. Over time, management is able to consistently demonstrate to analysts an ability to quantify how market events can impact their value. This can eventually lead to a higher "management multiple" for the company's stock price.

Risks are then quantified by "shocking" the baseline valuation with the financial impacts of a simulation involving individual risk scenarios as well as the combined impacts of multiple risk scenarios occurring simultaneously. The two "Value Impact" charts on the extreme right side of Figure 3.1 depict the results of both types of quantification.

The lower of the two charts (Individual Risk Exposures) shows the ranking of each individual key risk scenario by the primary metric—the impact on company value. This puts all types of risk on an apples-to-apples basis of comparison, in quantitative form, and serves as a prioritization and ranking of the key risks. For the key risks, this supplants the more rudimentary qualitative ranking relied on in the qualitative risk assessment portion of the risk identification process step. A modified case study example of the individual risk exposures chart is enlarged and shown in Figure 3.2.

This individual risk quantification exercise is quite revealing, especially the first time it is performed, in a way that is very surprising to management. Some risks that management had assumed to be of low significance turn out to be ranked highly, even among the top five risks, for example. Conversely, some risks thought to be high on the list turn out to be far less potentially impactful, sometimes due to their having already been over-mitigated, and some of these are occasionally even deleted from the key risk list.

This is a very exciting moment—one of the defining moments—in the ERM process. This is the first time that management sees a truly holistic list of key risks, from all sources, quantified in terms of their potential impact on company

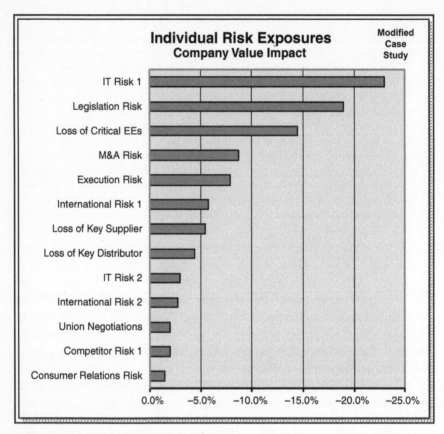

FIGURE 3.2 Individual Risk Exposures

value. This vision immediately shifts management's attention and focus, resulting in decision making to mitigate the largest potential threats (examples of case studies are highlighted in Chapter 5). There are three main reasons why this information leads to a clear and immediate shift in decision making. First, company value is a metric everyone in the company can understand. Second, it is also a metric that everyone knows they have to care about, both in protecting it and increasing it. Finally, each quantitative result is based on a risk scenario that is clearly documented and tangible, and as a result, this resonates with management.

This last point is in sharp contrast to traditional risk quantification methods, which commonly use convoluted formula-driven parameterized mathematical distributions combined with stochastic simulations to generate individual risk events. The results of such complex and abstract quantification are not easily traceable to specific risk scenarios that are concrete or, at times, even realistic. In fact, because the process involves random generation, the specific risk scenarios produced by these complex traditional approaches change every time. As a result, management has great difficulty getting comfortable with the information, and when people are uncomfortable, they hesitate to act.

Once calculated on the basis of the company value metric, the individual risk exposure graph is also readily available for any other key metrics (revenue growth, net income growth, etc., and for financial services companies, capital ratios). This is easily done, because to calculate company value, every other possible metric is required, so the value-based ERM model already has all the elements needed for producing these other key metrics.

In Figure 3.1, the chart just above the individual risk exposures chart is enterprise risk exposure. This is expressed in two forms. The first form is a graph of the distribution of impacts on company value from simulations involving one or more risk scenarios occurring simultaneously, including both upside and downside events. The enterprise risk exposure graph is enlarged and shown in Figure 3.3.

This illustrates a representation of the full range of potential outcomes, and their likelihoods, for all key risk scenario combinations, recognizing the interactivity of the risks. The horizontal axis is company value and the vertical

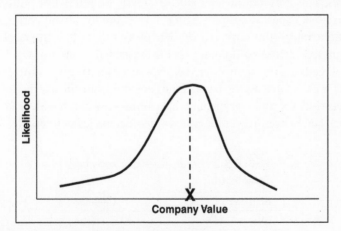

FIGURE 3.3 Enterprise Risk Exposure—Graph Form

axis is likelihood. The vertical dotted line in the middle intersects the horizontal axis at the baseline company value (represented by an X), which is what the company would be worth if they were to perfectly execute their strategic plan and everything were to go as they expected. To the extreme right, the value of the company is much higher, but with a very low likelihood; this is where many upside risk events would have to occur at the same time. Similarly, to the extreme left, the value of the company is much lower, but also with a very low likelihood; this is where many downside risk events would have to occur at the same time.

Unlike the individual risk exposures chart in Figure 3.2, it is difficult to gain much information from just looking at the enterprise risk exposure graph. The way this is used is to produce information about the likelihood of the company's "pain points," which are risk tolerance thresholds for which management wants the likelihood of crossing them to be quite small. Management is always well aware of what these are—they are the thresholds that, if crossed, would bring great scrutiny down upon them by the board of directors, shareholders, and other external stakeholders. Some examples of typical pain points include: a decrease in company value of 10 percent or more; a ratings downgrade; falling short of earnings expectations by more than 2 pennies per share; and so on.

Table 3.2 shows an example of the pain point information produced as a representation of enterprise risk exposure in table form. Each piece of information in the table (corresponding to each row) identifies a pain point and the associated likelihood of its threshold being crossed based on current exposures. This information is produced directly from the distribution in the enterprise risk exposure graph (Figure 3.3) as the likelihood corresponding to the area under the curve to the left of a vertical line intersecting the horizontal axis at the pain point. This is illustrated in Figure 3.4.

Analogous to the individual risk exposures chart, once enterprise risk exposure is calculated on the basis of the company value metric, both forms of enterprise risk exposure—graph and table forms—are also readily available for any other key metrics (revenue growth, net income growth, etc.).

TABLE 3.2 Enterprise Risk Exposure—Table Form

Pain Point	Likelihood
ΔValue $\leq$ 10%	15%
ΔValue $\leq$ 20%	3%

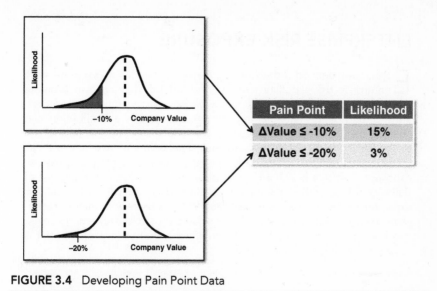

Pain Point	Likelihood
ΔValue ≤ -10%	15%
ΔValue ≤ -20%	3%

FIGURE 3.4 Developing Pain Point Data

This is the end of the risk quantification process. At this point, management now has all the current risk exposures—individual risk exposures and both forms of the enterprise risk exposures. The next step is risk decision making.

Risk Decision Making

We will discuss three aspects of risk decision making:

1. Defining risk appetite
2. Managing enterprise risk exposure to within risk appetite
3. Strategic planning and other business decision making

Defining Risk Appetite

The first step in risk decision making is for management to define risk appetite, which is sometimes referred to as risk tolerance. Risk appetite is the level of enterprise risk exposure with which management is comfortable, at the limit. Because the current level of enterprise risk exposure may be different from the desired level at any time, risk appetite represents the target maximum level of enterprise risk exposure.

ENTERPRISE **RISK EXPOSURE**

Earlier, we defined individual risk exposure metrics as separate from enterprise risk exposure metrics. And indeed, they are two separate types of information, used in different ways. However, technically, the former are included in the latter. Enterprise risk exposure is a distribution that contains the data points where one risk scenario occurs at a time (in addition to the far more robust and voluminous data points of two or more risk scenarios occurring simultaneously). Therefore, references to enterprise risk exposure, particularly in the context of metrics reviewed in the process of defining risk appetite, should be considered to include individual risk exposure information as well. Individual risk exposure information is presented separately because it can be calculated prior to the full enterprise risk exposure calculation (because risk correlations are not required), and it is usually treated as a distinct element.

The key step in defining risk appetite is the risk appetite consensus meeting. This is where the ERM committee (which may be called by various names, including the risk committee) gets together to review the enterprise risk exposure metrics (see "Enterprise Risk Exposure") and decide on the target level for enterprise risk exposure. In defining risk appetite, management is essentially attempting to discern the level of risk in the enterprise that is desired by the collective shareholders, which are often a highly diverse group with different perspectives, expectations, and investment needs.

Each person on the ERM committee brings a different perspective to this exercise. ERM committee members are individuals, and as such, each has a different emotional, gut-level feel for how much risk he or she feels the enterprise should be taking. However, intellectually, each person is looking at a consistent set of metrics, along with the unifying metric of company value, and this helps drive consensus on the definition of risk appetite.

Managing Enterprise Risk Exposure to within Risk Appetite

Once risk appetite is defined, the next step in risk decision making can take place. This is the most important exercise in enterprise risk management: moving enterprise risk exposure to within risk appetite. This is the primary purpose of ERM—not just to calculate and report risk exposures, but most critically to:

A. Measure what the overall volatility of the enterprise *is* (enterprise risk exposure)
B. To consciously decide on, and clearly define, what it *should be*, at the limit (risk appetite); and
C. To manage A to within B.

Enterprise risk exposure is a calculation, whereas risk appetite is a decision. This is a salient point, yet one that is missed by those who believe that both are mere calculations. This results in confusion and leads the ERM program down a twisted and tangled path, from which it is very difficult to find the way back.

Now, let's assume that the ERM Committee conducts the risk appetite consensus meeting, and decides that the current level of enterprise risk exposure is too high. In other words, the current level of enterprise risk exposure exceeds the target level of risk exposure, or risk appetite. In this case, there are only two things that management can do to decrease the level of enterprise risk exposure and to manage it to within the risk appetite:

1. Change strategy
2. Change (risk management) tactics

This is illustrated at the top of Figure 3.1. As you can see, changing strategy or tactics impacts the filters below. This in turn changes the calculations of enterprise risk exposure, as well as the calculation of the baseline company value. What this illustrates is that the value-based ERM process provides management with the ability to evaluate alternate risk decisions—strategic and tactical—before they are made, by quantifying their impact on the key metrics—enterprise risk exposure and the baseline company value. Decision making is fully supported because management is provided with the impact of each decision alternative on risk (enterprise risk exposure) and return (baseline company value). This is one of the most effective elements of the value-based ERM process and is certainly one of its most unique components. This combination of both risk and return elements is a key ingredient that supports decision making more generally.

To assist in the risk appetite consensus meeting, management usually supplements the enterprise risk exposure information provided to the ERM committee with some examples of how the enterprise risk exposure can be changed by readily available strategic or tactical maneuvers. Helping the ERM committee understand what is possible—how much the enterprise risk expo-sure needle can feasibly be moved—is not only helpful, it is advisable.

Defining risk appetite should only be done *after* enterprise risk exposure is calculated and, ideally, after getting some sense of the level to which it can be feasibly managed. Unfortunately, this advice is not followed by everyone implementing ERM, and it can lead to some difficulty. To see this, consider an example of a company doing it the other way around—defining risk appetite prior to knowing their current enterprise risk exposure. Imagine the following sequence of events:

1. The ERM committee conducts a risk appetite consensus meeting, without any quantitative information on enterprise risk exposure, and defines the firm's risk appetite.
2. Management reports risk appetite to internal stakeholders, and possibly to some external stakeholders as well, such as rating agencies.
3. Six months later, management calculates enterprise risk exposure and realizes that the enterprise risk exposure greatly exceeds their stated risk appetite; even more problematic, after evaluating some strategic and tactical changes designed to lower enterprise risk exposure, they realize that there is no viable way to manage it to within risk appetite.
4. Management restates its risk appetite to allow for a higher level of enterprise risk exposure.

The result of the unfortunate sequence of events in the example would likely be, at a minimum, a loss of some confidence in management's abilities in enterprise risk management. This can be easily avoided by calculating enter-prise risk exposure, and quantifying the impacts of potential strategic and tactical maneuvers to manage it, prior to attempting to define risk appetite.

Nevertheless, it is useful to get an early sense, at a high level, of manage-ment's thinking on risk appetite, prior to finalizing the quantification. This is only used for the ERM modeling team's internal purposes, in defining metrics and approximate breakpoints for the enterprise risk exposure pain points.

Strategic Planning and Other Business Decision Making

The value-based ERM framework provides an ability to quantify all key risks in terms of their impact on company value (and other key metrics) and supports the primary risk decision making in the ERM process—managing enterprise risk exposure to within risk appetite. However, it does far more than that. This framework supports all management decision making, by informing decisions with a more robust view on both the risk and return profile of any venture.

To see how, look once again at Figure 3.1. Imagine that you are standing to the left of the figure, looking to the right. What the value-based ERM framework appears to be doing is taking traditional ERM (identifying the risks and developing risk scenarios, on the left side) and marrying it pretty tightly to the company value metric (the value-based ERM model and value impacts, on the right side).

Now, imagine that you are standing to the right of the figure, looking to the left. From this vantage point, what this framework appears to be doing is taking the traditional practice of value-based management (understanding the drivers of company value and making the value of the company go up, on the right side) and marrying it to more rigorous scenarios (risk scenario development, on the left side). To see this, consider a key element of value-based management: the strategic planning process. Management devises a strategic plan, which, if properly executed, will increase the firm's value. The strategic plan is usually supported by a strategic plan financial projection. Unfortunately, the result of most strategic planning processes—the "Plan"—is a binder on a shelf. The Plan is a static, single scenario projection of the future, presented as if it will happen, just as expected, with 100 percent certainty. This is a little unfair because the work done to develop the Plan by the individual business segments often involves some excellent scenario analyses, including SWOT analyses (strengths, weaknesses, opportunities, and threats to the Plan) and sensitivity analyses, often with robust quantitative workups. However, these are usually done in very different ways throughout the company, by many different individuals, so that the scenario analyses cannot be used on an aggregate basis:

- One person's perspective of a worst-case scenario may be quite different from another person's (similarly, for all other scenarios, such as moderately pessimistic, best-case, etc.).
- Business segments, and even different individuals within business segments, may have different understandings of what is already embedded in the strategic plan's baseline scenario, and therefore, may have erroneously constructed risk scenarios (in terms of how much deviation there is from baseline in a given scenario).
- Business segments may be taking different bets on, or have different expectations of, the expected future environment (such as the direction of the economy in the near future).

What the value-based ERM framework does is to align everyone in the enterprise, in terms of what a best-estimate baseline projection of the future strategy is, what a worst-case scenario is, what the future expectations of the environment are, and so on, as well as how to define risk generally. The importance of this alignment cannot be overstated. Through this alignment, the value-based ERM approach provides management with a much more robust, consistent, and dynamic strategic planning process and strategic plan financial projection. The baseline company value is predicated on a set of business segment financial projections with a consistent view on what constitutes a best-estimate baseline scenario and future view of the internal and external environment. In addition, the scenarios are consistent for all universal assumptions (the economy, interest rate environment, currency exchange rates, weather, etc.) and are consistently defined for all risk scenarios (for example, the definition of a worst-case scenario is well understood, documented, and shared internally).

In addition to providing a dynamic strategic planning tool, the value-based ERM approach provides a valuable ad-hoc "what-if" tool, which can answer such questions as:

- If a moderately pessimistic scenario for economic conditions occurs, how would it impact revenues in each of our major business segments, and the enterprise in total, including adjustments for any cross-segment interactions?
- If our worst-case scenario for currency exchange rates is realized, how would it impact our earnings across the enterprise?
- If our moderately optimistic scenario for the competitive environment occurs, how would it impact our profit margins enterprise-wide?

These additional tools are not ancillary. Rather, they are critical to a successful ERM program. A successful ERM program must be integrated into key decision-making processes, such as strategic planning, strategic and tactical decisions, and transactions.

In Chapter 2, we offered a commonly used short definition of ERM, which offered a technical description of ERM:

The process by which companies identify, measure, manage, and disclose all key risks to increase value to stakeholders.

However, when ERM is implemented using a value-based approach, a better definition may be as follows:

A practical yet advanced approach to integrate both risk and return information into strategic planning and other business decision making.

OVERCOMING THE CHALLENGES BY USING A VALUE-BASED ERM FRAMEWORK

At the beginning of this chapter, we stated that traditional ERM frameworks often struggle to satisfy the 10 key criteria of an ERM program. We also highlighted three core challenges, which are subsets of the 10 key criteria, which are common symptoms of a suboptimal ERM framework. The emerging value-based ERM framework was designed to effectively address the challenges of traditional ERM programs, including these three core challenges. Now that we have described the value-based ERM approach, we will discuss how this emerging framework satisfies each of the 10 key criteria, and addresses the three core challenges.

Criterion 1: Enterprise-Wide Scope

One of the main obstacles to achieving a consistent enterprise-wide adoption of an ERM program is a limiting approach—an approach that simply cannot work in every part of the organization. This is most common when the ERM program is first developed with only the company's primary business segment in mind. This is especially common in financial services firms that have diverse businesses, some of which have to hold *required capital* on their balance sheets, and some of which do not.

Required capital is an amount of capital that is required to remain on the balance sheet in support of existing business on the books, and cannot be employed to support future growth. The amount of required capital is set by multiple stakeholders, including regulators, rating agencies, and management itself, where each has its own approach to defining and calculating the required amount. The company often holds the maximum of these amounts to ensure satisfying all stakeholders.

Financial services companies where banking or insurance is the primary business generally use a capital-based ERM framework; that is, they use capital as their key metric. It is understandable that these types of organizations would be drawn to a capital-based approach. It is an important metric for them. It is also a metric that is a product of risk management—the required capital levels are set based on assessing levels of risk in the firm. Unfortunately, this becomes a nonstarter for those financial services companies that also have non-financial services operations, in terms of achieving an enterprise-wide ERM program. A capital-based approach simply can't work in these non-financial services operations, because they don't have capital requirements.

For example, assume a bank holding company has a retail banking division and a consulting division. They institute a capital-based ERM program. Their key metric for quantifying risk exposure is the amount of additional required capital generated by the risk exposure. The consulting business clearly generates risk, yet it does not generate required capital, because this part of the enterprise is not subject to capital requirements. Capital requirements are not a universal currency that can be used to evaluate risks across the enterprise, and as a result, the company has an incomplete ERM program.

However, the value-based ERM program offers a metric that can, and does, work across both financial services and non-financial services operations. Company value is a unifying metric. Company value is the present value of distributable cash flows for both types of operations. Each has a slightly different definition for distributable cash flows, but once properly defined, they are fully comparable:

$$
\begin{aligned}
Distributable\ cash\ flow_{Non-financial\ services} \\
&= Net\ income \\
&+ Depreciation\ and\ amortization \\
&- Increase\ in\ working\ capital \\
&- Capital\ expenditures
\end{aligned}
$$

and

$$
\begin{aligned}
Distributable\ cash\ flow_{Financial\ services} \\
&= Net\ income \\
&+ Depreciation\ and\ amortization \\
&- Increase\ in\ working\ capital \\
&- Capital\ expenditures \\
&- Increase\ in\ required\ capital
\end{aligned}
$$

Criterion 2: All Risk Categories Included

One of the most important of the 10 key criteria is the inclusion of all risk categories in an ERM program. Ignoring a risk category, or not having a balanced focus among all risk categories, can expose the company to excessive risk and result in focusing limited risk mitigation resources on the wrong priorities. In addition, a lack of sufficient focus on certain risk categories can result in unpleasant surprises; management doesn't really care about *which* risk source takes them by surprise . . . they just don't want to be surprised. Unfortunately, the vast majority of traditional ERM programs focus all, or most, of their attention on financial risks, either ignoring or giving short shrift to the strategic and operational risks, which are actually responsible for far more firm volatility than the financial risks.

One of the main reasons for this imbalanced focus is an inability to quantify strategic and operational risks. *This is the first of the three core challenges to a successful ERM implementation, which we discussed earlier.* Let's examine this further.

Traditional Approach

There are three common approaches that traditional ERM frameworks use in attempting to quantify strategic and operational risks:

1. Qualitative only
2. Industry data
3. Risk capital

Qualitative Only The most common approach used in traditional ERM frameworks is simply to not quantify strategic and operational risks, but instead to develop qualitative information. This qualitative information takes the form of key risk indicators (KRIs). For example, a qualitative KRI for the risk of poor customer service might be the number of complaints per month.

KRIs can be useful. Changes in KRIs can indicate a potential underlying problem, either existing or emerging, and prompt management to investigate. However, KRIs are not enough to support ERM decision making; for example, choosing between two alternate mitigation approaches. Management needs numbers—quantitative data—to make decisions. Even quantitative data that require estimates, or even guesses accompanied by confidence ranges, are better than mere qualitative data.

Industry Data Another approach often used by traditional ERM frameworks is to rely on industry data to quantify strategic and operational risks. For some risks this may be useful. However, the vast majority of strategic and operational risks, and certainly the most important risks, cannot be quantified using this approach. This is because industry data is often either unavailable or inappropriate or both.

Industry data is often unavailable for these risks. For example, there is no industry data set that can quantify the potential impact of the company's strategic plan being flawed or the potential impact of poor strategy execution. Each company's strategy, or its ability to implement the strategy successfully, is a completely unique risk.

Industry data is often useful as anecdotal supplementary data for risk quantification. However, it is often inappropriate to rely on industry data as the primary basis for risk quantification. The net impact of risk on an organization varies significantly based on the risk mitigation tactics in place. For example, if one company has more insurance coverage or a superior risk culture than another apparently identical company, the first company will not suffer the same consequences from a given risk event as the second company. How a risk works its way through each organization can be radically different. Using an industry data set does not take into account the specific nature of the company and its risk management tactics.

Risk Capital   The third approach routinely used to address quantification of strategic and operational risks is the one that may initially seem to be the most rigorous quantitatively. Ironically, this is also the worst of the three traditional ERM approaches. This approach is only used by financial services companies that have capital requirements. This approach was introduced by Basel II, and involves setting aside capital for operational risk. This effectively means that the amount of required capital is increased to recognize balance sheet volatility caused by the operational risks.

The first and most obvious failure is that Basel II ignores strategic risks altogether. As shown in Chapter 2, strategic risks are more important than operational risks, and appear to be at least twice as important. However, even in terms of appropriately quantifying operational risks, there are significant problems with the risk capital approach. Under Basel II, there are two alternative methodologies:

Alternative 1: Set aside a percentage of revenues as operational risk capital.
Alternative 2: Use an internal model to calculate operational risk capital.

The vast majority of banks use alternative 1 and set aside approximately 15 percent of revenues as operational risk capital. A majority of insurance companies have copied this method as well. The 15 percent is not risk-based. The 15 percent, and therefore the amount of operational risk capital, is an arbitrary number, totally unconnected to the reality of operational risks in the business. This is not a risk-based approach. But that is the least of its problems. Worse still is the fact that this method produces an estimate of operational risk whose changes are often even *directionally* incorrect.

Consider the following example. You are the head of the consumer lending division of a large bank. The bank institutes an ERM program, and in an attempt to quantify operational risk, defines operational risk capital as 15 percent of revenues. You are given the additional responsibility for operational risk management for your division. You excel at your new risk management role. Within just the first year, you are a whirlwind of productivity, and by everyone's account, you have cut operational risk virtually in half. You have decentralized key offices, instituted a litany of good operational risk protocols, purchased more insurance coverage, and developed detailed business continuity plans. In addition, in your primary role over the past year, you have grown top-line revenues 25 percent. Congratulations: At year end, operational risk capital—the measure of how much operational risk there is in your division—goes . . . *up*! This is not even directionally correct. The actual risk was lowered by about 50 percent, yet the metric goes up 25 percent. Clearly, this makes no sense, yet this is a very common approach employed in the financial services sector.

Alternative 2 requires the bank to develop its own internal model to measure operational risk capital requirements. Banks use VaR models and insurance companies use economic capital models, both of which were defined in Chapter 2. These models are risk-based in that they are generally proportional to the risk: more risk means more risk capital, and less risk means less risk capital. In addition, they can be, and sometimes are, used to try to quantify strategic risks as well as operational risks. However, they do not fully capture the financial impacts of strategic and operational risks. The VaR and economic capital models are usually designed to quantify the impact of risks on the balance sheet, to show the net impact to capital (assets less liabilities) and to required capital. These models ignore the impact to future revenues and expenses, which is often the bulk of the impact of strategic and operational risks.

Consider the following case study. A large multinational insurance company is attempting to quantify the impact of a key risk involving a disaster at an internal conference where top salespeople and managers are among those killed. The key element to this risk quantitatively is that it significantly lowers the entire future revenue projection of the strategic plan.

Unfortunately, the insurance company's economic capital model woefully understates this risk. Because most economic capital models are capital-centric and therefore focus exclusively on balance sheet capital and required capital, revenues for all future new business are generally not included, and so are not available to be "shocked" downward to capture the full financial impact of the risk. The baseline economic capital model includes a future projection of revenues and expenses, but only those related to the current insurance business "inforce," or on the books. To add insult to injury, not only does the economic capital model fail to fully quantify the downside impact of this worst-case scenario, but it actually reports the event as *good* news, because it accounts for a reduced allocation of expenses (due to fewer employees).

Value-Based Approach

Now, we will discuss the value-based ERM approach to quantifying strategic and operational risks. After that, we will discuss how the value-based approach addresses the shortcomings of the traditional ERM approach to quantifying strategic and operational risks.

As discussed earlier, the ERM model projects distributable cash flows into the future, consistent with the strategic plan, and then out beyond the planning period in some reasonable way. The first metric calculated is the baseline company value, which discounts the baseline distributable cash flows to today, using the hurdle rate. The baseline company value is the price that an investor would pay today, if they believed the company was going to perfectly execute the strategic plan, and everything was going to go its way. Risk is then defined as anything that shocks this baseline company value, up or down.

Failure Modes and Effects Analysis (FMEA) Technique   The value-based ERM approach uses a technique called Failure Modes and Effects Analysis (FMEA), adapted from the manufacturing sector, to develop the individual deterministic risk scenarios for strategic and operational risks. There are four steps to the FMEA process:

1. **Identify interviewees.** The first step in the FMEA process is to identify the most appropriate internal subject matter experts for the risk in question. For some risks, this might be the most senior person involved with the risk, such as the executive risk owner, who has overall responsibility for the risk, enterprise-wide. This might be the case for certain litigation risks or human resources risks. However, the person closest to the risk is usually the most appropriate choice.

2. **Develop risk scenarios.** The second step is to begin the FMEA interview with the identified interviewees by soliciting from them a set of risk scenarios for the key risk in question. There are often several risk scenarios for each key risk. For example, a single key risk may have the following risk scenarios:

- Credible worst-case
- Moderately pessimistic
- Mildly pessimistic
- Baseline (represents no risk)
- Mildly optimistic
- Moderately optimistic
- Credible best-case

Not every key risk will have upside risk scenarios, but it is important to consider these.

Each of these scenarios is an individual deterministic risk scenario. In other words, these are hypothetical specific events. It is critical to develop specific deterministic scenarios. Imagining a specific event occurring makes it easier for interviewees to think through the sequential progression of likely events, as well as the consequences to the company.

It is best practice to begin with a credible worst-case scenario, by asking the subject matter experts, "When your head hits the pillow at night, what do you worry about?" This gets at something perhaps remote in likelihood, but not out of the realm of all possibility, yet something that is potentially very damaging to the company. Some of the less extreme risk scenarios are often developed by modifying the credible worst-case scenario (such as reducing its scale).

For each individual risk scenario, the FMEA process guides the experts into thinking the event through in detail, chronologically. A series of expert-led questioning extracts the internal subject matter expert's knowledge as to what eventualities in the external and internal environment would likely flow from the initial event. What would be the initial damage? What would be the secondary and tertiary repercussions? How would management respond, and how quickly could they respond?

3. **Assign likelihood.** The third step is to assign likelihood to the event. This is difficult because it is so uncertain. It is also difficult because the interviewees are often not accustomed to making such estimates, and usually do not speak the language of probability. They are unlikely to respond in terms such as, "There is a 15 percent chance of this risk event occurring this year." This is another area where skill in conducting the

FMEA process is required to bridge the gap between the qualitative language used by the interviewees and the quantitative language needed for the ERM model.

4. **Estimate quantitative impacts.** The final step in the FMEA interview is to develop estimates of the quantitative impacts of each deterministic risk scenario on the baseline company value. This is done step by step, using a series of questions: How would this impact revenues this year? Future years? What are the impacts on fixed expenses? Variable expenses? and so on. As with assigning likelihood, estimating quantitative impacts can be difficult from the standpoint of getting interviewees comfortable with making estimates. This is another reason why it is important to have someone with experience conducting the FMEA interviews. See "But Aren't These Just Guesses?"

An illustrative example is shown in Figure 3.5, which outlines the flow of the four-step FMEA exercise, as well as an abridged summary of the kind of information produced. Both the likelihood and the quantitative impacts become inputs into the ERM model for shocking the baseline company value, first to quantify individual risk exposures, and later to quantify enterprise risk exposure.

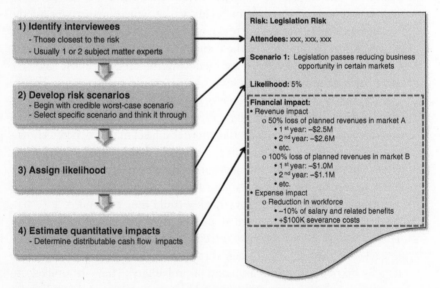

FIGURE 3.5 The FMEA Process and Sample Summary Output

BUT **AREN'T THESE JUST GUESSES?**

A common initial concern raised in early discussions of the FMEA technique is the claim that this information can't possibly be useful because it is all based on mere guesses. Although the latter is largely true—the process does involve guesses—the former statement is incorrect: This information does add quite a lot of value to the ERM process. There are several factors that more than compensate for the uncertain nature of the information:

- **Decisions happen anyway.** As discussed in Chapter 2, the reality is that strategic and operational risks must be quantified in some way. They are far more impactful to firm volatility than financial risks, and management must make decisions involving these risks each and every day, with or without the benefit of quantitative data. Management is far better off with estimates, even highly subjective estimates, than with no quantitative information at all.

- **Expert guesses.** Although these are guesses, they are expert guesses, made by those closest to the risks and often those with decades of personal experience and even more anecdotal knowledge of risk events in the industry. There are many brilliant people in the firm, and there is much valuable knowledge trapped inside their heads. The FMEA process extracts this useful information out of the heads of the subject matter experts and puts it on the page in a consistent quantitative form, for all key risks, all across the company. In many cases, the FMEA process is the first time the subject matter experts have being asked to think through the risk scenarios and potential mitigation, and this thought-provoking process produces better guesses than previously existed anywhere, even *inside* the experts' heads.

- **Ranges.** Ranges around the guess are used as a type of sensitivity analysis, which provides a level of comfort by showing how wrong the estimate could be. A case study illustrates this point. An ERM team presented a business opportunity, predicated on FMEA information, to a business unit, who initially objected based on the approximate nature of a single critical assumption. However, the business unit accepted the proposal once it was clear that, based on examining the ranges, the assumption would have to be off by a factor of 10 to negate the validity of the opportunity.[5]

   In addition, the ranges themselves reveal useful information. The point estimates for two different risks might be identical at $10 million. However, the range for the first risk might be $8 million to $12 million, whereas the range for the second risk might be $5 million to $50 million.

(continued)

(continued)

- ■ **Reduced bias.** Another factor that makes this information better than pure guesses is the fact that the results of the FMEA interviews are documented. This reduces bias. When people know that their name is formally attached to something, they tend to be even more careful about its quality. This occurred during the initial implementations of SOX. At the end of the first major effort to gather and assess a large amount of data, senior executives had to sign their first attestation regarding the accuracy of the risk assessments, control assessments, and the financial reports. It was at this stage that the quality of the information increased somewhat, as the executives began scrutinizing the information more closely to increase their level of comfort before affixing their signatures.

- ■ **A crowd of experts.** When the FMEA information is initially gathered, it is the product of just one or two experts. However, the FMEA information is published and shared with others in the company. This results in corrections and enhancements to the data, as others contribute their insights. This is much like the effect of Wikipedia, which benefits from shared knowledge leading to a collective consensus.[6]

- ■ **Relative comparisons.** The FMEA process provides the ability to make relative comparisons between risks. The FMEA exercise is performed in a consistent manner around the enterprise, for all risks, and expresses their potential impact quantitatively. Even though each individual risk scenario is quantified using subjective estimates, collectively this information becomes more powerful, because the relativities between risks are more reliable than any one estimate. The comparative analysis often leads to priorities shifting to those risks that are relatively more impactful.

Advantages of Value-Based Approach

Now that we have described the value-based approach to quantifying strategic and operational risks, we will compare the effectiveness of this approach with the traditional ERM approaches. As discussed earlier, the three traditional ERM methods used in attempting to quantify strategic and operational risks have several disadvantages:

- ■ Metrics don't support decision making.
- ■ Data are unavailable or inappropriate.
- ■ Approach is not risk-based.
- ■ Inability to fully quantify risk impacts.

The value-based approach addresses each of these issues.

Ability of Metrics to Support Decision Making The first traditional ERM method involves using only qualitative information, which leads to the inability to make decisions based on the information. In stark contrast, the value-based approach quantifies all key risks. In addition, the value-based approach quantifies them in terms of the impact on company value, which robustly supports decision making.

Availability and Appropriateness of Data The second traditional ERM method is to use industry data, which leads to the problem of unavailability and inappropriateness. The value-based approach resolves these issues as well. The data is available because the company is developing its own data primarily using internal personnel. This information is abundant, because management always knows who the one or two people are that are closest to a given risk, and certainly has access to them. In addition, the data developed is company- and culture-specific, because it is based on the specific situation within the firm.

Risk-Based Approach The third traditional ERM method involves using risk capital as the key metric. There are two alternative approaches: The first uses an approach that is not risk-based and, worse, is sometimes directionally incorrect in its measurement of changes in exposure. Clearly, the value-based ERM approach is risk-based, because it begins with the company-specific risk scenarios, and the ERM metrics properly rise and fall with the level of exposures.

Ability to Fully Quantify Risk Impacts In addition, the value-based approach allows for full quantification of the risks because the baseline company value captures the full projection of future revenues, expenses, and other components of distributable cash flow, and risk is measured as shocks to the baseline. In our example discussed earlier, a disaster at an internal conference results in the death of top salespeople and managers. The value-based ERM approach has in its baseline company value the future revenues that these salespeople were to generate. As a result, the quantification of the risk, which is the shock to the baseline, would fully reflect all of the lost revenues.

Figure 3.6 summarizes the comparison between traditional ERM and value-based ERM in terms of quantifying strategic and operational risks.

Traditional Approach		Value-Based Approach
Method 1: Qualitative	Cannot support decision making	Quantifies impact to value/ supports decision making
Method 2: Industry data	Often unavailable or inappropriate	Company/situation-specific
Method 3: Risk capital	▪ Not risk-based/often directionally incorrect ▪ Understates risk	▪ Risk-based ▪ Fully quantifies risk impacts

FIGURE 3.6 Quantifying Strategic and Operational Risks

In the section titled "Case Studies" in Chapter 5, several case studies will be discussed that more fully illustrate the value-based ERM methodology for quantifying strategic and operational risks, as well as demonstrate its effectiveness.

Criterion 3: Key Risk Focus

Many traditional ERM programs treat ERM as an expanded SOX exercise. This is partly a result of the familiarity of the risk folks in the firm with SOX. It is even more a result of the fact that the traditional ERM framework does not lend itself to much beyond risk mitigation. As a result, without anywhere else to go, management develops as comprehensive a laundry list of risks and risk controls as it reasonably can.

Because the value-based ERM approach uses company value as the key risk metric, it immediately focuses management on an appropriately limited number of key risks. The key risks stand out quite distinctly in terms of their potential impact—the amount of company value that they might destroy. This naturally avoids an unnecessarily long list of risks, most of which would have negligible impact on company value.

Criterion 4: Integrated across Risk Types

Risk management programs (precursors to ERM programs) almost always involve "silo" approaches to risk, meaning each type of risk is handled separately within the company. This leads to difficulties in three areas, as discussed in Chapter 2:

1. Completeness
2. Efficiency
3. Internal consistency

Unfortunately, although all traditional ERM programs tout an integrated approach as a key criterion, most of them still suffer from the same silo mentality as their risk management predecessors. However, the value-based ERM approach makes it easy to integrate an ERM program across risk types. Let's examine each of the three areas of potential difficulty regarding integration, and compare the traditional ERM approach to the value-based ERM approach.

Completeness

Traditional ERM programs using silo approaches are incomplete, because they ignore multiple risks occurring simultaneously and fail to capture their inter-activity—both offsets and exacerbations. In contrast, the value-based ERM approach fully reflects this by directly measuring multiple risks and their interactivity in the ERM model, producing the entire distribution of real-world outcomes in the enterprise risk exposure graph (see Figure 3.1).

Efficiency

The inefficiencies in many traditional ERM programs caused by the lack of centralized coordination and cross-departmental communication are resolved in the value-based ERM approach. The structure provided by the value-based ERM approach, as well as the unifying nature of the company value metric, ensure a high level of ERM coordination and cross-pollination. The risk scenarios are developed in a way that identifies and includes inputs from any relevant area of the firm. In addition, the value-based approach uses a central ERM model that can be used by business units anywhere in the firm to measure the marginal impact of any risk decision. Finally, the top-down approach to defining risk appetite, cascading down to risk limits, leads to coordinated approaches by type of risk, enterprise-wide.

Internal Consistency

The internal inconsistencies of traditional ERM programs employing a silo approach can manifest as conflicting projections of the internal and external environment (for example, the performance of equity markets). However, the value-based ERM approach clarifies where these exist and provides a single consistent view for the company. The construction of the ERM model and the calculation of the baseline company value correct these issues, as well as strengthen the strategic planning process. In addition, risk scenarios are developed in a way that includes all relevant viewpoints from anywhere in the firm, partly during the FMEA process itself, and partly by the documentation and internal sharing of the resulting risk scenarios.

Criterion 5: Aggregated Metrics

We will discuss two aspects of aggregated metrics:

1. Enterprise risk exposure and risk appetite
2. Top-down allocation of risk appetite to risk limits

Enterprise Risk Exposure and Risk Appetite

There are two key aggregate metrics required for ERM. The first one is enterprise risk exposure and the second one is risk appetite. The former is a calculated item, but the latter is a management-defined item. Enterprise risk exposure represents the current level of overall enterprise volatility. Risk appetite is the maximum limit of enterprise risk exposure to which management would like the company to be exposed.

The two aggregate metrics should be mirrors of each other, because the metric(s) used to define risk appetite should follow the metric(s) chosen for enterprise risk exposure. This is because risk appetite is simply management's defined limit for the maximum acceptable level of enterprise risk exposure. Recall that each of these aggregate metrics is actually an entire distribution of outcomes (see Figure 3.1), which may be represented by multiple metrics, each with multiple thresholds, and a corresponding likelihood for each threshold. For enterprise risk exposure, one expression of these threshold-likelihood pairs may be called a pain point. For example, one pain point expression of enterprise risk exposure, and its risk appetite counterpart, might be as follows:

> Enterprise risk exposure pain point expression: 1 percent chance of losing (amount X) of (metric Y)
>
> Corresponding risk appetite expression: 5 percent chance of losing (amount X) of (metric Y)

So, because one (risk appetite) follows the other (enterprise risk exposure), a key to producing these two aggregate metrics is that the enterprise risk exposure metric(s) must be expressed, and calculated, at an enterprise level. Without an aggregate level enterprise risk exposure, there is no aggregate level risk appetite.

Unfortunately, most traditional ERM programs do not have this. Instead, they commonly produce a large volume of key risk indicators (KRIs) to track the exposure for their key risks. Disparate KRIs metrics are used for different key risks. As a result, there is no single metric available to aggregate the exposures to the enterprise level, which, in turn, means that there is also no aggregate metric for risk appetite.

Without a quantitative definition of risk appetite, these companies complicate matters in their attempt to produce some type of risk appetite statement. What results is often a vague and confusing document. *This is the second of the three core challenges to a successful ERM implementation, which we discussed earlier: An unclear definition of risk appetite.* This leads to the inability to perform the primary function of ERM—managing enterprise risk exposure to within risk appetite. In addition, it also prevents the proper order of risk limit setting, which should be top-down. Lacking a cascading top-down approach to setting risk limits can sometimes lead to under-mitigation, which is potentially dangerous; however, an even more common result is wasteful over-mitigation. This was discussed in Chapter 2.

Unlike the traditional ERM programs, the value-based approach provides both of the key aggregate metrics. All key risks can be quantified in terms of their potential impact on company value. The company value metric works consistently, regardless of geography or accounting system, because it is based on distributable cash flow, which is a universal currency. It also works for all types of risks, because it is the only metric that can fully quantify all risks, particularly strategic and operational risks, which often impact future revenues and expenses. This allows the calculation of enterprise risk exposure in terms of company value as well, and as a result, risk appetite is easily expressed at the aggregate level, on the same basis.

This facilitates the main goal of ERM: managing enterprise risk exposure to within risk appetite. Both metrics are expressed consistently, so it is clear how to do this because they can be compared directly. For example, modifying our example discussed earlier, we might have the following:

Enterprise risk exposure: 1 percent chance of losing 30 percent or more in company value

Risk appetite: 5 percent chance of losing 30 percent or more in company value

Top-Down Allocation of Risk Appetite to Risk Limits

The value-based ERM approach also facilitates the appropriate top-down allocation of risk appetite to risk limits. This is due to the same attribute that allows the upward aggregation of individual risk exposures to enterprise risk exposure: The company value metric is a consistent metric appropriate for all key risks.

One way to visualize this is as a four-step process:

1. Upward aggregation of individual risk exposures to enterprise risk exposure (graph form)
2. Developing pain point data (representation of enterprise risk exposure in table form)
3. Defining risk appetite as a mirror of enterprise risk exposure (table form)
4. Downward cascading allocation of risk appetite to individual risk limits

This is illustrated in Figure 3.7. In Step A, the ERM model aggregates the individual risk exposures, using the risk scenario information developed in the FMEA process as well as the risk correlation data[7] by running simulations involving combinations of one risk event per simulation, two risk events per simulation, and so on, producing the graph form of enterprise risk exposure. In Step B, pain points are selected to produce the table form of enterprise risk exposure. Step C involves two parts. The first part involves mirroring the pain points from enterprise risk exposure, thus populating the left-hand column of the risk appetite table. In the second part of Step C, management defines the acceptable likelihood for each pain point during the risk appetite consensus meeting, thus populating the right-hand column of the risk appetite table.

Step D involves using the ERM model to reverse-engineer any desired risk limits, below enterprise level, which will aggregate to risk appetite at the enterprise level. Regardless of the type of allocation, or budgeting, of risk appetite—whether the limits are by source of risk, by business unit, by geography, and so on—the reverse-engineering aggregation is feasible, because all exposures are measured with the consistent metric of company value.

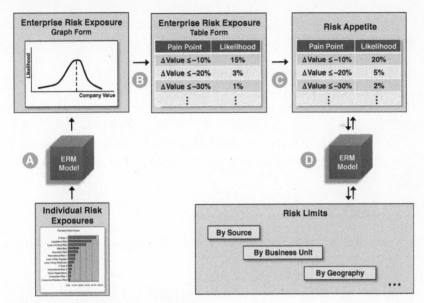

FIGURE 3.7 Aggregate Risk Metrics

Some illustrative examples of these types of risk limits may include:

- **By source.** No more than a 2 percent loss of company value from a risk event caused by technology failure
- **By business unit.** No more than a 5 percent loss of company value from risk events arising from our retail business unit
- **By geography.** No more than a 10 percent loss of company value from risk events arising from our international operations

An example is provided in Chapter 6, "How to Define Risk Limits."

Criterion 6: Includes Decision Making

The third step in the ERM process cycle is risk decision making, which is most central to the purpose of ERM—actually *doing* something about the risks, acting on the information gathered up to this point in the process. Sadly, the most common problem plaguing traditional ERM programs is the inability to integrate ERM into decision making. *This is the third, and final, of the core challenges to a successful ERM implementation, which we discussed earlier.*

There are three critical elements that must be in place for effectively integrating ERM into decision making:

1. ERM metrics that support decision making
2. Practical ERM models
3. Consensus buy-in from business segments

Let's evaluate both the traditional ERM approach and the value-based ERM approach in terms of whether, and to what extent, they satisfy these three critical elements.

Do the ERM Metrics Support Decision Making?

There are two aspects to having ERM metrics that support decision making:

1. Robust metrics for all types of risks
2. Metrics with both risk and return information

Traditional ERM programs do not have either of these in place, and therefore do not have ERM metrics that support decision making. However, the value-based ERM approach has both of these aspects and fully supports decision making.

Robust Metrics for All Types of Risks   Traditional ERM programs generally do not have robust metrics for all risks. The metrics for strategic and operational risks are either nonexistent or are simply not robust enough—not nearly as robust as the metrics for financial risks. This was discussed earlier in this chapter. As a result, the ERM metrics of traditional ERM programs cannot support any decision in the company that involves strategy or operations, which is the vast majority of important decisions. Essentially, traditional ERM programs are more like financial risk management programs than holistic ERM programs, and as such, their metrics are largely relegated to supporting decisions solely involving financial risks.

Unlike traditional ERM programs, the value-based ERM approach quantifies all types of risk, and does so in an equally robust way. All risks are quantified on a consistent basis in terms of their potential impact on company value (and other key metrics). As a result, all types of decisions can be informed by the value-based ERM metrics, including strategic decisions, tactical decisions, and transactions.

Metrics with Both Risk and Return Information   Traditional ERM metrics generally provide only half the picture needed for a business decision. Traditional ERM metrics are only geared for capturing the downside. For example, in financial services firms, they use capital loss or the increase in required capital to measure the impact of a risk. But a business person needs to balance risk and return to make risk–reward trade-off decisions. A decision cannot be made without an ability to compare, within the given metric(s), the downside and the upside of a decision.

Unlike traditional ERM programs, the central metric of the value-based ERM approach—change in company value—is suitable for combining the risk as well as the return side of the business decision-making equation. Not only that, this provides the single most rigorous business case one can ever make for a decision: the expected change in the company's value, and the level of certainty around achieving that change.

Are the ERM Models Practical?

Most traditional ERM models are overly complex. ERM models are designed, built, modified, expanded, and maintained by modelers. And modelers, by their nature, are like thoroughbreds—they love to run. It's as if they have all this pent-up capability and they are itching to unleash it. Modelers are tempted to go down a rabbit hole of ever-increasing expansion of the model's level of detail, in a misguided belief that they are perfecting the model. However, this is counterproductive to the whole point of the exercise, which is to support decision making.

In contrast, value-based ERM models are not overly complex; rather, they have an appropriate balance between robustness and practicality. The value-based approach is designed specifically for connecting risk management to business decision making. As a result, every aspect of the approach is tailored and trimmed to keep it sleek and practical with this singular focus in mind, and the model itself is no exception.

We will discuss four aspects of ERM model practicality:

1. **Reliability.** Traditional ERM models tend to be unreliable in terms of their quality. Traditional ERM models require a large volume of inputs, which makes them cumbersome to update every period. By the time the model is refreshed, it is time to update the inputs again. As a result, the model grows burdensome and the quality of updates deteriorates. In addition, the voluminous and tangled programming code makes the model prone to errors.

However, value-based ERM models are highly reliable in terms of their quality. These models use a reasonable number of inputs, which makes them easier to maintain, keeping the quality of the updates high. In addition, the simplicity of the programming code makes the model less prone to errors.

2. **Speed.** The response time for traditional ERM models is too slow to keep up with the pace of business. In the financial services sector, these models can literally take weeks to complete a single run. There are not many decisions in the organization that can wait that long for an answer. In addition, modifications to the model often require a lengthy time period and a significant allocation of resources.

   However, the response time for value-based ERM models is fast enough to support business decision making even at the highest levels, where a faster pace is required. Run time is usually kept to within a handful of hours. With such a quick turnaround time, virtually all decisions can be feasibly supported. In addition, modifications to the model can be made rapidly, because the programming code is relatively straightforward.

3. **Transparency.** With a traditional ERM approach, the quantification methodology is so murky that it tends to make management skittish at the prospect of relying on it for use in decision making. For example, risk scenarios might be based on a convoluted set of formulae, which are used in conjunction with a stochastic process that generates new and abstract risk scenarios every time. The lack of tangible risk scenarios can be disconcerting.

   However, with a value-based ERM approach, the methodology is highly transparent to management, which gives them more comfort in relying on it for decision-making purposes. For example, the underlying individual risk scenarios that give rise to the entire set of exposure metrics are tangible, specific, deterministic scenarios. Management can review them directly, and even challenge the choice of assumptions, which gives the approach a very concrete feel. This accelerates management's adoption of ERM into decision making.

4. **Balance of significant digits.** Traditional ERM models have an imbalance of significant digits in their calculation and presentation of results (this was discussed in Chapter 2). Traditional ERM models purport to provide enterprise risk exposure calculated to a high level of accuracy. However, these models cling to a hyper-accurate measurement of financial risk while giving short shrift to the (more important) strategic and operational risks, either ignoring them or estimating them crudely. Yet, studies (discussed in Chapter 2) show that strategic and

operational risk exposures generally represent the bulk of a firm's aggregate enterprise risk exposure. Therefore, claiming such a high level of accuracy when reporting enterprise risk exposure is a violation of the significant digits rule.

In contrast, the value-based ERM approach uses an appropriate balance of accuracy in the calculation and reporting of its results. It uses a consistent level of accuracy for both the financial risks and the strategic and operational risks. The value-based ERM approach develops aggregate information that is correctly presented as approximate, by its nature, and is also balanced, and thereby respectful of the significant digits rule.

Is There Consensus Buy-In from Business Segments?

In most traditional ERM programs, there is a lack of buy-in by the business segments that ERM is something that is good for the business. This is all too often the bane of the ERM program leader, who is faced with the task of "selling" ERM to the business segments, whose receptivity remains cool. Sometimes this is due to an ERM program that is, or is perceived to be, per-petrated on the business segments by the corporate department. Perhaps there was not enough input by the business segments in the risk identification or risk quantification stages of the ERM process. Alternatively, the program may be, or may be perceived to be, too compliance oriented.

This is another area in which the value-based ERM approach excels. There are two features of the value-based ERM approach that result in rapidly building consensus buy-in from the business segments:

1. Appropriate level of input by business segments
2. Support of business segment goals and initiatives

Appropriate Level of Input by Business Segments   Most traditional ERM programs involve too much development exclusively within the bounds of the corporate ERM team, particularly risk scenario development. Their thinking is that if they first build a robust model fully populated with data and assumptions, and then unveil it, when people see what it can do, they will buy in to the process. Unfortunately, this doesn't work. Those closest to the risks—which are largely those in the business segments—must be heavily involved, particularly with risk scenario development.

The value-based ERM approach has an appropriate balance between business segment and corporate input. The value-based approach uses the

FMEA process (described earlier in this chapter). The majority of the inputs required for the FMEA process involve strategic and operational risks. Those closest to these risks are mostly associates in the business segments, who provide the bulk of the input. However, the corporate ERM team has a right and responsibility to push back on some assumptions, to ensure a consistent and credible process. For example, corporate ERM may know that one of the FMEA interviewees is a particularly risk-averse individual, and may tend to exaggerate the risks; alternatively, they may know that another FMEA interviewee is a risk taker, and usually downplays the importance of potential negative events. Or, someone else may be the champion for a mitigation project under consideration, and that may color his or her perspective. Knowing the people involved, and also seeing the FMEA exercise across the enterprise, puts Corporate in a position to provide valuable input.

Support of Business Segment Goals and Initiatives   Although most traditional ERM programs speak a lot about linkage to decision making, the reality is that they are mired in mitigation. Knowing this, the business segments are leery at the notion of inviting the risk folks into their business discussions, lest they get in the way by throwing up risk roadblocks to progress. The value-based approach is the diametric opposite to this. Its focus on decision making permeates every step in the ERM process. One of the best examples of this is during the FMEA risk scenario development exercises.

The FMEA interview is usually attended by business segment subject matter experts who are closest to the risk, the interviewer (an ERM specialist with experience in FMEA interviews), and representation from the corporate ERM team. The subject matter experts will often exhibit unreceptive body language at the outset of the meeting, leaning back in their chairs with arms folded, looking at their watches, thinking (if not verbalizing):

> This is just another corporate effort. You're going to collect information and then try to use it to handcuff me in some way, imposing limits or controls on what you call "risk taking" but what I call doing business. So, let me get back to my work of running the business, because I'm generating the earnings that are paying all of your corporate salaries anyway.

This begins to change as the meeting unfolds. From the very beginning of the FMEA process, the subject matter experts are being asked for all the inputs: What could go wrong? What do you worry about? How bad might it be? How fast would we recover? And so on. The subject matter experts are appropriately respected for the knowledge they have. Feeling this, they loosen up a little bit. Arms become uncrossed.

Next, the ERM model, which quantifies the risks based on the risk scenario inputs, is another potential barrier to business unit buy-in. Models are usually a "black box," or nontransparent to those not in control of it. However, the value-based approach uses a simpler, more accessible model that can be easily explained. In addition, subject matter experts gain additional comfort when they are told that they will have a chance to review the outputs and revisit their inputs if results appear odd. They determine the inputs. They understand the internal mechanics. They get to review the outputs. Suddenly, this begins to feel like they own the model, and essentially they do. The buy-in builds further. They are now sitting up straight.

Finally, at the end of the meeting, the subject matter experts from the business segment are asked, "Is there any mitigation that you feel is needed, or is there any project you had planned related to this risk scenario?" About a third of them will pound their fist on the table, and exclaim, "Yeah, we know we need such-and-such, but we just couldn't make the business case and Corporate did not approve it." The corporate ERM folks are in a position to respond, "Well, maybe we can help you. The ERM model is written in the language of changes in company value, which is the strongest business case possible. We can help you model the proposed decision, including its upside and downside exposures, based on the marginal impact to the firm (including any offsets elsewhere in the firm) and show you where the 'edges' are—what revenues or cost savings are needed to make this viable." Now the buy-in goes into full gear. Now the subject matter experts lean all the way forward in their chairs. Now they love you, because you are helping them get their project accomplished. You are helping them achieve their goals, keep their jobs, and get their bonuses. It is at this point that rather than pushing ERM into the business segments, there actually begins to be a pull from them, once they see how it can serve their needs.

The shift in consensus buy-in can be rapid and dramatic. As an example, a financial firm was piloting the value-based approach in business segment A before rolling it out to business segments B and C. After witnessing the rapid shift in consensus buy-in resulting from this process, the CFO told me, "This is fun. I thought I would have to push ERM into business segments B and C. But once they heard what business segment A was getting, they were banging on my door to get it, too." As a result, the company moved quickly to implement the value-based ERM approach enterprise-wide.

TABLE 3.3 Supporting Decision Making: Traditional ERM versus Value-Based ERM

	Traditional Approach		Value-Based Approach	
Do metrics support decision making?	NO	■ Not for operational or strategic risks ■ Only risk, not return	YES	■ Metrics for all risks ■ ΔValue = rigorous business case
Do ERM models work?	NO	■ Unreliable quality ■ Slow response time ■ Lack of transparency ■ Violates significant digits rule	YES	■ Reliable quality ■ Fast response time ■ Transparency ■ Balance of significant digits
Is there buy-in from business units?	NO	■ Corporate-driven ■ Compliance-oriented	YES	■ Business unit-driven/ Corporate for consistency ■ Supports business unit goals/initiatives

Table 3.3 summarizes the comparison between traditional ERM and value-based ERM in terms of supporting decision making.

Criterion 7: Balances Risk and Return Management

Traditional risk management was exclusively about downside risk protection. Though ERM is supposed to equally treat downside and upside volatility, most traditional ERM programs lack the ability to deal with upside volatility. The value-based ERM approach easily handles both, through its unifying metric—changes in company value. Using the same language (value) for both risks and opportunities clears the path for complete integration of both sides of risk–return management.

Not only does the value-based ERM approach resolve this historical problem with traditional risk management and even traditional ERM programs, but it also solves a problem more generally for business management. One of the oldest and most used business phrases is "risk–reward" or "risk–return" management. Incredibly, this is rarely done, at least not in a robust way. Most companies have their reward or return management (e.g., strategic planning) completely segregated from their risk management (e.g., internal audit, corporate risk unit, etc.). Value-based ERM finally fulfills the promise of balancing risk and return and integrating both into considerations of business decisions, starting with strategic planning and cascading down through the organization.

Criterion 8: Appropriate Risk Disclosures

The purpose of financial reporting is to inform investors about the potential risks and opportunities of the company. As alluded to in Chapter 2, the most defensible approach is to inform the development of risk disclosures with a quantification of the potential impact of key risks on company value. After all, the primary stakeholder is the shareholder, and company value is their primary metric.

Unfortunately, companies using a traditional ERM approach are unable to do this, because they do not measure exposures in terms of the potential impact on company value. However, companies using a value-based approach are easily able to inform the risk disclosures with this type of information. The potential impact on company value is a central output of the value-based approach.

Criterion 9: Measures Value Impacts

The ability to find the actions that truly add value depends fundamentally on the activity of measuring value. Surprisingly, as discussed earlier in this chapter, few companies measure company value. So, to fulfill the portion of the ERM definition that describes its purpose as "to increase value," an ERM program would have to bring with it a measurement of value. Unfortunately, traditional ERM programs do not do this. For example, at financial services companies, most traditional ERM programs are capital-centric—they use the change in balance sheet capital or the increase in required capital as the primary metric.

In comparison, the value-based ERM approach is all about value. Company value is the central metric. The value-based ERM approach fully supports both measuring the upside of value volatility (reward) as well as the downside of value volatility (risk). This puts management in the best position possible to manage value. Because value is fully measured, it can be fully managed.

Criterion 10: Primary Stakeholder Focus

Most traditional ERM programs focus on downside protection, and in that tradition, they tend to focus more on satisfying rating agencies than on satisfying any other stakeholder. This is especially true for financial services companies, which are, at times, overly focused on capital requirements. Maintaining an appropriate level of capital is critical. However, focusing too heavily on capital needs does not always lead to decisions that increase company value.

A better approach is to focus on the primary stakeholder, who, for most public companies, is the shareholder, and treat all other stakeholders as secondary. Secondary stakeholders should only be satisfied to the extent that it optimally increases company value. The value-based approach provides the framework to do just that. Every decision is viewed in terms of how it impacts company value. See "Managing Secondary Constraints for Maximal Value."

In Chapter 10, we generalize the definition of the value-based ERM approach to show how it can be adapted for entities that do not have public shareholders and are not focused on company value or distributable cash flows.

MANAGING **SECONDARY CONSTRAINTS FOR MAXIMAL VALUE**

The value-based ERM approach takes secondary stakeholders into account as constraints to be managed in the process of increasing company value. All types of decisions as to the optimal level of resources to expend in satisfying secondary stakeholders can be evaluated by the impact on company value. There is a "sweet spot" the company must find for the amount of resources to use in satisfying each such secondary stakeholder. The following two examples will illustrate this point:

Rating Agencies

- If the company does too little, in the extreme, then the likelihood of a ratings downgrade increases. A ratings downgrade risk scenario would include an increase in the cost of debt capital (i.e., interest expense), decreasing distributable cash flows, and lowering company value. This risk scenario may rise in the key risk ranking, which would increase the enterprise risk exposure. If the enterprise risk exposure is increased enough, this would imply a higher cost of equity capital, further lowering company value.

- If the company does too much, in the extreme, it may take the form of expensive risk mitigation efforts related to some issue about which the rating agency has expressed concerns, or abandoning plans for aggressive new ventures about which the rating agency had negative, perhaps overly conservative, views. This would directly result in higher-than-expected expenses or lower-than-expected revenues,

- respectively, decreasing distributable cash flows and directly lowering company value.
- There is an optimal balance of efforts that maintains the desired rating at an appropriate cost, which results in the best risk–return trade-off, maximizing company value.

Charities

- If the company does too little, in the extreme, it increases the risk of negative media coverage resulting in reputational damage. This risk scenario may include a decrease in revenues due to loss of customers, an increase in expenses to fund an expensive public relations advertising campaign to mitigate the damage, or both, decreasing distributable cash flows and lowering company value. This risk scenario may rise in the key risk ranking, which would increase the enterprise risk exposure. If the enterprise risk exposure is increased enough, this would imply a higher cost of equity capital, further lowering company value.
- If the company does too much, in the extreme, it will overspend on charitable donations. This would directly result in higher-than-expected expenses, decreasing distributable cash flows and directly lowering company value.
- There is an optimal balance of efforts that satisfies the company's image as a decent corporate citizen at a reasonable level of donations, which results in the best risk–return trade-off, maximizing company value.

 ## SUMMARY

Traditional ERM frameworks do not satisfy many of the 10 key ERM criteria, and often fail to achieve most of them. In addition, traditional ERM programs have three core challenges to successful ERM implementation, which are like flags, or symptoms, identifying those companies that are using a suboptimal ERM framework, and as a result, are struggling to satisfy the 10 key criteria. These three core challenges are:

1. Inability to quantify strategic and operational risks
2. Unclear definition of risk appetite
3. Lack of integration of ERM into decision making

The value-based approach was designed to address these shortcomings. Through a synthesis of ERM and value-based management, the value-based approach offers an advanced yet practical ERM approach that fully satisfies all 10 key ERM criteria, including the three core challenges.

Now that we have provided the recent historical context for ERM (Chapter 1), properly defined both risk and ERM (Chapter 2), and presented the value-based ERM framework (this chapter), we conclude Part I, "Basic ERM Infrastructure." We are now ready to explore Part II, "ERM Process Cycle," where we will discuss the four steps in the ERM process cycle: risk identification (Chapter 4), risk quantification (Chapter 5), risk decision making (Chapter 6), and risk messaging (Chapter 7).

 NOTES

1. Insurance risks are another category, primarily for insurance companies, but also for other companies offering certain types of guarantees.
2. Some non-key risks also receive quantitative treatment, but not in the same robust manner as described in the remainder of this section. Identifying "emerging risks"—those risks that may become key risks in the future—is a process that includes some quantitative analysis of risk scenarios for certain non-key risks.
3. This is very different from traditional ERM methods, which attempt to generate risk scenarios from continuous distributions, most of which must be artificially developed specifically to enable this approach.
4. This only represents the portion of the volatility arising from the key risks, because these are the only ones quantified.
5. See Chapter 6, "Integrating ERM into Business Decision Making," "Dealing with Soft Assumptions" for more detail on this case study.
6. See also *The Wisdom of Crowds*, a book by James Surowiecki, which discusses how collective information can improve even the estimates of the smartest individual expert.
7. Correlation data adjusts for the fact that some risks are more likely to occur together (positively correlated) than the multiplication of their probabilities would otherwise indicate, whereas other risks are less likely to occur together (negatively correlated). Risk correlations are discussed in more detail in Chapter 5.

II

PART TWO

ERM Process Cycle

CHAPTER FOUR

Risk Identification

The dangers of life are infinite, and among them is safety.

Goethe

ONCE AN ERM framework is chosen, and after at least some basic risk governance is established, the four-step ERM process can begin. Risk identification is the first step in this process, which, as discussed in Chapter 2, is a continuous, evolving, and integrated process.

COMPONENTS OF RISK IDENTIFICATION

There are three components to the risk identification ERM process step, as performed using the value-based ERM approach:

1. Risk categorization and definition
2. Qualitative risk assessment
3. Emerging risk identification

The first time these three components are conducted, they must be performed in the order shown, because the outcome of each preceding component is used as input into the following one.

Before we discuss these three components, we will discuss the five keys to successful risk identification.

FIVE KEYS TO SUCCESSFUL RISK IDENTIFICATION

Many companies have at least begun the ERM process and have at least completed the first step in the ERM process cycle—risk identification. Therefore, many believe that common practices in risk identification are, by now, best practices, and that this step is fairly straightforward. Unfortunately, quite the contrary is true. There are several aspects of risk identification that are still routinely performed in a suboptimal way. Not only does this hamper the risk identification process step, but it also significantly impacts the quality of the entire ERM program, because every other step in the ERM process is downstream from the risk identification step, relying on information from it.

To avoid these problems, ERM programs must employ the following five keys to a successful risk identification process step:

Key #1: Define risks by source
Key #2: Categorize risks evenly
Key #3: Define metrics clearly
Key #4: Gather data appropriately
Key #5: Identify risks prospectively

The first two keys to success are primarily related to the risk categorization and definition component of risk identification. The last three keys to success are primarily related to the qualitative risk assessment component of risk identification. These keys to success will be discussed later, within the context of their corresponding component.

We will now discuss the three components of the risk identification ERM process step, starting with risk categorization and definition.

RISK CATEGORIZATION AND DEFINITION

The risk categorization and definition component of the risk identification process step consists of constructing a comprehensive list of known potential risks. The result is the risk categorization and definition (RCD) tool. The RCD tool includes a risk categorization hierarchy including risk categories, risk subcategories, risk divisions, the risks themselves, and a definition clarifying the scope of the risk. Table 4.1 shows a partial sample of an RDC tool.

TABLE 4.1 Partial Sample of Risk Categorization and Definition (RCD) Tool

Risk Category	Risk Subcategory	Risk Division	Risk	Definition
Operational	Human resources	Talent management	Ability to recruit or retain	Ability to recruit or retain staff not matching expectations
Operational	Human resources	Talent management	Succession planning	Ability to develop new leadership not matching expectations
Operational	Human resources	Talent management	Critical employee(s)	Unexpected loss of employee(s) with critical and rare knowledge or skills
Operational	Human resources	Talent management	Labor or producer relations	Employees or producers take unexpected action against the company (e.g., union strike)
⋮	⋮	⋮	⋮	⋮
Operational	Technology	Data security and privacy	External attack	External attack (e.g., phishing) steals company or customer data, including privacy data, and/or destroys programs or data
Operational	Technology	Data security and privacy	Internal attack	Internal attack steals company or customer data, including privacy data, and/or destroys programs or data
Operational	Technology	Data security and privacy	Accidental breach	Employee accidentally exposes company or customer data, including privacy data, and/or destroys programs or data

The risk categorization in the RCD tool should be reasonably comprehensive in terms of categories and subcategories, but certainly not in terms of individual risks. A full list of categories and subcategories is needed to serve as a prompt to participants in the qualitative risk assessment interviews, to trigger them to consider myriad potential key risks that may lie within each category or sub-category. However, it is not advisable to attempt to construct a comprehensive list of all potential risks. Even if such a task were possible, the list of risks would be too long. In addition, any list that purports to be comprehensive in terms of risks tends to lower the level of imagination used by participants in the qualitative risk assessment. Rather than meditate for a while on the business and its risks, they simply look down the list and check off the ones that look relevant.

The main risk categories, and their definitions, are as follows:

Financial risk. Unexpected changes in external markets, prices, rates, and liquidity supply and demand. This includes market risk, credit risk, and liquidity risk

Strategic risk. Unexpected changes in key elements of strategy formulation or execution

Operational risk. Unexpected changes in elements related to operations, such as human resources, technology, processes, and disasters

There is one additional risk category—insurance risk, which generally applies only to insurance companies. Insurance risk involves poor performance of the pricing, underwriting, reserving, or setting of required capital for insurance products.

An example of some common risk categories and subcategories, and their definitions, is shown in Table 4.2.

TABLE 4.2　Common Risk Categories and Subcategories

Risk Category	Risk Subcategory	Definition
Financial		A category of risks related to unexpected changes in external markets, prices, rates, and liquidity supply and demand. See also market risk, credit risk, and liquidity risk.
Financial	Market	Unexpected changes in external markets (such as stock markets), prices (such as commodity prices), or rates (such as interest rates), related to (a) general market movements (although the source for this is often economic risk) or (b) a specific asset on the company's balance sheet. Some examples include equity market risk, interest rate risk, and currency risk.

Financial	Credit	Unexpected changes in credit markets (availability), prices (credit spreads), or credit-worthiness of issuers, related to (a) general credit market movements (although the source for this is often economic risk) or (b) a specific issuer of a fixed-income security on the company's balance sheet or (c) a counterparty to whom the company has extended credit.
Financial	Liquidity	Unexpected changes in liquidity supply or demand, related to three different levels of impact on the company: (a) untimely asset sales; (b) inability to meet contractual demands; or (c) default. A change in liquidity supply involves an unexpected change in the ability to sell assets as expected in the market, in terms of price, volume, or timeliness. A change in liquidity demand involves an unexpected change in demand for liquidity by option holders, such as bondholders exercising early put options or "run-on-the-bank" situations for financial services companies, where account holders suddenly request the withdrawal of funds from their accounts, en masse.
Strategic		**A category of risks related to unexpected changes in key elements of strategy formulation or execution. This is highly variable by company and must be customized.**
Strategic	Strategy	Viability of strategy—such as choice of products, distribution channels, markets, or value proposition—does not match expectations. This is highly variable by company and must be customized.
Strategic	Execution	Strategy is not implemented as expected. This is highly variable by company and must be customized.
Strategic	Governance	Governance is not functioning as expected.
Strategic	Strategic relationships	Unexpected change in strategic relationships, such as a parent company or joint venture partner.
Strategic	Competitor	Unexpected change in competitive landscape, such as new entrants, aggressive competitor actions against the company, price wars, and so forth.
Strategic	Supplier	Unexpected changes in supplier environment, such as supplier capacity, supplier failure, or change in the cost of goods or services. This also includes unexpected changes in rating agency ratings or regulatory licenses.
Strategic	Economic	Unexpected changes in the economy. This is often the source of risk that triggers multiple simultaneous unexpected changes in other items, such as consumer

(continued)

TABLE 4.2 (*continued*)

Risk Category	Risk Subcategory	Definition
		disposable income (impacting demand for the company's products or services), employment markets (impacting the company's fixed expenses), inflation/deflation (impacting the company's variable costs), items related to market risk, and items related to credit risk.
Strategic	External relations	Unexpected changes in the company's relationship with external stakeholders with public voices, such as the media, consumer advocates, equity analysts, rating agencies, regulators, and politicians.
Strategic	Legislative/ regulatory	Unexpected changes in laws or regulations.
Strategic	International	Unexpected changes in the business environment of foreign countries in which the company operates, such as unexpected changes in the government's stability, attitude toward foreign companies, and tariffs.
Operational		**A category of risks related to unexpected changes in elements related to operations, such as human resources, technology, processes, and disasters.**
Operational	Human resources	Human resources (i.e., people) are not performing as expected, such as unexpected changes in talent management, performance, productivity, and conduct.
Operational	Technology	Technology not performing as expected. Some examples include data security, data privacy, data integrity, capacity, and reliability.
Operational	Litigation	Unexpected civil suits or judgments against the company.
Operational	Compliance	Level of compliance not matching expectations, such as financial reports are not as accurate as expected.
Operational	External fraud	Unexpected change in the amount of fraud by external parties.
Operational	Disasters	Unexpected natural or man-made disasters, such as weather-related (such as hurricane, flood, tornado, earthquake, and drought), health-related (such as pandemic), accidental (such as fire), general acts of destruction (such as war, terrorism, and rioting), and specific acts of destruction against the company (such as product tampering, attack on employees, and sabotage). This also includes unexpected man-made disasters caused by company employees or agents, such as environment damage.
Operational	Processes	Company processes not functioning as expected.

Nomenclature

Although it is important for the RCD tool to include a comprehensive list of risk categories and subcategories, it is not particularly important that its nomenclature conform to any external standard. What is important regarding RCD nomenclature is that it be clearly defined and consistently used throughout the organization. In fact, internally, it is often best *not* to use an externally defined standard for RCD nomenclature. External standards are often poorly constructed; for example, they are not consistently defined by source. In addition, it is preferable to customize the nomenclature with terminology already in use by the businesses, which can help to pave a smoother path toward adoption and integration of the RCD tool, specifically, as well as ERM generally.

RCD Tool Applications

The RCD tool provides a uniform lexicon for risks throughout the enterprise. This assists the development of risk culture, which is the integration of ERM into key company processes. Having a consistent language for risk is critical to a uniform adoption and integration of ERM into the organization over time. The importance of having a common language for risk cannot be overstated, and will be further explored later, during discussion of the first two keys to successful risk identification. Suffice to say that there are many ways that the categorization and definition of risks can go awry, and the RCD tool helps keep this on a consistent track.

As a result of this unifying quality, the RCD tool becomes a natural focal point for many aspects of the ERM program, and is commonly used in several ways. The main applications for the RCD tool include the following:

- Catalyst
- Collection and coordination
- Monitoring
- Reporting
- Comparative analysis
- Recording

Catalyst

Often, the very first use of the RCD tool is as a catalyst in the qualitative risk assessment phase of the risk identification process step. The RCD tool is part of the advance communication provided to the qualitative risk assessment survey participants. This helps trigger survey participants' imagination of potential key risks to consider. At a minimum, it confronts survey participants with the specific risks listed in the RCD tool, and calls on them to consider whether these are potential key risks for their business or for the enterprise as a whole. In addition, the reasonably comprehensive nature of the RCD tool reminds survey participants of risks that they may well know, but that may have otherwise slipped their mind during the qualitative risk assessment exercise. Finally, for qualitative risk assessments subsequent to the initial one, the RCD tool shared with survey participants is often populated to show which risks were identified as potential key risks in the prior qualitative risk assessment, as well as their consensus ranking and likelihood-severity scores. This helps survey participants consider whether, and to what extent, the importance of these previously identified risks has changed.

This also gets qualitative survey participants to think in terms of risk defined and categorized in a consistent manner. The RCD tool illustrates the proper way to define risks by source and to categorize risks evenly.

Collection and Coordination

The RCD tool is useful for the collection of data and coordination of activities during the qualitative risk assessment. The RCD tool is easy to use as a template to populate risks as they are identified by survey participants during the qualitative risk assessment. In addition, it helps interviewers as they interpret and document the risks provided by survey participants. Often, the risks, as stated by survey participants, are either not worded clearly or are not properly defined as a source of risk (see later "Key #1: Define Risks by Source"). By mapping the inputs provided into the RCD tool, interviewers can quickly identify any problems. When the qualitative risk assessment is performed via live interviews, the RCD tool helps interviewers identify any issues in real time, which affords them the immediate opportunity to ask clarifying questions of survey participants, and to make any necessary corrections.

In addition, when interviews are used for the qualitative risk assessment, the RCD tool facilitates coordination among multiple interviewers. In addition to their uniform interview script, all interviewers have the same RCD tool, which serves as a central touchstone keeping all interviewers aligned. Also, as new potential risks are identified by survey participants in early interviews, interviewers can quickly and easily coordinate with each other to include the additional risks in the RCD template, making them more complete for the remaining interviews.

Finally, the RCD tool is used to coordinate the qualitative risk assessment consensus meeting. This is where the individual results of the qualitative risk assessment are aggregated and shared with all survey participants, and a meeting is held to clarify any results with significant dispersion and enhance the level of consensus before finalizing results.

Monitoring

After the qualitative risk assessment, the RCD tool is used to store all the results—key risks as well as those risks confirmed as risks in the consensus meeting, but which did not rise to the level of *key* risks on the basis of their likelihood-severity scores. In between periodic reperformance of the qualitative risk assessment, the fully populated RCD tool is used to monitor any potential changes in the importance of any of the risks listed therein. This is part of emerging risk identification.

Reporting

The RCD tool can also be used as part of the internal reporting of key risks to management and to the board of directors. Seeing the key risks listed within the RCD tool provides a context within which to better understand the key risks. This highlights those risks selected as key risks, and contrasts them against those risks *not* selected as key risks. This provides more information and elicits the kind of engaged dialogue that builds risk awareness and risk culture at senior levels. In addition, using the RCD tool for internal reporting provides a standard report format that can be sustained over time.

Comparative Analysis

Another useful application of the RCD tool is to provide a basis for conducting a comparative analysis between the company's own risk disclosures and that of its key competitors. When available, competitors' risk disclosures are examined and the risks are mapped into the RCD tool. This puts the disparate formats and terminology on a consistent basis, which allows direct comparison. This analysis often reveals interesting information, such as the following:

- Risks disclosed by the company and by competitors
- Risks disclosed by the company but not disclosed by competitors
- Risks disclosed by competitors but not disclosed by the company
- Relative emphasis placed on certain risks by competitors and how that differs from the company's relative emphasis

Recording

The RCD tool is also useful as a platform for the risk event database, which records actual occurrences of risk events impacting the organization. The risk event database captures various information about the events, including, for example, originating source of the risk, how the event emerged and unfolded, management's actions, and the ultimate financial impacts. This is used for two purposes. The first is to capture information that can be used to enhance the development of risk scenarios. Capturing historical experience related to a specific risk can inform the estimates of future likelihood as well as future severity of impact. A second purpose is to enhance the entire ERM program through what is often referred to as "risk learnings."[1] Risk learnings are the lessons learned from the risk event, including, for example, answers to the following questions:

- Was the originating source for the risk event on our radar? If not, can we improve our risk identification process?
- How did the risk emerge? Should we have caught it earlier on?
- How did the risk event unfold, and what financial impacts occurred? Can we use this information to enhance our risk scenario development process?
- Was there any existing pre-event mitigation in place (i.e., fraud detection systems) to make the event less likely or less impactful, and was it effective?
- Was there a management reaction plan in place (e.g., business continuity plan), did management follow it, and was it effective?
- Was there post-event mitigation (e.g., insurance coverage) and did it perform as expected?

For the RCD tool to be effective, its construction must reflect the two related keys to successful risk identification, listed earlier:

Key #1: Define risks by source
Key #2: Categorize risks evenly

Key #1: Define Risks by Source

Most ERM programs fail to properly define all risks by their source. Typically, they define some risks by their source, but they define others by their outcome. For example, here is a sample list of seven risks:

1. Competitor risk
2. Supplier risk

3. Technology risk
4. Regulatory risk
5. Terrorism risk
6. Reputational risk
7. Ratings downgrade

Unfortunately, these risks are inconsistently defined. The first five risks are defined by their source, but the last two risks are defined by their outcome.

Let's look first at reputational risk. Clearly, protecting their reputation is a major concern for most companies, and this is a risk that is very commonly included in company's key risk lists. However, reputation risk is not a risk. That is, it is not stated in the form of a source of risk. Rather, reputational damage is a result, an outcome, which can occur as a direct result of several distinct sources of risk. Product quality may not be living up to expectations or to company advertising campaigns. Customer service may have deteriorated past a tipping point. A significant case of internal fraud may be discovered, or an internal scandal may become public. Company management of external relations may have gone awry. There are various risk events that are the originating sources, or root causes, that lead first to negative media coverage, and then, possibly, to reputational damage.

In fact, not only is reputational damage not a true source of risk, it is also not even the true outcome, at least not the outcome that matters most. Reputational damage is only relevant to the point that it actually causes financial consequences, which are the ultimate outcome in terms of importance. To matter, reputational damage must manifest in some financial way, either in lowering future revenues, increasing future expenses, and/or increasing the cost of capital. At least one of these must occur for company value to be reduced. So, reputational "risk" is only a stopover—an intermediate outcome—along the way. Figure 4.1 illustrates these relationships in terms of their flow from multiple true sources of risk to negative media coverage and then reputational damage, and, finally, to the true outcome of financial impacts. See "LifeLock."

A similar observation is presented for the second of the two risks from our earlier example, which was the risk of a ratings downgrade. Companies with public debt are concerned with their debt ratings assigned by rating agencies. And it is quite common to find "ratings downgrade" on a company's key risk list. Yet, as in the situation for reputational risk, ratings downgrade is not a source of risk. Rather, a ratings downgrade is an intermediate outcome that

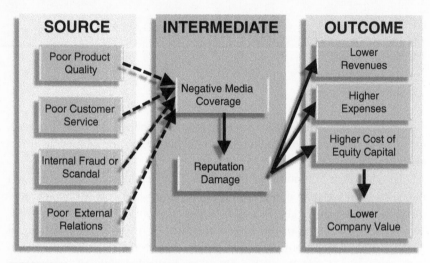

FIGURE 4.1   Reputational Risk Can Result from Several Different Risk Sources

LIFELOCK

Risk events involving reputational damage do not always result in large financial impacts. This is often the case for companies with lesser-known brands, which tend not to generate a sustained level of media interest after a story initially breaks. This is also often the case for risk events for which people tend not to hold the company accountable. However, a risk to avoid would be one that betrays the core branding of the company. For example, if a home security alarm company suffers a break-in at its headquarters, it can be very bad for business. A company called LifeLock got itself into such a situation.

Founded in 2005, LifeLock became one of the leading names in identity theft protection in the United States, using a marketing campaign with CEO Todd Davis' social security number painted on the side of a truck. In May 2007, the *Phoenix New Times*, a free weekly newspaper in Phoenix, ran an article indicating that Robert J. Maynard, Jr., a cofounder of LifeLock, may have stolen his own father's identity to get an American Express card, and used it to make $150,000 in fraudulent charges. Maynard resigned within days. In May 2010, the same newspaper ran another article revealing that Todd Davis had himself been a victim of identity theft at least 13 times since 2007. LifeLock's earnings are not public, but this could not have been good for business.

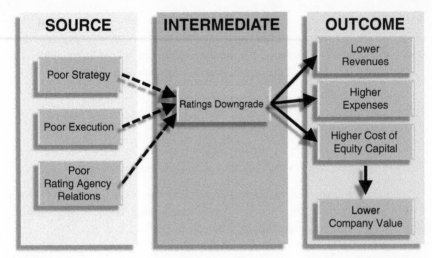

FIGURE 4.2 A Ratings Downgrade Can Be Triggered by Several Different Risk Sources

can be triggered by many different sources of risk. The strategy itself may be flawed. Management may be struggling to effectively implement the strategy. Management may have a deteriorating relationship with one or more of the rating agencies.[2] These are examples of true sources of risk that can give rise to a ratings downgrade. The ratings downgrade is a direct result of one or more of these sources of risk. Once it occurs, the ratings downgrade is merely an intermediate outcome; it can then lead to financial impacts, including lower revenues, higher expenses, and/or a higher cost of capital. Figure 4.2 illustrates these relationships in terms of their flow from multiple true sources of risk, to the intermediate outcome of a ratings downgrade, and on to financial impacts.

Another example is equity market risk. This is a common risk found on key risk lists for companies that have equities among their invested assets, particularly financial services companies. Yet, most of the time, this is not the source of risk, but rather merely one expression—an intermediate outcome—of the true source of risk, which is volatility in the economy. Identifying the true source for market risk has additional implications beyond the earlier examples of reputational risk and ratings downgrade. In this example, economic volatility is not the only possible source driving equity market volatility, but it is perhaps the primary one. The more important distinction here, though, is that the single source of risk—economic volatility—drives multiple intermediate outcomes, many of which impact each other, in complex ways, and all of which ultimately can impact the financial components of company value. The intermediate outcomes of economic volatility include, for example:

- Equity market risk (unexpected changes in equity markets)
- Credit risk (unexpected changes in credit markets)
- Unexpected inflation or deflation
- Unexpected changes in employment levels
- Unexpected changes in consumer spendable income

Figure 4.3 illustrates the basic order of these relationships in terms of their flow from the single true source of risk highlighted here, to the multiple intermediate outcomes, and on to financial impacts.

Failing to define all risks consistently by source lowers the quality of three of the ERM process steps:

- Risk identification
- Risk quantification
- Risk decision making

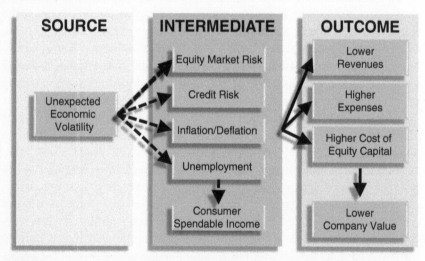

FIGURE 4.3   Economic Volatility Is Often the Source of Equity Market and Other Risks

Impact on Risk Identification

Failing to define all risks consistently by their source lowers the quality of the qualitative risk assessment component of the risk identification process step. The qualitative risk assessment involves asking survey participants to assess potential key risks by providing a qualitative ranking (e.g., high, medium, or low) for both likelihood and severity. To have meaningful survey results, survey participants in the qualitative risk assessment must have a clear definition and consistent understanding of the risks they are assessing. Unfortunately, when risks are defined by their outcome, this often causes confusion. In considering a given risk defined by its outcome, different survey participants may be imagining a different corresponding source of risk, and as a result, the likelihood and severity scores will be provided on an inconsistent basis. This inconsistency is even more insidious to the ERM process, because it usually goes undetected.

Impact on Risk Quantification

Failing to define all risks consistently by their source also impedes the risk scenario development portion of the risk quantification ERM process step. It does so in three ways:

1. **Inability to identify subject matter experts.** When risks are improperly defined by outcome, it is even difficult to identify the appropriate subject matter experts to begin with, because this depends on the source of risk. Risk scenarios for reputational damage caused by poor product quality should involve subject matter experts from the quality or production areas. However, risk scenarios for reputational damage caused by poor customer service should involve those from the customer service center.
2. **Difficulty imagining risk scenarios.** The ambiguity of a risk that is improperly defined by outcome makes it difficult to imagine individual deterministic risk scenarios. Something amorphous such as reputation risk does not immediately bring to mind a specific risk scenario. In fact, this just leads those responsible for developing the risk scenarios—subject matter experts—into an attempt to identify a source of reputational risk on an impromptu basis. Trying to trace this back to a source of risk does not belong in the risk scenario development exercise. In this forum, the subject matter experts are likely to omit one or more potential sources of risk.
3. **Incomplete risk scenarios.** Defining risks by their outcome can lead to incomplete risk scenarios. When the true source of risk is not identified, it

is easy to omit other intermediate outcomes that would naturally accompany the outcome identified in a given scenario. Consider our earlier example of equity market risk. As Figure 4.3 shows, if equity market risk was the only item identified, the risk scenario would include only the financial impacts from equity volatility. However, in most cases, economic risk (unexpected economic volatility) is the true source of risk. Realistic economic scenarios include impacts on multiple intermediate outcomes (credit risk, inflation/deflation, etc.), all of which have varying, and interacting, financial impacts, each of which must be included.

Impact on Risk Decision Making

Failing to define all risks consistently by their source also inhibits the risk mitigation portion of the risk decision-making process step. Although some risk mitigation relates to the outcome (for example, insurance coverage), most mitigation is performed at the source of risk. As a result, it is difficult to evaluate mitigation options for risks when you don't know the source. For example, if management became concerned about a ratings downgrade, their actions to mitigate this risk would depend on what is driving this concern. Is it a poor strategy? If so, what aspect(s) of strategy must be corrected? Is it poor execution of strategy? If so, what aspect(s) of execution must be better managed? If the source is not identified, then management is hard-pressed to come up with a vision of the mitigation options to consider.

Consistently defining risks by their source resolves all of these issues. It allows for consistent scoring provided by survey participants in the qualitative risk assessment, because they all have a common understanding of the specific source for each risk. It makes it easy to identify the appropriate subject matter experts responsible for developing risk scenarios for each individual risk source. It provides a smooth path for imagining the specific risk scenarios, which can flow logically from their originating source. It provides the ability to construct complete risk scenarios. And, finally, it enables consideration of all mitigation options, which occur mostly at the source.

Now, let's look at the second key to success, which must be reflected in the construction of the RCD tool.

Key #2: Categorize Risks Evenly

Many RCD lists do not categorize risks at an even level of abstraction. Some portions of the RCD tool are often categorized at too high a level, and others are often categorized at too low a level. Either one of these problems lowers the quality of the risk identification process step. Those categorized at too high a level can lead to failure to consider subcategories (or divisions or individual risks) within the category (or subcategory or division) identified. As an example consider the risk division "Talent management" shown in Table 4.1. If the RCD tool had only identified this division and not identified any of the risks below it, it is possible that some of the risks under this division may have been missed, such as "Critical employee(s)."

Similarly, some portions of the RCD tool are categorized at too low a level, which can lead to failure to consider the divisions above the identified risks, as well as some of the individual risks to which they correspond. As an example, again consider the risk division "Talent management" shown in Table 4.1. If the RCD tool had only identified some of the individual risks, such as "Ability to recruit or retain" and "Succession planning," it is possible that the overarching division, "Talent management," may have been missed. This might result in omitting other risks within the division such as "Critical employee(s)" or "Labor or producer relations."

QUALITATIVE RISK ASSESSMENT

Once the RCD tool is properly constructed, the main activity in the risk identification process step can take place: the qualitative risk assessment. The qualitative risk assessment is the second component in the risk identification ERM process step. We will describe the qualitative risk assessment by its purpose, its process, and its product.

Purpose

The primary purpose of the qualitative risk assessment is to prioritize the list of potential risks and narrow them down to the list of key risks. The key risk list is a list of approximately 20 to 30 of the most important risks, which will be advanced to the next step in the ERM process cycle: risk quantification. A secondary purpose of the qualitative risk assessment is to support the emerging risk identification process.

Process

The process of the qualitative risk assessment involves soliciting input from internal personnel regarding the organization's key risks, and a high-level qualitative scoring of each potential key risk's likelihood of occurrence and severity of impact. The qualitative risk assessment is conducted in a four-step process:

Step 1: Participant identification
Step 2: Advance communication
Step 3: Qualitative risk assessment surveys
Step 4: Consensus meeting

Step 1: Participant Identification

The first decision in the participant identification step is the number of survey participants to include. This does vary somewhat by size and complexity of the organization. However, it is best to keep the number to a manageable size, keeping in mind that this exercise must be repeated periodically, and possibly annually, depending on the dynamic nature of the internal and external environments. For most companies, an appropriate number of survey participants may be between 25 and 35. This number may naturally flow from the second decision, which is selection of the survey participants themselves, but it is helpful to begin with at least a target number in mind, to prevent the list from growing so large that the process becomes unworkable.

The second decision is selection of the most appropriate survey participants. This is unique to each company. However, a partial list of suggested individuals to include, as well as the perspectives they offer, is shown in Table 4.3.

Political concerns are, as always, a consideration. If there is a segment of the organization, or individual, with whom there is a need or desire to accelerate the pace of buy-in for the ERM program, it may be wise to include a key representative from that segment, or the specific individual, as a survey participant.

Step 2: Advance Communication

After the qualitative risk assessment survey participants have been identified, the next step in the qualitative risk assessment is to send them an advance communication. The advance communication should be designed to achieve the following objectives:

- Request participation
- Prepare participants
- Schedule time

TABLE 4.3 Suggested Participants for Qualitative Risk Assessment Survey (Partial List)

Suggested Survey Participant	Perspective Offered
Independent director (1 or 2)	Objective
Chief executive officer (CEO)	Enterprise-wide
Chair of audit committee and head of internal audit	Knowledge gained through audit activities
General counsel	Litigation risk
Chief risk office (CRO) or equivalent	Enterprise-wide
Heads of major business segments and one of their lieutenants	Risks in the business segments; lieutenants are often closer to the risks and offer more insights
Head of human resources	Human resources risk
Chief technology officer (CTO)	Technology risk
Head of marketing	Brand risks
Head of investor relations	Investor relations risk
Head of compliance	Compliance risks
Chief financial officer (CFO)	Financial reporting risk
Head of strategic planning	Enterprise-wide
Chief investment officer (CIO)	Financial risk
Personnel with long experience in the industry (1 or 2)	Industry-related risks
Personnel with longevity in the organization (1 or 2)	Organizational risks

Request Participation   Although requesting the participation of the invitee may be the most obvious goal of the advance communication, the approach is not necessarily straightforward. It must be done skillfully. If not crafted properly, it could have the opposite of its intended effect: it might produce resistance. However, if constructed carefully, it can garner participation and begin to build the buy-in process for the ERM program. To do this, the advance communication must effectively convey the following:

- High-level support for the ERM program
- Importance of the qualitative risk assessment
- Critical need for their input

- Finite time commitment
- Level of confidentiality

Communicating the level of endorsement for the ERM program signals to invitees that this should be given some priority, and to make time in their schedule. This can include support from the board of directors, the CEO, other senior executives, as well as any leader(s) of the survey participant's particular business segment. Explaining the importance of the qualitative risk assessment to the overall ERM program provides the context for the exercise and the linkage of survey participant efforts to the overall ERM program. Stressing the need for their valuable input—based on their industry knowledge, their experience, and their expertise—expresses respect for survey participants, and sets a tone that is conducive to building consensus buy-in. Describing the specifics of the required activities—before (preparation), during (survey), and after (follow-up and consensus meeting)—including the logistics and time commitment, gives invitees a level of comfort that the exercise will not suffer from "scope creep," where the time and effort far exceed initial expectations. Finally, stating the level of confidentiality up front helps establish trust.

Prepare Participants   The advance communication should include four types of information to properly prepare the survey participant for the qualitative risk assessment survey:

1. **Inputs needed from survey participants.** The advance communication should include a clear description of what survey participants will be expected to provide during the survey; for example:
   - The type of key risks they should identify
   - The number of key risks they should provide (e.g., three to five)
   - The *credible worst-case scenario* for each key risk (this will be discussed later; see "Key #3: Define Metrics Clearly")
   - The likelihood score for each key risk they identify
   - The severity score for each key risk they identify
   - Likelihood and severity scores for the risks identified by other survey participants
2. **ERM background.** The qualitative risk assessment survey participants have varying levels of knowledge of the ERM approach and ERM terminology. To maintain a consistent level of quality in the survey, it is necessary to provide some background information on ERM, or at least the portion of ERM relevant to this exercise. A very brief primer on ERM can be provided. This can be provided in various forms, such as a

document, a brief video, or a brief webinar. Whatever the form, it is useful to include the following items:

- Basic outline of the ERM framework and process cycle
- How the qualitative risk assessment fits into the ERM program
- How information from the qualitative risk assessment will be used
- ERM approach to defining risk, in general (e.g., by source)
- ERM approach to defining key risks (e.g., top 20 to 30 threats)
- Explanation of the company value metric
- ERM terminology

3. **Risks to consider.** To get survey participants thinking about the potential key risks to the enterprise, it is helpful to provide them with the RCD tool, and this should be done as part of the advance communication. This serves two purposes: As a prompt to help participants consider key risks, and to illustrate the ERM approach to defining risk.

   As discussed earlier, the RCD tool is a catalyst to help trigger the participant's imagination of potential key risks to consider, as well as, at a minimum, get them thinking about the specific risks listed in the RCD tool. In addition to providing a reasonably comprehensive list of risk categories, risk subcategories, risk divisions, and a good number of individual risks as well, the RCD tool may be used to provide additional fodder. The RCD tool may indicate the list of risks, including key risks, identified in the prior qualitative risk assessment (if available). Finally, the RCD may also be populated with the company's disclosed risks, and, if available from a comparative analysis, the disclosed risks of key competitors.

   In addition, the RCD tool offers participants a clear illustration of the proper way to think about risks. Risks are defined by source. Also, risks are categorized at a consistent level of abstraction. Finally, risks are prospective future events (discussed later; see "Key #5: Identify Risks Prospectively").

4. **Definition of metrics.** For the advance communication to be effective, it must define the likelihood and severity metrics clearly. This was the third of the five keys to successful risk identification listed earlier: Key #3: Define metrics clearly.

Key #3: Define Metrics Clearly Survey participants are asked to consider the likelihood and severity of the potential risks, and provide these scores in the qualitative risk assessment survey. Guidance for these qualitative metrics is traditionally provided to participants in the form of the likelihood and severity scoring criteria to ensure a consistent form of input from participants. A typical example of likelihood and severity scoring criteria are shown in Table 4.4.[3]

TABLE 4.4 Example of Traditional Likelihood and Severity Scoring Criteria

Likelihood			Severity		
5	Very high	1-in-5 or greater chance of occurring	5	Very high	> $200 million
4	High	1-in-10 chance of occurring	4	High	$50 million–$200 million
3	Medium	1-in-20 chance of occurring	3	Medium	$20 million–$50 million
2	Low	1-in-50 chance of occurring	2	Low	$10 million–$20 million
1	Very low	1-in-100 or less chance of occurring	1	Very low	< $10 million

For the qualitative risk assessment results to be meaningful there must be consistency in how it is conducted. Participants must have a consistent understanding of the qualitative metrics and how to assign the qualitative scores to the risks, for both likelihood and severity. Unfortunately, when traditional criteria such as those in Table 4.4 are provided without further clarification, participants do not have a consistent interpretation of either the likelihood or the severity metrics. To correct this, both the likelihood and severity metrics must be clearly defined.

Let's begin with the qualitative likelihood metric. Participants are not given clear guidance on how to consistently assign the qualitative likelihood score. Participants are asked to qualitatively score the likelihood of the potential key risk . . . but there is usually no guidance on the type of risk scenario. Each risk can occur under a number of wide-ranging scenarios. Is it an Armageddon scenario? Is it a "most likely" downside scenario? Something else? Each participant, in considering the same risk, may be imagining, and providing a qualitative likelihood score for, a different scenario. As a result, the qualitative scoring of likelihood is inconsistent across participants, significantly lowering the quality of the survey.

For example, imagine that you are a participant in the qualitative risk assessment survey, and you have just been asked to provide a qualitative score for the likelihood of a data breach risk event occurring. The first thing you must do is imagine the data breach scenario. But you are given no guidance on this. You might imagine a disaster scenario, where an unencrypted file containing the privacy data for all the company's customers is stolen with intent to use it. You might estimate that such a rare event has only a 1-in-1,000 chance of occurring this year. Alternatively, you might imagine a moderately pessimistic scenario, where an encrypted file containing privacy data for 1 percent of the company's customers is merely lost. You might estimate that this event has a 1-in-10 chance of occurring this year. Or, you might imagine any number of other risk scenarios across the spectrum of possibilities. The qualitative score you assign to likelihood will depend entirely on your chosen risk scenario. Similarly, other participants' qualitative likelihood scores will depend on their chosen risk scenarios. Without any guidance, the risk scenarios imagined tend to vary significantly from participant to participant, rendering the survey results practically meaningless.

A best-practice solution does exist which can correct the problems inherent in a lack of guidance on what type of risk scenario to envision for the qualitative scoring of likelihood. Instructing participants to imagine, and then provide scores for, a credible worst-case scenario tends to ensure a reasonable level of consistency in scoring, yet is not overly prescriptive to the point of impinging upon survey participants' freedom to provide their own input. A credible worst-case scenario is not the most unlikely of events, but neither is it a common event. It is somewhat in between, but still represents a fairly pessimistic scenario with a severe impact. A depiction of the credible worst-case scenario is shown in Figure 4.4.

One advantage of using a credible worst-case scenario is that it is not a worst-case scenario that may be so unlikely as to engender a lack of confidence in the exercise, yet it is a robust enough risk scenario to capture the full impact

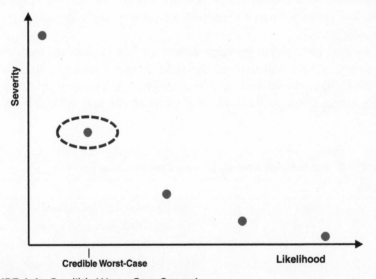

FIGURE 4.4 Credible Worst-Case Scenario

of this type of risk. Another advantage is that this bit of guidance is flexible enough to accommodate varying types of risks. A worst-case scenario for one type of risk, such as technology risk, may be far more likely than a worst-case scenario for litigation risk, yet they are both within the guidance and both may be defined as a credible worst-case scenario, even though their consensus qualitative likelihood scores may differ significantly.

Now, let's address the lack of consistency involving the qualitative severity metric and caused by traditional criteria, such as those in Table 4.4. Typically, participants are not given a clear definition of the qualitative severity metric. The severity criteria do provide a specific range of dollar impacts, but they often do not clarify what is impacted. A $10 million impact on . . . what metric? Is it the balance sheet? Is it earnings? If so, is it just this year's earnings or the cumulative impact over multiple years? Is it company value? Is it revenues? Participants will have varying interpretations of this, and as a result, the quality of the survey declines precipitously.

A best-practice solution is to clearly define the severity metric, and to define it using a single, unifying metric, which can fully and appropriately capture all financial impacts, including those to the income statement, balance sheet, and cost of capital. The solution is to define the qualitative severity metric as the financial impact on company value.[4] This results in a subtle but critical change to the severity scoring criteria shown earlier in Table 4.4. Tables 4.5 and 4.6 illustrate two examples of value-based severity scoring criteria.

Because most survey participants will not have a firm understanding of the company value calculation, the ERM primer provided in the advance communication should include a brief description. However, the company value metric is surely intuitive—the value of the firm is something that

TABLE 4.5   Value-Based Severity Scoring Criteria: Dollar Form

Severity		
5	Very high	> $200 million loss in company value
4	High	$50 million–$200 million loss in company value
3	Medium	$20 million–$50 million loss in company value
2	Low	$10 million–$20 million loss in company value
1	Very low	< $10 million loss in company value

TABLE 4.6 Value-Based Severity Scoring Criteria: Percentage Form

Severity		
5	Very high	> 10% loss in company value
4	High	2.5%–10% loss in company value
3	Medium	1.0%–2.5% loss in company value
2	Low	0.5%–1.0% loss in company value
1	Very low	< 0.5% loss in company value

everyone understands. To make the company value metric even more tangible, it may be analogized to market capitalization, which is similar in magnitude. This may serve the purpose, because the qualitative risk assessment survey is a broad tool with the sole intent of approximating the relative importance of potential key risks. Additionally, a couple of examples may be provided to illustrate how different types of risks can impact company value.

There is another dimension to consider scoring when conducting the qualitative risk assessment. See "Time Horizon."

TIME **HORIZON**

In addition to likelihood and severity, some qualitative risk assessments use an approach where a third dimension is added to the scoring criteria: the time horizon. Qualitative risk assessment survey participants are asked to indicate whether the speed of onset corresponding to the risk is fast or slow, or whether the risk is a near-term risk event (such as in the next three years) or a long-term risk event (such as beyond three years). Although this makes the time-to-onset more explicit, this potentially complicates the interpretation of the likelihood scores. Likelihood of occurrence must correspond to a time horizon. By allowing survey participants to provide a time horizon score, survey participants may also be providing likelihoods corresponding to a variety of time horizons, some near-term and some long-term. For example, risk A may have a 10 percent chance of occurring next year, but risk B may have a 10 percent chance of occurring in 10 years. These likelihoods cannot be compared directly. The survey participant, if asked, may have estimated

(continued)

(continued)

the likelihood of risk B occurring in the next year to be *less than* 10 percent. It is not an apples-to-apples basis of comparison. Allowing a separate time horizon score can still work, but it requires combining two pieces of data, both time horizon and likelihood, to properly interpret.

An alternate approach is to capture the time horizon, but not to use it as an explicit additional dimension in the scoring criteria. In this approach, the time horizon is defined as near-term only (such as the next three years), and whenever possible, just the coming year. For the vast majority of the risks, survey participants provide the likelihood corresponding to the risk occurring in the coming year. For those risks not expected to occur until later years, the time to onset is captured in the credible worst-case scenario, and the likelihood corresponds to the earliest possible time of onset, but still limited to the near-term time horizon. For example, the risk of a union strike might be considered as occurring at the next contract negotiations, scheduled two years from now. For some high-severity risks which develop slowly, over several years, the likelihood of occurrence within the near-term may be zero. These will receive the lowest likelihood score, which is fine, because they will still be accounted for through their high severity score. If the risk does not rank highly enough on a combined likelihood-severity basis to become a key risk, it will remain on the non-key risk list, and will be monitored over time as part of the emerging risk identification process.

Schedule Time   There are a few factors to consider when scheduling time with survey participants. Their calendars are usually booked several weeks in advance; these are busy people. As a result, advance planning is necessary to avoid having a gap in the ERM implementation time line. Also, if possible, it is more efficient to schedule all interviews sequentially, rather than having some simultaneously, because risks identified in earlier interviews may be incorporated into subsequent interviews. Further, interviews should not be scheduled back-to-back. An interval of time should be allotted between interviews to clarify and document meeting notes, and to make any required changes to the RCD tool prior to the next meeting. Finally, the period over which all the interviews are conducted—from the first interview to the last one—should be as short as possible, to reflect a consistent snapshot in time; as time goes by, the environment may change, which can skew the results between those interviewed prior to the change, versus those interviewed afterward. This is true even for small changes in the environment that merely change the mood of personnel; it is best to capture all participants' impressions when they are in a relatively similar point in time and frame of mind.

Step 3: Qualitative Risk Assessment Surveys

The third step in the qualitative risk assessment is conducting the surveys. The last two of the five keys to successful risk identification, discussed earlier, relate to the qualitative risk assessment surveys:

Key #4: Gather data appropriately
Key #5: Identify risks prospectively

Key #4: *Gather Data Appropriately*   Gathering data appropriately means collecting the right data, at the right time, in the right way. Unfortunately, most qualitative risk assessment surveys do not satisfy these criteria.

For a survey to be most effective, it must focus its requests exclusively on the data truly needed. Survey designers are often tempted to include some of the "nice to have" data, but must be ever-vigilant in identifying and eliminating extraneous portions of the data request. Survey participants have limited time and limited patience for unnecessary efforts. Unfortunately, most qualitative risk assessment surveys have data requests that are far more extensive than they need to be. These data requests include not only some "nice to have" data, but also some "no need to have" data. An example of such a larger-than-necessary data request commonly used in qualitative risk assessment surveys includes the list of items shown in Table 4.7 requested for each identified risk.

TABLE 4.7 Example of Larger-Than-Necessary Data Request

Item #	Data Request Item
1	Likelihood score
2	Severity score
3	Historical experience data
4	Mitigation in place
5	Mitigation planned
6	Person(s) responsible for mitigation
7	Effectiveness of mitigation
8	Name of risk owner
9	Risk and mitigation documentation
10	Other data

Some of this data is not needed during the qualitative risk assessment, and most of this data is actually not even needed at all in the ERM process. The sole purpose of the qualitative risk assessment is to prioritize and rank the potential key risks. To accomplish this, the only data needed from Table 4.7 are Items 1 and 2—the likelihood and severity scores. One additional item not appearing in Table 4.7 is needed when employing the best-practice approach for consistent likelihood scoring: a brief description of the credible worst-case scenario.

Some of the remaining items in Table 4.7 are needed, but only later, during the risk scenario development portion of the risk quantification ERM process step. At this later stage, the mitigation in place should be captured, which is Item #4 in Table 4.7. The historical data experience, which is Item #3, is needed as well, although rather than document this, it is merely drawn upon by the subject matter expert in estimating the potential financial impacts as part of the Failure Modes and Effects Analysis (FMEA) exercise.

There are three disadvantages of gathering this data in the qualitative risk assessment exercise. First, as discussed earlier, making the survey longer than necessary annoys survey participants, and inevitably lowers the quality of the survey. In addition, gathering this information earlier than it is needed often results in portions of it being out of date by the time it is needed; this necessitates a repeat data request to refresh the information, which, aside from further aggravating survey participants is also inefficient. Finally, gathering this data too early—in the qualitative risk assessment survey rather than during the FMEA risk scenario development interviews—results in more inefficiency, collecting far more data than is needed. This is because it causes these data items to be collected for *all* identified risks, which may be upwards of 80 to 100 risks. However, this data is only needed for those risks that will advance to the risk quantification process step—the *key* risks—which may be between 20 and 30 in number.

A more appropriate data request that is more efficient and effective includes only the data needed at the time of the qualitative risk assessment survey. An example of an effective data request is shown in Table 4.8, which is requested for each identified risk.

TABLE 4.8   Appropriate Data Request

Item #	Data Request Item
1	Likelihood score
2	Severity score
3	Credible worst-case scenario

This data request is all that is needed to prioritize and rank the risks identified in the qualitative risk assessment survey. Once the key risks are identified and promoted to the risk quantification ERM process step, additional data will be needed, but only for the key risks, which are fewer in number. At that point, during the FMEA risk scenario development interviews, additional data will be collected.

Now that we have discussed gathering the right data at the right time, we will address gathering data in the right way. Although there are many variations employed in conducting surveys, there are two basic methods that are commonly used. One is templates and the other is interviews.

A template approach to conducting the qualitative risk assessment survey is the more commonly used of the two survey methods. This involves sending templates or questionnaires to survey participants and requesting that they complete and return them. There are some advantages to a template survey:

1. **100 percent consistent communication to participants.** Using a template survey ensures 100 percent consistency in terms of what is communicated to the survey participants. Unlike interviews, where multiple interviewers may deviate from a script, or have varying levels of skills, a template is a controlled and uniform communication.
2. **Easily scalable.** Templates are easily scalable from the point of view of the ERM team. Once the template is designed, it is nearly as easy to send it to 60 individuals as it is to send it to 30. Templates also make the collection and compilation of data easier, from the perspective of the ERM team, because survey participants must use a standard format within which to populate the data requested.

Unfortunately, the template survey method has several disadvantages, which far outweigh the advantages:

1. **Not well received.** Templates are not well received by survey participants. Rather than building buy-in for the ERM program and advancing the risk culture, they produce resistance and resentment among survey participants. Consider their perspective. One day, they open an e-mail from the ERM team and it is a request for data, along with a template and instructions on how to complete it. Someone, whom they may not know, just gave them one more task to complete. This is not a good first impression. The instructions are lengthy, and participants feel like they are on their own to figure it out and do all the work. This comes across as impersonal and inconsiderate. Data requests using templates tend to be

more extensive, because adding items to the request is easy for the ERM team, and survey participants wonder if all this is really necessary. This casts a shadow on the credibility of the entire ERM effort.

2. **Inconsistent time and effort.** There is an inconsistent level of time and effort given to completing the templates. Some survey participants diligently focus on the exercise, carefully reading the instructions, thoughtfully pondering the business and its potential key risks, and gathering all the ancillary data requested. Other survey participants just complete it quickly to get it done and out the door. This results in an inconsistent level of quality in survey results. Although it is apparent when reviewing the populated templates that the quality varies, at this point, after the fact, there is little or no recourse for the ERM team.

3. **Difficult to fix errors.** Many survey participants, despite the advance communication provided to them, are not ERM-savvy. Some participants will identify risks that are not properly defined by source. Some will identify risks that are clearly not *key* risks. Others will identify risks that are too detailed or not detailed enough. Some will identify risks that are retrospectively focused (discussed later; see "Key #5: Identify Risks Prospectively"). Many will misinterpret the definition of ERM metrics and improperly score the qualitative likelihood and severity metrics. Correcting these errors may not be feasible for the ERM team, or, at a minimum, will require much iterative effort.

4. **Less confidential.** Templates are usually conducted on a nonconfidential basis. Confidentiality can be achieved with templates, but the nature of completing documents with names attached and sending them to another department makes anonymity more difficult to ensure, and offers survey participants less comfort. As a result, the free flow of information suffers, and some of the most important risks may remain hidden or underemphasized.

Rather than use templates, the best-practice method for conducting the qualitative risk assessment survey is through interviews. First, let's address the shortcomings of this method:

1. **Less than 100 percent consistent communication to participants.** Unlike the template approach, when using interviews, it is more difficult to maintain 100 percent consistency in terms of what is communicated to the survey participants. However, this can be mitigated in one of two ways. One way is to use a small number of interviewers with similar levels of ERM

training, experience, and expertise, and having them stay in close communication. Another way is to use just one interviewer, which is feasible given the reasonable number of interviewees. Though this lengthens the time required to complete the qualitative risk assessment, the trade-off may be worthwhile, assuming time constraints allow this.

2. **Not as easily scalable.** Interview surveys are not easily scalable. To survey more participants requires more time or more qualified interviewers, and adding more interviewers lowers the consistency of messaging, as discussed earlier. However, this is a minor issue. The scalability of templates is only gained at the expense of quality. In addition, for most organizations, 25 to 35 survey participants are usually enough to produce robust survey results.

Now, let's discuss the advantages of using interviews as opposed to templates:

1. **Well received.** Unlike the template approach, the interviews are well received by survey participants. Conducting interviews tends to build buy-in for the ERM program and advance the risk culture. It builds good will with survey participants. Unlike templates, which feel like an impersonal request to do work on behalf of the ERM team, the interview is personal—a face-to-face, one-on-one interaction.[5] This gives a good first impression. Rather than leaving survey participants stuck to figure out the instructions on their own and do all the work, the interviewer is present, spending his or her time as well; this is a highly personal approach. The interviewer reiterates highlights from the advance communication, answers any questions, and dynamically guides the survey participant through the interview. In addition, rather than requiring the survey participant to populate a template themselves, the interviewer takes notes, documents the interview in a set of minutes, and sends them to the interviewee to confirm accuracy. This creates an atmosphere of collaboration, and is respectful of the survey participant's time. Finally, data requests using interviews tend to be more focused, because adding items to the request would make more work for the ERM team as well, and survey participants appreciate the minimalist attitude. This enhances the credibility of the ERM effort.

2. **Consistent time and effort.** Using interviews compels a more consistent level of time and effort by each survey participant. Unlike templates, where the ERM team is not present to verify the level of care used to complete the

survey, the ERM team member is present during the interview, and ensures that a consistent level of effort is put forth for each survey. This consistency enhances the quality of the survey results.

3. **Easy to fix errors.** Interviews provide an opportunity to compensate for the lack of ERM-savvy among many survey participants. Interviewers can dynamically correct any errors immediately, during the interview. Whether someone fails to identify a risk by its source, identifies risks that are too detailed or not detailed enough, identifies risks that are retrospectively focused, or misinterprets the definition of ERM metrics, the interviewer is present to correct it on the spot. This significantly enhances the quality of the exercise, and is also highly efficient, eliminating the need for iterative corrections.

4. **More confidential.** It is easier for interviews to be conducted on a confidential basis, meaning that survey results are not attached to participant names, but merely reported anonymously. Compared to templates, a personal, one-on-one, closed-door interview, where only one set of notes exists, is easier to conduct on a confidential basis. More importantly, survey participants feel more confident in the anonymous nature, become more relaxed, and, as a result, tend to share more information. In particular, they are most likely to identify risks which are not usually discussed openly, and these kinds of risks can be of the most value in this exercise. Ideally, the interviewer is not an employee but rather a consultant, which offers an even higher level of anonymity.

Key #5: Identify Risks Prospectively The last of the five keys to successful risk identification is to identify risks on a prospective basis during the qualitative risk assessment. This may seem obvious. Certainly, risks are not in the past, but in the future. Risk is the uncertainty of achieving our future goals. However, there are usually some risks that appear which are actually retrospectively identified, in that they are rooted in the past. This problem is commonly diagnosed as "fighting the last battle" syndrome. Continuing the medical analogy, the underlying cause of this disease is an overemphasis, during the qualitative risk assessment, of recent past risk occurrences. This is often present when a recent past event caused significant trauma to the organization, hemorrhaging in the financial results, and psychological scarring to management. The main symptom is the appearance of identified risks in the qualitative risk assessment that seem overly specific in nature, that precisely match the source of risk that caused a recent negative event still etched in management's collective consciousness, and that are often already well mitigated, possibly even over-mitigated. Despite this being a past event, management is simply not comfortable unless such risks appear on the risk list. The prognosis of this disease, if left untreated, is that the qualitative risk assessment scoring will be skewed, overemphasizing risks with recent occurrences. In addition, the inclusion of these risks, many of which should be excluded, can crowd out some other risks that should be on the radar.

When a risk is suspected of being identified on a retrospective basis, some simple questioning can be helpful. Ask about the past events that may have caused this risk to be overweighted in the mind of the survey participant. What was the event? What were the financial impacts? What did management do in response? What mitigation is in place to lower the likelihood or mitigate the severity of this risk? If the inquiries confirm suspicions that this risk may not belong on the risk list, presenting the case for its removal to the participant who raised it may resolve the issue. If not, there are two other opportunities to resolve this issue: the other participants may not score it highly, or this may be resolved by raising and addressing the issue at the consensus meeting.

In addition to the two keys to successful risk identification related to the qualitative risk assessment survey—Key #4: Gather data appropriately and Key #5: Identify risks prospectively—there are additional techniques that are helpful. See "Additional Techniques" for two examples.

ADDITIONAL **TECHNIQUES**

There are two additional techniques that are helpful when conducting the qualitative risk assessment surveys:

1. **Collect two perspectives.** The first technique is simply to ask survey participants to identify potential key risks from two perspectives: the overall enterprise perspective and the perspective pertaining just to their area of responsibility or expertise. Getting survey participants to look from both of these vantage points adds value to the survey. Participants with areas of responsibility or expertise that are not enterprise-wide can identify potential key risks related to their areas of specialty, and they can also bring a fresh perspective that may highlight new potential key risks for the overall enterprise. Consider an example where the survey participant is the head of a business segment. Although most risks that are significant to a single business segment may not rank highly from the

(continued)

(continued)

enterprise perspective, some do rank highly. For example, a risk origi-nating within a single business segment can impact other business segments or the enterprise as a whole. In addition, a participant usually focused on a single business segment may bring a bit of an "outsider" perspective when viewing the overall enterprise, and may identify an important potential key risk that, once identified, receives a high consen-sus ranking in the qualitative risk assessment.

2. **Use a retrospective-outcome provocation.** Earlier, we discussed the importance of employing five keys to success when conducting the qualitative risk assessment. We will now briefly discuss a technique that temporarily seems to violate two of these: Key #1: Define risks by source, and Key #5: Identify risks prospectively. It is important to follow these keys for best results, but it is also helpful to step outside of these rules, for a brief moment, to allow for a provocation from a different perspec-tive that may help identify risks as yet uncovered. Although it is always important to categorize and define risks prospectively and by source, and initially ask survey participants to think of risks prospectively and by source, sometimes this may not capture all the known risks, because this is not the usual way in which people think.

   Toward the end of the survey, once you have captured all the risks that you can with this "prospective-source" approach, it is helpful to switch, temporarily, to a "retrospective-outcome" approach, using the following provocation: Ask the participant questions such as, "In the past, what events resulted in a large decrease in revenues? In earn-ings? In company value?" These types of questions are more tangible and will lead to very specific discussions. For each such discussion, you must trace the story provided by the survey participant back to the event's originating source of risk. This reverses the outcome-driven aspect of the provocation, and we arrive, once again, at the source of the risk. Once this is done, you can compare the risks identified by the provocation to the initial list of risks provided by the participant and by others to determine if this technique results in any newly identified risks. For any such newly identified risk, the next step is then to examine whether it is a viable *prospective* risk, which reverses the retrospective-driven aspect of the provocation. Those risks that ad-vance past both of these reversal stages are then added to the potential key risk list and will be included in the remaining individual surveys, as well as the consensus meeting.

   One cautionary note for the retrospective-outcome provocation: Use it judiciously. It should only be used with survey participants who are ERM-savvy and have more immunity to the "fighting the last battle" syndrome.

Step 4: Consensus Meeting

The fourth and final step in the qualitative risk assessment is the consensus meeting. The qualitative risk assessment survey produces a list of risks that typically number in the range of 80 to 100, each of which is scored by both likelihood and severity. The next step is the consensus meeting, which includes all survey participants and relevant members of the ERM team. The consensus meeting has two purposes:

1. Enhance consensus
2. Select key risks

Enhance Consensus The first goal of the consensus meeting is to enhance the level of consensus for qualitative scores, either for likelihood or severity, which meet both of the following conditions:

- Scoring data has a high level of dispersion
- Scoring data corresponds to a risk with a high ranking

The reason for selecting scores with a high level of dispersion is that those are the scores for which there is not a strong level of initial consensus. The reason for limiting the focus to those with high rank is to be respectful of survey participants' time. The main purpose of the risk identification exercise is to identify the key risks. The key risks will be those 20–30 or so risks that have the highest rank. Enhancing consensus on all risks is nice to have, but this is only necessary for scores corresponding to risks ranked highly enough that they might become key risks.

To determine which scores meet both of these criteria, the ERM team must perform the following three tasks:

1. **Define the risk-ranking criteria.** The ERM team must define the risk-ranking criteria. The risk-ranking criteria are either rules or guidelines for combining the qualitative likelihood and severity scores into a single number which is used to rank all the risks identified in the qualitative risk assessment. The first step is often to convert the qualitative scores into numeric scores. An example of a nonproportional conversion is shown in Table 4.9.

   Another approach is to use a conversion scale proportional to the actual relative values from the midpoint of the ranges in the scoring

TABLE 4.9 Example of Nonproportional Conversion of Qualitative to Numeric Scoring

Qualitative Score	Numerical Score
Very High	5
High	4
Moderate	3
Low	2
Very Low	1

criteria, an example of which was shown in Table 4.4. The conversion for the highest score must be made somewhat arbitrarily, because it has no upper bound. An example of a proportional conversion is shown in Table 4.10.

There are numerous methods for defining the risk-ranking criteria. One set of methods involves weighting each nonproportional numerical score separately and then adding them together. Usually, the weights are either equal—producing a straight summation of the two numerical scores—or a higher weight is assigned to the severity scores. Another method involves multiplying the proportional numerical scores together. This is equivalent to calculating a probabilistic expectation. Another

TABLE 4.10 Example of Proportional Conversion of Qualitative to Numeric Scoring

Qualitative Likelihood Score	Numerical Likelihood Score	Qualitative Severity Score	Numerical Severity Score
1-in-5 or greater chance of occurring	25%	> $200 million loss in company value	$250 million
1-in-10 chance of occurring	10%	$50 million–$200 million loss in company value	$125 million
1-in-20 chance of occurring	5%	$20 million–$50 million loss in company value	$35 million
1-in-50 chance of occurring	2%	$10 million–$20 million loss in company value	$15 million
1-in-100 or less chance of occurring	0.5%	< $10 million loss in company value	$5 million

method first excludes all risks not meeting a minimum numerical score for likelihood or severity; the likelihood minimum may be different from the severity minimum. Yet another method is to plot the average likelihood and severity scores on a graph and draw a line or a curve separating out the 20 to 30 risks with the higher scores; an example of this will be shown later.

2. **Rank the risks.** The ranking criteria are applied to the risks identified in the qualitative risk assessment to produce a tentative ranking. The ranking is reviewed for reasonability by the ERM team, and any odd results are noted and discussed at the consensus meeting. One example of an odd result would be a risk that received a low ranking whereas the ERM team, based on their extensive experience, would have expected it to receive a high ranking.

3. **Conduct a dispersion analysis.** A dispersion analysis is performed on both the likelihood and severity scores to identify any scores for which there is not a clear initial consensus. These scores are identified by a high level of dispersion, and generally appear in one of two forms—bimodal or highly disparate. A bimodal result indicates two distinct opinions within the group of participants. For example, consider a risk for which survey participants scored the severity as shown in Figure 4.5. There is clearly not a single consensus among participants, but rather two distinct clusters of votes; one group of participants thinks the severity is low but another group believes the severity is high.

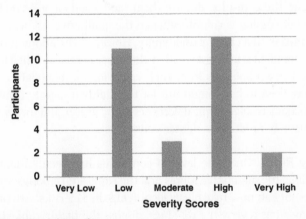

FIGURE 4.5 Bimodal Results

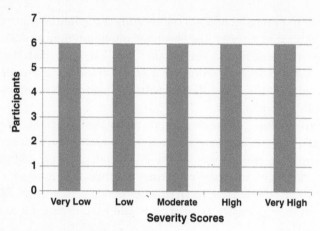

FIGURE 4.6 Highly Disparate Results

A highly disparate result indicates that there is no consensus at all. For example, consider a risk for which participants scored the severity as shown in Figure 4.6. There is no consensus at all among the participants.

Now, the ERM team is in a position to determine which scores meet both of the criteria specified earlier: scores with a high level of dispersion and that correspond to a risk with high ranking. The first goal of the consensus meeting is to examine these results, discuss them, and conduct a second round of scoring. The discussion is voluntary when the qualitative risk assessment has been performed with a cloak of anonymity. However, the anonymity is mainly about who identified which risks, rather than the scoring. It is helpful to solicit at least one or two opinions from each camp for the bimodal results. More opinions may need to be brought out for the highly disparate results. A brief discussion usually resolves some differences in the group, and the second round of scoring usually produces a tighter consensus.

Select Key Risks Once the level of consensus has been enhanced to the extent possible, the qualitative scores and the resultant rankings are finalized. The main event can now take place: identifying the key risks. Attendees of the consensus meeting review the rankings, discuss the highly ranked risks, and decide on where to delineate between key and non-key risks. The cutoff point should be in the neighborhood of the 20 to 30 most highly ranked risks. One

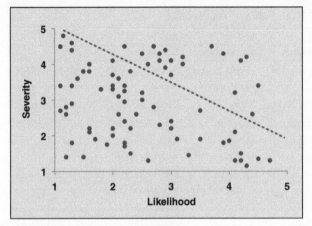

FIGURE 4.7 Example of Selecting Key Risks

example of how this is conducted is illustrated in Figure 4.7. Those risks to the upper right of the line are the key risks. Attendees of the consensus meeting must decide where, literally, to draw the line: how far to the upper right versus lower left to draw it, and also at what angle to draw it.

Product

There are three main results, or products, of the qualitative risk assessment. The first and most important is the key risk list. The second is the tool to monitor any potential changes in the importance of any of the risks. Both of these products follow the format of the RCD tool. The third result is an advancement of the organization's risk culture. The qualitative risk assessment has involved key personnel from all corners of the enterprise, and enhanced their knowledge of, and experience with, enterprise risk management. This is one of the first steps in developing consensus buy-in for the ERM program.

An example of a key risk list is shown in Table 4.11. There are three important characteristics of the key risk list. First, it is a short list—the example shown has just 20 key risks. Second, it follows the consistent hierarchical format and nomenclature of the RCD tool. Third, and surprising to some, it does not include the likelihood-severity scores. It has shed them. The reason for this is that the likelihood-severity scores are only useful in helping to identify the key risks. That was their sole purpose, and that has now been achieved. Going forward, the ranking of the key risks will no longer

TABLE 4.11 Example of Key Risk List

Rank	Risk Category	Risk Subcategory	Risk Division	Risk
1	Strategic	Legislative/ regulatory	Product/services-related	Product Y impacted by new regulation
2	Strategic	Economic	Economic risk	U.S. economic downturn
3	Strategic	Supplier	Supplier failure	Supplier partial failure
4	Operational	Human resources	Talent management	Loss of critical employees
5	Strategic	Strategic relationships	Joint ventures and alliances risk	Joint venture risk
6	Strategic	Execution	M&A risk	International M&A risk
7	Strategic	Execution	Product execution risk	Product quality risk
8	Strategic	Competitor	Struggling competitor(s)	Price war
9	Strategic	Supplier	Supplier relationships	Cost of goods/services increases
10	Strategic	Strategy	Channel strategy risk	Change in performance of intermediaries
11	Strategic	Competitor	Innovation	Competitor introduces new features
12	Operational	Human resources	Performance	Research & development (R&D) risk
13	Operational	Human resources	Talent management	Labor relations risk
14	Operational	Disasters	Environmental damage	Environmental damage at Site X
15	Operational	Litigation	Litigation risk	Class action lawsuit
16	Strategic	Supplier	Supplier relationships	Change in status of regulatory licenses
17	Strategic	Strategy	Channel strategy risk	Distribution channel risk
18	Operational	Technology	Data security and privacy	External attack
19	Operational	Human resources	Talent management	Inability to recruit enough to support growth plans
20	Financial	Credit	Counterparty risk	Change in creditworthiness of counterparties

be based on the qualitative scores. The key risks are now advanced to the risk quantification ERM process step, which provides quantitative metrics—a far superior tool for prioritization and ranking.

The second product—the tool to monitor any potential changes in the importance of any of the risks—is simply the entire list of risks from the qualitative risk assessment. This list retains the likelihood-severity scores. This is used in the ongoing emerging risk identification work, discussed next.

 ## EMERGING RISK IDENTIFICATION

Emerging risk identification consists of two components:

1. Monitoring known risks
2. Environmental scanning for unknown risks

Monitoring Known Risks

The first component of emerging risk identification is to monitor known non-key risks for any changes which might increase their ranking enough to become key risks. There are two aspects to this. One aspect is monitoring any changes in the internal and external environment that would make the risk event more likely to occur. Another aspect is monitoring changes that would increase the severity of the risk event. Monitoring for severity changes is sometimes supported by conducting limited quantification exercises for these risks. These exercises must be kept to a limited effort, because there are a large number of identified non-key risks, often in the range of 50 to 80. One way to do this is to simply take the credible worst-case scenario obtained in the qualitative risk assessment and quantify that one scenario for each non-key risk, or, more feasibly, for selected non-key risks.

Monitoring known risks is a reasonably straightforward and doable exercise. It consists of targeted monitoring of a limited and defined set of risks—those identified in the qualitative risk assessment. As mentioned earlier, the RCD tool, which houses these risks, is used for this purpose.

Environmental Scanning for Unknown Risks

The second component of emerging risk identification is environmental scanning for unknown risks. Unlike monitoring known risks, this task is not at all straightforward and can never be completed. There is no definitive science for identifying unknown risks. In addition, the sources of potential risks that someday might become key risks are virtually limitless.

Unfortunately, a common and dangerous misconception of ERM is that it can indeed effectively perform environmental scanning for unknown risks, and afford a good level of protection against such surprises. This false belief is partly fostered by the fact that these types of risks are the most feared. The sudden emergence of a risk event that takes us by surprise is a primal fear. The fact that many people hold the false belief that ERM can protect them from unknown risks is evidenced by the fact that chief risk officers are often fired after a major risk event occurs. This would be warranted in cases where the ERM program was poorly designed or implemented and where the risk event that materialized was one that should have been known, more highly prioritized, or more effectively mitigated. Although some firings have taken place under these circumstances, this has not always been the case. In these other cases, either senior management falsely believed that ERM *can* protect the firm from unknown risks, or they believed that shareholders hold such a fantasy.[6]

It is an inescapable truism of our existence that we will always be exposed to the element of surprise. ERM is not designed to prevent unknown events from emerging that can damage or even destroy the organization, nor could it, or any other system, be so designed. It is critical for the CRO and the ERM team to set proper expectations right from the start of ERM adoption and implementation. ERM cannot predict the future. It cannot know the unknown. All it promises is to make better sense out of how we make risk–reward decisions, and to organize and leverage information about the risks we do know about.

Unfortunately, because we, as humans, have such a high utility for avoiding negative surprises, we are tempted to believe those who present a system that can make us safe. Naturally, there are those that prey on these temptations, claiming that they have a system capable of identifying unknown risks. They often present elaborate and esoteric methods and claim that advanced mathematics can capture hidden information, leading to better identification of unknown risks. The seduction of such promises must be strongly resisted. Any system that involves the randomness of human behavior, such as your business does, can never be reduced to an automatic mathematical system that can determine unknown risks. Upon close examination, the façade of these approaches always falls away to reveal a delicate array of assumptions that must be constructed by the subject matter experts to begin with. This leads right back to your people and their best guesses regarding unknown risks.

Knowing all this, we must resign ourselves to the fact that all we can do is institute a simple approach in attempt to discover unknown risks as early as possible. Therefore, this component—environmental scanning for unknown risks—is a more mundane but realistic approach: conducting vigilant advance scouting for risks that are not currently on the risk list but that might suddenly become key risks. This consists of one or more of the following activities to gather information and intelligence from multiple sources:

- Attend industry conferences
- Research industry journals
- Serve on industry committees
- Conduct comparative analysis of competitors' disclosed risks
- Read ERM surveys
- Make other investments in information and intelligence gathering

 ## KILLER RISKS

There are two particular types of risks that warrant highlighting separately because of their special nature. These risks share three qualities. They are:

- Politically difficult to introduce
- Easily identifiable
- A leading indicator of high-severity risk events

Two such risks which we will discuss are arrogance and concentration risk.

Arrogance

Let's discuss each of the qualities listed earlier, and then briefly examine possible risk mitigation.

Politically Difficult to Introduce

Arrogance, whether present in one particular business segment or a characteristic shared enterprise-wide, is certainly a difficult risk to mention to management. Who likes to hear that they are arrogant? Even more relevant, who likes to be the one to have to tell someone else that he or she is arrogant? To suggest such a risk internally is tantamount to challenging the culture within the organization: not a happy prospect for a corporate employee.

Easily Identifiable

Another seemingly difficult aspect of this risk is recognizing it in the first place. What company has the collective clarity and objectivity to recognize that they are arrogant, as well as the level of maturity to admit it? Fortunately, arrogance is easily identifiable. The companies or areas that exude arrogance are usually those that have some basis for it, such as having achieved external recognition of their superiority. They may have dominant market share, awards for quality or innovation, or something similar. Internal talking points are often laced with evidence that there is a belief in their own superiority. There may be an undue amount of fanfare and celebration of achievements, which is noticeable by its excess. This may also take the form of self-satisfaction or a lack of self-criticism. This is combined with a dismissive attitude toward competitive analysis, fueled by the belief that all eyes are on them and that nothing can be learned from the competition. This can be easily observed as a lack of participation on industry committees or shrinkage in the budget for competitive analysis. In addition, there is a marked tendency to overestimate their strengths and underestimate weaknesses. This can be seen by examination of the strengths, weaknesses, opportunities, and threats (SWOT) analysis performed as part of the strategic planning process. Finally, it is often apparent to those outside the organization or business area that there is an attitude of arrogance present, and a simple inquiry with external parties can quickly identify the presence of this risk.

Conversely, it is often easy to spot the companies that do *not* succumb to arrogance. They may be leaders in their field but they are never satisfied. They are always examining what they can do better. They still fear the competition. They are never complacent. A good illustration is from the sports world. The team that is excellent but not arrogant has a relentless focus on areas to improve. Even after a victory by a wide margin, the coach of such a team will remain focused on what they can do better next time. Rather than strut or crow about a victory, the team is humble and vigilant, which is, in part, what keeps them on top.

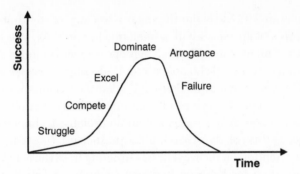

FIGURE 4.8 Arrogance Is a Leading Indicator of Failure

A Leading Indicator of High-Severity Risk Events

Arrogance is a leading indicator of one or more high severity risk events. This is a risk that can do much damage, and often does. This is a natural recurring cycle that is visible in organizations, in people, and even in countries that achieve some level of success. The organization begins by struggling to survive. After a while, it becomes competitive and eventually starts to excel. Eventually, it gets to the top and begins to really dominate its field. This is where arrogance can take hold. When it does, it is a leading indicator of failure. This cycle is exhibited in Figure 4.8.

When arrogance takes root, it can sprout many different types of risk events. Arrogance is like dropping one's guard. Once you unknowingly drop your guard, attacks can come in any form. One example is that it might lead to a lack of innovation in developing products and services. Another example is that it might lead to a feeling of entitlement which encourages bad behavior or abuses by management.

Possible Risk Mitigation

The cycle illustrated in Figure 4.8 is not inevitable. Even for those organizations or areas already suffering from arrogance, if this is identified in time and properly treated, it can be corrected. Sometimes, this is only possible after an embarrassing and public incident that hints at the fact that the organization or area may be slipping off its perch, and gets people murmuring.

One example of this is the United States, which, after victory in World War II, had arguably entered into a phase of arrogance, leading to complacency. In 1957, Russia, the main adversary of the United States at that time, was first into space with a satellite called Sputnik. This was a wake-up call for the United States. Through appropriate recognition of the problem, an ability to admit it publicly, and strong leadership by President Kennedy, the United States enhanced its math and science curriculums and reinvigorated its space program. As a result, the United States was able to regain a competitive position in space exploration and related technologies.

Addressing this risk directly is unlikely to succeed. One way to approach it is to focus attention on the weaknesses resulting from the behavior without having to mention the behavior itself. An example is to challenge whether the organization is performing enough competitive analysis. This can be addressed either directly through the business segments, or indirectly through the ERM team, via the emerging risk identification exercise. Another example is to challenge the amount of benchmarking being performed where results are measured against key competitors. This can help get the culture back a quantum of realism, and get away from an insular attitude.

Concentration Risk

Concentration risk is another risk that warrants special attention. First, we must define it. One popular definition of concentration risk is a lack of diversification in the investment portfolio, resulting in too much risk exposure in one area. A common example is a high percentage of assets invested in one particular asset class, such as real estate in one location. Another example is a concentration of a bank's loans in one industry sector.

Technically, this definition does not conform to the approach discussed earlier in this chapter for properly defining and categorizing risks by source. The level of concentration is no more than an expression of the level of exposure of a given source of risk. For example, concentration risk related to equities is properly defined and categorized as equity market risk, where the concentration aspect of this risk merely points up a concern for the *level* of equity market risk exposure.

Nevertheless, we will temporarily depart from our convention of categorizing and defining risks by source, but only for the purposes of discussing a set of risks that meet our definition of killer risks. However, we will not define concentration risk in terms of poor diversification of investments. Rather, we will define concentration risk here as an unhealthy level of internal or external concentration of *power*. Power can take many forms, including authority, information, access to markets, and so on.

There are two types of power concentration risks: internal and external. There are numerous examples. We will first discuss two internal examples followed by three external examples.

1. **Rainmaker.** A rainmaker is an individual or group that achieves outstanding results; for example, growing revenues or profits. One example of a rainmaker power concentration risk is a "golden boy" unit, described in Chapter 2, which generates such a high level of revenues or profits that its authority appears to be above the rules.
2. **Mastermind.** A mastermind is someone who stands out in terms of his or her intellectual abilities. There are two main types of mastermind power concentration risks. One is an executive with an entire fiefdom, and the other is a sole individual, perhaps in middle management.
3. **Critical Supplier.** A critical supplier is a provider of a necessary set of goods or services operating in a supplier market without a sufficient level of competition. An extreme example is a sole-source supplier, which means there is currently only one active supplier with which the organization currently has, or is able to have, a business relationship.
4. **Large Customer.** A large customer is one that represents a significant portion of the business. One example is a large customer of the organization's core business. However, another example is a minor business segment's customer that is so large that its loss could significantly damage the business and possibly destroy it.
5. **Large Distributor.** A large distributor is one that controls a significant portion of the customer's access to its markets. As with the large customer situation, this can either relate to a significant portion of a core business, or a large enough portion of a non-core business such that its loss could be catastrophic for that business.

Let's again discuss each of the qualities listed earlier for killer risks, and then briefly examine possible risk mitigation.

Politically Difficult to Introduce

Clearly, the internal power concentration risks are also politically challenging to bring up. By definition, you are threatening a very powerful entity. Their demonstrated abilities in amassing power prove them to be formidable players. Though external power concentration risks are usually politically easier to discuss, these can sometimes be treacherous as well; these external entities may have internal allies with a vested interest in maintaining the status quo.

Easily Identifiable

There is one easily recognizable characteristic that virtually always accompanies any concentration of power, including our five examples: arrogance. The lack of competition leads to an arrogant attitude, which was discussed earlier as its own killer risk.

Rainmaker   Everyone is aware of the rainmakers in the organization, the special treatment they receive, and the financial rewards lavished on them. They often have a peacock-like attitude, which makes them nearly impossible to ignore.

Mastermind   Masterminds are highly respected and widely known internally, and often externally, for their knowledge and skill in a specific area of expertise. Ironically, this risk is often evident by its highly prized nature. It is often touted as an advantage. Management often feels proud of their mastermind. They feel comfortable knowing they have this reliable and valuable resource. Yet, having so much to lose, all in the person of one individual, is itself a risk.

Critical Supplier   Management is well aware of their critical suppliers, particularly the sole-source suppliers. Supply chain management is part and parcel of routine management activities.

Large Customer   Large customers are not hard to identify. Management is aware of the large customers of its core businesses, and will often visit with them to maintain the relationship. Customers large enough to be significant to individual business segments are top-of-mind to local management, and a list of them can easily be obtained.

Large Distributor   Similar to large customers, large distributors are well known internally, either at the executive or local management level.

A Leading Indicator of High-Severity Risk Events

All power concentration risks are leading indicators of potential high-severity risk events. The higher the concentration of power, the more severe the ultimate risk event can be.

Rainmaker   There are countless stories of rainmakers, either individuals or groups, that emerge, become highly successful for a time, and then crash and burn, sometimes taking the organization with them. The Financial Products division of AIG is only one recent example. Generating huge growth for AIG through its sales of credit default swaps (CDSs), the Financial Products division used this power to ignore internal phone calls from corporate personnel responsible for oversight . . . until the division bankrupted AIG through massive losses, contributing to the global financial crisis that began in the United States in 2007. The natural progression of these types of stories often seems to be in three steps:

1. Recognition of talent
2. Massive, rapid growth
3. Implosion

Initially, the rainmaker talent is identified by its early success. It is the next step that fuels the high-severity nature of this power concentration risk. Growth is difficult to achieve. It is management's excitement at the prospect of dramatic growth that leads them to quickly scale up a business producing dramatic results. Blinded by the potential rewards, they often either ignore the risks, or, more commonly, they do not thoroughly examine the risks. This urge to grow quickly is what transforms a simple risk into a killer risk. Often, the more inordinately large the returns, the more everyone wants to believe that this is a good business to expand, and yet, the more likely it is that the risks are also inordinately large.

Just as with arrogance, when a concentration of power exists, it can result in manifold types of risk events. The risks involved with rainmaker individuals or groups are mainly a lack of scrutiny, transparency, and accountability, which encourages bad behaviors or abuses by management. The normal checks-and-balances of power, such as internal audit or an ERM program, are not permitted to properly monitor the goings-on within the unit. Sometimes the high-severity risk event takes the form of internal fraud or theft. In the aftermath of an investigation uncovering such events, and the ensuing criminal prosecution, it is common for the perpetrators of the crime to convey feelings of entitlement that led them to believe the normal rules did not apply to them. In many cases, this is such a compelling factor leading to the crime, that even after a criminal conviction, the wrongdoers rationalize that their contribution to the company entitled them to what they usurped.

Other times, this takes the form of excesses in terms of perquisites. Management is often overly trusting of rainmakers, giving them anything and everything they desire. Once exposed, these excesses can lead to negative media coverage, potential reputational damage, and the resultant negative financial impacts.

In addition, the sheer nature of the pressure to continue to perform at a consistently miraculous level can lead to excessive risk taking or even outright fraud. It is human nature to want to avoid falling off from a peak performance period, which means losing the high level of recognition and financial rewards. Sometimes, this leads to desperation and an at-all-costs mentality to maintain personal status.

Mastermind   Masterminds are also common; most companies have at least one. The existence of a midlevel manager mastermind is not as risky as an executive mastermind with a fiefdom. A larger level of responsibility leads to a higher level of risk severity. The high level of dependency the organization has on this individual can lead to an imbalance in leverage, resulting in similar risks as with the rainmaker: a lack of scrutiny, transparency, and accountability, which can lead to bad behavior or abuses by the mastermind or his or her staff. Another example of risk exposure is a sudden and hard-to-fill vacuum in this area of expertise should the mastermind fall ill, pass away, or retire. Worse still, this can also lead to competitive risk if the mastermind is lured away by a competitor. An example will help illustrate the level of potential damage.

A Fortune 500 company was very proud of their chief financial officer (CFO). He was well known in the industry. He was highly respected internally. He was a high performer. The company considered him a competitive advantage, and thought they were getting quite a lot for their money. They were aware, however, that his interpersonal skills chased away many others with whom he worked. He was very arrogant and often verbally abusive of others. Nevertheless, the company figured he was well worth the trade-off.

One day, the CFO left the company. He retired. In addition to the large hole he left in the CFO position, the company learned, over time, that there were many other holes. The CFO didn't like to be challenged, and filled all his supporting positions with weak players. When the CFO retired, the entire department virtually collapsed. Several of the individuals simply could not perform their jobs without the prior CFO around. Many projects languished for months or years. It took the company several years to fully recognize what had happened and to effectively repair and rebuild the department.

Critical Supplier A power concentration in a single critical supplier exposes the organization to high-severity risk events. Three examples are discussed here. The first example is a temporary loss of the critical supplier's capacity, for example, due to a fire. This can result in a temporary inability to sell goods and services and/or a temporary failure to adequately serve the existing customer base or even honor contractual commitments. This can result in decreased revenues due to a lack of sales for a period of time, and increased expenses due to attempts to work around the situation or due to litigation. An even more damaging possibility is a permanent loss of market share due to reputational impacts: The market may interpret the event not as a one-time incident, but as an instability in the organization or its management.

The second example is a permanent loss of a sole-source supplier. Where other suppliers are available, it may take a while to establish a business relationship. This down time can result in the same financial impacts described earlier for the temporary loss example. In addition, expense margins will increase further due to the lack of negotiating leverage with the new supplier. However, in some cases, a backup supplier simply may not exist. This may require a major change to the goods or services sold by the company, which can dramatically exacerbate the severity of the event.

The third example involves a supplier to whom the company has extended a large amount of credit, or who holds a large amount of company assets. One recent example of such a situation has the distinction of also satisfying our definition of both a rainmaker and a mastermind, except that it was not an internal entity. For decades, Bernie Madoff supplied asset management services to companies as well as individuals. For many investors, Madoff was a critical supplier with whom they had an extremely high concentration risk. Some individuals even invested all of their assets with Madoff. The high level of returns Madoff appeared to generate qualified his business as a rainmaker. In addition, the ability to generate these returns routinely, with little or no volatility, despite turbulent market conditions, made him seem like a legitimate mastermind. According to Business Insider[7], HSBC had approximately one billion dollars invested with Madoff. This is significant exposure, even for a bank the size of HSBC; it represented approximately 15 percent of HSBC's post-tax profits for 2008. According to Bloomberg, Ascot Partners LLC, a money management firm, had invested nearly all of its $1.8 billion in assets with Madoff.[8] There is a long list of other companies and individuals that had large concentration risk exposure to Madoff's firm. Bernie Madoff was arrested in December 2008 for what is now known as the largest Ponzi scheme in history. The consequences for the companies and individuals whom Madoff served as a critical supplier were high-severity events, and often catastrophic; some companies, including Ascot, went bankrupt, and some individuals committed suicide.

Large Customer   Having a large customer brings with it great risk. The loss of a large customer immediately leads to a loss in company value equal to the corresponding loss of future profits. In addition, if the customer is lost to a competitor, this may be taken by the market as a signal that something is amiss, leading to a lack of confidence in management, a further loss of market share, and possibly an exodus of key employees. This can lead to a downward spiral, magnifying the loss further.

Large Distributor   A large distributor is an example of a concentration of power in the form of access to markets. The loss of a distributor can instantly destroy a large amount of value. First, there is the loss of value corresponding to the proportion of expected future sales through that distributor. In addition, depending on the nature of the goods or services the company provides, the distributor may be able to immediately move the entire existing book of business to a competitor. For example, an association promoting a service to its membership base might encourage members to immediately switch over to its new provider. In addition, just as with the loss of a large customer, the loss of a large distributor may be taken as a negative signal by the market and/or by key employees, leading to a downward spiral that magnifies the loss.

Possible Risk Mitigation

Let's briefly explore risk mitigation possibilities for each of our five examples of power concentration risks.

Rainmaker   As with arrogance, addressing the rainmaker power concentration risk directly is tantamount to corporate suicide. Even addressing it indirectly is still a rough road. There are only two indirect mitigation approaches discussed here that may be of some, although still limited, use.

The first mitigation approach is intended to combat the lack of scrutiny, transparency, and accountability that often protects rainmakers. An indirect form of mitigation is to embed, in the audit plan or ERM program, an explicit recognition that rapid growth, in and of itself, generates risk, and therefore must be subject to additional examination. It is a fundamental precept in finance that risk and return go hand in hand. You cannot have higher returns without higher risk (except for arbitrage opportunities, which evaporate quickly in a reasonably efficient market). Capturing the rainmakers, including any golden boy units, under the umbrella exercise of examining all high-growth areas, may make it slightly easier to penetrate the cloak of secrecy that usually envelops rainmakers.

The second mitigation approach is intended to negate arguments such as, "Don't worry about the risks here, we are generating far more value than other departments." An indirect form of mitigation is for the ERM team to offer to measure the value as well as the risks. This is possible when the ERM program employs a value-based ERM approach, which is described in Chapter 3. The value-based ERM approach measures risk and return on an integrated basis, because risk is defined as volatility—both upside and downside—in company value. This approach can provide the proper analysis as to whether the extra returns generated are indeed worth the additional risk exposures.

Mastermind For the mastermind power concentration risk, one way to approach it is to highlight this type of problem generally as a talent management issue, and define an approach to identify and remediate such situations. Getting broad buy-in for the approach can then lead to a committee or team to implement it. The implementation might scan the enterprise to identify all such areas of "rare talent concentration risk," emphasizing the invaluable nature of the individuals identified. Committee suggestions for mitigation might include ensuring the development of a strong cast of supporting players for succession planning.

Critical Supplier For the critical supplier power concentration risk, there is likely to be a fatalistic attitude in the company. Management is well aware of the situation, and the feeling may generally be that not much can be done about the situation. This is another area where a value-based ERM approach can enhance mitigation efforts. Once this risk is quantified, in terms of the devastating impact it can have on the value of the firm, it tends to ratchet up the level of attention and spurs more urgent and aggressive actions. An example of this is given in a case study discussed in the section titled "Case Studies" in Chapter 5. Mitigation efforts certainly include the obvious: attempting to get one or more additional suppliers, or at least to line up a backup supplier. When this is not possible, and where the likelihood and severity of losing the supplier is dire enough, it may be worthwhile to at least explore the possibility of deliberately diversifying the strategy—new goods and services, other markets, different distribution channels, and so forth—to dampen the risk. Alternatively, the company could explore the possibility of increasing its scale, through a merger or acquisition, to decrease the severity of this risk to a more acceptable level.

Large Customer For the large customer power concentration risk, management is usually focused on preserving the customer relationship. Business segment management is aware of their largest customers, and their incentives are highly aligned to keeping this business. However, upper management may not always appreciate business segment management concerns about these large customers, and may not always approve unusual measures proposed to keep these customers happy. What can help, similar to the critical supplier risk, is to quantify the impact of this risk on company value. Putting the risk in terms of the potential value lost allows a proper assessment of which mitigation actions are worthwhile.

Large Distributor The mitigation suggested here for large distributor power concentration risk is similar to a combination of that proposed for the prior two examples of power concentration risk. There may be a pervasive feeling that not much can be done about this risk. However, once this risk is quantified, in terms of its potential disastrous impact on company value, it tends to precipitate action. Efforts to gain additional distributors are undoubtedly constantly underway, because this increases revenues and is fully aligned with incentives. Barring that, mitigation to consider may include diversifying the strategy or increasing scale through merger or acquisition. Either of these can decrease the severity of this risk exposure to a more acceptable level. In addition, the quantification of this risk highlights another mitigation opportunity. Framing the risk in terms of the potential impact on value allows for a more informed decision by management as to which mitigation actions, intended to maintain a beneficial relationship with the distributor, are advisable.

 SUMMARY

Risk identification, the first step in the ERM process cycle, consists of three components: risk categorization and definition; qualitative risk assessment; and emerging risk identification. Despite being the most commonly performed ERM process step, there remain several aspects of risk identification that are routinely performed in a suboptimal way. This significantly impacts the quality of the entire ERM program, because every other step in the ERM process is downstream from the risk identification step. To avoid these problems, ERM programs must employ the five keys to a successful risk identification process step: define risks by source; categorize risks evenly; define metrics clearly; gather data appropriately; and identify risks prospectively. The first two keys to success relate to the risk categorization and definition (RCD) tool, which has several applications in an ERM program. The remaining three keys to success relate to the qualitative risk assessment. In addition to taking care to employ the five keys to successful risk identification, there are two killer risks that companies must be vigilant against: arrogance and concentration of power.

With the conclusion of risk identification, the ERM program arrives at a major milestone: identification of the key risks. The key risks are those that will advance to the next step in the ERM process cycle, which is the topic of our next chapter: risk quantification.

 ## NOTES

1. Standard & Poor's uses this term in their ratings guidance.
2. This refers to deterioration in the relationship itself, due to personal friction, as opposed to, for example, impatience with management's ability to address issues raised by the rating agency. This indicates a failure of external relations.
3. The absolute amounts in the severity column will vary by size of the organization.
4. In the qualitative risk assessment, both severity and likelihood are typically scored on a net risk exposure basis.
5. Some interviews may need to be conducted by videoconference or phone, due to the remote location of some survey participants.
6. Of course, other possibilities include the political expedience of offering a scapegoat to deflect criticism, as well as the psychological benefits of taking some action that gives the appearance of restoring safety and preventing a recurrence.
7. Businessinsider.com, Henry Blodget, December 23, 2008.
8. Bloomberg.com, Joshua Fineman, December 19, 2008.

CHAPTER FIVE

Risk Quantification

Any intelligent fool can invent further complications, but it takes a genius to retain, or recapture, simplicity.

E.F. Schumacher

T HE RISK QUANTIFICATION ERM process step is the lynchpin of the ERM process cycle. It enhances the key risk ranking and prioritization performed in the prior ERM process step—risk identification—and it also provides the information necessary to perform the next ERM process step—risk decision making. The key linkage performed in this step is the connection of risk and value by quantifying risk in terms of its value impact. This is the bridge between risk and return.

In this chapter, we will address risk quantification as performed using the value-based ERM approach. Risk quantification is performed with the value-based ERM model. By model, we mean a financial model in the form of a spreadsheet-based tool. The model receives input of data and assumptions, performs calculations, and produces output of results.

Before we discuss the risk quantification activities, we will emphasize the most critical overriding characteristic of the value-based ERM model: practicality.

168

PRACTICAL MODELING

The single most important characteristic of the value-based ERM model is that it is practical. All aspects of the model—inputs, calculations, and outputs—are kept simple, with the sole purpose, constantly in mind, of supporting decision making. As was discussed in some detail in Chapter 3, there are four aspects to this practicality:

1. **Reliability.** The inputs are few in number and so are more easily maintained at a high level of quality. In addition, simplicity in the calculations reduces the number of errors.
2. **Speed.** Simplicity in the calculations also translates to fast run times. The model provides answers in hours rather than the typical days or weeks for traditional ERM models.
3. **Transparency.** Simplicity in methodology means easier scrutiny by management. For example, tangible individual deterministic risk scenarios can be reviewed directly, unlike formula-generated, difficult-to-understand, and ever-changing stochastic risk scenarios. Deterministic and stochastic scenarios are discussed later in this chapter (see "The Power of Deterministic Risk Scenarios").
4. **Balance of significant digits.** The level of rigor is balanced with the inherent lack of precision in the assumptions. The value-based approach recognizes that a high level of complexity is simply not warranted, in light of the significant digits rule.

It is paramount to keep these four aspects of practicality constantly in mind when building the model. A perpetual vigilance is required against adding complexity. There is a natural tendency to build out additional complexity, often merely because the person trained in modeling is able to do it, enjoys doing it, and, it is actually much easier than keeping it simple. It is good to keep the following quotes in mind:

Perfection is achieved, not when there is nothing more to add, but when there is nothing left to take away.

Antoine de Saint-Exupéry

Simplicity is the ultimate sophistication.

Leonardo da Vinci

There is also another force that continually pushes people toward over-modeling. Those performing the modeling find it difficult to believe that something simpler can be better. See "Can Simpler Actually Be Better?"

CAN **SIMPLER ACTUALLY BE BETTER?**

Technical professionals, including modelers, tend to want to add complexity. It's encouraged by their training. It's aligned with their skills. It's in their DNA. Additional technological sophistication *is* useful, but only if it increases utility (it is used more) and enhances performance (results improve). However, technological complexity is often in direct opposition to those two criteria. One such example, highlighted in an article by *The New Yorker*,[1] is presented here, and comes to us from the field of obstetrics.

In the United States, in the 1950s, the field of obstetrics was in poor shape. One out of every thirty babies was stillborn (3.3 percent). Despite the availability of an abundance of individual detailed metrics on the health of the baby, there was poor care of newborns deemed "too sick to live." This included babies that were thought to be too small or had poor coloring or were not breathing well at the time. These babies were simply listed as stillborn, placed out of sight, and allowed to die.

In 1953, Dr. Virginia Apgar introduced a new metric to gauge the viability of newborns in an attempt to improve newborn care and, as a result, the mortality rate. The Apgar score was a zero-to-10 point scale: two points for pink all over, two for crying, two for good breathing, two for limb movement, and two for a heart rate over one hundred beats per minute.

Imagine the reaction of the technical professional in obstetrics at the time: "This metric is ridiculously simplistic and cannot possibly capture a baby's viability. It oversimplifies the complexities of each individual metric already available to us, and equates them all to each other in importance. Is breathing really only as important as crying? How could the Apgar score be of any value?"

In fact, the Apgar score is widely credited with revolutionizing the field of obstetrics. It was adopted globally, and succeeded in its goals to improve newborn care and the mortality rate. How can this be? How could simpler have been better? Simplicity translated into practicality, and practicality drove results. The Apgar score was easy to measure without sophisticated tools or know-how. It could be calculated by anyone that could count to 10. It was easy to compare results, from one baby to the next, from one doctor to the next, and from one hospital to the next. Availability and comparability drove competition to improve scores. This led to experimentation and eventually to standardized improvements. The Apgar score led to hundreds of improvements in newborn care now known as the "obstetrics package." One example was the shift away from general anesthesia to epidural anesthesia during childbirth once this was shown to improve Apgar scores. To date, in the United States alone, the Apgar score has saved literally millions of lives; for full-term babies, the stillborn rate is now just 1 in 500 (0.2 percent).

What is the lesson here? It's partly about seeing the bigger picture, staying focused on how technical information will work in practice, and, when necessary, letting go of unnecessary detail and complexity. Rather than getting caught up in the detailed individual pieces of data, and the new and more advanced equipment available to *some* hospitals and usable by *some* doctors, Apgar realized that a less accurate but more accessible metric could drive improvements and save lives. Whereas technical professionals often indulge personal desires to employ their most complex techniques, the businesspeople they serve more often just need practical metrics that are easy to calculate, easy to understand, and easy to use in practice. The lesson for those building ERM models: Trying to perfect the model by increasing its complexity may in fact kill it. If they choose to downshift their intellectual capabilities a bit, they may actually gain more traction. Or, using a different analogy, when ERM model builders are invited to the business table, they need to bring more than their stochastic forks and knives. They need to develop practical, marketable solutions that will catch on.

There are a few guidelines to help achieve and maintain a practical level of ERM modeling. If these guiding principles can become a mantra to those performing the model building, then the ERM model can become, and continue to be, a valuable element supporting decision making:

- Start fresh
- Expand judiciously
- Consider practicality

Start Fresh

When building the value-based ERM model for the organization for the first time, the model must be built anew, using basic principles as opposed to using a generic model. Generic models are, by their nature, overly complex. A generic model is designed to handle all the different types of businesses that it may encounter. As a result, generic models contain a lot of excess coding and functionality that is not needed for the specific entity that uses it.

Expand Judiciously

When building the value-based ERM model for the first time, or expanding the model over time, the model must be expanded judiciously. Model capabilities should only be developed to the extent needed to match their intended usage. Consider what decisions the model must support, and how quickly the results must be provided.

Although it is important to be vigilant against unnecessary model expansions, there are three main types of expansions that are both valid and natural to the development of the value-based ERM model:

1. Business segments
2. Value drivers
3. Outputs

Business Segments

The value-based ERM model must be expanded to include detail at the level of business segments or sub-segments appropriate to the risk quantification exercise. At one level, it is important to include the same breakdown as that used in other key business processes, such as strategic planning or internal reporting. This makes it easier to integrate ERM into key company processes. At another level, a more detailed breakdown may be required depending on key risk scenarios. For example, if a risk scenario impacts a major product line within a business segment, it may be necessary to break the business segment projection into two parts—one for the major product line and one for the remainder of the business segment.

Value Drivers

The model must also be expanded to include a level of detail sufficient to support the dynamic nature of the business by including value drivers. For example, if the company has salespeople, rather than model revenues as a single line item, revenues should be broken up into its detailed value driver components, such as:

- Number of new salespeople hired
- Retention rate of salespeople

- Average number of items sold per salesperson
- Average price of items sold per salesperson

In addition, more detail may be required if some of these components are not homogeneous enough; for example, retention and productivity may vary significantly by salesperson experience level.

Outputs

The company value metric is the dominant metric, and the primary set of outputs is expressed in these terms. However, management usually requests that outputs be expressed in terms of at least three or four additional key metrics. The model must be expanded to accommodate these. Examples of additional key metrics include revenue growth rate, net income growth rate, earnings per share growth rate, and, for financial services companies, capital ratio.

Consider Practicality

When faced with each new request or decision point related to potentially increasing the level of model complexity designed to "increase accuracy," consider its appropriateness. Stop, take a breath, and carefully think it through. Ask yourself, "Is it worth it?" Balance the desire for robustness against the need for practicality. Is the enhancement truly needed? What is gained and what is lost? Consider that every time the model is made more complex to better address one specific additional item, it puts the overarching goal of practicality slightly more at risk. Does the change make the model less reliable? Does it slow down the response time? Does the methodology on which calculations are based become less transparent? Is the added complexity mathematically appropriate in light of the significant digits rule?

This last question in particular—regarding significant digits—should always be top-of-mind. Consider the weakest link in the calculation chain, the lowest common denominator of inaccuracy, if you will. Is the enhancement merely an illusion of more accuracy, because the approximate nature of one of the assumptions overwhelms the equation anyway? Would it be insincere, and potentially misleading, to embed model calculations implying a higher level of accuracy than can possibly be achieved in the result?

COMPONENTS OF RISK QUANTIFICATION

There are three distinct components in the risk quantification ERM process step:

1. Calculate baseline company value
2. Quantify individual risk exposures
3. Quantify enterprise risk exposure

The value-based ERM model evolves with each of these sequential activities.

 CALCULATE BASELINE COMPANY VALUE

The first activity in the risk quantification ERM process step is to calculate the baseline company value. In the value-based ERM approach, risk is defined and quantified in terms of a deviation from expectations. A company's expectations are represented by its strategic plan. The baseline company value is an internal valuation based on achieving the strategic plan.

We will discuss three aspects of calculating the baseline company value:

1. Input of data and assumptions
2. Model calculations
3. Output of results

Input of Data and Assumptions

The data and assumptions needed to calculate the enterprise baseline value include the following three items:

1. **Strategic plan financial projection.** The first item needed as input for the calculation of the baseline company value is the strategic plan financial projection. This is a financial projection that extends out to the end of the formal planning period; for example, a three-year period. This should include the latest version of the official strategic plan projection as well as any detailed supporting documents. This should also include any information available internally regarding projections or expectations beyond the formal planning period; this is often limited to additional revenue growth, expense reduction, and known or scheduled changes in investments.

2. **Recent financials.** The second item needed as input for the calculation of the baseline company value is recent financial results that are normalized for any one-time or anomalous items. This includes the income statement, balance sheet, cash flow statement, and, for financial services companies, required capital calculations. In addition, this includes the detailed data supporting the construction of the financials; for example, rates of returns on invested assets, tax rates, and so forth.

3. **Discount rate.** The third item needed as input for the calculation of the baseline company value is the discount rate, or cost of equity capital. This is the rate that will be used to discount all future distributable cash flows back to the present time in the calculation of company value. This is the return on investment assumed to be demanded by the collective shareholders. This is based on the long-term average required return. For a discussion on determining an appropriate discount rate, see "Setting the Discount Rate."

SETTING **THE DISCOUNT RATE**

There are numerous methods of determining an appropriate discount rate. One popular method is to use the capital asset pricing model (CAPM).[2] The various methods will not be explored here for three reasons. One reason is that this is basic corporate finance, and is not unique to enterprise risk management. A second reason is that the discount rate is readily available, because it is already used in routine corporate budgeting decisions as a hurdle rate.

A third reason that it is not worth spending much time on this is, again, the significant digits rule. Much time and effort can be spent tinkering with different methodologies for estimating the cost of equity capital, yet its true value cannot really ever be known with much accuracy. The cost of equity capital is the weighted average of the return required from every single shareholder, ranging from day traders to institutional long-term holders, and everyone in between. Even if you were able to individually ask each of these investors, "What is the return you require from your investment in our stock?" the following would be true:

■ The answers would vary from investor to investor.

■ The answers would probably change from day to day.

■ Many investors would not be able to give you a definitive answer.

(continued)

(continued)
Given the elusive nature of the discount rate, and in consideration of the high level of uncertainty in so many of the inputs into the value-based ERM model, it is a much better use of time to simply estimate the discount rate using some reasonable approach or use the readily available hurdle rate, and move on.

Model Calculations

The baseline company value calculation involves a common valuation approach and can be considered in three parts:

1. Build a dynamic reproduction of the strategic plan financial projection to project financials to the end of the formal planning period (e.g., three years), and modify it to create a distributable cash flow projection.
2. Project the distributable cash flows beyond the formal planning period (e.g., up to model year 20) and add a terminal value.
3. Discount the distributable cash flow projection back to time zero using the discount rate.

Before we present an illustrative example, we will discuss three aspects of this calculation:

1. **Company value formula.** We will discuss four aspects of this formula:
    1. **General formula.** The general formula for the calculation of company value was presented in Chapter 2 (see "Company Value"), and is repeated here:
    $$Company\ value = \sum_{n=1}^{\infty} \frac{DistCF_n}{(1+d)^n}$$
    Where:
    - n = year of projection
    - $DistCF_n$ = distributable cash flow for projection year n
    - d = discount rate, which is management's estimate of the rate of return required by the shareholders for their investment, i.e., the cost of equity capital

There are many variations of this formula. Different companies define value differently. It is up to management to determine what is appropriate, based on the unique characteristics of the organization.

2. **Distributable cash flow.** Distributable cash flow is king. To investors, it is distributable cash flow that matters, as opposed to representations made by any particular accounting system. Cash flow is the universal equation for value. If I ask you to invest in my business, you will only take into account the following factors in valuing the opportunity[3]:

   ■ How much cash you must give me
   ■ When you must give cash to me
   ■ How much cash I plan to give to you in the future
   ■ When I plan to give cash to you
   ■ How likely you think I am to achieve my plans to give cash to you (in terms of amount and timing)

   Whatever accounting basis is used for the strategic plan financial projection, the distributable cash flow formula essentially removes the accounting and reduces everything to cash flows.

   Distributable cash flow (DistCF) is calculated as:

   Net income + Depreciation and amortization − Increase in working captial − Capital expenditures

3. **Truncated formula.** As a practical matter, to limit the projection to N years, a *terminal value* is used to truncate the calculation:

$$Company\ value = \frac{DistCF_1}{(1+d)^1} + \frac{DistCF_2}{(1+d)^2} + \cdots \frac{DistCF_N}{(1+d)^N} + \frac{TV_N}{(1+d)^N}$$

   Where:

   ■ $DistCF_n$ = distributable cash flow for period n
   ■ TV_N = terminal value at end of period N
   ■ d = discount rate
   ■ N = final year of projection

4. **Terminal value formula.** The terminal value represents the value remaining at the end of the projection period. This is used as a truncation, to limit the number of years projected in the model. There are various methods of calculating the terminal value. One common approach is to assume that the distributable cash flow from the final year of the projection, year N, continues to grow annually, in perpetuity, at a constant growth rate. This results in the following shorthand formula:

$$TV_N = \frac{DistCF_N \times (1+g)}{(d-g)}$$

Where:

- TV_N = terminal value at end of period N
- $DistCF_N$ = distributable cash flow for period n
- g = growth rate
- d = discount rate
- N = final year of projection

As with calculations of the discount rate, we will not further explore the alternate methods for calculating the terminal value. Terminal value is a standard component of valuation techniques and is not unique to enterprise risk management.

2. **Projection.** The distributable cash flow projection derived from the strategic plan financial projection only extends to the end of the formal planning period. The model calculations must project beyond that for several more years. For example, if the formal planning period is three years, and there is a desire to project distributable cash flows for 20 years, the projection must be extended an additional 17 years.

To do this, we must build two features into the model calculations:

1. **Dynamic relationships.** Developing a dynamic relationship involves identifying the financial line items in the distributable cash flow projection, or the value driver components, that drive other financial line items, and finding a way to dynamically estimate their relationship. One simplified example is identifying revenues as a driver of variable expenses, and representing future variable expenses in the projection as a percentage of revenues. Another example is identifying that one year's fixed expenses are a driver for the following year's fixed expenses, along with inflation, and representing future fixed expenses in the projection as the prior year's fixed expenses increased for inflation.

2. **Reasonable trend lines.** The distributable cash flow projection must have reasonable trend lines for key financial line items such as revenues and expenses. There are two projection periods involved—the strategic plan projection period and the period beyond that. Strategic plan projections have a tendency to include revenue growth that exceeds that achieved in recent years. In addition, strategic plan projections have a tendency to be overly optimistic in the ability to achieve sudden expense reductions that have not been possible previously. Examining the trend lines in the recent financial data and comparing them to those of the projection during the strategic planning period can serve as a reasonability check.

For the period beyond the financial plan projection period, the trend lines must be created. This is done using a combination of the recent financial data, the strategic plan projection, and information about expectations for the industry sector, such as growth prospects. A conservative set of steady trend lines are then developed for projecting beyond the strategic plan period.

3. **Reasonability check.** A reasonability check can be performed on the baseline company value calculation by comparing it with market capitalization. Market capitalization is the market's estimate of the company value, and is calculated as follows:

Market capitalization = Outstanding shares × Stock price per share

The relationship between the baseline company value and market capitalization varies by situation. However, in many cases, the baseline company value is 5 to 15 percent higher than the market capitalization. Whatever the percentage, the relationship should make sense in light of the company's circumstances and market conditions.

Illustrative Example: Pear Inc.

Pear Inc. is a hypothetical competitor to Apple in the handheld electronic device market. Pear manufactures smartphones and sells them through retail outlets in the United States. Its major competitive advantage is a more sophisticated network called InfinityG.

Input of Data and Assumptions   Last year, Pear had 5,000 salespeople, each selling an average of 750 units annually, based on a $250 purchase price per unit. The purchase price is expected to remain constant in the future. Pear tends to lose 15 percent of its salespeople each year. Last year, Pear hired 1,000 new salespeople. Starting this year, Pear plans to grow more aggressively. Each year going forward, Pear plans to hire 100 more new salespeople than the year before. Pear earns net investment income at an earned rate of 4.5 percent on invested assets of $150 million.

Pear's variable costs—its costs of goods sold (COGS)—are equal to 67 percent of sales. Last year, research and development costs (R&D) were $50 million, and this is expected to remain constant in the future. Last year, Pear's fixed expenses—its selling, general, and administrative (SG&A) expenses—were $35 million, and are expected to increase with an annual inflation rate of 3.5 percent. Pear pays interest expense of

6 percent on long-term debt of $150 million. Pear's effective tax rate is 35 percent.

Pear uses a discount rate of 13 percent for internal valuations, believing that this fairly represents the long-term average required return of the collective shareholders.

Pear has 200 million shares outstanding. The current stock price is $8.75 per share, resulting in a market capitalization of $1.75 billion.

Calculation of Baseline Company Value   For our illustrative example, we will make the following simplifying assumptions:

- There are no items of depreciation, amortization, change in working capital, or capital expenditures; this equates net income with distributable cash flow.
- All net income is paid out in shareholder dividends.
- The extension of the strategic plan projection beyond the formal planning period uses the same trend lines as the strategic plan projection itself.
- The projection period is twenty years.
- The growth rate for distributable cash flows beyond the projection period (used for calculating terminal value) is 0 percent.

The first three years of Pear's distributable cash flow projection is shown in Table 5.1.

Pear's baseline company value calculation is as follows:

$Company\ value_{Baseline}$

$$
= \frac{DistCF_1}{(1+d)^1} + \frac{DistCF_2}{(1+d)^2} + \cdots \frac{DistCF_N}{(1+d)^N} + \frac{TV_N}{(1+d)^N}
$$

$$
= \frac{DistCF_1}{(1+d)^1} + \frac{DistCF_2}{(1+d)^2} + \cdots \frac{DistCF_N}{(1+d)^N} + \frac{DistCF_N \times (1+g)/(d-g)}{(1+d)^N}
$$

$$
= \frac{\$147M}{(1.13)^1} + \frac{\$155M}{(1.13)^2} + \frac{\$165M}{(1.13)^3} + \cdots \frac{\$468M}{(1.13)^{20}} + \frac{\$468M/0.13}{(1.13)^{20}} = \$1.91B
$$

Performing a reasonability check by comparing baseline company value to market capitalization reveals that the former is higher than the latter by 9.0 percent:

$$
\frac{1.91B}{1.75B} - 1 = 9.0\%
$$

TABLE 5.1 Pear's Distributable Cash Flow Projection

(in $ millions)	Projection Year 1	Projection Year 2	Projection Year 3	. . .	Projection Year 20
Sales	955	995	1,045		2,552
Net Investment Income	7	7	7		7
Total Revenues	**962**	**1,002**	**1,052**		**2,559**
Cost of Goods Sold (COGS)	640	667	700		1,710
Research & Development (R&D)	50	50	50		50
Selling, General & Administrative Expenses (SG&A)	36	37	39		70
Interest Expense	9	9	9		9
Total Expenses	**735**	**763**	**798**		**1,839**
Income Taxes	**79**	**84**	**89**		**252**
Net Income	**147**	**155**	**165**		**468**
Distributable cash flow	**147**	**155**	**165**		**468**

Although we are not given enough information in this illustrative example to determine if this is within reasonable bounds, it is within the common range provided earlier of 5 to 15 percent.

Output of Results

The main output is the baseline company value itself. This is the price that investors would pay today if they believed that the organization was going to perfectly execute its strategic plan and that everything was going to go its way. The first time this is calculated is an exciting moment. For most companies, the most important metric is company value. Up until this point in time, management has relied on equity analyst valuations or market capitalization as a proxy for company value. Now, management has their own valuation, which has three main advantages over external estimates of company value. It is:

1. More accurate
2. More detailed
3. More dynamic

More Accurate

The baseline enterprise valuation has the potential to be a more accurate estimate of company value than market capitalization or analyst valuations. As discussed in Chapter 3, the internal baseline enterprise valuation leverages inside information—the information so valuable that rogue stock traders want to get their hands on it. Nobody can know with certainty what the future financial results will be. However, each local manager is in the best position to make an informed estimate as to what their part of the business is likely to generate, as well as ranges around that estimate. Collecting these estimates and ranges from local managers all around the company, in a consistent manner and in as unbiased a way as possible, and aggregating them into a single valuation model, results in a powerful tool and a more accurate estimate of company value.

The baseline company value calculation is also less volatile than external valuations such as market capitalization. This is a direct consequence of its being more accurate. The market tends to initially overreact to new information in both directions, causing additional volatility. Sometimes the market initially reacts broadly, for example, regarding bad news in an industry sector, and only some time later differentiates the reaction between individual stocks. The baseline company value calculation doesn't share this extra volatility. Management is more knowledgeable about the impact of new information on the company, and therefore doesn't overreact.

Virtually every time I have seen this done, the initial internal calculation of the baseline company value exceeds the market capitalization. This makes sense. It is the job of management to grow the value of the firm. Management sets the strategy and supporting objectives that, if and when achieved, will increase company value. However, an *excessively* optimistic strategic plan projection produces a baseline company value that is less, not more, accurate than external valuations. Later activities in the risk quantification ERM process step, such as the calculation of enterprise risk exposure, serve to strengthen the strategic planning process. These activities can help identify an achievable strategic plan, as well as a separate strategic plan that is most likely and which facilitates a baseline company value calculation that delivers on the promise of a more accurate measure of company value.

There are numerous applications of a more accurate calculation of company value. Two are discussed here. One application is to support better decision making. For example, having a more accurate estimate of company value than the general market supports more advantageous decisions regarding stock issuance or buy-back. A more advanced version of this basic company value model, in the form of the fully evolved value-based ERM model, and its ability to support decision making, is discussed in Chapter 6. Another application is to support better communications with external stakeholders. For example, having an internal stock valuation that is more accurate than the one used by equity analysts supports more effective communications with them. This will be further discussed in the section titled "Communications with Stock Analysts" in Chapter 7.

More Detailed

Unlike an external valuation of the company, which offers one number representing firm value, the value-based ERM model provides more detail. The value-based ERM model provides an ability to estimate the portion of company value attributable to parts of the company below enterprise level. Each business segment or sub-segment for which the value-based ERM model has detail has its own valuation. In addition, if desired, a valuation can be produced for any portion of business, or even individual projects, for which the corresponding financial information can be isolated and incorporated into the value-based ERM model.

This information offers a new way to look at the business that can result in a shift in management focus and attention. Consider the following hypothetical example. A technology company, SFX Computers, manufactures computers and accessories and has five business segments:

1. Laptop
2. Notebook
3. Workstation
4. Server
5. Accessory

Historically, SFX has given priority, of attention and budget, to each business segment roughly in proportion to recent earnings. This relative emphasis is shown in Figure 5.1, which highlights business segment earnings for the prior year. SFX management had been giving about half of its time and attention to the Laptop business segment, which represented half of its earnings, with the remainder evenly split between its other business segments.

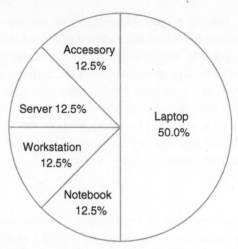

FIGURE 5.1 SFX Prior Year Earnings by Business Segment

However, recently SFX performed a baseline company value calculation, with details supporting valuations for its five business segments. The results of the calculation are shown in Figure 5.2.

The attribution of SFX's company value into its five business segments reveals the true relative value of the segments. The Laptop and Workstation

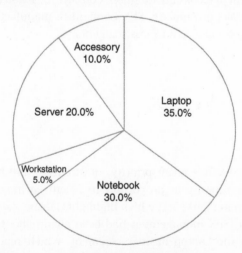

FIGURE 5.2 SFX Company Value by Business Segment

segments are less important than their prior year earnings would indicate, reflecting SFX's expectation, contained in the strategic plan projection, that demand for laptops and workstations will decline over the next several years. Similarly, the Notebook segment is more than twice as important as prior year earnings might suggest, reflecting SFX's expectations that demand for notebooks will increase significantly in the coming years. Changes in the relative importance of the Server and Accessory segments reflect SFX expectations related to shifting trends in revenue growth and profit margins.

With a clear picture of the relative contributions to company value made by each business segment, SFX management has since shifted its focus. This shift is reflected in the amount of attention and budget now afforded to each segment.

More Dynamic

External estimates of company value are not as dynamic as internal calculations of company value. External valuations only reflect information that is publicly available, whereas internal valuations reflect any inside information available to management. Having an internal valuation model allows management to revise the baseline company value calculation for new developments or decisions that change future expectations. New developments in the external or internal environments may either be unknown to the public or the public may not yet realize, or appreciate, the significance of the information vis-à-vis a specific company's future prospects. However, management may have this information, is in a better position to interpret its impact on the company's future distributable cash flows, and can revise its internal calculation of the baseline company value as necessary.

This dynamic internal valuation model can be used for decision making. For any decision, management can determine its marginal impact on the distributable cash flow projection, or the discount rate, and then recalculate the baseline company value. Having a valuation of the enterprise on a pre- and post-decision basis provides a dynamic basis for decision making.

 ## QUANTIFY INDIVIDUAL RISK EXPOSURES

The second step in the risk quantification ERM process step is to quantify the individual risk exposures. This involves the quantification of multiple deterministic risk scenarios for each key risk, in terms of its potential impact on the baseline company value. The baseline company value represents the expectations embedded in the strategic plan. Risk, in the value-based ERM approach, is defined in terms of deviation from expected. We will first discuss three aspects of quantifying individual risk exposures:

1. Input of data and assumptions
2. Model calculations
3. Output of results

Following this discussion, we will present several case studies.

Input of Data and Assumptions

We will discuss the following aspects of developing inputs for the individual risk quantification exercise:

■ The power of deterministic risk scenarios
■ Range of individual risk scenarios
■ Labeling of individual risk scenarios
■ Approaches to developing individual risk scenarios

The Power of Deterministic Risk Scenarios

There are two basic approaches used to generate risk scenarios: stochastic and deterministic. The stochastic approach involves some type of automation. It is designed to generate a large number of random scenarios without human involvement beyond setting up the process. Setup involves developing a formula, which attempts to capture the shape of the risk distribution, and a random number generator. The deterministic approach involves human judgment to select and define each individual risk scenario.

Deterministic scenarios offer four advantages over stochastic scenarios. Deterministic scenarios produce more robust scenarios, produce more accurate scenarios, enhance risk culture, and support decision making.

1. **Produce more robust scenarios.** The stochastic approach automates scenario generation, which means that it doesn't require additional thinking. Unfortunately, additional thinking is precisely what is needed to develop robust risk scenarios. There are numerous variables that require consideration, and these can only be brought to light by having subject matter experts think through each risk scenario individually. This is what

the deterministic approach does best. Subject matter experts are asked to think through, step by step, the downstream consequences flowing from an originating risk source. Having a specific, deterministic scenario to work with is a powerful catalyst in sparking dialogue with the subject matter experts and in extracting their good knowledge of how the specific situation would likely play out. Imagining a specific event actually occurring makes it easier for them to think through the sequential progression of likely events and the consequences to the organization.

One type of variable to consider is that each risk scenario may trigger different types or levels of mitigation. For example, different levels and/or causes of damage to company property may activate different levels of insurance coverage. Another example is that each scenario, for a given risk, may involve a different level of management response; higher levels of management may be involved at higher levels of severity, bringing more corporate resources to bear in mitigating the impacts of the risk event.

Another type of variable to consider is that certain scenarios, particularly those of extreme severity, may trigger secondary events that are usually associated with separate risk sources. This allows for the incorporation and reflection of correlations between risks, within the risk scenario itself. For example, a worst-case pandemic scenario may trigger an economic downturn.

2. **Produce more accurate scenarios.** A deterministic approach results in more accurate risk scenarios by reducing errors and bias, avoiding unrealistic scenarios, and producing better "tail" scenarios.

   1. **Reducing errors and bias.** With a stochastic approach, risk scenarios cannot be easily documented and shared with others. The risk scenarios can change with every run of the model; documentation would involve providing formulae rather than specific scenarios. However, with a deterministic approach, risk scenarios can be easily documented and widely shared, because they are specific and well defined. This reduces errors and bias in deterministic scenarios. Dissemination of deterministic risk scenarios leverages the knowledge of the wider group, providing opportunities to identify and correct errors. For example, a risk scenario may include an assumption about mitigation in the form of an insurance contract, and the risk manager in charge of these contracts can review the documentation and provide any needed corrections (e.g., the insurance coverage may have recently been modified). In addition, the enhanced transparency reduces bias. The subject matter experts developing the risk scenarios

are aware that their assumptions will be reviewed by others, which provides an extra incentive to be as accurate as possible.

2. **Avoiding unrealistic scenarios.** The stochastic approach often uses interpolation, particularly for strategic and operational risks, for which there is less data. The stochastic formula automatically generates future risk scenarios by relying on interpolation to construct risk scenarios in between available data points. Unfortunately, this can produce unrealistic scenarios. Some risks, or aspects of risks, can only occur in two discrete states. For example, a scandalous internal event either becomes public knowledge or it does not. The severity of the former can be much higher than the latter, with media coverage causing reputational damage. Interpolating between these two, in terms of impact severity, is not realistic. In contrast, the deterministic approach avoids producing such unrealistic scenarios. It does not rely on unthinking interpolation based on historical data points. Each risk scenario is consciously, thoughtfully, and prospectively developed by subject matter experts.

3. **Producing better "tail" scenarios.** Stochastic approaches have become less popular since the global financial crisis that began in the United States in 2007. A major reason is that they failed to produce good "tail" scenarios—extremely pessimistic scenarios that are in the tail portion of the distribution. Stochastic methods rely on formulae to represent the shape of the risk distribution. The inherent inaccuracy of formula-fitting to historical data is exacerbated when this is blindly followed into areas with very few data points, of which the tail portion of the distribution is an example. Leading up to the financial crisis, scenarios that were described by stochastic methods as extremely rare were actually occurring fairly routinely, exposing a glaring weakness of this approach. Rather than follow a mathematical method into statistical silliness, the deterministic approach relies on subject matter experts to individually think through each tail scenario, and to assign a reasonable likelihood. Although the experts do review the limited historical data points, the tail scenarios rely more on their judgment, which results in more sensible tail scenarios.

3. **Enhance risk culture.** The stochastic approach, by its design, engages fewer people from the business segments. It relies more on a few financial personnel, leveraging historical data and mathematical formulae to produce a scenario-generating machine. In contrast, the deterministic approach engages more people. This is a good thing. This enhances the risk scenarios by leveraging the knowledge of the subject matter experts, those closest to the risks. However, this also enhances the organization's

risk culture. The deterministic approach to risk scenario development involves a broad range of people throughout the organization, exposing them to ERM and getting them thinking more about risk in general. This is particularly true for strategic and operational risks, which require subject matter experts beyond the finance departments into human resources, strategic planning, legal, information technology, external relations, and other areas. In addition to educating personnel about ERM concepts, the interactive dialogue generated in the risk scenario development exercises helps build buy-in for the ERM program.

4. **Support decision making.** There are two critical characteristics that scenarios need to effectively support decision making:

1. **Transparency.** Stochastic scenarios are not easily accessible to management. They involve formulae and mathematics that are not intuitive to non-financial personnel. The mysterious nature of a risk scenario generator, humming away in a "black box," generates more than scenarios . . . it generates suspicion. Management cannot "touch and feel" the risk scenarios and see how they are developed. Without the ability to scrutinize, management hesitates to use the information for decision making.

   However, scenarios produced with a deterministic approach are fully transparent. Each specific individual risk scenario, along with all of its assumptions, is clearly laid out in easy-to-read, concise documentation. The scenarios are tangible, and resonate with management. The scenarios can easily be reviewed, and management can challenge and sensitivity-test any assumption. This engenders trust. As a result, management becomes comfortable relying on the information and using it for decision-making purposes.

2. **Stability.** Risk scenarios generated by a stochastic approach tend to change every time the ERM model is run. That is the nature of the randomizing function. This produces "noise" in the ERM model results. This causes some discomfort with management. Eyebrows are raised when they see changes to results when no explicit changes have been made to the model. The ever-shifting nature of the stochastic risk scenarios causes an uneasy sense of instability and a decreased desire to use the information in decision making. In contrast, deterministic scenarios have stability. They tend to remain unchanged, unless a change to the business occurs, necessitating valid updates. This consistency gives management the comfort they need to incorporate the information into decision making.

Range of Individual Risk Scenarios

There are often several risk scenarios for each key risk. Some key risks will have both upside and downside scenarios, some will not have any upside scenarios, and all will have a baseline scenario.

Upside and Downside Scenarios   Some key risks will have both upside and downside scenarios. One example is competitor risk. New competitors may enter the field, which may be a downside risk scenario, or a competitor may fail, which may be an upside risk scenario. Several risk scenarios might be developed for this risk, such as:

- Extremely pessimistic
- Moderately pessimistic
- Baseline (represents no risk occurring)
- Moderately optimistic
- Extremely optimistic

No Upside Scenarios   Some risks will not have any upside scenarios. These are risks for which there is no expectation (in the strategic plan) for the event to occur. One example may be a terrorist attack. There is usually no expectation that a terrorist attack will occur that will directly impact the company. The risk scenarios might include the following:

- Extremely pessimistic
- Moderately pessimistic
- Mildly pessimistic
- Baseline (represents no risk occurring)

Although most companies will not have any upside risk scenarios for terrorist attacks impacting the company, this would not be true for all companies. A company that operates in a conflict region may well have a baseline expectation built into their strategic plan, and resulting distributable cash flow projections, that a certain number of terrorist attacks will occur. In such a case, downside risk scenarios are those where the experience is worse than expected—higher than expected frequency and/or larger than expected impact. The upside risk scenarios here would be those where the experience is *better* than expected—lower than expected frequency and/or smaller than expected impact.

Another example of a company that might have upside risk scenarios for terrorism risk is an insurance company that provides coverage for this risk. The insurance company will have expectations, reflected in its pricing and embedded in its strategic plan and resultant distributable cash flow projections, regarding the likelihood and severity of terrorist attacks. Downside risk scenarios are those where the experience during the period is worse than expected, resulting in higher-than-expected claims payments. Upside risk scenarios are those where the experience during the period is better than expected, resulting in lower-than-expected claims payments.

Baseline Scenario   All key risks have a baseline scenario. This is the scenario when no risk event occurs, but instead, the expectations of the strategic plan, and resultant distributable cash flow projection, are met. Technically, this is not a risk event at all. However, it is important to keep this as a placeholder. This will be useful in the next, and final, activity in the risk quantification ERM process step: quantifying enterprise risk exposure. At that point, we will address simulations where multiple risk scenarios can occur simultaneously. One of the inputs needed for this is the likelihood of each individual risk scenario, and the baseline scenario has its own likelihood to take into account. In addition, the mechanics of the calculation are easier to visualize and perform if the baseline scenario is treated as just another individual risk scenario.

Labeling of Individual Risk Scenarios

The ranking of an individual risk scenario implied by its label, such as "worst-case," may not always be borne out by the risk quantification. When initially crafting the individual risk scenarios, the labels attributed to each risk scenario are based on an early impression of the severity of impact. However, this does not necessarily match the actual calculated financial impact. The risk quantification is a complex calculation. It involves projecting financial impacts into future years, interactivity between dynamic financial line items, and the effect of discounting for the time value of money over multiple years. In addition, different mitigation arrangements come into play. Finally, risks impact different business segments differently; for example, some regulations may negatively impact one business segment, while simultaneously positively impacting another business segment. How all these complexities play out is not always apparent at the outset.

The good news is that the labeling of individual risk scenarios doesn't matter. All that is needed here is to produce an array of individual risk scenarios that adequately represent a robust range of possible events for each key risk. The results of the individual risk quantification—quantifying each risk scenario in terms of its potential impact on the baseline company value—will determine its ultimate rank position.

Approaches to Developing Individual Risk Scenarios

There are two different approaches to developing individual risk scenarios:

1. **Approach for risks with mostly objective inputs.** The risks with risk scenario inputs that are mostly objective are those for which a large amount of objective external quantitative experience data is readily available. These are typically financial risks. One example is equity market risk, which is a financial risk for which there exists decades of experience with daily (and intraday) data on its volatility (i.e., the volatility of the major stock markets).

   Developing discrete risk scenarios for these risks is relatively straightforward. A richly detailed distribution of historical risk scenarios is available from which to choose discrete risk scenarios. This distribution provides fodder for both the individual risk scenarios themselves as well as their likelihood. Several discrete risk scenarios are selected to represent the shape of the distribution, including its inflection points. The likelihood of each discrete scenario is obtained by mapping it to a portion of the nearly continuous historical distribution and summing the corresponding likelihood.[4]

2. **Approach for risks with mostly subjective inputs.** The risks with risk scenario inputs that are mostly subjective are those for which a large amount of objective external quantitative experience data is *not* readily available. These are typically strategic and operational risks. One example is execution risk, which is a strategic risk, and for which there is no external objective data available. The ability to execute the strategic plan as expected is a completely unique risk to each company.

   Developing discrete risk scenarios for these risks is relatively more involved, in that it requires expertise in a specific technique. The technique used to do this is an adaptation of a technique from the manufacturing sector called Failure Modes and Effects Analysis (FMEA), which was described in Chapter 3. The technique involves identifying the appropriate internal subject matter experts and interviewing them to define the risk scenario event, assign likelihood, and estimate the quantitative impacts. An example showing a summary of the results of a FMEA interview is shown in Figure 3.5 in Chapter 3. The results of the FMEA interviews include all the inputs needed for quantifying individual risk scenarios, including changes, or shocks, to the items impacting the distributable cash flow projection. For most key risks, this typically includes the following:

- Changes to revenues, for one or more years
- Changes to variable expenses, for one or more years
- Changes to fixed expenses, for one or more years

For risks that materially change the company's risk profile, a change in the discount rate is also included.

The subject matter experts will often provide these inputs in terms of ranges. For example, they may estimate that revenues next year would be decreased by "approximately 10 to 20 percent." The midpoint of the range is typically used as the main input for the quantification and the endpoints of the ranges are used for sensitivity analysis.

To enhance the development of risk scenarios, the ERM team supplements the subject matter experts' knowledge, where appropriate, with the information collected in the risk event database. This information will include, for the risk in question, the historical occurrences of the risk event at the company (which helps form the likelihood assumption), how the event unfolded as well as management's actions (which helps form the risk scenario event itself), and the ultimate financial impacts (which helps form the impact assumptions).

Model Calculations

The value-based ERM model evolves along the way with each of the activities in the risk quantification ERM process step. In this activity—quantifying individual risk exposures—the model from the prior activity—calculating baseline company value—is expanded to include two new capabilities: (1) shocks to baseline and (2) stakeholder actions.

Shocks to Baseline

We have now finally arrived at the most fundamental element in the value-based ERM approach: quantifying individual risks. Individual risks are quantified by their potential impact, or shock, to the baseline company value (and other key metrics, also derived from the distributable cash flow projection). Our definition of risk is any deviation from expectations. Expectations are defined as the baseline company value (or, equivalently, its baseline projected distributable cash flows).

The value-based ERM model is expanded to reflect shocks to the baseline company value. This involves shocks to any element in the value-based ERM model that impacts the baseline company value, which includes the distributable cash flow projection and the discount rate. This affords a before-and-after look at the baseline company value (and supporting key metrics).

Although this can be done manually by editing the baseline company value model, that would be a crude, tedious, and error-prone approach. In addition, it would not support the evolution of the model needed for the next risk quantification activity—quantifying enterprise risk exposure—where an efficient mechanism is needed to run numerous simulations that include multiple simultaneous shocks. Therefore, it is necessary to modify the value-based ERM model to efficiently accommodate shocks in an elegant manner.

A key aspect of having an efficient ability to shock the baseline is to isolate and highlight any elements that may change. By necessity, this evolves as the work progresses to develop risk scenarios for the key risks. As new risk scenarios are developed, new elements will be identified that will require "shocking" in the model. One example of this is where a risk scenario only impacts a sub-segment of one of the business segments, in a situation where the model had, up to this point, only included detail broken out at the business segment level. In some cases, it may be advisable to modify the model to include the additional detail, breaking out that one business segment into two components, to isolate the business impacted by the risk scenario. Another example is where a risk scenario impacts the different strata of salespeople in different ways. Imagine that the strata differentiation is related to experience level. It may be necessary to expand the model to separately track and project recruitment, retention, and production levels for each stratum separately, to efficiently handle the related risk scenarios.

Stakeholder Actions

In quantifying individual risk exposures, we are shocking the baseline company value for those elements identified in the risk scenario development exercise. This is no longer a static projection like the baseline valuation model used to calculate the baseline company value. We are shocking the system, moving from a baseline scenario to a new, post-risk event scenario, or shock scenario. However, there is more to producing a shock scenario than merely adjusting for the elements identified in the risk scenario development exercise. We must also adjust for the dynamic reality of stakeholder actions.

Stakeholder actions are reasonably predictable actions expected to be taken by internal stakeholders, such as management, and external stakeholders, such as rating agencies, in response to triggers created in shock scenarios. An example of internal stakeholder actions is where, as a result of the risk scenario, the amount of available capital falls to a level that precipitates management actions to raise capital. The value-based ERM model must take into account this reality, and modify the calculations to dynamically reflect this. An example of external stakeholder actions is where revenue declines to a level that precipitates a ratings downgrade by rating agencies. Again, the value-based ERM model must reflect such dynamic actions, triggered not from the individual risk scenario itself, but from the fallout of its impact on other key financial line items, such as capital, revenue, expenses, and such.

Output of Results

There are three main types of outputs we will discuss for the individual risk quantification activity:

1. Shock of key metrics
2. Attribution of shocks
3. Comparative ranking of shocks

Shock of Key Metrics

The output of results from quantifying one individual risk scenario typically includes the values for the key metrics, on both a baseline and a shock scenario basis. To illustrate some common outputs, we continue our earlier example of Pear, Inc., and consider the following individual risk scenario:

Risk: Execution of product strategy

Risk scenario: InfinityG, Pear's sophisticated network, is found to have technological problems

Partial summary of impacts from FMEA risk scenario development exercise:

- Pear is forced to permanently lower its average price per unit from $250 to $225.

TABLE 5.2 Individual Risk Scenario Quantification Outputs: Pear's Product Strategy Execution Risk Scenario

(in $ millions)[5]	Enterprise Value	Five-Year Revenue CAGR[6]	Five-Year eps[7] CAGR
Baseline Scenario	1,907	7.98%	10.86%
Shock Scenario	1,571	5.03%	6.39%
Absolute Change	−336	−295 bps[8]	−447 bps
Percentage Change	−17.6%	−37.0%	−41.2%

- Annual sales per salesperson permanently decrease from 750 to 725.
- Pear is forced to permanently increase SG&A expenditures 10 percent, to fund additional marketing.

Some common individual risk scenario quantification outputs are shown in Table 5.2 for this risk scenario.

At this point, all we have done is individually quantify the risk scenarios. We have not yet calculated any interactivity between risk scenarios, which is part of the next risk quantification activity—calculating enterprise risk exposure. Yet, this is still quite valuable information, and it immediately spurs management action. Once management sees the potential impact to company value, they take actions. These actions are further informed by the attribution information discussed next. In addition, several case studies illustrating this point are presented later.

Attribution of Shocks

By itself, calculating the shock impact of individual risk scenarios on company value is powerful information. It shows management the connection of risk to value, focusing priorities and clarifying a business case for decision making involving mitigation. However, specific mitigation actions are further informed by calculating an attribution of the individual risk scenario shocks to company value. This reveals how much each component risk driver contributes to the overall shock to company value. For example, assume a risk scenario includes two component drivers—one being a reduction in revenues and another being an increase in variable expenses. The attribution would show how much of the total value shock was separately caused by each component driver: the value shock from the revenue decrease and, separately, the value shock from the variable expense increase.

There are several ways to calculate attribution for each component driver. Two examples of methodologies are as follows:

Method #1. Each component driver can be introduced, by itself, into the baseline model, and the value shocks recorded separately; if the component value shocks do not add up to the total value shock (due to interactivity) then the remainder is allocated to the drivers, in proportion to the magnitude of each component driver. Some component drivers may be judiciously excluded when it is clear that allocation to those drivers is not warranted.

Method #2. Each component driver can be cumulatively introduced into the model, one at a time, in some chosen order, with each marginal value shock attributed to the newly introduced driver.

As an illustration, we will perform an attribution calculation using our earlier example of Pear's product strategy execution risk scenario. The attribution is detailed in Table 5.3. We use attribution method #1. The initial attribution's results, prior to allocation of any interactivity, are shown in Column 1. The sum of the individual component driver shocks to company value add up to a reduction of $344 million, which does not equal the total company value shock from our earlier example, which is a reduction of $336 million. This is due to the interactivity of the component drivers. In this case, the combined impact is *less* than the sum of the parts. We allocate the interactivity only to the first two component drivers: reduction in average price per unit and reduction in annual sales per salesperson. These two are the cause of the interactivity: The first one lowers the average revenue on sales, but the second one reduces the amount of sales, which offsets the impact somewhat. Column 2 in Table 5.3 shows an allocation by magnitude between the first two component drivers. Column 3 verifies that the final attribution does indeed sum to the total company value shock of $336 million. Column 4 shows the relative percentage contribution, in percentage form, of each component driver to the company value shock. This attribution helps management focus as they consider mitigation opportunities. The case studies presented later will expand on this point.

Comparative Ranking of Shocks

Once the calculations are completed for all the individual key risk scenarios, comparative outputs can be produced. The most important of these is a

TABLE 5.3 Attribution of Company Value Impact: Pear's Product Strategy Execution Risk Scenario

Column: (in $ millions)	(1) Initial Attribution	(2) Allocation of Interactivity	(3) Final Attribution	(4) Percentage
Reduction in average price per unit	−240	+6	−234	70%
Reduction in annual sales per salesperson	−80	+2	−78	23%
Increase in SG&A due to marketing costs	−24	—	−24	7%
Sum of component drivers	−344	+8	−336	100%

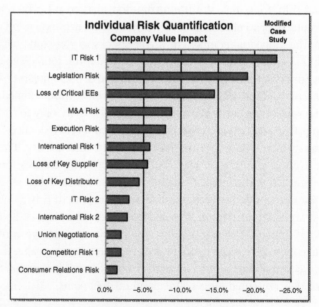

FIGURE 5.3   Ranking of Individual Risk Scenario Exposures

ranking of all individual risk scenario exposures in terms of their potential impact on the baseline company value. This was illustrated in Figure 3.2 in Chapter 3, and is repeated here as Figure 5.3. Once this is available for the company value metric, it is also immediately available on the basis of the other key metrics.

This is a very important output, as was discussed in Chapter 3. This is the first time management sees a holistic view of all key risks—from all sources including strategic, operational, and financial—quantified in terms of their impact on a single consistent metric. This immediately shifts management attention to the most highly ranked risks. In addition, this replaces the rudimentary ranking produced by the qualitative risk assessment exercise performed in the risk identification ERM process step. The first time this is done, there are typically some surprises: Some risks thought to be large turn out to be quite small or negligible, and other risks thought to be minor end up ranked highly, sometimes even in the top five.

Case Studies

Five case studies are presented here to illustrate the quantification of individual risk scenarios using the value-based ERM approach. These case studies will illustrate the approach as well as the impact of the information: the power of quantification, particularly in terms of the potential impact on the baseline company value, to support management decision making. The case studies presented focus on strategic and operational risks rather than on financial risks, because approaches to quantifying the latter are fairly straightforward, whereas a practical approach to quantifying the former has been, up to this point, elusive for most ERM practitioners.

Case Study #1: Technology Data Security and Privacy

This case study involves an operational risk related to technology data security and privacy. A midsize financial services company was surprised to see that a risk scenario involving an external attack on their technology ranked #3 in terms of its potential impact on company value. The risk scenario envisioned a computer worm entering an unprotected device such as a handheld device. The company had a policy in place to protect all such devices but was aware that the policy was not widely enforced, leaving them vulnerable. The risk scenario illustrated here is an extremely pessimistic one, which involved almost every bad event imaginable:

- Entire e-mail system disabled
- All programs and files, and their backups, deleted
- Customer lists stolen and sold to competitors for poaching
- Customer credit card data stolen and fraudulent purchases made
- Customer privacy data stolen

However, upon examining the attribution, it was immediately apparent that the vast majority of the impact on company value was due to the last item—customer privacy data stolen—and took the form of notification and monitoring[9] costs. The reasoning, as thought through during the FMEA risk scenario development exercise, was as follows: Customer privacy data for millions of people resides on several dozen computers, though the company was unsure which computers they were. Because all programs and files would be deleted, it would be impossible to determine whether all or only a portion of the privacy data was actually stolen. As a result, the company would have to pay for notification and monitoring costs for *all* those whose privacy data was on their computers.

As a result of this individual risk quantification information, management immediately made two decisions, both related to mitigation. They launched an initiative to identify and secure the several dozen computers on which resided the customer privacy data. This lowered the likelihood of the risk scenario. In addition, realizing that they had unnecessarily maintained privacy data for ex-customers, they decided to purge this data from their computers. This immediately reduced the severity of the risk scenario by nearly half.

There are three main lessons illustrated by this case study. The first lesson is that quantifying risk scenarios in terms of their potential impact on value supports decision making. This risk exposure existed at the company for some time, but management did not take action until they were shown the magnitude of the risk expressed in terms of the potential impact on value. The second lesson is that calculating the attribution by component driver focuses management on mitigation opportunities. The attribution clearly highlighted the privacy data on the computers as the largest driver of the magnitude of this risk. As a result, management was able to immediately focus mitigation efforts on this area, leading to two initiatives to mitigate the risk. The third lesson is that the FMEA risk scenario development process develops robust scenarios. This risk scenario reveals the kind of thoughtful detail that can only be gotten by getting the internal subject matter experts to think through specific risk scenarios, as well as the valuable nature of such an exercise.

Case Study #2: Loss of Critical Employees

This case study involves an operational, human resources risk related to losing critical employees. A large insurance company was quantifying risk scenarios of situations where valuable employees are gathered together, leading to a high concentration of exposure. In particular, they began to focus on the risk scenario involving a plane crash on the way to a conference for sales leaders. The company had a policy limiting the number of key employees on any one flight but was aware that the policy was not always enforced, particularly for these conferences. The sales leaders' conferences were attended by high-powered individuals who often wanted to fly on the same aircraft together. In addition, these conferences were usually held at exotic locations for which fewer flights were available. The risk scenario included the loss of the following types of individuals:

- Top salespeople
- Sales managers
- A few senior executives

Upon review of the attribution, it became clear that, although the loss of the top salespeople was significant, the larger portion of the value impact came from losing their sales managers. The reasoning, as thought through during the FMEA risk scenario development exercise, and as quantified by the value-based ERM model, was as follows: Sales managers are the most difficult to replace. They are extremely rare individuals. The salespeople are very loyal to their sales managers, and may have even come to the company in the first place by following the sales managers. As a result, the retention of salespeople would suffer in those offices where a sales manager is lost. The productivity of the remaining salespeople in that office would also deteriorate.

As a result of this individual risk quantification information, management immediately made a decision related to mitigation. They decided to strengthen the enforcement of the travel limitations policy for concentration of key employees on flights, particularly in relation to sales managers. In addition, they reviewed other travel policies to uncover any additional mitigation opportunities related to other modes of transportation.

There are three lessons illustrated by this case study. The first is that calculating attribution by component driver focuses management on mitigation opportunities. It was not at all clear, until this exercise, that the sales managers represented the largest part of this risk exposure.

The second lesson is that value-based quantification is superior to the traditional capital-based quantification common at insurance companies. Had the insurance company used a traditional approach to quantifying risk, using an economic capital model, it likely would have significantly underestimated the impact of this risk scenario, causing it to remain unmitigated. This is because most economic capital models ignore future revenues and expenses related to new business in their baseline projection; instead they simply project revenues and expense for the "inforce," which is the business currently on the books. Unfortunately, for this risk scenario and for the majority of strategic and operational risk scenarios, the impacts are largely on future revenues and expenses, as opposed to capital.

The third lesson is that despite the fact that the arithmetic is simple a value-based ERM model is needed to project out the risk scenario impacts on value, discount them to the current time, and produce a final calculation, including attributions. An intuitive estimate cannot suffice. It is impossible to correctly rank the risks, identify the largest component driver, and take appropriate mitigation actions without crunching the numbers.

Case Study #3: Money Laundering

This case study involves an operational, human resources risk related to a potential money-laundering incident. A leading U.S. nonpublic insurance company was spending a significant amount of money on mitigation known as anti–money laundering (AML). The spending got to the point where a senior executive halted all further mitigation activities pending an analysis. He thought that the mitigation might be excessive, particularly in light of the risk in question. He asked, "How bad could this risk even be?" As a result, the company requested a quantification of this risk. The risk scenario illustrated here is a very pessimistic one:

- A severe money-laundering violation occurs
- Fines are levied on the company
- Criminal prosecutions follow
- Media coverage is triggered

▪ Customer retention decreases significantly, more than what would be expected at other companies, because the violation shatters the company's brand positioning as one of high integrity

The quantification revealed that the event would destroy nearly half (45 percent) of the company's value. When management learned of the magnitude, their response was decisive: they immediately resumed their spending on anti-money laundering efforts. They instantly became comfortable with this decision. They didn't ask about the level of precision in the calculation. They also did not even ask, nor care, about the estimated likelihood of the risk scenario. It didn't matter. Until this risk quantification exercise, they had no idea that the potential impact on value was even on this order of magnitude, which was a level for which they had the proverbial "zero tolerance."[10]

There are two lessons highlighted by this case study. The first lesson is that the value metric leads to decision making. The shock to company value is one that hits home. Value is the language of business decision-makers, and when you speak their language, they understand: There is a significant threat to something they have to care about. The second lesson is that the risk quantification exercise adds value, despite its lack of precision. In this case, the approximate nature of the calculation did not inhibit the usefulness of the information to senior management. They became comfortable with their decision and acted swiftly.

Case Study #4: Supplier Disruption

This case study involves a strategic risk related to a potential supplier failure. A leading U.S. cleaning products manufacturer was quantifying their key risks. One of the risks included losing a sole-source supplier to a fire. Some time earlier, management had made a strategic decision to eliminate a backup supplier for one of their minor product lines. This resulted in a sole-source supplier situation, but this did not engender much concern, and was allowed to continue unchecked for a long time. Just prior to the risk quantification exercise, management was querying the sole-source supplier about their mitigation procedures against fire damage. Their response was, "Hey, we're great at it. In fact, we're so good at it that we cannot even share the details with you, because it is highly confidential. We consider it a competitive advantage." In reaction to this, management decided that, as part of their fiduciary duties, perhaps they should quantify this risk.

The quantification of a risk scenario in which a fire totally destroys the supplier's facilities revealed that this was, by far, the number one risk of the company, in terms of its potential impact on company value. The impact was approximately 12 percent of company value, whereas the next most impactful risk had a potential impact of only about 9 percent. The reasoning, as thought through during the FMEA risk scenario development exercise, and as quantified by the value-based ERM model, was as follows: The loss of the sole-source supplier would completely wipe out one of their minor product lines. However, in addition, this would result in a loss of market share in one of their major product lines. This major product line was in a market with a very tough competitor who would swoop in and take away a significant portion of their market share, which they would never fully recover. The leveraging impact of the loss of market share on a permanent basis, for all future projection years, is quite large, even after discounting to the present time.

Management was surprised by this information, but also pleased. This was good news. They immediately made a mitigation decision to begin the process to qualify a backup supplier. This would take about one year and only about two million dollars, which for them was very minor. This meant that they would be able to report the #1 key risk, along with the others, to the board of directors, and then within a relatively short time frame they would be able to virtually eliminate the #1 key risk. With a backup supplier in place, the likelihood of this risk scenario becomes so remote that this would be removed from the key risk list.

There are two lessons demonstrated by this case study. The FMEA process is an invaluable way to translate and share the knowledge of the subject matter experts, those closest to the risks. In addition, the value metric is needed to fully quantify risks. In this case, the full projection of lost revenues is required to appropriately quantify this risk scenario.

Case Study #5: Poor Strategic Planning

I am often asked the question, "Aren't there some risks that just cannot be quantified?" The traditional notion that some risks simply cannot be quantified seems to permeate much of the ERM literature and is pervasive among traditional ERM practitioners. As discussed throughout this book, a value-based ERM approach, in theory, allows for the quantification of any risk. This is also borne out by actual experience, rather than mere theory. The case studies above offer some evidence of this. However, one of the risks that may appear to be the most difficult to quantify is the risk of a poor strategic plan. After all, how can one gauge whether their strategic plan is poorly devised? That is why this case study is one of my favorites. It illustrates one such situation, and how this was done.

This case study involves a strategic risk related to poor strategic planning. A global leader in the technology sector began implementing an ERM program. They had just completed the risk identification ERM process step and wanted to pilot a value-based ERM approach for the risk quantification ERM process step. To test its viability, they chose what they believed to be one of the most difficult risks to quantify: the risk of poor strategic planning. Management was aware that they had a very entrepreneurial culture, and that they tended to develop strategic plans that were extremely aggressive. They were usually unable to achieve the strategic plan goals, but this failure was a result of unrealistic goals, rather than poor execution of the strategy.

The quantification of this risk was elevated to an even higher level of difficulty, like an Olympic high diver adding another twist to the dive, by the fact that the company refused to provide us, their consultants, with their strategic plan. Despite our having signed a nondisclosure agreement, their strategic plan was deemed too confidential to share, as a matter of policy. Because the first step in the value-based ERM quantification approach is to develop a baseline valuation model, this was not the best of news. However, we did have their public financial reports, and management did provide some public statements they had made about their growth prospects. Using this information, we developed a high-level baseline valuation of the company, as well as a value-based ERM model to quantify the risk.

The risk scenario development meeting was conducted using the FMEA method. The risk scenario illustrated here involves failures related to four specific strategic plan elements that management knew were particularly questionable in terms of their feasibility. One was an inability to achieve and maintain the same price premium, which they had been able to charge in their main market, in the new markets into which they had recently ventured. Another was weaker-than-expected supplier relationships. The remaining two elements were related to an inability to achieve expense reductions expected from the integration of acquisitions. The quantification of this risk scenario revealed a potential decrease of 20 percent of their baseline company value.

There are two interesting aspects of this case study. The first one relates to an interaction that occurred at the meeting where we first presented the baseline valuation. On seeing the baseline valuation, including the distributable cash flow projection, the project leader pulled her team aside for a hushed discussion. Following this sidebar, they expressed their concern that perhaps we had somehow obtained a copy of their strategic plan. Apparently, the baseline valuation resonated so well, even though it was constructed at a very high level and relied on even more simplifying assumptions than usual, that they found it difficult to believe we did this without their actual strategic plan. We were able to persuade them that, in fact, we only used public information. The interesting point here is that, as discussed earlier, many modelers believe that ERM models must be highly detailed, and use only precise assumptions, to be at all useful. This is simply untrue, both in theory and in practice.

The second interesting aspect of this case study relates to the quantification of the risk scenario. The magnitude of the shock—a 20 percent decrease in baseline company value—was just about equivalent to how much their employee stock options were out-of-the-money.[11] This revealed the level of bias in the strategic planning process. It is management's job to grow the value of the company, and in this case, one of their deep-seated needs was to increase the stock price to the level at which the stock options would be back at-the-money[12]. In other words, the market was implicitly saying, "We don't believe in your strategic plan," to the extent that they inferred what it was, "but rather we think you will fail to achieve key elements of it" (perhaps the very same four strategic plan elements of which management was skeptical). Essentially, management, through their strategic plan, was saying, "We think we are worth our baseline company value," and the market was saying, "No, we think you are worth about 20 percent less." Who is right? If management perfectly executes its strategic plan, then they will have been correct, and the market capitalization should increase about 20 percent. If the risk scenario discussed here ends up occurring, with management missing four of its strategic plan elements, then the market's valuation will have turned out to be accurate. The truth may turn out to be somewhere in between. However, the cost of not achieving the strategic plan was now quantified. In addition, the attribution revealed the relative contribution of achieving each of the four strategic plan elements in question. This gave management insights into the added value of additional efforts to achieve strategic plan goals, in the aggregate, as well as the marginal relative benefits of focusing on any one of the four individual strategic plan elements. This helped prioritize management efforts, as well as make the business case for any proposed additional initiatives to support the strategic plan goals.

There are four lessons highlighted by this case study. First, any risk can be quantified, even one as challenging as the risk of poor strategic planning. Second, the quantification of individual risk scenarios, including the calculation of baseline company value upon which it is predicated, need not be hyper-accurate to achieve their purpose. In this case, the ERM model resonated with management to a high degree, despite its total lack of inside information in constructing the baseline enterprise valuation. Third, using the value metric allows ERM information to be related to other key metrics, such as, in this case, employee stock options (and their strike price). This makes a smoother path for integrating ERM into key company processes, including decision making (Chapter 6) and risk messaging (Chapter 7). Fourth, the attribution of shocks into their component drivers facilitates management focus and prioritization of actions.

QUANTIFY ENTERPRISE RISK EXPOSURE

The third step in the risk quantification ERM process step is to quantify enterprise risk exposure. We will discuss three aspects of quantifying enterprise risk exposure:

1. Input of data and assumptions
2. Model calculations
3. Output of results

Input of Data and Assumptions

Enterprise risk exposure, in its graph form (see Figure 3.3 in Chapter 3), represents the full range of possible outcomes:

- Baseline is achieved (no risk events)
- One risk scenario at a time
- Two risk scenarios at a time
- Three risk scenarios at a time, and so forth

The graph is a distribution where the horizontal axis represents severity, or impact on baseline company value (or some other key metric), and the vertical axis represents likelihood. Therefore, the enterprise risk exposure calculation requires two types of inputs—those related to quantifying the severity of individual risk scenarios and those related to likelihood. Data and assumptions related to severity are already available, because they were developed as inputs to the individual risk quantification.

There are two types of inputs related to likelihood:

1. Likelihood of individual risk scenarios
2. Correlation between individual risk scenarios

Likelihood of Individual Risk Scenarios

The first input related to likelihood—the likelihood of each risk scenario—is also readily available. The more difficult part—estimating the likelihood of each individual non-baseline risk scenario, for each key risk, was developed in the risk scenario development exercises, which utilizes the FMEA technique. The easy part is estimating the likelihood for the remaining scenario— the baseline scenario. This is calculated as 100 percent less the sum of the likelihoods of the other individual non-baseline risk scenarios.

Correlation between Individual Risk Scenarios

The second input related to likelihood is the correlation between individual risk scenarios. This must be developed. Most traditional attempts to incorporate correlations into risk modeling have been debunked during the global financial crisis that began in the United States in 2007. Most traditional approaches are used in combination with stochastic risk scenarios, and, as a result, require a generic automatic assumption about correlations between risk sources, which is assumed valid across all of their corresponding individual risk scenarios, rather than customizing the correlation assumptions for each pair of individual risk scenarios. This means that traditional methods are attempting to encapsulate the correlation between two distinct risk sources using a single correlation assumption. This would require that all risk scenarios resulting from those two risks share the same correlation behavior. This is too crude of an estimate. During the financial crisis, it was demonstrated that, when extreme risk scenarios are at play, such correlation assumptions break down. Correlations between risks behave quite differently "in the tail," that is, at the extreme negative edge of the distribution, which corresponds to the realization of two or more simultaneous highly pessimistic risk scenarios.

With a value-based approach, which is used in combination with deterministic risk scenarios, we avoid this difficulty. Rather than attempt to paint correlations broadly, as if they are uniform by risk source, we produce an assumption for each pair of individual risk scenarios. This may initially appear to be a daunting task, because there may be over 100 individual risk scenarios. However, the vast majority of individual risk scenario pair combinations are independent, which means they are uncorrelated, that is, they have a correlation of zero. The vast majority of key risks are strategic and operational risks, as opposed to financial risks. Most strategic and operational risks are independent of each other. For example, the risk that the strategy is flawed is uncorrelated with an information technology failure, which is uncorrelated with a regulatory change, and so on. Although it is necessary to consider each pair-wise combination, wide swaths of this work are instantly completed using this realization.

For those individual risk scenario pairs that *are* correlated, the correlation must be estimated. For those risks for which objective external data is readily available, which are usually financial risks, the correlation data is available from the investment department. For the remaining ones, a simple approach is to simply guess at it, using the appropriate sign and rough magnitude.

Why is this reasonable? Because correlations in general, and even correlations for risks for which objective external data is readily available, are mysterious relationships that (a) nobody can honestly claim to know with much certainty, particularly in regard to how they behave when you most need to know this, that is, "in the tail," and (b) do exist, and should at least have some accounting for them in the calculation of a distribution of outcomes, such as enterprise risk exposure.

So, if two individual risk scenarios are thought to be moderately positively correlated, assign a value to the correlation. It is naturally going to be a fairly arbitrary value, but it should at least reflect the direction of the correlation (in this case, positive), and the correlation's magnitude should at least reflect, in relative terms versus the assignment of other correlations, the degree of correlation (in this case, moderate).

Model Calculations

The calculation of enterprise risk exposure consists of the following three steps:

1. Selecting simulations
2. Calculating impact
3. Calculating likelihood

Selecting Simulations

Each simulation represents one possible future for the organization. A simulation may be visualized as a vector, whose length is equal to the number of key risks, and where each vector position indicates the risk scenario selected for its key risk. An example of this is shown here:

$$Simulation_i = (Risk_1 Scen_i, \ Risk_2 Scen_i, \dots Risk_n Scen_i)$$

Where:

- i = the simulation number
- $Risk_x Scen_i$ = the risk scenario from key risk x that was selected in simulation i; this can include one of the pessimistic scenarios, one of the optimistic scenarios (if any exist), or the baseline scenario for this key risk (which means that no risk event occurred)
- n = the number of key risks

The number of simulations required to run every possible combination of risk scenarios developed, for the key risks selected, gets prohibitively large very quickly after a handful of key risks and risk scenarios. Shortcuts are used to select the set of simulations that will produce a representation of the enterprise risk exposure distribution that is sufficiently robust as well as stable. This is somewhat of an art form, and various techniques can be used to do this.

One example of a practical approach to selecting an appropriate but manageable set of simulations involves the following three steps:

1. **Set maximum run time.** The first step is to decide on the maximum desired model run time. Ideally, the value-based ERM model should be able to perform the enterprise risk exposure calculation within a matter of six to eight hours, although some companies find a run time of up to 12 or even 24 hours an acceptable time frame. The run time must be short enough to be practical in terms of running multiple iterations of the model when needed. In addition, it must be rapid enough to be practical in terms of effectively supporting decision making, particularly at the highest levels, where speed is of utmost importance.

2. **Determine maximum number of feasible simulations.** The maximum run time decided on in the first step is used to back into the maximum number of simulations that can be feasibly calculated within that time frame. For example, assume the maximum run time is set at six hours. Run the model with 10,000 simulations, and record the run time. If the run

time is one hour, then 60,000 is the maximum number of simulations that can be run within the six hour maximum time frame.[13]

3. **Determine simulations needed for stability.** In this step, an initial number of simulations—well below the maximum number of feasible simulations—are randomly generated, using stochastic techniques, and then run through the value-based ERM model to calculate a first value for enterprise risk exposure. It is important to note that the stochastic element here is only involved with the *selection* of which deterministic risk scenarios will populate the simulation vectors, rather than using stochastic techniques to actually *construct* the risk scenarios. After this first value is calculated, a second value is calculated using a new set of randomly generated simulations. The values are then compared to see if they are within a reasonable tolerance level of each other. If there is reasonable stability, then the initial number of simulations becomes the final number of simulations. However, if the first value is not within an acceptable tolerance level from the second value, the process must be repeated, each time increasing numbers of simulations, until stability is achieved.

If the final number of simulations required for stability exceeds the maximum number of feasible simulations, there are a few options. If the increase in the number of simulations required results in a minor increase in run time, management may simply choose to accept this. However, if the run time is unacceptably long, one option is for management to allocate more computing resources, using parallel processing to shorten the run time to a reasonable level. Another option is to revise the calculation to include a number of deterministic simulations, along with the stochastic ones, to make the calculation more stable with fewer numbers of stochastic simulations. Such deterministic simulations typically include those simulations which are more significant, either due to high likelihood and/or high severity.

Once the simulations are selected, they are locked into the model, and not allowed to change from one model run to the next.[14] This adds further stability, by avoiding the "noise" that would be present if the stochastic simulations were refreshed with each model run.

Calculating Impact

Once the simulations are determined, each simulation is run through the value-based ERM model to calculate its impact on the baseline company value (and other key metrics), and the results are recorded. Simulations that have more than one risk scenario occurring simultaneously will have their shock inputs, from the FMEA risk scenario development exercises corresponding to each risk scenario, aggregated together. The value-based ERM model will then calculate the integrated impact of the multiple risk scenarios occurring together. This is a powerful aspect of the model: the ability to see how multiple risk scenarios interact, and to measure the net impact on the organization.

Calculating Likelihood

The likelihood of a simulation is calculated by multiplying the likelihood of each individual risk scenario in the simulation vector, initially assuming independence of all risk scenarios, and then multiplying this by a correlation adjustment factor.

$$P(Sim_i) = P(Risk_1 Scen_i) \times P(Risk_2 Scen_i) \ldots \times P(Risk_n Scen_i) \times \text{CAF}$$

Where:

- $P(x)$ = probability of x
- Sim = simulation
- i = the simulation number
- $Risk_x Scen_i$ = the risk scenario, from key risk x, that was selected in simulation i; this can include one of the pessimistic scenarios, one of the optimistic scenarios (if any exist), or the baseline scenario for this key risk (which means that no risk event occurred)
- n = the number of key risks
- CAF = correlation adjustment factor

Adjustments must be made to account for correlations wherever the simulation includes the occurrence of two risk scenarios that are not independent. There are numerous methods that may be used to do this, ranging from the simple to the complex. A simpler approach is preferable, because it avoids the pretence that the true correlations can really be known with much certitude. This is another example where the rule of significant digits comes into play. Many risk modelers spend a significant amount of time and effort refining their correlation approaches and assumptions further and further, as if this is the differentiator between success and failure of an ERM program. Although the interaction between multiple risks is a key factor in

ERM, there is more than one way to reflect risk interactivity, and the correlation adjustment is the least important of all of them. See "Capturing Interactions."

One simple way to perform this adjustment is to use a correlation adjustment factor that is the multiplicative product of individual pair-wise correlation factors. For example, if a simulation includes only one pair of risk scenarios that are correlated, a single individual pair-wise multiplicative factor is applied to the simulation probability. When a simulation includes more than one pair of risk scenarios that are correlated, each individual pair-wise correlation adjustment factor is similarly applied multiplicatively to the simulation probability. The formula showing the correlation adjustment factor as the multiplicative product of individual pair-wise correlation adjustment factors is shown below:

$$CAF = IPCAF_{Risk_d Scen_i; Risk_f Scen_i} \times IPCAF_{Risk_r Scen_i; Risk_m Scen_i} \times \cdots$$

Where:

- CAF = correlation adjustment factor
- $IPCAF_{Risk_x Scen_i; Risk_y Scen_i}$ = individual pair-wise correlation adjustment factor, for the combination of risk x scenario i occurring simultaneously with risk y scenario i

There are four different situations involving the individual pair-wise correlation adjustment factor (IPCAF):

1. If the two risk scenarios are *positively correlated*, then the IPCAF will *increase* the simulation probability (i.e., the IPCAF will be greater than 1).
2. If the two risk scenarios are *uncorrelated*, then the IPCAF will *not change* the simulation probability (i.e., the implied IPCAF will equal 1, though technically no IPCAF applies unless the pair are correlated).
3. If the two risk scenarios are *somewhat negatively correlated*, then the IPCAF will *decrease* the simulation probability (i.e., the IPCAF will be greater than 0 but less than 1).
4. If the two risk scenarios are *100 percent negatively correlated*, meaning that it is impossible for them to occur together, then the IPCAF will *zero-out* the simulation probability, eliminating it entirely (i.e., the IPCAF will be zero and therefore the CAF will also be zero).

CAPTURING **INTERACTIONS**

Traditional approaches to ERM determine risk scenarios, and measure them, in silo form, or one at a time. After that, there is an attempt to capture all the risk interactivity through a correlation adjustment to likelihood. This is not enough. One of the key ERM criteria is to have an integrated approach that fully captures the interaction between two or more risks. This was discussed as Criterion 4 in Chapters 2 and 3. There are three techniques that the value-based ERM approach uses to account for these interactions:

1. Risk scenarios
2. Impact calculations
3. Correlation adjustments

Risk Scenarios

The first technique to address risk interactivity is to reflect it directly in the risk scenarios themselves. In the value-based ERM approach, deterministic risk scenarios are developed using the FMEA technique. This involves a thought-provoking process where subject matter experts are asked to think through individual risk scenarios for key risks that are defined by their source. This allows the experts to consider all the downstream impacts flowing from the risk source, including those that are primary, secondary, and so on. Some of these impacts include triggering other risk scenarios related to different risk sources, which are then incorporated directly into the risk scenario. For example, an extremely pessimistic pandemic risk scenario may be assumed to trigger an economic downturn risk scenario, which then has its own set of cascading impacts and implications, which will be embedded directly in the pandemic risk scenario.

This is one of the two most powerful ways to reflect the interaction between risks. It provides a realistic portrayal of the risk interaction and how it would occur in the real world. This draws out the knowledge of the subject matter expert, who is closest to the risk and to the business. In addition, this provides a tailored approach to examining risk interactivity. As opposed to a formulaic approach using a single correlation metric across all risk scenarios for a given risk, this allows us to incorporate customized risk interactivity assumptions for each specific risk scenario.

Impact Calculations

The second technique to address risk interactivity is to reflect it directly in the calculation of the impact on company value (and other key metrics). The value-based ERM approach allows the quantification of two or more risk scenarios directly within the value-based ERM model.

This is the other of the two most powerful ways to reflect the interaction between risks. This affords the clearest picture of how the risks will interact, including the amount that some combinations may offset each other, as well as the amount that other combinations may exacerbate each other. The net effect on the projected distributable cash flows, the baseline company value, and any other key metrics can be observed directly. In addition, an attribution calculation reveals the individual component drivers and their corresponding contribution to any interactivity between risks.

Correlation Adjustments

The third technique to address risk interactivity is risk correlation adjustments. These are multiplicative modifiers to the simulation likelihood. These do serve to recognize one aspect of the relationship between two risk scenarios: their tendency, or lack of tendency, to occur together. However, this is the least important of the three techniques. For the majority of risks that are correlated, this is a highly arbitrary assumption. What is useful about this technique is that, for risk scenarios where there is a known or strongly held belief as to the general nature of their correlation, this allows at least a directionally correct adjustment.

Output of Results

There are four types of outputs from the enterprise risk exposure quantification:

1. Enterprise risk exposure—graph form
2. Enterprise risk exposure—table form
3. Downside standard deviation
4. Other outputs

Enterprise Risk Exposure—Graph Form

The first, and primary, type of output is the enterprise risk exposure in graph form. This is a representation of the full distribution of all possible outcomes (see "Caveats," discussed later in this chapter). This was shown in Chapter 3, Figure 3.3. All other exposure-related results are derived from this graph. The types of information that can be derived include, but are not limited to, the following four items:

Item #1. The likelihood of a decrease in company value of X percent or more

Item #2. The likelihood of company value being within the range of +/− X percent of the baseline company value

Item #3. The likelihood of an increase in company value of X percent or more

Item #4. The impact of each individual risk scenario on company value

Each of the above is also available for all key metrics, not just for the company value metric. Examples of commonly used key metrics include the following:

- Company value
- Revenue growth rate (e.g., three-year or five-year CAGR[15])
- Net income growth rate (e.g., three-year or five-year CAGR)
- Earnings per share (eps) growth rate (e.g., three-year or five-year CAGR)
- Capital ratio (for financial services companies); for example, the ratio of actual capital to required capital, where required capital is the capital needed as a buffer against the current level of risk

Items #1, #2, and #3 typically form the basis for the enterprise risk exposure table form output, which is the primary data used to inform the most important decision in ERM: defining risk appetite.

A subset of item #3 is the likelihood of achieving or exceeding strategic plan goals. This can be seen by plugging in zero as the percentage. This is a very interesting result. This is a measure of the confidence level in the strategic plan, or, put another way, a measure of the level of difficulty in achieving plan goals and initiatives. The first time this is calculated, management is initially surprised at the value of this metric. It is usually significantly lower than 50 percent, and often in the neighborhood of 35 percent. However, upon examination, this makes sense. More things can go wrong than can go right. This is visually presented in the graph form of enterprise risk exposure as a "fat tail" distribution. There is more area under the curve to the left of the dotted vertical line (representing the strategic plan being achieved) than to the right.

Ironically, and perhaps a bit confusingly with our terminology, risk is measured as deviation from expected, where *expected* is defined as the perfect realization of the strategic plan, and its corresponding distributable cash flow projection. However, this is not the *probabilistic* expectation, or the mean. The actual probabilistic expectation for company value, or the mean company value, is usually somewhat lower than the baseline company value.

Item #4 is the set of individual risk exposures discussed earlier. However, as indicated in Chapter 3 (see "Enterprise Risk Exposure"), the individual risk exposures are technically a subset of the enterprise risk exposure, because it already includes the one-at-a-time risk scenarios.

Enterprise Risk Exposure—Table Form

As discussed in Chapter 3, the table form of enterprise risk exposure is derived from the graph form. The table form consists largely of items such as those listed earlier, in "Enterprise Risk Exposure—Graph Form," as items #1, #2, and #3, where the values selected as the percentages define the pain points. This is the primary data used to inform the most important decision in ERM: defining risk appetite. Table 5.4 shows a modified case study of a table form of enterprise risk exposure.

Downside Standard Deviation

A traditional measure of volatility that is easily calculated for a given distribution is the standard deviation. The higher the standard deviation, the higher the level of dispersion away from the mean, or average value. The formula for standard deviation is as follows:

$$\sigma = \sqrt{\frac{1}{n}\sum\nolimits_{x=1}^{n}(x - \bar{x})^2}$$

Where:

- σ = standard deviation
- n = number of data points in the distribution
- x = a data point in the distribution
- $\bar{x}$ = mean of distribution (note that if the metric used here is company value, this is the probabilistic expectation of company value)

TABLE 5.4 Enterprise Risk Exposure—Table Form

	Modified Case Study
Pain Point	**Likelihood**
Decrease in company value of more than 15%	8.5%
Falling short of this year's planned revenue growth by more than 200 basis points	13.2%
Falling short of this year's planned earnings by more than 2¢ per share	10.4%
Ratings downgrade of one level	7.6%

The standard deviation metric does not suit our purposes. First, standard deviation is defined in terms of deviation from the *mean*. For ERM purposes, we define risk as deviation from the *baseline*, or strategic plan expectations. Second, standard deviation captures all volatility—volatility resulting in deviations below the mean, as well as volatility resulting in deviations above the mean. This is appropriate where all deviations from the mean—both upward and downward—are equal in importance as well as symmetrical, such as in the bell-shaped curve of a normal distribution. For ERM purposes, we do define risk as all volatility. However, not all deviations are created equal. Downside volatility—producing results that fall short of the strategic plan expectations—is the bad volatility, but upside volatility—producing results that exceed strategic plan expectations—is the good volatility. Although in reality the two are connected, management would prefer to decrease downside volatility, but they would prefer to increase upside volatility. In addition, enterprise risk exposure is generally not a symmetrical distribution. It is generally a "fat tail" distribution. As such, it is important to distinguish the downside volatility from the upside volatility.

We will define a new volatility metric, called downside standard deviation ($\sigma_{downside}$, or DSD). The higher the downside standard deviation, the higher the level of dispersion below the baseline, or strategic plan expectations. The formula for downside standard deviation is as follows:

$$\sigma_{downside} = \text{DSD} = \sqrt{\frac{1}{m}\sum\nolimits_{y=1}^{m}(y - \bar{\bar{x}})^2}$$

Where:

- $\sigma_{downside} = \text{DSD} =$ downside standard deviation
- $m =$ number of data points in the distribution that correspond to a result that falls short of baseline expectations
- $y =$ a data point in the distribution that corresponds to a result that falls short of baseline expectations
- $\bar{\bar{x}} =$ baseline, or strategic plan expectations

This is a very important metric with several advantages. It is a single number. It is prospective. It incorporates all the downside risk from the enterprise risk exposure calculation. It is readily available. It can be easily recalculated to assist in the evaluation of potential decisions.

In addition, the downside standard deviation can be used as a relative guide to changing a key input to the value-based ERM model: the discount rate.

Changes to the discount rate may be needed when calculating a revised baseline company value (upon periodic updates); quantifying individual risk exposures; or for decision-making purposes. Although it is not worthwhile spending a lot of time developing the assumption for the absolute value of the discount rate, it is important to include a thoughtful approach to determining any relative *changes* in the discount rate. Whatever the absolute value of the discount rate, based on the current level of riskiness in the firm, the following two statements are true:

1. Any increase in riskiness of the firm will increase the discount rate.
2. Any decrease in riskiness of the firm will decrease the discount rate.

This merely indicates that the return on investment required from shareholders is proportional to the level of risk. This is fairly straightforward. However, what does require a bit more care is deciding which changes to the firm actually do rise to the level of materially changing the riskiness of the firm, and what should be the nature of the relationship between change in risk, as measured by downside standard deviation, and changes in the discount rate. Whatever management decides regarding this relationship, it should be consistently followed in all activities in the risk quantification and risk decision making ERM process steps.

Other Outputs

The two forms of enterprise risk exposure (graph form and table form) and the downside standard deviation are the major outputs from the enterprise risk exposure calculation. However, there are two other useful outputs that are readily available, or can be easily derived, from the calculation of enterprise risk exposure:

- Likelihood of failure
- Economic capital

Likelihood of Failure   There are numerous ways to define varying degrees of failure, and generally, the pain points can be counted among them. The pain points are thresholds, defined in terms of failing to achieve selected company goals regarding key metrics, for which management wants the likelihood of crossing them to be appropriately low. However, in addition to the typical pain points, there are other types of failures, whose likelihoods are readily available and which management finds useful, but are not always selected for inclusion as one of the formal pain points. Some examples of such failures include the following:

- A one-level ratings downgrade
- A two-level ratings downgrade
- Bankruptcy, defined as default on debt payments
- Capital ratio falling below some extreme threshold level
- All capital being exhausted

Economic Capital   Economic capital is a key metric for financial services companies. In Chapter 2, we defined economic capital as the amount of capital needed on hand today to limit the probability of ruin, over a given time horizon, to within a small predefined likelihood. One of the major benefits of a value-based ERM approach for financial services companies is that the value-based ERM model can serve a dual purpose as an economic capital model. This can be referred to as a "value-based economic capital model." Because the value-based ERM model can produce a distribution of outcomes for any definition of ruin, it can simply be run iteratively, by varying the initial level of capital, to determine the level of capital that limits the probability of ruin to the desired predefined likelihood.

Having a value-based economic capital model to replace, or preclude the need to develop, a traditional economic capital model offers three advantages:

1. **Enhances coordination.** At most financial institutions, such as banks and insurance companies, there is a lack of efficient coordination between the value-based models and the economic capital models. The value models—e.g., the strategic plan projection models, or the embedded value[16] models—are in one department, such as corporate planning, and the economic capital models are in another department, such as corporate risk management. This means that they are likely to have some differences that may conflict. The models may have inconsistent assumptions or calculations. In addition, any existing friction between the departments, due to differing political agendas or incentives, may result in a lack of coordination in usage of the models.

   However, introducing a value-based ERM approach resolves this issue completely. Those using a value-based economic capital model have in their possession a single, integrated tool that has automatic coordination and consistency, because both the value model and the economic capital model reside within a single model.

2. **Moves beyond the tail.** Traditional economic capital models typically only examine extreme risk scenarios, or tail events, such as a one-in-a-thousand risk scenario. Such an unlikely risk scenario is based on the least credible data. There are (luckily) precious few of these historical events. In addition, this is the least actionable information. There are very few opportunities (again, luckily) for management to have to deal with such situations.

    However, the value-based economic capital moves beyond the tail to include the full range of risk scenarios, both upside and downside, including those near the baseline expectation. This is far more credible information, because it is based on volatility for which more experience exists. In addition, this information is far more valuable to management, because it deals with the kind of volatility they are more likely to encounter, as opposed to the Armageddon scenarios.

3. **Satisfies key ERM criteria.** The value-based economic capital model satisfies all of the 10 key ERM criteria, and in particular, it satisfies several criteria or sub-criteria that a traditional economic capital model fails to satisfy, the five most important of which are discussed here:[17]

    1. **Full quantification of strategic and operational risks.** Most traditional economic capital models significantly underestimate the impact of some risks. For their baseline, rather than use a full projection of future distributable cash flows, they use current capital levels, or a partial projection of future distributable cash flows.[18] This is a particularly poor way to measure strategic and operational risks, which often have their largest impact on future revenues and expenses. A value-based economic capital model resolves this problem, because it uses the full projection of future distributable cash flows as its baseline.

        For more detail, see Chapters 2 and 3, "Criterion 2: All Risk Categories Included."

    2. **Integration of multiple simultaneous risks.** Most economic capital models do not use an integrated approach. They measure one source of risk at a time, and then construct an elaborate correlation matrix in an attempt to formulate an equation that captures risk interactivity. This is suboptimal, as discussed earlier (see "Capturing Interactions"). The value-based economic capital model resolves this issue by capturing interactions in three ways (see same sidebar).

For more detail, see Chapters 2 and 3, "Criterion 4: Integrated across Risk Types."

3. **Metrics that support decision making.** Traditional economic capital models do not have the metrics to fully support business decision making. These models cannot support decisions involving strategy or operations, because they either do not fully quantify strategic and operational risks, or simply omit them altogether. In addition, these models usually only present the risk (capital) aspect of the equation, and ignore the return (value) aspect. Business decision-makers require both risk and return information to make decisions.

However, value-based economic capital models resolve both of these issues. They can support all types of decisions, including those related to strategy and operations, because their quantification approach fully quantifies all risks, including strategic and operational risks. In addition, these models provide an integrated look at both risk and return information, because risk is expressed in terms of its value impact. All decisions are supported by information showing the potential impact on expected value, as well as the likelihood of achieving that value change, which is a rigorous business case for any decision.

For more detail, see Chapters 2 and 3, "Criterion 6: Includes Decision Making."

4. **Practical modeling.** Most traditional economic capital models are not practical. They tend to be unreliable, they have slow response times, they lack transparency, and they violate the significant digits rule. As an example related to response time, some companies have models that can only manage a single run, using hundreds of computers, in a period of several weeks.

In contrast, the value-based models are highly practical. They are reliable, they have fast response times, they are highly transparent, and they respect the significant digits rule. As an example related to response time, the value-based economic capital model usually runs in a handful of hours.

For more detail, see Chapters 2 and 3, "Criterion 6: Includes Decision Making."

5. **Balance of risk and return.** The lack of connection between traditional economic capital models and traditional value-based models at financial services companies was discussed earlier, in "Enhances coordination." This leads to an incomplete picture being provided to management, which causes inaction. Those presenting the results of the value

models may hear concerns such as, "Yes, that's nice to see how much value is created by this venture, but what about the risks?" Those presenting the results of the economic capital models may hear concerns such as, "Yes, that's nice to see how much risk, in the form of economic capital, is created by this venture, but what about the opportunities it generates?" Risk–return, or risk–reward, is one of the most common phrases in business, yet these two aspects of the business are not properly integrated at most financial services companies.

However, the value-based economic capital model integrates these two models together. As a result, risk and return can be managed together, because the value-based economic capital model provides information on both the risk (change in economic capital or value volatility) and the value (change in baseline company value) marginally produced by any single venture or by the enterprise as a whole.

For more detail, see Chapters 2 and 3, "Criterion 7: Balances Risk and Return Management."

Caveats

There are several caveats that, although required for practicality and appropriate for the intended usage, should be disclosed when presenting results derived from the enterprise risk exposure information. Examples of the type of caveats that may be applicable are as follows:

- Represents volatility from key risks (not all risks)
- Includes the first possible occurrence of each risk event (does not include multiple occurrences of the same risk event in successive years, unless embedded within a specific risk scenario)
- Includes a representative sampling of simulations (not all possible risk scenario combinations)

SUMMARY

The second step in the ERM process cycle, risk quantification is the lynchpin, quantifying risk in terms of its value impact and bridging the gap between risk and return. The value-based approach to risk quantification offers numerous advantages. The practical approach to modeling, the use of deterministic risk scenarios, and the ability to quantify risk scenarios by impact on company value is a powerful combination, the value of which is demonstrated through several case studies in this chapter. In addition, the value-based approach also provides a superior ability to capture risk interactions in the calculation of enterprise risk exposure. Finally, the value-based approach also improves economic capital models used in financial services companies.

Now, we are ready to move on to the next chapter, where we will discuss the main thrust of a value-based ERM approach: making better risk–return decisions.

 NOTES

1. Atul Gawande, "The Score: How Childbirth Went Industrial," *The New Yorker*, October 9, 2006.
2. Using the capital asset pricing model (CAPM) approach, the cost of equity capital is calculated as follows:

$$COEC = R_f + \beta_s \times (R_m - R_f)$$

Where:
- COEC = cost of equity capital
- R_f = risk-free rate
- β_s = the stock's beta, i.e., the relative movement of the stock in relation to the general stock market
- R_m = stock market return rate

3. This excludes synergies related to your (the investor's) other dealings (e.g., tax advantages, natural hedges to other investments, etc.).
4. If the nearly continuous historical distribution were represented graphically, for example by a curve, the likelihood corresponding to an individual risk scenario would be a portion of the area under the curve, near and around the representative individual risk scenario.
5. The number of significant digits shown in this table is higher than warranted by the data, but is displayed for illustrative purposes.
6. Compound annual growth rate
7. Earnings per share
8. Basis points
9. The company would be required to pay for the costs of performing notification and monitoring related to the detection of any identity theft that may result from the stolen privacy data.
10. The term *zero tolerance* is in quotes because, though often used, the term is usually inaccurate. Often, there is a non-zero chance of something happening. But it sounds nice, so people like to use this term. What people

often are implying is that they have precious little tolerance for the event in question.

11. The term *out-of-the-money* refers to stock options for which the strike price (the price at which one may purchase the stock upon exercising the option) is *above* the current stock price.

12. The term *at-the-money* refers to stock options for which the strike price (the price at which one may purchase the stock upon exercising the option) is *equal to* the current stock price.

13. In practice, this is not precisely linear.

14. Technically, this converts the stochastic simulations to deterministic ones, because although the stochastic simulations were initially randomly generated, once they are no longer allowed to change with each run, we are deterministically selecting those particular simulations.

15. Compound annual growth rate

16. At an insurance company, an embedded value model quantifies the value of the organization, based solely on the business "inforce" which is a run-out of the insurance policies already on the books, and excludes new business expected to be sold in the future.

17. In addition, Criteria 9 and 10 are also enhanced by the conversion of a traditional economic capital model to a value-based economic capital model.

18. Insurance company economic capital models typically project distributable cash flows corresponding to "inforce" business, which includes insurance policies already on the books, but excludes new business expected to be sold in the future.

CHAPTER SIX

Risk Decision Making

Often the difference between a successful person
and a failure is not one has better abilities or ideas,
but the courage that one has to bet on one's ideas,
to take a calculated risk—and to act.

André Malraux

URING THE BREAK at an ERM roundtable discussion of chief
financial officers and chief risk officers of leading U.S. companies
implementing ERM programs, I overheard the following exchange
between a few of the attendees: "Are you making different decisions based
on your ERM information? Are you doing anything differently because of
ERM?" Unfortunately, as discussed earlier, most ERM programs suffer from
an inability to integrate ERM into decision making. Yet, this should be the
most important step in the ERM process. If you are not acting differently,
making different choices, as a result of implementing an ERM program, then
you have misspent a good deal of time and energy. As described in Chapter 3,
the value-based ERM approach resolves these issues, allowing a full integration of ERM into decision making.

There are two major categories of risk decision making that we will discuss:

1. Defining risk appetite and risk limits
2. Integrating ERM into decision making

DEFINING RISK APPETITE AND RISK LIMITS

We will discuss each of the following two topics separately:

1. Defining risk appetite (risk exposure thresholds at the enterprise level)
2. Defining risk limits (risk exposure thresholds below enterprise level)

Defining Risk Appetite

Defining risk appetite is the first and most critical decision in the risk decision making ERM process step. This facilitates the basic purpose of ERM, which is managing enterprise risk exposure to within risk appetite. In addition, with a value-based ERM approach, defining risk appetite is also the key that unlocks the far more expansive ability of ERM to support all decision making.

Many mistakenly believe that defining risk appetite is part of the risk quantification ERM process step. In other words, they believe that risk appetite can be defined by a calculation. It cannot. Risk appetite is an expression of judgment by management, or more specifically by the ERM committee, as to the level of enterprise risk exposure, at the maximum limit, with which the shareholders are comfortable. This is an exercise that requires thoughtful discussion, debate, and, ultimately, a consensus opinion among the members of the ERM committee.

SampleCo Illustration

To illustrate the process of defining risk appetite, we will use a modified case study of a Fortune 1000 company we will call SampleCo. We will discuss the following aspects of this process:

■ ERM committee
■ Information for risk appetite consensus meeting
■ Risk appetite consensus meeting
■ Risk appetite definition

ERM Committee SampleCo's ERM committee had 12 members:

1. Chief executive officer (CEO), chair of ERM committee
2. Head of ERM program, functioning as chief risk officer (CRO), and will be referred to as CRO herein
3. Chief financial officer (CFO)
4. Head of business segment #1
5. Head of business segment #2
6. Head of business segment #3
7. Head of business segment #4
8. Head of business segment #5
9. Chief legal counsel
10. Head of compliance, nonvoting; invited quarterly
11. Head of tax, nonvoting; invited quarterly
12. Head of internal audit, nonvoting

Information for Risk Appetite Consensus Meeting SampleCo's ERM committee scheduled a risk appetite consensus meeting to define its risk appetite. To assist the ERM committee in defining risk appetite, the ERM team provided them with the following information:

- Enterprise risk exposure—table form
- Individual risk scenario exposures
- Mitigation options

Enterprise Risk Exposure—Table Form The table form of SampleCo's enterprise risk exposure is shown in Table 6.1.

TABLE 6.1 SampleCo Enterprise Risk Exposure—Table Form

	Modified Case Study
Pain Point	**Likelihood**
Decrease in company value of more than 15%	8.5%
Falling short of this year's planned revenue growth by more than 200 basis points	13.2%
Falling short of this year's planned earnings by more than 2¢ per share	10.4%
Ratings downgrade of one level	7.6%

The information shown in Table 6.1 served only as an initial draft of the table form of enterprise risk exposure. The metrics, and particularly the corresponding break points that comprise the pain points, were selected based on initial guidance from key members of the ERM committee, as well as the results of the enterprise risk exposure calculation itself. Changes to the pain points are often discussed and finalized during the risk appetite consensus meeting. To prepare for this possibility, and to further assist the ERM committee in arriving at a consensus risk appetite definition, a member of the ERM team attended the risk appetite consensus meeting ready to provide dynamic changes to the pain points, along with their associated likelihoods, using the value-based ERM model.

For illustration purposes, this case study was modified to include only a subset of the information contained in the actual table form of SampleCo's enterprise risk exposure. In addition to the more extreme pain points shown, SampleCo used other, more moderate, pain points. It was not just the extreme pain points about which management was concerned, but also significant deviations from results that management expected would occur more frequently. An example of a more moderate pain point than those shown in Table 6.1 is a decrease in company value of more than 10 percent.

This is a common practice of companies implementing a value-based ERM approach, and a significant advantage over traditional ERM approaches. Traditional approaches to ERM, particularly in financial services companies, do not construct the full distribution of outcomes, but rather only produce pain points for the most extreme of events, far more in the "tail" than those shown in Table 6.1. This is suboptimal, because there is far more information that can be provided to management regarding the volatility closer to baseline results. The value-based approach includes this, and thereby paints a more complete picture of the enterprise risk exposure.

Individual Risk Scenario Exposures SampleCo's individual risk scenario exposures, quantified in terms of their potential impact on company value, are shown in Figure 6.1. The individual risk quantification was also provided in terms of two additional key metrics: revenue growth and earnings per share growth. This is shown in Table 6.2. Note that the risk ranking changes based on the key metric through which it is viewed.

Although the company value metric is the dominant one, the other key metrics are also important, and reviewing individual risk scenario exposures in terms of multiple key metrics may provide additional insights in defining

FIGURE 6.1 SampleCo Individual Risk Scenario Exposures—Company Value Metric

risk appetite. It is also particularly helpful for stimulating discussion, and ultimately consensus, because not all members of the ERM committee may put the same emphasis on each key metric, based on their unique perspective.

As additional support, the ERM team supplemented the information in Figure 6.1 and Table 6.2 with summaries of the risk scenarios as developed during the FMEA interview process. This concise, tangible documentation of risk scenarios enhanced the level of comfort with the information, and helped smooth the path toward consensus.

TABLE 6.2 SampleCo Individual Risk Scenario Exposures—Multiple Key Metrics

Modified Case Study

	Risk	Δ Company Value	Δ Revenue Growth	Δ EPS Growth
1	Execution Risk 1	**−28.5%**	**−21.1%**	−19.9%
2	Loss of Key Supplier	−22.0%	−0.0%	**−20.0%**
3	Execution Risk 2	−17.4%	−6.8%	−13.7%
4	IT Risk 1	−14.2%	−3.6%	−3.3%
5	Economic Risk 1	−8.2%	−11.2%	−10.4%
6	Product Strategy Risk	−7.4%	−2.7%	−2.5%
7	Loss of Critical Employees	−4.9%	−5.9%	−5.4%
8	Joint Venture Risk 1	−4.5%	−4.4%	−4.0%
9	IT Risk 2	−3.9%	1.7%	−1.0%
10	Competitor Risk	−3.3%	−1.9%	−1.8%
11	Regulatory Risk 1	−2.7%	−0.0%	−1.8%
12	Disaster Risk	−2.6%	−0.0%	−0.0%
13	Regulatory Risk 2	−2.2%	−0.0%	−0.5%

Mitigation Options It often happens that an ERM committee attempts to define risk appetite without having first quantified enterprise risk exposure. This involves skipping the risk quantification ERM process step and advancing directly to the risk decision making ERM process step. This is inadvisable. Without the quantification of enterprise risk exposure, the ERM committee has no information on how large it may actually be. Without the quantification of enterprise risk exposure, the ERM committee may set risk appetite at an unrealistic level. In these situations, after enterprise risk exposure is quantified and the ERM committee realizes that risk appetite, as initially defined, is unachievable, they are forced to amend the definition. Such attempts to revise the risk appetite definition can erode confidence in the ERM committee, the ERM process, or both.

Similarly, it is helpful to quantify at least some mitigation options, and to provide this information to the ERM committee for use during the risk appetite consensus meeting. If, upon reviewing the enterprise risk exposure information, the ERM committee wishes to define risk appetite at a level below the current enterprise risk exposure, it would be helpful for them to know, in advance, that enterprise risk exposure can actually be brought to within risk appetite through mitigation. If the ERM committee defines a risk appetite that cannot be realized, the ERM program risks losing credibility with both internal and external stakeholders. For this reason, the ERM team often provides an illustration of the ability of some mitigation options to lower the enterprise risk exposure. Because risk appetite has not yet been defined, the ERM team cannot know for certain how much, if at all, the enterprise risk exposure may need to be reduced. However, the ERM team takes educated guesses, along with advance guidance from one or two key ERM committee members, to make reasonable suggestions regarding the mitigation options.

Risk Appetite Consensus Meeting   With all of the information in place, SampleCo held its risk appetite consensus meeting. The ERM committee reviewed the information provided, and a facilitated discussion began. As co-facilitators, the CRO and I, as their consultant, played a key joint role in this meeting, because the risk appetite consensus meeting is a challenging one to manage. Different members of the ERM committee brought different perspectives to the discussion. This is natural, because they have different roles in the company, different goals for their areas of responsibility, and different incentives in their compensation formulae. Ultimately, however, they arrived at a consensus risk appetite definition.

Risk Appetite Definition   The result of the risk appetite consensus meeting was a risk appetite definition that required SampleCo to lower its enterprise risk exposure. Table 6.3 shows the main portion of the risk appetite statement.

TABLE 6.3   SampleCo Risk Appetite

Modified Case Study

Enterprise Risk Exposure		Risk Appetite	
Pain Point	Likelihood	Likelihood—Soft Limit	Likelihood—Hard Limit
Decrease in company value of more than 15%	8.5%	10%	15%
Falling short of this year's planned revenue growth by more than 200 basis points	13.2%	15%	25%
Falling short of this year's planned earnings by more than 2¢ per share	10.4%	10%	15%
Ratings downgrade of one level	7.6%	5%	10%

Table 6.3 shows that the risk appetite definition includes both soft and hard limits. The hard limits are set as maximum limits that should rarely, if ever, be exceeded. The soft limits can be crossed, occasionally, for a temporary period of time. The soft limits are set as triggers for escalating levels of attention, to carefully monitor, and ultimately lower, the enterprise risk exposure back to within the soft-limit threshold. For example, when a soft limit is crossed, it triggers a requirement that any actions which would further increase the risk exposure metric must be approved by a higher-level authority. In addition, corporate ERM may become automatically involved and begin working with management to evaluate and select mitigation options that are expected to lower the risk exposure back to within the soft limit.

The risk appetite definition reveals that SampleCo's ERM committee was comfortable with the current level of enterprise risk exposure in terms of the first two pain points—those involving the company value metric and the revenue growth metric. However, they were uncomfortable with the last two pain points. They defined risk appetite with soft limits that require a reduction in the likelihood of the "Falling short of this year's planned earnings by more than 2¢ per share" pain point, from 10.4 percent to 10.0 percent. In addition, the soft limits require the risk exposure as expressed in the pain point "Ratings downgrade of one level" to be reduced from 7.6 percent to 5.0 percent. The hard limits are defined in a way that does not urgently require mitigation actions, because they are set above the current enterprise risk exposure level.

In addition, the risk appetite statement includes one additional key point. Upon reviewing the individual risk scenario exposures, the ERM committee decided that a hard limit should be put in place limiting exposure of any single risk scenario to a maximum of a 10 percent impact on company value. They came to this decision largely from reviewing Figure 6.1, which shows that just four individual risk scenarios had exposures that exceeded a 10 percent potential impact on company value. As a result of this additional limit, SampleCo immediately began investigating the feasibility of mitigation options for each of these four risk scenarios.

Defining Risk Limits

Once risk appetite is defined at the enterprise level, it may be allocated down to lower levels of the organization through what are referred to as risk limits. This may be thought of as a budgeting process, where a risk budget is created and corresponding risk exposures for this allocation must stay within budget. One example is a risk limit set for each business segment. We will address two aspects of risk limits:

1. Why risk limits are used
2. How to define risk limits

Why Risk Limits Are Used

There are four reasons why risk limits are used:

1. **Diversification.** There is much uncertainty in the ERM information, particularly in any one piece of information, and as such, additional measures of prudence are appropriate. The risk limits act to diversify the risk exposures, preventing too much concentration of exposures in any one area, such as a single business segment, or even a single source of risk.
2. **Risk–return management.** Risk limits can be used to manage the risk–return balance for portions of the business below the enterprise level, such as business segments. The process of defining risk limits can produce an attribution of the downside standard deviation metric for a given business segment. This is a holistic measure of the marginal level of downside risk that the business segment produces. Management analyzes this in relation to the returns generated by the business segment to determine any necessary actions to better manage the risk–return profile of the business segment. For example, if the level of risk is judged to be too high, the business segment may be required to produce higher returns; alternatively, a decision may be made to lower the level of risk generated by the business segment, and risk limits may be defined to facilitate this reduction.
3. **Managing enterprise risk exposure.** In a value-based ERM approach, the ERM model is readily available as a dynamic tool to manage enterprise risk exposure to within risk appetite. Management can easily access the ERM model, quickly evaluate the marginal impact of any potential decision on enterprise risk exposure, and obtain any necessary reviews and approvals, including that of corporate ERM and the ERM committee, who ensure that the overall enterprise risk exposure is maintained within risk appetite. However, in a traditional ERM approach, such an accessible, dynamic tool is typically unavailable. As a result, companies use risk limits to allocate, or budget, enterprise risk exposure.

4. **Habit.** A fourth reason that risk limits are used is simply that they are a familiar habit. The concept of an enterprise risk management approach is a new one. It is a drastic change to shift from independently managing risks in silos to managing them in an organized, top-down fashion. Up until the point that ERM is introduced into an organization, risk management is performed on more of a local level. In the absence of ERM aggregate metrics, such as enterprise risk exposure and risk appetite, companies manage their risks with risk limits, often established by business segment or business unit. These risk limits are a long-established and familiar concept. It is difficult to let go of this, even though it may not be needed any longer. Although, as discussed earlier, risk limits do have their purposes, these purposes can be satisfied with one or two forms of allocations—such as by business segment and by source of risk. However, some companies maintain multiple sets of risk limits that go beyond this, and which persist for the simple, though hard-to-justify, reason of satisfying an old habit.

How to Define Risk Limits

Companies implementing ERM use a wide range of practices to define their risk limits. Unfortunately, most of these companies use practices that are long-standing historical practices, and that pre-date the implementation of ERM. Some companies use slightly modified versions of these practices in an attempt to connect the risk limits to their new ERM framework.

The main problem with these common practices is that they rarely involve top-down allocation of risk appetite. Before adopting ERM, the majority of these companies used risk limits that were based on loose rules of thumb, often set by local management. These risk limits were not related to an aggregate measure of risk exposure for the company because aggregate metrics such as enterprise risk exposure and risk appetite did not yet exist. As a result, not only are most companies' risk limits not top-down, but they are also not even bottom-up. They don't add up. It is not even possible to add them up, because various risk exposures have disparate risk metrics. There is no common metric with which to aggregate.

This issue is discussed in depth in Chapter 3 (see "Criterion 5: Aggregated Metrics"). The problem originates with an unclear definition of risk appetite, which is the second of the three core challenges in successfully implementing an ERM program. Figure 3.7 in Chapter 3 illustrates a process for developing appropriate aggregate metrics—both enterprise risk exposure and risk appetite—and a general approach for a downward-cascading allocation of risk appetite to risk limits. An example of how to perform such a top-down allocation is presented in "Top-Down Allocation: An Example."

TOP-DOWN **ALLOCATION: AN EXAMPLE**

Companies that have implemented a value-based ERM approach and that have the appropriate aggregate metrics—enterprise risk exposure and risk appetite—are in a position to define their risk limits using a top-down allocation of risk appetite. For these companies, there are many variations on how to do this, and one approach is presented here.

In this example, let's make four simplifying assumptions about the company:

1. The company would like to set risk limits for its business segments, and corporate is considered an additional business segment.
2. There are no separate hard and soft limits, but rather only one risk appetite limit.
3. Company value is the only key metric, and only one pain point is used: a decrease in company value of more than 10 percent, which is currently $500 million.
4. Enterprise risk exposure is calculated as an 8 percent likelihood, and risk appetite is defined as a 15 percent likelihood, of hitting the pain point.

One approach to a top-down allocation of risk appetite to risk limits involves a three-step process:

1. Attribution analysis
2. Risk–return adjustment
3. Scaling up

Attribution Analysis

The first step is to conduct an attribution analysis to identify the portion of the current enterprise risk exposure that is attributable to each business segment. There are several different approaches that can be used to do this. We will only discuss one approach here, because this will suffice to illustrate the concept. Let's discuss how to perform an attribution analysis for one particular business segment which we will call the Alpha business segment.

In attribution analyses, a common problem is how to address the interactivity between individual contributors toward the overall result. In other words, when the sum of the parts does not equal the whole, how do you allocate the remainder? An attribution analysis for the marginal contribution of the Alpha business segment toward enterprise risk exposure is particularly challenging in this regard. There are several aspects of interactivity involved in calculating enterprise risk exposure, including the following:

- Risks originating in the Alpha business segment but whose severity of impact on company value is larger due to the presence of other business segments, such as a risk that triggers reputational issues impacting the entire enterprise
- Risks originating in the Alpha business segment but whose *likelihood* is larger due to the presence of other business segments, such as a risk that would not have as high a likelihood of triggering reputational issues related to negative media coverage were it not for the other business segments; in other words, the size of the firm makes it more likely to receive media attention
- Risks originating in the Alpha business segment but whose severity of impact on company value is *smaller* due to the presence of other business segments, such as a risk that would be more severe if the Alpha business segment were not a part of the larger firm and benefiting from funding, a strong rating, and other corporate support
- Risks originating in the Alpha business segment but whose *likelihood* of impact on company value is *smaller* due to the presence of other business segments, such as a risk whose likelihood is inversely proportional to economies of scale
- Risks impacting the entire enterprise, such as a natural disaster
- Correlations between risks[1] originating in the Alpha business segment and those originating in other business segments
- The interactions of risks originating in the Alpha business segment with risks originating in other business segments by virtue of their inclusion together in the simulations comprising the enterprise risk exposure calculation (see Chapter 5, "Capturing Interactions").

It is complicated and challenging to address each of these interactions one by one. One simple though imperfect way to address this is to hold fixed the values of the business segment in the value-based ERM model, delete the risks originating solely in the business segment, and recalculate enterprise risk exposure. This is a measure of what the enterprise risk exposure

(continued)

(continued)
would be if the Alpha business segment had zero risk associated with it; in other words, if the Alpha business segment distributable cash flow projection always remains equal to its baseline projection. The difference between the actual enterprise risk exposure and the recalculated enterprise risk exposure with the Alpha business segment excluded is what we'll call the initial attribution of enterprise risk exposure to the Alpha business segment. The formula for the initial attribution is as follows:

$$Initial\ ERE_{Alpha} = ERE_{Firm} - ERE_{Firm\ where\ Alpha\ has\ zero\ risk}$$

Where:

- ERE = enterprise risk exposure

The next step in the enterprise risk exposure attribution analysis is to calculate the initial attribution for every other business segment. This allows the calculation of the remainder, which represents the contribution to enterprise risk exposure not yet accounted for with this approach. The remainder is calculated as follows:

$$Remainder = ERE_{Firm} - \sum_{i=1}^{n} Initial\ ERE_i$$

Where:

- i = the business segment
- n = the total number of business segments

To calculate the enterprise risk exposure attribution for the Alpha business segment, we must first allocate the remainder among all the business segments. There are various ways of doing this. One way is to allocate the remainder to each business segment in proportion to the relative size of its initial enterprise risk exposure allocation. In this case, the allocation of the remainder to the Alpha business segment is calculated as follows:

$$Remainder_{Alpha} = Remainder \times \frac{Initial\ ERE_{Alpha}}{\sum_{i=1}^{n} Initial\ ERE_i}$$

Now we can calculate the attribution of enterprise risk exposure to the Alpha business segment as follows:

$$ERE_{Alpha} = InitialERE_{Alpha} + Remainder_{Alpha}$$

The enterprise risk exposure attribution can be expressed in terms of the contribution to the likelihood of hitting the pain point, either in absolute terms or in percentage terms. Let's assume that the enterprise risk exposure attribution for the Alpha business segment accounts for 2 percent of the total enterprise risk exposure 8 percent likelihood. Expressed as a percentage, the enterprise risk exposure attribution for the Alpha business segment is 25 percent (2/8) of the total enterprise risk exposure.

A similar attribution can be performed for the downside standard deviation (DSD) metric.

Risk–Return Adjustment

In the second step, management analyzes the risk–return balance for the Alpha business segment, comparing the returns Alpha generates to the marginal contribution to risk exposure as expressed through the two metrics calculated in the attribution analysis: the enterprise risk exposure attribution for Alpha and the downside standard deviation for Alpha.

Let's assume that management is not satisfied with the risk–return balance, in light of the Alpha business segment risk–return profile in relation to that of the entire enterprise. As a result, management would like to see Alpha's contribution to enterprise risk exposure reduced from 25 percent to 20 percent. This is not a threshold, but merely suggests an appropriate risk exposure level commensurate with Alpha's expected returns. For this exercise, let's refer to the 20 percent as the optimal level for Alpha's contribution to enterprise risk exposure.

Scaling Up

Up to this point, we have measured Alpha's current contribution to enterprise risk exposure as well as its optimal contribution to enterprise risk exposure. Now we must scale up from enterprise risk exposure to risk appetite. This is because we are defining risk limits and risk limits are a subset of risk appetite, just as the Alpha enterprise risk exposure attribution is a subset of enterprise risk exposure. We are moving from exposures and an attribution of exposures to risk appetite and an attribution of risk appetite, which is the risk limit.

We calculate the Alpha business segment risk limit as follows:

$$Risk\ limit_{Alpha} = Optimal\ ERE\%_{Alpha} \times Risk\ appetite$$
$$= (20\%) \times (15\%\ likelihood)$$
$$= 3\%\ likelihood$$

INTEGRATING ERM INTO DECISION MAKING

The term *risk culture* is an ERM phrase that has almost as many definitions as there are people attempting to define it. Some define risk culture as a supportive environment within which ERM can flourish. Others define risk culture to include risk governance, in that a proper hierarchical organization is conducive to ERM adoption.

However, culture is not something that exists on paper, such as a governing document. Culture is the way in which ideas and theoretical concepts actually take shape in real life. It is the same with *risk* culture. Risk culture—the way in which ERM is embraced by company employees—is measured by the extent to which ERM is integrated into key internal company processes. We will define risk culture as a combination of the following two items:

1. The extent to which ERM is integrated into decision making (discussed in this section)
2. The extent to which ERM is integrated into business performance analysis and incentive compensation (discussed in the "Internal Risk Messaging" section in Chapter 7)

We are now at the summit of the value-based ERM approach. Although there are many benefits to implementing a value-based ERM program, the single most important purpose is to make better decisions. By integrating both risk (enterprise risk management) and return (value-based management), we are now in a position to make better risk–return trade-off decisions, which increases company value.

We will discuss three aspects of integrating ERM into decision making:

1. Decision making with ERM
2. Risk-priority decision making
3. Return-priority decision making

Risk-priority decision making involves decisions whose primary goal is related to managing the level of risk to an appropriate level (up or down); an example of risk-priority decision making is managing enterprise risk exposure to within risk appetite. Return-priority decision making involves decisions whose primary goal is related to increasing company value; an example of return-priority decision making is strategic planning.

Decision Making with ERM

The process of making risk–return trade-off decisions with ERM information, in general, is virtually identical for both risk-priority and return-priority decisions. This is an important point. The fact that a single approach to decision making can be used for any type of decision—whether related to managing risk or enhancing value—is evidence that the value-based ERM approach delivers on its promise of bridging the gap between ERM and value-based management. A single decision-making process provides a strong business case for risk-priority decisions, by expressing risk in terms of its potential impact on company value, and also for return-priority decisions, by providing more rigor around the scenario analyses.

As discussed in Chapter 3, and illustrated in Figure 3.1, in the risk decision making process step of a value-based ERM framework, there are two types of decisions that management can make: They can change strategy or they can change tactics. As can be seen from Figure 3.1, a change in either will change the filters and, thereby, change the calculation of the risk and return metrics, informing the potential viability of the decision. Expanding the framework to emphasize the decision-making portion, and to incorporate our categorization of decisions into risk-priority and return-priority decisions, we arrive at the modified value-based ERM framework shown in Figure 6.2.

In the modified version of the value-based ERM framework shown in Figure 6.2, we expand on the original, representational framework and reveal two important nuances. First, regardless of the type of decision (strategic or tactical) or its primary intent (risk-priority or return-priority), any decision can impact either (or both) of the two filters shown in Figure 6.2. This means that any decision can lead to a change in the selection of key risks (represented by changes to the first filter), as well as in the level of risk mitigation for the key risks (represented by changes to the *second* filter). A return-priority decision can change the selection of key risks (e.g., an acquisition of foreign business adds sovereign risk as a new key risk) or can change the level of mitigation for an existing key risk (e.g., an acquisition of a countercyclical business mitigates economic risk). A risk-priority decision can change the selection of key risks (e.g., backward integration eliminates a supplier risk) or can change the level of mitigation (e.g., hurricane insurance mitigates hurricane risk).

The second nuance revealed in Figure 6.2 is that, in addition to changing items related to the two filters, a decision can also impact additional items, such as the key risk scenarios and the baseline company value. In Figure 6.2, this is indicated by the arrows with the broken lines.

The decision-making process, for both risk-priority and return-priority decisions, is a two-step process:

1. Recalculate risk and return metrics
2. Evaluate risk–return trade-off

Recalculate Risk and Return Metrics

A five-step procedure is used to recalculate the risk and return metrics:

Step 1: Revise distributable cash flow projection. The first step in the procedure to recalculate the risk and return metrics is to revise the baseline company value distributable cash flow projection. This captures how the decision is expected to impact future revenues and

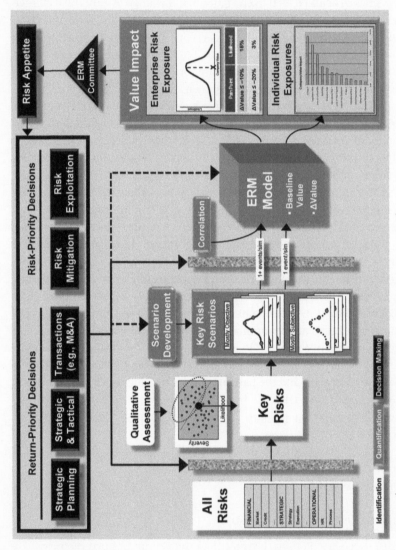

FIGURE 6.2 Value-Based ERM Framework Modified to Highlight Decision Making

242

future expenses. For risk-priority decisions, which are usually mitigation, expenses are often the only item impacted. For return-priority decisions, both revenues and expenses are usually impacted.

Step 2: Revise discount rate. The second step in the procedure is to revise the discount rate used in the baseline company value calculation. A change in the discount rate would reflect a change in the riskiness of the firm. At this stage, an estimate of any change in the discount rate would need to be tentative, pending review of changes to enterprise risk exposure, and, in particular, the downside standard deviation. This is, by necessity, iterative (just once), because the baseline company value must be recalculated prior to recalculating the risk metrics—enterprise risk exposure and downside standard deviation.

Step 3: Recalculate baseline company value. The third step is to perform a tentative (pending finalization of the discount rate) recalculation of the baseline company value, using the revised distributable cash flow projection and the revised discount rate. The (tentative) revised baseline company value is used as the basis for recalculating enterprise risk exposure. In other words, all risk is now defined as deviations from this revised baseline.

Step 4: Revise key risk scenarios. The fourth step in the procedure is to revise the key risk scenarios. One aspect of this is to review existing key risk scenarios, determine if any revisions are needed, and if so, make the revisions, using FMEA interviews with selected subject matter experts if warranted. Another aspect of this is to identify any new key risks introduced, and if so, develop appropriate risk scenarios for them, using the FMEA technique.[2] In addition, some key risks or key risk scenarios may need to be removed.

Step 5: Recalculate enterprise risk exposure. The fifth step involves recalculating enterprise risk exposure. This involves running the simulations through the value-based ERM model using the revised baseline company value and revised key risk scenarios. The outputs include the following items:

■ Enterprise risk exposure[3]
■ Downside standard deviation
■ Probabilistic expectation of company value

The impact on the downside standard deviation must now be compared to the tentative revision to the discount rate used in the baseline company value recalculation. Any material increase (or decrease) in the downside standard deviation should correspond to an increase (or decrease) in the discount rate. For example, all things being equal, if the firm becomes more volatile, then investors will require a higher rate of return, which equates to a higher discount rate in the enterprise valuation, which lowers company value. If the initial change in the discount rate does not properly reflect the change in riskiness implied by the impact on downside standard deviation, then the discount rate must be adjusted to make it so. If the discount rate is adjusted at this stage, the procedure must be repeated one more time, starting at the second step.

Evaluate Risk–Return Trade-off

Once the risk and return metrics are recalculated, management has the information it needs to evaluate the risk–return trade-off of any decision. A decision must be evaluated in terms of its impact on both the risk metrics (the first two in the following list) and the return metrics (the last two in the following list):

1. **Impact on enterprise risk exposure.** The impact on enterprise risk exposure will be the first item considered for *risk*-priority decisions, in cases where the enterprise risk exposure either exceeds risk appetite (either hard or soft limit) or is too far below it. In these situations, management evaluates decisions (risk mitigation options in the former situation, and risk-taking options[4] in the latter) with an eye towards how effectively they manage exposures to the appropriate level. *Return*-priority decisions must also review the impact on enterprise risk exposure to ensure that it does not violate risk appetite limits; however, this will not be the first item considered.[5]
2. **Impact on downside standard deviation.** The impact on downside standard deviation is another way to look at the impact of a decision on the level of firm risk. If the change in this metric is considered out of bounds, particularly in terms of its implications for the discount rate and the resultant impact on the baseline company value, then the decision may be invalidated.
3. **Impact on baseline company value.** The impact on the baseline company value is the first item considered for return-priority decisions, and is always the overriding consideration, even for risk-priority decisions. Management should only be making decisions that preserve or increase value, and this equates to maintaining a neutral or positive change in the baseline company value. In addition, all things being equal, management should be making those decisions that generate the largest increase in value.
4. **Impact on probabilistic expectation of company value.** The impact on the probabilistic expectation of company value should also be considered, because it provides another view on whether the decision being considered is adding value. In a perfect world, this should be the dominant metric, as

opposed to the baseline company value, for determining a value-added decision. Based on probability theory, this is the expected value of the company. However, despite what the probabilities say about "expectation," management is committed to achieving the strategic plan, and this must be their working expectation; therefore, changes to the baseline company value usually carry more weight in determining a go/no-go decision.

The risk–return trade-off analysis provides management with the information needed to select the best risk–return trade-off decisions and increase company value. Prior to finalizing any decisions, management obtains any reviews and approvals that may be required by ERM policies and procedures.

The elements of the risk–return analysis are fundamental to the rules of basic finance. However, the type of information made available by the ERM process, with its rigor in calculating baseline (pre-decision) and revised (post-decision) risk and return metrics, is unprecedented. The ERM process provides a uniform approach for making all decisions, whether for risk-priority decisions (adding a requirement to preserve or increase value) or for return-priority decisions (adding robustness to the sensitivity analyses). Enhancing and joining both the risk and return information improves the risk management decisions, such as mitigation, as well as routine business decisions, such as strategic planning, strategic and tactical decisions, and transactions.

Risk-Priority Decision Making

We will discuss two topics on risk-priority decision making:

1. Managing enterprise risk exposure to within risk appetite
2. Mitigation decisions

Managing Enterprise Risk Exposure to within Risk Appetite

Once risk appetite is defined, the primary function of ERM—managing enterprise risk exposure to within risk appetite—can be performed. From here forward, for convenience sake, we will use the term *risk appetite* to collectively refer to both risk appetite (risk exposure thresholds at the enterprise level) and risk limits (risk exposure thresholds below enterprise level), unless specified otherwise. The first time that enterprise risk exposure is measured and risk appetite is defined, management will find itself in one of the following four situations:

1. Enterprise risk exposure exceeds the hard limit of risk appetite.

2. Enterprise risk exposure is at, or exceeds, the soft limit of risk appetite, but is below the hard limit.
3. Enterprise risk exposure is excessively below the soft limit of risk appetite.
4. Enterprise risk exposure is in a reasonably comfortable range below the soft limit of risk appetite.

These four situations are listed in decreasing order of priority, in terms of management actions needed to change the enterprise risk exposure. In the first situation, there is an urgent need to reduce exposures to below the hard limit, because the hard limit should rarely, if ever, be violated. In the second situation, management may take some immediate actions to reduce exposures to a comfortable range below the soft limit, although management may also allow selected exposures to slightly exceed the soft limit for awhile, depending on the upside opportunity that accompanies this. In the third situation, management takes action to *increase* risk exposure; this is often referred to as risk exploitation (see "Risk Exploitation"). In such situations, management often knows, even prior to this exercise, that they are not taking enough risk, and therefore not achieving competitive returns, but it is at this moment—when they see a quantification of how much room they have for additional risk taking—that they are in a confident position to take on more risk. In the fourth situation, management does not take risk-priority actions, because the enterprise risk exposure is precisely where it ought to be.

RISK **EXPLOITATION**

In form, risk exploitation is no different from any routine business decision that simply involves taking on more risk. However, in context, risk exploitation refers to the conscious decision to take on additional risk exposure as part of a risk-priority decision. Risk exploitation can have one of two motives. It may be to increase the enterprise risk exposure of the firm, to move it closer to the soft limit of risk appetite for a better overall risk–return profile. Alternatively, it may be to increase one particular individual risk exposure to move it closer to its risk limit, where the company has a competitive advantage in taking such exposure and expects a profitable risk–return trade-off. Both of these motives, however, are only acted on if management finds appropriate risk–return trade-off business opportunities.

In the first two situations, management must act to reduce enterprise risk exposure to within risk appetite. These actions are more traditionally thought of as being within the realm of ERM[6] and are clearly risk-priority decisions. Yet, all of the first *three* situations require actions, or decisions, that are of the risk-priority type, because the risk level is not where management would like it to be. All of these decisions are evaluated using the procedure discussed earlier (see "Decision Making with ERM"). The fourth situation, where the risk level is reasonable, is the one in which companies hopefully spend the majority of their time, and where most of the important decisions are *return*-priority decisions, which, as with all decisions, are evaluated using the same procedure discussed earlier (see "Decision Making with ERM").[7]

There are two types of ERM information routinely provided to maintain an appropriate level of enterprise risk exposure:

1. Exposure information
2. Key risk indicators (KRIs)

Exposure Information Exposure information and the corresponding thresholds are routinely reported to the board of directors, management, and the ERM team, in support of maintaining an appropriate level of enterprise risk exposure. The information includes a comparison of enterprise risk exposure to risk appetite. In addition, any and all risk exposures below enterprise level (individual risk exposures, business segment risk exposures, etc.) are compared to their corresponding risk limits. The information is reported to those with the corresponding level of authority to oversee, direct, or take actions to manage the exposure to within its tolerance limit. The reporting frequency varies according to the volatility of the exposures, to afford a reasonable time frame for action.

Key Risk Indicators (KRIs) Along with the actual exposures, key risk indicators (KRIs) are also commonly provided in support of maintaining an appropriate level of enterprise risk exposure. The most useful KRIs are leading indicators which are highly correlated with the exposure metric and serve as an advance warning to management about a likely impending change in the level of exposure.

Some examples of KRIs, and the corresponding risk exposure for which the KRI may be a leading indicator, are shown in Table 6.4.

TABLE 6.4 Examples of Key Risk Indicators

Key Risk Indicator (KRI)	Corresponding Risk Exposure
Attempted attacks on information technology	Risk of a data security breach
Calls to customer service	Risk of poor product/service quality
Lawsuits filed against the company	Litigation risk
Unemployment rate	Disability insurance risk[8]
Complaints related to human resources issues, within a single business unit	Risk of employment-related lawsuit or scandal

Most of the KRIs commonly used seem fairly obvious but some are unusual. However, as long as the KRI is highly correlated to the level of risk exposure, it can be a useful early warning sign regardless of how curious it might seem. An interesting example of an unusual but effective KRI comes from outside the corporate sector. See "The Intuition KRI."

THE **INTUITION KRI**

New York's Bryant Park, located behind the New York Public Library, is a popular site for New Yorkers. Business people eat their lunches at tables that ring the park, summer sunbathers lie on the grass, and the park is the site of various social festivities. The park is largely maintained through private funds provided by local business owners. According to an article in *The New Yorker*,[9] as part of efforts to keep the park in good condition, there is daily monitoring of an unusual KRI that serves as an early warning sign of worsening conditions. Once every workday, at lunchtime, a monitor walks around the park with a clicker, counting the number of men and women. The KRI is the ratio of women to men. A healthy ratio is over 50 percent. When the ratio begins changing to a preponderance of men, park management take this as a signal that action is needed to improve park cleanliness, safety, or other conditions. The explanation given is that women are more perceptive of subtle indicators—such as crumbs left on a table or the presence of homeless people—and when women start avoiding an area, it is correlated with an imminent change in the character of the park.

Mitigation Decisions

We will discuss four aspects of mitigation decisions:

1. Types of mitigation decisions
2. Leveraging existing risk management models
3. Determining the value of mitigation in place
4. Integrating ERM into internal audit plans

Types of Mitigation Decisions   Mitigation decisions reduce the likelihood of occurrence of a key risk scenario, the severity of its impact, or both.

Mitigation can be used to reduce the likelihood of a key risk scenario occurring. In most cases, such preventive mitigation also reduces the severity of impact. For example, lobbying efforts may prevent harmful legislation altogether, or they may reduce the severity of the impact of the legislation that does get passed. Some examples of such mitigation, along with the type of risk whose likelihood they reduce, are shown in Table 6.5.

Some of the examples in Table 6.5 may seem less like mitigation decisions and more like they are part and parcel of simply conducting business. That is why it is helpful to have a single decision-making process in place that can be used consistently for all types of decisions, regardless of whether they seem like pure mitigation, partial mitigation, or just routine business

TABLE 6.5   Examples of Mitigation Reducing the Likelihood of a Key Risk Scenario

Mitigation	Reduces Likelihood of . . .
Lobbying efforts	Legislative/regulatory risk
Initiative to identify critical employees and develop customized retention programs for them	Loss of critical employees
Process-mapping project to identify and secure weak points in financial reporting	Risk of financial reporting restatement
Stricter rules on employees regarding securing data and usage of wireless devices	Data privacy breach
Enhanced succession plan	Weakened leadership
Strong compliance personnel focused on regulatory compliance	Risk of regulatory fines
Training program for employees on protecting intellectual property	Failure to protect intellectual property

decision making. Such a process was described earlier (see "Decision Making with ERM").

In addition to trying to prevent a key risk scenario from occurring to begin with (reducing likelihood), mitigation decisions can also be used to reduce the severity of impact if the risk scenario were to occur. For example:

- The purchase of a hurricane insurance policy to partially mitigate a key risk scenario of a hurricane destroying the company headquarters.
- A hedging program put in place by the investment department to partially mitigate a foreign exchange key risk scenario.
- A business continuity plan put in place to partially mitigate a pandemic key risk scenario.
- Discontinuing operations in a particular country to completely mitigate a key risk scenario related to local unrest. This is an example of risk avoidance.

In Chapter 5, we discussed five case studies of individual risk quantification. Let's briefly examine whether the mitigation resulting from each case study reduces likelihood, severity, or both.

Case Study #1 involved an operational risk related to technology data security and privacy. The key risk scenario was an external attack on information technology. Management made two mitigation decisions. The first mitigation decision was to identify and secure the computers containing privacy data. This reduces the likelihood of occurrence; more secure computers imply a less likely breach. However, this also reduces the severity of impact; if a privacy data breach were to occur, it would likely be less severe due to the additional security protocols. The second mitigation decision was to purge ex-customer privacy data from the computers. This reduces the severity of impact; if a breach were to occur, it would impact the privacy data of fewer customers.

Case Study #2 involved an operational, human resources risk related to losing critical employees. The key risk scenario was a plane crash on the way to a conference for sales leaders. Management made a mitigation decision to strengthen the enforcement of the travel limitations policy for concentration of key employees on flights, particularly in relation to sales managers. This reduces the severity of impact; if a single plane crash were to occur, it would impact fewer salespeople, and particularly, fewer sales managers.

Case Study #3 involved an operational, human resources risk related to a money-laundering incident. The key risk scenario was a very pessimistic money-laundering event. Management made a mitigation decision to restart their anti–money laundering (AML) efforts. This reduces the likelihood of occurrence; AML efforts are preventative. However, this also reduces the severity of impact; if a money-laundering event were to occur, it would likely be less wide ranging across the enterprise due to AML controls instituted.

Case Study #4 involved a strategic risk related to supplier failure. The key risk scenario was losing a sole-source supplier due to a fire. Management made a mitigation decision to qualify a backup supplier. This reduces the severity of impact; if a fire were to destroy the sole-source supplier, a rapid shift to the backup supplier implies minimal supplier disruption.

Case Study #5 involved a strategic risk related to poor strategic planning. The key risk scenario involved failures related to four specific strategic plan elements that management knew were particularly questionable in terms of their feasibility. The implied mitigation decision included additional efforts to achieve the strategic plan, focusing in priority order on the more impactful strategic plan elements. This reduces the likelihood of occurrence; the additional efforts are preventative. However, this also reduces the severity of impact: If management suffers a failure in relation to one or more of the four strategic plan elements, it would likely be by less of a margin due to the additional efforts.

In each of the case studies discussed, the individual risk quantification of key risk scenarios resulted in so large a potential impact on company value that it sparked immediate management action in the form of one or more mitigation decisions. The procedure for decision making, whether involving risk-priority decisions (e.g., mitigation) or return-priority decisions (e.g., strategic planning), was outlined earlier (see "Decision Making with ERM"). However, for each of these case studies, management *implicitly* followed this procedure, but did not feel the need to formally go through all of the recalculations. In such cases, the individual risk exposure is so extreme, and the need for action so clear, that management only requires the following information for the mitigation options:

- Cost of mitigation
- Reduction in likelihood due to mitigation
- Reduction in severity due to mitigation

Management selected mitigation if the cost was reasonable and it produced a satisfactory result. Examples of satisfactory results included the following:

- An elimination of the key risk corresponding to an individual risk scenario due to the reduction of likelihood or severity
- A reduction in the ranking of an individual risk scenario due to a reduction of likelihood or severity
- A reduction of the exposure below the risk limit[10] for an individual risk scenario

Some interpret these actions as management having "zero tolerance" for exposures that exceed risk appetite or risk limits. Another way of looking at this is that management was implicitly making a judgment that the risk exposure, if left unchecked, would result in a higher discount rate, thereby lowering value. Implicitly, then, the decision-making process outlined earlier was actually followed, although the situation was so clear that management chose to skip the formality of performing some of the recalculations.

Leveraging Existing Risk Management Models ERM is not risk management. ERM is a strategic, integrated process involved with the key risks, which are just the top 20 to 30 or so threats to the enterprise. ERM can be considered a high-level, top-down approach. ERM models are simple, handle multiple interacting risks, and are not designed for evaluating mitigation decisions for lower-level risks.

In contrast, risk management is a tactical, silo-based approach involved with a large volume of risks, the vast majority of which are not significant threats to the organization. Risk management can be considered a detailed approach. Many risk management models are highly detailed, largely focus on one risk at a time, and are not able to aggregate risk exposures to the enterprise level.

However, ERM models and risk management models do relate to each other. The ERM approach leverages existing risk management models, to the extent appropriate. The interaction involves an efficient division of labor where each type of model is allocated the task that suits it best.

The ERM model is appropriate to use for prioritization of risk management efforts. The ERM model quantifies enterprise risk exposure, which includes individual risk exposures for the key risks, and defines risk appetite and risk limits for the enterprise as a whole, using a top-down, integrated approach. This can be considered *strategic* risk management in that it sets the high-level risk strategy. This defines *what* to do, in terms of which key risk scenarios to concentrate on, and in what priority order.

Risk management, or *tactical* risk management, then focuses on the key risk scenarios prioritized in the risk strategy provided by ERM. Risk management defines the *how*, in terms of how best to mitigate the key risk scenarios. Risk management models are in a much better position, for some risks, to analyze the specific alternative mitigation options in detail.

However, the risk management models cannot properly measure the marginal impact of any decision on the firm. This is because they are silo-based, usually only handling one risk at a time. The ERM model is equipped to measure risk interactivity, including exacerbations and offsets. For this reason, the individual risk management models are most often used only for developing *inputs* for the ERM model for each potential mitigation decision. These involve any changes to inputs for the individual risk scenarios or the baseline company value. The ERM model is then used to determine the marginal change in the risk and return profile, which informs the decision. However, some decisions are straightforward enough that the individual risk management model will suffice.

This is depicted in Figure 6.3. In step 1, the ERM model calculates enterprise risk exposure, which, when compared with risk appetite and risk limits, sets the strategic priorities for risk mitigation decisions. In step 2, management identifies potential alternative mitigation options for evaluation. In step 3, the existing risk management model is leveraged, producing the

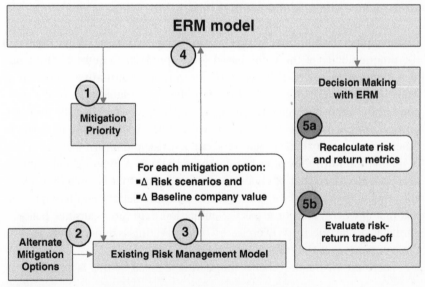

FIGURE 6.3 Leveraging Existing Risk Management Models

changes to the individual risk scenarios and to the baseline company value. In step 4, these items are used as inputs back into the ERM model. Step 5 involves the process used for decision making with ERM, where step 5a is the recalculation of the risk and return metrics and step 5b is the evaluation of the risk–return trade-off, to arrive at a final decision.

Consider the following example. An ERM model indicates that currency risk is a key risk whose exposure exceeds its risk limit, and that mitigation is therefore required. This information is then handed down to an existing risk management model, which is leveraged to evaluate alternate mitigation options, such as which type of hedge against currency risk would be best to purchase. This is appropriate because the investment department has a risk management model with far more detail related to evaluating currency risk than the ERM model. Each risk mitigation option is evaluated in terms of how it would change the currency risk scenarios (changes to likelihood and severity), as well as the baseline company value (changes to distributable cash flows and the discount rate). The changes for each mitigation option are then uploaded back to the ERM model for making the best risk–return decision. The ERM model recalculates values for the net marginal impact on risk and return metrics, reflecting risk interaction of multiple key risks for each mitigation option. The risk–return trade-offs for each mitigation option are evaluated and a final decision is made.

Determining the Value of Mitigation in Place   In Chapter 3, we discussed the unique ability of the value-based ERM approach to quantify the value of mitigation in place. This refers to a rigorous quantitative approach to demonstrating the value added by any mitigation-related area of the company or the value of specific risk mitigation. This involves using the decision-making process (see "Decision Making with ERM") in reverse, so to speak. In other words, rather than compare the current risk and return metrics to that of a potential future decision, we compare them to a hypothetical undoing of a prior decision: that of choosing the mitigation that is already in place. For any mitigation in place, whether it is an entire department (compliance, risk management, etc.) or a specific mitigation item (an insurance policy, a financial hedge, etc.) this exercise involves creating a hypothetical view of the company as if the mitigation were *not* in place.

There are two main benefits that can be derived by this technique:

1. **Establish the value of a mitigation-related department.** This technique can be used to establish, for the first time, the value of a department

or unit whose role is mitigation related. The value is measured directly as the impact on the baseline company value. This is calculated as follows:

$$Value\ of\ mitigation = CoValue_{Baseline} - CoValue_{Excl\ Mitigation}$$

Where:

- $CoValue_{Baseline}$ = baseline company value
- $CoValue_{Excl\ Mitigation}$ = recalculated company value based on excluding mitigation

The value of mitigation in place will be positive if its contribution to company value due to lower risk exposure (as expressed by a lower downside standard deviation and, more directly, a lower discount rate) is greater than its detraction from company value due to higher costs. As discussed earlier, another metric that provides a different perspective on value added is the probabilistic company value, and this may be used as well.

This is a quantum leap forward for these areas, as well as the companies that attempt to effectively manage them. Until a value-based ERM approach is instituted and these values are calculated, management has difficulty developing reasonable approaches to goal setting, performance measurement, and incentive compensation for mitigation-related personnel. However, the value-based ERM approach provides a common set of risk and return metrics to support decision making related to all mitigation-related areas, which is also the same common set of metrics used for all other decision making in the firm, whether for risk-priority or return-priority decisions.

2. **Evaluate appropriateness of specific mitigation items.** This technique can also be used to evaluate an individual existing mitigation item, such as an insurance policy or a hedge. Again, the exercise involves recalculating the risk and return metrics under the assumption that the mitigation is no longer in place. This is used to evaluate past mitigation decisions that were made without the benefit of the rigorous quantification afforded by the value-based ERM approach, but based merely on rules of thumb or subjective management judgment, whose quality may vary from area to area across the enterprise.

This evaluation will either confirm the appropriateness of a specific mitigation item, or identify the amount of over-mitigation. Management often harbors long-held suspicions that certain mitigation efforts have been excessive in light of their benefits. This technique allows management to test these notions and, if validated, provide a strong quantitative business case for paring back these efforts and redirecting resources where they can be put to better use.

Integrating ERM into Internal Audit Plans The value-based ERM approach provides a single rallying point—the potential impact on the baseline company value—for prioritization of risk management efforts, wherever they may be in the enterprise. One of the main risk management areas that can be enhanced through this alignment is the internal audit function. Internal audit provides much value in detecting and deterring certain types of risks, such as fraud, financial reporting errors, and so on. However, historically, the internal audit function has not been fully utilized to its maximum benefit. Management often feels that internal audit is focusing on too many minor items. The value-based ERM approach changes this. By integrating ERM information into the internal audit process, the internal audit plan can be prioritized to focus more resources on the key risks, which are those with the largest potential impact on company value. The internal audit team elevates their focus to items of more strategic importance to the firm. This is valuable, because the company benefits through more efficient prioritization of risk mitigation resources.

One example where this occurred was at a manufacturing company that was ranked among the top three in its sector and was implementing a value-based ERM program. The head of internal audit, who was acting as the de facto chief risk officer, reprioritized the internal audit plan in alignment with the value-based ERM information and had the following comment afterwards: "This is great! My boss has been telling me for years that I am always 'down in the weeds,' spending my resources looking at the small stuff. This gives me a way to fix that, and focus on the biggest priorities for the company."

Return-Priority Decision Making

One of the most appealing aspects of the value-based ERM approach is its ability to enhance routine business decision making. The decision-making process used for these, and indeed any, decisions, was described earlier (see "Decision Making with ERM"). We will discuss the integration of ERM into the following return-priority decision-making processes:

- Strategic planning
- Business decision making

Integrating ERM into Strategic Planning

The value-based ERM process strengthens the strategic planning process in three major ways:

1. Aligns baseline assumptions
2. Aligns scenario assumptions
3. Converts static document into dynamic planning tool

Aligns Baseline Assumptions There are five distinct activities in the risk quantification ERM process step, performed as part of a value-based ERM approach, that serve to better align the baseline assumptions in the strategic plan:

1. **Aggregating projections.** The process of aggregating the individual business segment projections that support the strategic plan, and any other detailed supporting documents, into a baseline company value model allows a more thorough vetting of the assumptions and clarification of any conflicting items. This process helps align assumptions related to the external environment as well as those related to the internal environment.

   Some of the most important assumptions relate to the external environment (future economic conditions, expectations about the stock and bond markets, etc.), which can affect the entire enterprise. Aligning external environment assumptions helps ensure that any related business segment decision making, such as a "bet" on market directions, is cohesive and rational for the company in the aggregate and is not being made at cross-purposes.

   The process of gathering together the different component projections and combining them into a single dynamic baseline valuation model can also help identify inconsistencies in assumptions related to the internal environment. A case study will help illustrate this.

   A midsize company was manufacturing and selling its products through its own dedicated sales force. Their strategic planning process was not rigorous. They had developed a high-level, top-down strategic plan financial projection that projected slow but steady growth over the plan period of three years. However, they also had a separate, more detailed financial projection related to the sales force, including salespeople hired, salesperson retention, and productivity. When the more detailed sales force plans were integrated into a dynamic strategic plan financial projection, it became clear that there were inconsistencies. The more detailed sales force projections revealed that revenues were actually going to *shrink* over the coming three years. In addition, the integrated model revealed that to achieve the planned growth shown in the original high-level strategic plan financial projection, management would have to adopt a far more aggressive strategy toward its sales force, such as more hiring, improved retention, and/or higher productivity. The CFO and CEO were presented with the discrepancy, and their reaction was, "We had a sense that there was a disconnect somewhere, but we didn't know exactly where, or how bad it was." They proceeded to modify their sales force strategy, making it consistent with supporting the plans for growth.

2. **Analyzing trends.** The trend analyses, performed as part of the development of the baseline valuation model, tend to reveal any potential discontinuities that warrant further examination. Discontinuities are identified by comparing strategic plan period projections to recent financials, as well as to projections beyond the formal planning period. Comparing these trends to consensus industry expectations regarding growth rates, by sector, provides additional insights. Finally, comparing trends across business segments can generate additional conversations that lead to higher levels of comfort, or possible changes, in the assumptions.

3. **Analyzing the valuation.** The calculation of the baseline company value itself has a tendency to stimulate productive discussions and reviews of the baseline assumptions. The valuation translates the baseline strategic plan assumptions into the language of business decision-makers: value. Showing the implications of the baseline assumptions, in terms of the resulting value of the company, generates a visceral response by management, which spurs some basic but useful analyses. Management compares the baseline company value to any preconceived notions they may have of its value. In addition, management performs a reasonability check, comparing the baseline company value against market capitalization. Finally, management reviews the valuation by business segment or sub-segment. These valuation analyses often shine a bright light on any suspicious results, leading to further scrutiny of any questionable assumptions, particularly aggressive growth or expense reduction assumptions.

4. **Documenting and disseminating.** Traditionally, the assumptions supporting the baseline strategic plan, and the resultant distributable cash flow projection, are often viewed and understood by only a handful of financial personnel. This inhibits a common understanding, and overt acceptance, of the baseline assumptions by those making decisions based

on their understanding of the baseline strategic plan. The quantification process in the value-based ERM approach involves a wider range of management, and puts the information in a format and language that can be more easily shared and understood. The baseline company value calculation, including the distributable cash flow projection and all related assumptions, is documented and shared consistently throughout the organization. Due to its connection to the broader ERM effort, a broader range of management is in tune with the goings-on that produced this information, and has a stronger tendency to focus on it. In addition, the expression of the baseline strategic plan in the language of value makes the information more accessible to management. Having a common understanding that is more broadly shared, especially among key business decision-makers, helps to politically tease out and resolve any disputed items in the baseline assumptions.

5. **Developing stress tests.** The process of developing key risk scenarios, which are essentially stress tests, also helps align the baseline strategic plan assumptions. Developing and examining upside and downside deterministic key risk scenarios, which occurs at a later stage during the FMEA process, also strengthens the understanding of what is, and what is not, included within the baseline assumptions. This occurs as subject matter experts, many of whom reside within the business segments, think through various scenarios, producing detail on the critical components within the business plan and how they can vary under different stress situations. This may produce an iterative pass back to the calculation of the baseline company value whenever any issues are uncovered.

Aligns Scenario Assumptions   The value-based ERM approach to the risk quantification ERM process step improves the alignment of scenario assumptions in the strategic plan in three ways:

1. **Consistent rigor in risk scenario development.** At any company, the subject matter experts include individuals with varying levels of ERM knowledge and skill. If left to their own devices to develop risk scenarios, the level of quality would vary to a degree that would impact the usefulness of the information. The value-based ERM approach avoids this problem by using a guided process—the FMEA interviews. The FMEA interviews ensure a consistent approach to the development of risk scenarios. It is used across all business segments (and corporate) and for all key risks. In addition, the uniformity of the interviews is further enhanced by the

continuous presence of the interviewers, who are skilled in the FMEA technique.

2. **Standardized definitions of risk scenarios.** Typically, risk scenarios are developed as part of the strategic planning process, including sensitivity analysis; stress testing; and/or strengths, weaknesses, opportunities, and threats (SWOT) analyses. These traditional methods for developing risk scenarios often lack consistency in terms of how scenarios are defined. One person's definition of a very pessimistic stress test may not match someone else's definition. In contrast, the FMEA interview method solicits the development of a range of risk scenarios, and, rather than leave it up to the subject matter expert to provide a subjective label, such as *very pessimistic*, relies on more objective elements to define each risk scenario. The ranking of a risk scenario is used as its automatic standard label, and the ranking depends on quantitative metrics, including, primarily, the severity—such as the potential impact on company value—and, to a lesser extent, the likelihood of occurrence, such as a 1-in-100 chance.

In addition to ensuring consistency, using a more objective standardized approach to defining risk scenarios serves another purpose: avoiding errors. It is quite common for a subject matter expert to describe one risk scenario as *very pessimistic* and another as merely *pessimistic* during the FMEA interview process, only to see later that the former has a lower severity than the latter. This is because the risk quantification calculations performed in the value-based ERM model, although based on fundamental finance theory, are difficult to perform in one's head. The calculations involve projecting and discounting, and sometimes these results are different than initially imagined. Fortunately, the FMEA approach does not rely on the subject matter expert's label, but merely collects a range of risk scenarios and uses standardized quantitative metrics for defining the risk scenarios.

3. **Uniform external environment assumptions.** The FMEA approach ensures consistent assumptions regarding the external environment, such as future economic conditions, expectations about the stock and bond markets, and so on. The FMEA interview approach is guided by individuals that are continuously present to identify all such usage of these assumptions and to ensure that they are uniform enterprise-wide. In addition, FMEA interviews are documented and shared, providing another opportunity to identify and reconcile any external environment assumptions that differ.

In addition to providing the proper alignment of assumptions to ensure a valid risk quantification ERM process step, with uniform external environment assumptions in place, management gains a useful "what-if" model for the company. Management can get an answer to questions such as, "If the economy worsens (to a specified degree), how would it impact the key metrics for the enterprise as a whole, as well as for each business segment?"

Converts Static Document into Dynamic Planning Tool   In most companies, the strategic planning process is an annual event. It is a formal event that consumes significant resources over several weeks. At the end of the exercise, what results is a thick binder that contains the strategic plan. A key element is how all the pieces of the strategy, including supporting tactics or initiatives, will achieve the financial results to which management is committed. These financial results are expressed in the form of a strategic plan financial projection, often for three or five years into the future. The strategic plan is a static document that is at least partly outdated by the time it is completed. Most CEOs dream of a day when their management continually lives and breathes strategic planning and uses a dynamic, ongoing, and nimble approach to developing and executing strategic decisions, rather than a static, once-a-year, and cumbersome approach. This would be a true competitive advantage.

One of the most valuable outcomes of a value-based ERM approach is an ability to finally achieve this dream. The value-based ERM approach connects enterprise risk management to value-based management. Another way of saying this is that the value-based ERM approach converts the heart of the strategic plan—the strategic plan financial projection—from a static projection into a dynamic model. Changes in the external or internal environment or changes in strategy or tactics can be readily reflected in the value-based ERM model, revealing the impact on projected financial results. In addition, any hypothetical change or decision can also be easily reflected. Even more importantly, the value-based ERM model transforms the strategic plan from a single-scenario projection into a distribution of likelihood-severity outcomes based on a large volume of simulations representing combinations of well-defined deterministic key risk scenarios. What this means is that it provides a much more robust picture of where the baseline company value is likely headed, as well as confidence intervals for varying ranges around the baseline company value.

After one full cycle of the value-based ERM process, companies tend to take advantage of this, and move to a more dynamic strategic planning process, increasing the frequency of many of their strategic planning activities from annually to quarterly or simply ad-hoc throughout the year, as conditions warrant. This increase in planning frequency is not accompanied by a magnification in effort to support it; quite the contrary. The agile value-based ERM model is relatively easy to update, residing in a single spreadsheet-based tool. In addition, the consistent approach to developing assumptions—both baseline and scenario assumptions—more easily aligns risk scenario development and maintenance.

This is the crowning example of the benefits of an ERM approach that, rather than treating risk as a separate stand-alone function, creates an approach where not only are risk and return, or risk and reward, married to each other, in fact they cannot exist without each other. Risk cannot be defined except in terms of the deviation of results from baseline company value, and value cannot be defined without the discount rate, which is a function of the downside standard deviation, which, in turn, is informed by enterprise risk exposure and its underlying key risk scenarios. This irrevocably connects risk management to strategic planning and decision making. The value-based ERM approach and model supply the strategic planning process with the rigor to enhance credibility and the dynamism to endow the process with vigor.

Integrating ERM into Business Decision Making

The value-based ERM process can be easily integrated into the full range of business decision making, including strategic, tactical, and transactional decision making. The basic way in which the value-based ERM process enhances day-to-day decision making in the business segments is no different from the way in which it is used to support the strategic planning process. The fundamentals are the same. Therefore, we will merely highlight the following selected aspects of integrating ERM into business decision making:

- The need for speed
- Dealing with soft assumptions
- Stock buyback or issuance
- Prioritizing between stakeholders
- Mergers and acquisitions

The Need for Speed   Many important business decisions must be made quickly, without the luxury of time for the kinds of detailed analyses management would prefer to do. This is because most financial models that are available for these analyses are too cumbersome, and cannot be adapted for a new type of decision in a short time frame. As a result, management often takes actions supported only by instinct, experience, and a back-of-the-envelope analysis of the numbers.

The value-based ERM approach and model typically usher in a new era in decision support. The equilibrium between robustness and fast flexibility of the value-based model strikes the right balance for supplying a "what-if" tool that can support any type of decision, even in the shortest of time frames.

A modified case study will help illustrate this point. A major technology firm was in the early stages of risk quantification when a major business issue arose. Some of their largest customers were collectively renegotiating their contracts and made a sudden demand. This large group of customers insisted that because the technology firm handled their data transfers, if a privacy data breach were to occur, they expected the company to cover the liability. In addition, the customers expressed that they were unwilling to pay for this liability coverage. The ERM personnel were told that in just 10 calendar days, the president of marketing and sales would be meeting with the CEO to decide on a response, and they were asked if they could provide any input to assist with the decision.

Instead of a technology firm, if they were a typical financial services company with a traditional, heavy ERM model laden with complexity, their answer would probably have been, "Sure, we can provide some insights. We'll hire back the consultants from whom we licensed the software, make modifications to the model, do some parallel testing, and then run some scenarios. We should be ready in about 10 to 12 weeks, if we hurry." If that had been the answer provided by this ERM team, do you think senior management would ever knock on their door again in a similar situation? Certainly not. It is crucial that once the ERM team is invited in and asked if they can help, and do so within the time frame required, the ERM team must be in a position to answer positively. Fortunately, that was the position in which this ERM team found itself, having the beginnings of a value-based ERM model at its disposal, which is spreadsheet-based, is quickly adaptable to support new business decisions, and has extremely fast run times.

The ERM team began by setting up the decision options and outlining the consequences. One option was to refuse to comply with the demand. On the upside, this would keep the company free from the potentially unlimited liability of covering privacy data breaches for these customers. On the downside, this option could result in losing customers to a competitor willing to take on such a liability. This represented a significant risk, because these customers collectively accounted for hundreds of millions of dollars in profits. A second option, on the other extreme, was to comply with the demand. On the upside, this decision would not cause them to lose any business. On the downside, the company would be saddled with a large liability, and they had no idea (yet) how large it could be. A third option was to offer to cover the liability only under certain conditions, which was somewhere between the other two options.

Once the decision options and their categories of consequences were defined, they followed the procedure outlined earlier in "Decision Making with ERM," to the extent possible. They had not yet fully quantified enterprise risk exposure, so they were not able to perform all the steps fully. However, for each decision option, they revised the distributable cash flow projection, revised the discount rate, and recalculated the baseline company value. In addition, they developed risk scenarios for the data breach risk, using the FMEA interview technique. All the initial risk scenarios were developed within the first two business days. They quantified the impact of the risk scenarios, under each decision option, in terms of their impact to the baseline company value.

Once all the risk–return trade-off information was assembled well within the required time frame, the senior member of the ERM team and his lieutenant attended the decision-making meeting and provided this ERM information in support of the decision-making process. After the decision was made, the feedback from the CEO was that the ERM information was much appreciated, that it helped them make the decision, and that this was a unique perspective that was unavailable from anywhere else in the firm. As you can imagine, after this event the ERM team began to get pulled into many more decisions of strategic importance, which greatly expanded the influence and funding of the ERM efforts.

Dealing with Soft Assumptions To make decisions, businesspeople need more than qualitative musings about the difference between two alternate choices. Business decision-makers need numbers. Hard numbers—those for which there is a high level of confidence in their accuracy—are preferred, but in their absence, estimates based on soft assumptions—those for which there is lower level of confidence in their accuracy—can also help support decision making. By necessity, the very nature of ERM information—which is focused on future forecasts and the level of uncertainty in them—is such that it must involve some estimates based on soft assumptions. In the section titled "But Aren't These Just Guesses?" in Chapter 3, we rebutted the typical objections to the use of soft estimates and discussed their advantages. We now present a modified case study illustrating one of the ways to make decisions based on soft assumptions.

A major telecommunications company had adopted a value-based ERM approach, and was beginning to use the ERM information to identify opportunities to make better decisions. The ERM team identified such an opportunity in one of its business units where they were about to implement a decision involving a new initiative and its accompanying package of security protocols. The ERM team approached management with a recommendation to make a different decision incorporating a different package of protocols. After reviewing the ERM information, management flatly rejected the ERM team's recommendation. Management argued, "This recommendation is based on a bunch of soft assumptions, and, in particular, is largely predicated on just one critical assumption, which had to have been pulled out of thin air, because there was no way that the ERM team could estimate it with much accuracy."

The ERM team responded by admitting to virtually every statement that management made in its response, although they still argued for, and succeeded in getting, management's acceptance of their recommendation. Yes, the recommendation was based on several soft assumptions. Yes, the one critical assumption was indeed the lynchpin of the recommendation. Yes, the ERM team could not, in fact, estimate the critical assumption with much accuracy. However, the ERM team did not need much accuracy to prove their case. The ERM team performed a sensitivity analysis that illustrated how wrong the estimate of the critical assumption would need to be in order to negate the recommendation. When management saw the results of the sensitivity analysis, which revealed that the ERM team would have to have been off by a factor of 10 for the recommendation to be nullified, management accepted the ERM team's recommendation. Management responded, "Okay. We get it. We're on board. We know that you are not off by a factor of 10."

Stock Buyback or Issuance   For many companies adopting a value-based ERM approach, one of the key benefits is an ability to make opportunistic stock buyback or issuance decisions. The risk quantification ERM process step provides two pieces of information that are helpful in supporting such decisions. The first piece of information is the baseline company value. As discussed in Chapter 5, if done properly, this is a more accurate valuation of the company than market capitalization. If management has full confidence in the accuracy of its baseline enterprise valuation, then when the market capitalization is lower than the baseline company value, this represents a viable opportunity for buying back stock. The market price is cheap relative to the true underlying value of the stock, which will be proved over time as management successfully executes the strategy, realizing the future distributable cash flows projected in its internal valuation. Conversely, when the market capitalization is *higher* than the baseline company value, this represents a viable opportunity for *issuing* stock. The market is paying a premium over and above what management believes to be the true underlying value of the stock.

The second piece of information that helps support these decisions is the enterprise risk exposure. The enterprise risk exposure provides confidence ranges around the baseline company value. For example, management can estimate the chances of achieving or exceeding the baseline company value. In addition, management can estimate the chances of being 10 percent or 15 percent off in their valuation. This is useful, because it is rare for management to have full confidence in its baseline company value calculation; this would be equivalent to management saying that they are 100 percent certain that they can meet or exceed the strategic plan goals.

Consider the following illustrative example of how management uses this information to opportunistically buy back some of its outstanding shares. The general stock market drops 25 percent. Share prices drop indiscriminately across most sectors and the company's stock price drops as well. Management believes that this is panic and that the decrease in company stock is without a valid rationale. Sensing a stock buyback opportunity, management compares the current market capitalization to its baseline company value calculation. The former is lower than the latter by 30 percent. Management believes that its enterprise risk exposure is a fair indication of the ranges of company values and their corresponding likelihoods. The enterprise risk exposure indicates that management has only a 40 percent chance of achieving or exceeding plan. Based on this estimate, management is not fully comfortable relying on the baseline company value as the sole basis of comparison for a stock buyback opportunity. However, management uses the enterprise risk exposure to estimate the chance of company value meeting or exceeding the current market capitalization, and finds this likelihood to be 75 percent. This instills a higher level of confidence that a stock buyback is a good bet, and management proceeds.

Prioritizing between Stakeholders   One of the challenges of running a company is prioritizing between multiple stakeholders. Shareholders demand a level of return commensurate with the level of risk. Rating agencies, representing bondholders, want solvency, or security of interest payments and the repayment of principal. Regulators desire a high level of compliance. And there are other stakeholders to deal with as well. Some decisions favor one stakeholder over another. Although shareholders are primary, it is not always clear how such trade-offs—gaining favor with one stakeholder while, simultaneously, falling into disfavor with another—balance out. This is because they are interrelated; for example, if rating agencies become so unhappy with management that they downgrade the company, this can lower the company value, hurting shareholders.

A value-based ERM approach can help management make such difficult decisions. It does this by valuing the trade-offs directly. The level to which any stakeholder may become displeased is measured directly, by quantifying the change in the baseline company value. There is no intrinsic value in maximally satisfying secondary stakeholders. Secondary stakeholders must only be satisfied to the point that it benefits the primary stakeholder, by increasing company value, which is the central focus and key metric of the value-based ERM approach. A modified case study illustrates this point.

A large private company implementing a value-based ERM approach arrived for the first time at the risk decision making ERM process step. Management decided to use the value-based ERM model to evaluate the viability of a decision that senior management was about to make. Senior management was considering implementing a new strategic initiative that was expected to generate significant revenue growth in one of their markets. However, if adopted, management was certain that the company would receive a ratings downgrade which would last five years. The downgrade would hurt them in some of their minor markets, where they would be forced to lower prices, and would also result in a higher cost of capital. Management was not sure whether the initiative would be viable, after all the dust settled between the various constituencies and their conflicting needs.

The value-based ERM approach was used to sort out all these moving parts. Management followed the steps indicated earlier (see "Decision Making with ERM"). They revised the baseline company value calculation to reflect the additional revenues generated in one market, as a permanent change, and the lower prices in some of the minor markets, and the higher cost of capital, as a five-year change, and the resulting higher discount rate. In addition, they revised a handful of key risk scenarios to reflect the lower rating. Finally, they recalculated enterprise risk exposure, and performed a reasonability check on the initial change in the discount rate. The risk-return trade-off evaluation clearly identified the initiative as a viable option which would generate a significant increase in company value.

Mergers and Acquisitions   Mergers and acquisitions are prime candidates for decisions that can be improved with a value-based ERM approach. Most studies show that the majority of these transactions actually destroy shareholder value. So, what goes wrong? Why do these decisions have such a poor track record?

One reason is that, due to the internal pressure, or perceived pressure, to get the deal done, internal financial projections of the benefits that will be generated by the transaction are continually tweaked toward increasingly optimistic assumptions. Another reason is that these assumptions, and those generating them, are never held to account after the fact, because their tracks are covered through the messy integration and reorganization process.

The value-based ERM approach changes all that. Because major decisions follow a standard and well-documented approach (see "Decision Making with ERM") that becomes part of a shared dynamic strategic planning model, there is nowhere to hide. It becomes clear, early on in the deal-making process, that whatever assumptions are used to support the decision to green-light the transaction will be around for awhile. As a result, those setting the assumptions, knowing that they are more likely to be held accountable if the transaction does not generate the benefits they project, have more incentive to keep their assumptions reasonable.

This results in more accurate pricing of mergers and acquisitions. This may also result in the company winning fewer deals, because their bids may tend to be lower than the other competitive bids. However, when this is synonymous with passing on more deals that would have destroyed shareholder value, then this is more than acceptable—it is preferable.

For this to work properly, those developing the assumptions for the financial projections of the transaction must have incentive compensation that is aligned with increasing company value. A modified case study highlights this issue. A technology company that was a dominant leader in its field was analyzing its poor performance in acquisitions, which had become part of their growth strategy over the past five years. They had an abysmal track record of overpaying on acquisitions, where some of the resulting losses were staggering in their magnitude. In focusing on one large acquisition, the source of the problem came quickly into focus.

The company had recorded the assumptions used during the deal-making process as a 10×10 grid of the estimated value of the transaction—the maximum bid warranted—based on two varying assumptions. The 10 columns showed the span of assumptions for revenue growth, ranging from most pessimistic at the extreme left to most optimistic at the extreme right. Similarly, the 10 rows showed the span of assumptions for expense savings, ranging from most pessimistic at bottom to most optimistic on top.

So, the most optimistic of all combinations was the upper right corner of the grid, which contained the largest possible bid the company could rationally offer. This box contained the price of $2 billion.

Just above and to the right of the table, just beyond the most optimistic bid, was the handwritten number "$2.4 billion." I asked, "What is that number?" They responded, "Well, that's the price we actually paid for the acquisition." I then asked, "Why would you pay more than you knew the acquisition was worth, even under the most optimistic combination of your assumptions?" Their response essentially indicated that their incentive compensation was based on total business segment revenue growth and not on company value. Their incentive was growth, not profitable growth.

 ## SUMMARY

The third step in the ERM process cycle, risk decision making, is the pinnacle of the value-based ERM approach. The primary purpose of this approach is to make better decisions by integrating risk (enterprise risk management) and return (value-based management), thereby increasing company value. The first step in risk decision making is to define risk appetite and risk limits. With these in place, we have a solid framework for managing exposures to within risk tolerances. However, we have so much more: a universal protocol for all decision making, whether risk-priority or return-priority. The ERM-infused decision-making protocol is agnostic as to the initiating driver behind a proposed decision. It uses a single standard for evaluating any decision: whether or not it increases company value. This opens the door to the value-based approach providing myriad other benefits, such as enhancing the strategic planning process; supporting stock buyback and issuance opportunities; enhancing M&A decisions; better prioritizing internal audit efforts; quantifying the value of compliance departments and other mitigation in place; better prioritizing between stakeholders; and generally supporting business decision making, even when speed is paramount and the assumptions are soft.

Risk culture is the acid test of an ERM program, because it gauges the extent to which ERM is actually integrated into key company processes. The integration of ERM into strategic planning and business decision making was addressed in this chapter. In the next chapter, we will discuss the integration of ERM into business performance analysis, incentive compensation, and communications to external stakeholders.

NOTES

1. The term *risks* is shorthand here for the individual risk scenarios, because this is the level at which correlations are handled in the value-based ERM approach.
2. When new key risks are introduced, an additional step that will be required is to revise the simulations used for the enterprise risk exposure calculation.
3. Enterprise risk exposure is comprised of enterprise risk exposure—graph form; enterprise risk exposure—table form; and individual risk scenario exposures.
4. Also referred to as *risk exploitation* (see "Risk Exploitation").
5. Enterprise risk exposure must also be monitored to ensure that it does not fall too far below the soft limit of risk appetite; this is necessary for those less common events where return-priority decisions somehow reduce enterprise risk exposure.
6. In our value-based ERM approach, these lines are happily blurred, because risk and return are properly integrated.
7. This is not to say that no risk-priority decisions take place. They do. However, they are less urgent, and are more in the nature of serving to maintain the appropriate levels of enterprise risk exposure.
8. There is a correlation between the unemployment rate and an increase in disability claims, as workers see disability as a safe haven against the possibility of being laid off.
9. Nick Paumgarten, *The New Yorker*, September 7, 2007.
10. Risk limits had not yet been formally set by management at this stage. Management made the mitigation decisions on learning of the potential impact of the key risk scenarios on company value. This occurred during individual risk quantification, which precedes the definition of risk appetite and risk limits. However, management's reaction to these high individual risk exposure levels revealed, implicitly, a tentative level for the risk limits, which were ultimately determined, and formally set, later in the ERM implementation process.

CHAPTER SEVEN

7

Risk Messaging

The greatest problem of communication is the illusion that it has been accomplished.

George Bernard Shaw

R ISK MESSAGING IS the fourth step in the ERM process cycle. In this chapter, we will discuss two types of risk messaging: internal risk messaging and external risk messaging.

 ## INTERNAL RISK MESSAGING

Internal risk messaging refers to incorporating ERM information into performance measurement and management.

There are two aspects of internal risk messaging:

1. Integrating ERM into business performance analysis
2. Integrating ERM into incentive compensation

Embedding ERM information into business performance analysis and incentive compensation signals all levels of management that there is a strong commitment to the ERM program. Effective internal risk messaging is necessary to drive the appropriate ERM activities in the risk identification, risk quantification, and risk decision making ERM process steps. If internal risk messaging is ineffective or nonexistent, management realizes that they themselves are being measured on the same basis that pre-dated ERM; as a result management begins to minimize ERM efforts or ignore them altogether.

Internal risk messaging—integrating ERM into performance measurement and management—along with integrating ERM into decision making (discussed in Chapter 6), constitute what we are defining as *risk culture*.

Integrating ERM into Business Performance Analysis

We will discuss how ERM enhances two traditional methods for analyzing business performance: financial results and balanced scorecards.

Financial Results

We will first examine the traditional approach to using financial results for business performance analysis, along with its deficiencies, and then we will discuss how the value-based ERM approach enhances this form of business performance analysis.

Traditional Approach　The primary traditional approach for evaluating the performance of the business is to analyze the prior single-period financial results. These largely consist of an income statement, balance sheet, and cash flow statement. Typically, the prior single-period financial results are compared to the strategic plan goals, or "Plan." Actual revenues are compared to Plan revenues, actual expenses are compared to Plan expenses, actual earnings are compared to Plan earnings, and so forth.

The benchmark—the Plan—is set using a form of risk adjustment. In setting Plan goals, management implicitly or explicitly sets higher goals for riskier businesses. However, there are two shortcomings with this traditional approach: It lacks rigor and it is incomplete.

Lacks Rigor　Management sets risk-adjusted goals either implicitly or explicitly. Both approaches usually lack rigor. In cases where management *implicitly* sets higher revenue and earnings goals for riskier businesses, their approach is often both subjective and inconsistent. In these situations, management often uses their gut-level feel for how much more should be required from the riskier businesses. They are not basing this decision on quantitative information. This is also an inconsistent approach. Different managers may be setting the goals for different businesses, and each may have a different subjective perspective on risk. In addition, without an objective standard, other factors enter into goal setting, such as negotiating leverage, which also varies by business segment, further skewing the implicit risk adjustment.

In most cases, management *explicitly* sets higher goals for riskier businesses. Goals may be set based on varying targets, such as a hurdle rate for return on assets or return on investment. We will illustrate this with an example. Consider a company that recognizes that its international business is more risky, and that its mature business is less risky, than the bulk of its domestic steady-growth business. As a result, management decides to vary its 15 percent hurdle rate, which, up until now, has been required for every business segment. They decide to increase the 15 percent hurdle rate a little for the riskier business, and decrease it a little for the less-risky business. Using judgment, as opposed to quantitative analysis of the risk, management sets the following explicitly defined hurdle rates for its business segments:

- Domestic steady-growth business segment: 15 percent return on investment
- International aggressive-growth business segment: 18 percent return on investment
- Mature business segment: 12 percent return on investment

Unfortunately, these targets are often set improperly, in two ways:

1. **The hurdle rates are often set arbitrarily.** The hurdle rates are usually set without knowledge of the actual level of underlying risk in each business segment, because it is not quantified. In our illustrative example, management merely began with the 15 percent hurdle rate for all of its businesses, and made a simple 3 percent upward adjustment for its higher-than-average-risk business, and a 3 percent downward adjustment for its lower-than-average-risk business.
2. **The investment metric—the base to which the hurdle rate is applied to determine target earnings—is poorly defined.** At non-financial services companies, the investment metric is often defined as an allocation of equity. At financial services companies, the investment metric is often defined as required capital. In either case, this only accounts for a portion of the shareholder's investment. The total investment is company

value. The company value calculation includes the present value of all future distributable cash flows. Equity, or required capital, usually represents only a small portion of company value.

However, even if we assume that equity, or required capital for financial services companies, *is* an appropriate definition of the investment, there are other problems with the way it is typically defined.

At non-financial services companies, the investment is often defined as allocated equity, which in some cases may just be the amount of equity maintained in the legal entity containing the business segment. This may have no relationship to the actual level of required investment; for example, there may currently be excess equity held in the legal entity.

At financial services companies, the investment is often defined as required capital. Required capital is the amount financial services companies set aside, in addition to reserves, as a buffer against bad performance related to the risk inherent in their existing commitments. Required capital is defined by management, and is often set in consideration of one or more of the following:

1. Regulatory capital
2. Rating agency capital
3. Economic capital[1]

Unfortunately, each of these is a poor way to define the investment metric for a business segment.

Regulatory capital and rating agency capital are not calculated based on the company's risks. They are determined formulaically, using an approach based on broad industry statistics. They are not customized to the specifics of the company, let alone to the specifics of each business segment.[2]

Traditional economic capital models are a step in the right direction, but they are also seriously lacking. These models use a company-specific approach to measuring risk, using risk scenarios and projecting their impact on company financials. However, there are two major problems with the way traditional economic capital models calculate risk exposure:

1. **Missing future new business.** Most economic capital models exclude future new business. They were originally designed to focus on balance sheet capital (hence the name), examining how it changed under stress conditions. As such, they do not look forward, and do not include future distributable cash flows for the firm as a going concern. This results in

economic capital models omitting the majority of the risk exposure. The majority of risk exposure comes from strategic and operational risks. Strategic and operational risks primarily impact future revenues and expenses. These cannot be captured properly using a traditional economic capital model, because these models do not project revenues and expenses for future new business in their baseline scenario, and do not reflect changes to future revenues and expenses in their risk scenarios.

2. **Missing integrated impacts.** Most economic capital models do not capture the integrated impacts of two or more risk scenarios occurring simultaneously. Instead, they measure each risk one at a time and attempt to adjust for interactivity using correlation adjustments, which is inadequate, as discussed in "Capturing Interactions" in Chapter 5. Omitting multiple simultaneous risk occurrences results in failing to capture some of the largest loss events (see "Omits the Largest Threats" in Chapter 2).

Incomplete Even more problematic than the lack of rigor is the fact that this approach is incomplete. It only measures the changes in the past period, for example, in terms of revenues, expenses, and earnings. This completely ignores the changes that occur during the year that may alter the trajectory of *future* revenues and expenses, versus the baseline strategic plan projection. Similarly, it also ignores the changes that occur during the year that may alter the riskiness of the firm, changing the enterprise risk exposure, the downside standard deviation, and, thereby, the discount rate. These missing items can easily be more significant than past period results.

Value-Based ERM Approach The value-based ERM approach provides multi-period metrics to support an analysis of business performance that is both rigorous *and* complete.

Rigorous With a value-based approach, the business performance is measured by the amount that company value is increased, over the past period, in comparison to the increase expected in the strategic plan. This is quite rigorous, since the value-based ERM approach strengthens the strategic plan and the strategic planning process. In addition, the value-based ERM approach provides rigorous risk and return metrics.

Complete In addition, this approach is complete in that it fully captures all future impacts on value as well as the impacts over the prior single period. This approach captures all of the following:

- Changes that occur during the year that impact distributable cash flows during the year
- Changes that occur during the year that alter the trajectory of *future* distributable cash flows
- Changes that occur during the year that alter the riskiness of the firm

In addition to being rigorous and complete, there are two additional desirable aspects to using the change in company value as a metric for performance analysis. First, in addition to the enterprise level metrics, an analogous set of calculations produces this information in support of an analysis of performance at the business segment level, or for any other level. Second, an attribution analysis can be performed to determine the relative contribution of any value driver of the past year's business performance. For example, the portion of the gains attributable to an increase in customer retention can be quantified.

Balanced Scorecards

Balanced scorecards are commonly used to evaluate business performance. The key feature of balanced scorecards is the use of several non-financial measures along with financial measures to analyze business performance. The premise is that there are numerous, less-tangible items that impact the value of the business, and simply achieving past period financial results that meet (or exceed) the strategic plan goals is not enough, because these other items also affect the value of the firm; if not now, then in the near future. This premise is valid. Unfortunately, there is a fundamental flaw in the way balanced scorecards are used, which leads to opportunity losses in company value.

The fundamental flaw with balanced scorecards is in the relative weight, or emphasis, placed on each of the scorecard elements. They are developed in a fairly arbitrary way. Some firms place a higher weight on the financial goals and equally distribute the remaining weights among the non-financial goals. Others use equal weights for all goals. Still others set different weights for each of the goals. However, all companies define these weights without a rigorous approach. They are more or less merely conjured up out of thin air.

Let's assume that management believes that the weights will be taken seriously by senior management. This would mean that management believes that the weights (corresponding to balanced scorecard goals) will somehow— either explicitly or implicitly—be reflected in their performance reviews and incentive compensation. If this is the case, then management will expend efforts to achieve the results of each scorecard element in proportion to these weights. However, to the extent that these weights do not match the true relative contribution to company value attributable to each scorecard element, this will result in a smaller increase in company value than would have been achieved with a correct set of weights. Because the weights used in the balanced scorecards are set somewhat arbitrarily without a rigorous approach to measuring the true relative contribution of each scorecard element to company value, the ironic result is that balanced scorecards are fundamentally, and destructively, *unbalanced*.

This problem can be solved using the value-based ERM approach. The value-based ERM approach can be used to directly calculate more appropriate weights for the balanced scorecard. It converts the less-tangible, non-financial items into tangible items that can be quantified in terms of financial results.

First, let's firmly establish the premise, which is not inconsistent with the balanced scorecard premise, that the only important item to the company is distributable cash flow, or, more precisely, the present value of all future distributable cash flows. This is the only result that matters to the shareholders. Unless a result impacts distributable cash flows now, or impacts them later, or impacts the discount rate, shareholders do not care about it. The reason the balanced scorecard introduces the non-financial metrics is that the prior single-period financial results do not capture all of this. Looking only at prior period results ignores the impact of changes during the past year that will impact the future distributable cash flows or the discount rate.

The dynamic strategic planning tool, embodied in the value-based ERM model, can be used to quantify each of the balanced scorecard elements in terms of its marginal impact on company value. For example, assume that one of the non-financial balanced scorecard items is "an increase in employee satisfaction." Management can make estimates, using an approach analogous to a FMEA exercise, to develop risk scenarios for quantifying the impact of this change on the baseline company value. A given increase in the employee satisfaction index can be equated with some level of increase in employee retention and/or employee productivity. These are value drivers in the dynamic value-based ERM model, and changing them will translate into an impact on the baseline company value. This is performed for each balanced scorecard item. Even the "financial results" balanced scorecard element itself must go through a (simple) calculation to put it on the basis of a change in baseline company value: It must be discounted to the present time using the discount rate.

Once the relative marginal increases in company value are calculated for a unit of improvement in each of the balanced scorecard items, they are used to define more appropriate weights. The weights are defined in proportion to the relative contribution toward company value. This results in a significant shift in the weights. The change from arbitrary weights to meaningful, quantitatively derived weights also increases the level of credibility of the balanced scorecard with management. For companies whose management takes the balanced scorecard seriously, this should lead to larger increases in company value going forward.

It should be noted that if the "change in company value" metric is used to analyze the performance of the business in the first place, then the balanced scorecard would not really be needed at all. All that the balanced scorecard would add at this point would be a simple rule of thumb that provides an approximate equivalency between a given level of improvement in one particular value driver and the resulting increase in company value. See "Balance or Distraction?"

Integrating ERM into Incentive Compensation

One of the basic tenets of good business practice is to use incentive compensation to align management interests with those of the shareholders. A common claim is that including stock or stock options in management's incentive compensation effectively achieves this alignment. The theory offered is that if management is awarded stock, or stock options, their

BALANCE **OR DISTRACTION?**

Some argue that the balanced scorecard helps management focus on a wide range of value drivers by requiring improvement in each balanced scorecard element. However, this is a hollow contribution. Shareholders are indifferent as to the source of an increase in company value. They just want it to increase and to keep increasing over time. There is no inherent benefit in forcing an attempt to squeeze an increase in company value specifically out of this source or that source. In fact, this tends to *slow* the increase in company value. Management must be free to achieve the largest possible increase in value from wherever the opportunity arises. Artificial constraints on these opportunities result in an opportunity loss in company value versus what could otherwise have been generated.

incentives are to drive up the stock price. If this "stock award alignment" theory were valid, then why do we still have so many instances where management is enriched while shareholders suffer losses? Part of the reason for this mismatch is that this simple theory has two holes in it:

1. Information mismatch for award value
2. Poor metrics for calculating award amount

We will discuss each of these holes, as well as how integrating ERM information into incentive compensation can plug them.

Information Mismatch for Award Value

The first hole in the stock award alignment theory is that there is a mismatch of information between management and the stock market which management can exploit. The value of the stock or stock option awards is based on the stock price. But this is not the best measure of the value of the organization. As discussed in Chapter 5 (see "Calculate Baseline Company Value"), an internal enterprise valuation is more accurate. This is, to a large extent, based on the fact that management has a better sense of the value of the enterprise than does the market, because it has access to inside information. With large amounts of stock or stock option awards already in hand, management has great incentive to use their information mismatch to drive up the market value, in some cases for long periods of time, without actually doing the hard work of increasing the underlying value of the firm, either by increasing future distributable cash flows or lowering the riskiness of the firm.

One solution is to replace actual stock and stock option awards with phantom stock based on ERM information, where the baseline company value calculation is used as the basis for the phantom stock value. To be effective, the unit in charge of calculating the phantom stock price must have a high level of independence and access to information, and they must be scrutinized by internal and external auditors and be reviewed by an independent valuation firm. Another option is to use an independent valuation firm to perform the calculations. Either way, this approach eliminates much of the mismatch of information. Management may still have great incentive to maintain some of this information mismatch, but it is far more difficult to hide information internally than it is to hide it from the market, particularly when someone is in charge of uncovering it.

Poor Metrics for Calculating Award Amount

The second hole in the stock award alignment theory is that there are poor metrics used to calculate the *amount* of the awards. The metrics that are typically used to calculate these awards are the traditional approaches that were discussed earlier (see "Integrating ERM into Business Performance Analysis"), along with their shortcomings. These traditional approaches include comparing past single-period financial results with Plan results and the use of balanced scorecards.

The solution to the shortcomings of these approaches was also discussed earlier: Use ERM metrics, which more properly capture the actual performance (of the enterprise, business segment, business unit, or individual), in terms of the change in baseline company value. The actual *amount* of the initial award is at least as important as the value of the award, which was addressed in the prior section. However, with both the amount of the award, as well as the value of the award based on the baseline company value calculation, there is superior alignment between management and shareholders. Management's true contribution to company value, in the past year, determines their award *amount*, and their future contribution to company value determines the sustained *value* of their award.

EXTERNAL RISK MESSAGING

External risk messaging refers to communicating ERM information to external stakeholders. There are four external stakeholders we will discuss:

1. Shareholders
2. Stock analysts
3. Rating agencies
4. Regulators

Communications to Shareholders

Communications to shareholders, or to potential investors and the general public, are referred to generally as risk disclosures. We will discuss two categories of risk disclosures:

1. Voluntary risk disclosures
2. Mandatory risk disclosures

Voluntary Risk Disclosures

Voluntary risk disclosures refer to ERM communications that management chooses to share publicly, for example in the annual report to shareholders, based on the belief that the ERM program constitutes a competitive advantage. Companies with advanced ERM programs, such as the value-based ERM approach, should include descriptions, and evidence of, their ERM activities in their voluntary risk disclosures. This can signal to investors a superior ability to properly understand and balance risk and reward, as well as to successfully execute their strategic plan.

The appropriate information to provide shareholders varies from situation to situation. In addition, the way in which the information is crafted must be done with care. A balance must be struck. Enough information must be given to convey the message, but without a high degree of specificity. However, some examples of typical items that may be appropriate to voluntarily disclose include the following:

- The comprehensive nature of the ERM program in terms of its enterprise-wide scope and its inclusion of all sources of risk
- The strategic focus of the ERM program and how it focuses management on the largest potential threats, whether from a single risk event or from combinations of simultaneous risk events
- Management's use of aggregate metrics—understanding risk exposures at the enterprise level, as well as defining risk appetite at the enterprise level—and thereby its ability to effectively manage risk exposure to within risk appetite
- The practical business applications of a value-based ERM program, and the competitive advantage gained from making better risk–reward decisions by linking ERM to value-based management
- How business performance analysis is enhanced using ERM information
- How management incentives are better aligned with shareholders using ERM information
- How risk governance is enhanced, providing additional comfort that key risk exposures are well understood and managed

In addition, it is advisable to include selected stories about the lessons learned through the adoption of the ERM program, and how it helped advance the risk culture. Specific stories of the enhanced sophistication gained from ERM strengthen the level of investor confidence. Flowery generalities of alleged competitive advantages tend to fall flat, whereas actual stories of success speak for themselves. The stories should include incidents where management made better decisions after producing ERM information. Some examples may include the following:

- Previously hidden exposures that were uncovered by the ERM program, immediately prioritized, and then mitigated
- A level of enterprise risk exposure that was quantified, deemed too risky, and reduced to an acceptable level
- Exposures that were identified as wastefully over-mitigated and where management produced significant cost savings by reducing the level of mitigation
- A change in the strategic proportions of the business toward a more shock-resistant portfolio, leveraging offsetting risk sources; for example, finding business opportunities that were countercyclical and strategically increasing the level of exposure to them
- A change in the strategic proportions of the business away from those identified as having a subpar risk–return profile and toward those with an acceptable or superior risk–return profile

Mandatory Risk Disclosures

We will discuss three Securities and Exchange Commission (SEC) requirements regarding risk disclosures:

1. Disclosure of risk factors
2. Disclosure of risk governance
3. Disclosure of risky incentive compensation programs

Disclosure of Risk Factors The SEC requires annual risk disclosures in form 10-K, Item 1A. Risk Factors.[3] The SEC requires "a discussion of the most significant factors that make the offering speculative or risky." The value-based ERM approach satisfies this requirement in a way that ensures compliance and also provides a competitive advantage. In addition to providing an ability to emphasize the biggest threats to shareholder value, the value-based ERM approach also provides the ability to properly categorize and define risks by their source, identify the most impactful component drivers of the key risk scenarios, and evaluate and select the most cost-effective mitigation actions. The risk disclosures offer another opportunity for management to showcase its leading practices in managing risk to protect shareholder value. These skills can be conveyed by crafting risk disclosures using the following three techniques:

1. **Categorize and define risks by source.** Most risk disclosures confuse risks sources with risk outcomes (financial impacts). This can be seen by the mention of reputational risk, or the risk of a ratings downgrade, as if each of these represented individual sources of risk. In addition, most risk disclosures demonstrate scrambled thinking about risk by confusing a single discussion with multiple sources of risk. This can be seen by selecting a single paragraph that should be discussing one source or group of sources of risk, but instead rambles on in a discussion across multiple sources of risk, crossing from strategic to operational and back again, sometimes all in the same run-on sentence. For an example of this, see "Muddled Risk Disclosure."

MUDDLED **RISK DISCLOSURE**

As an example of a single paragraph in a risk disclosure that discusses multiple risk sources in the same breath, consider the following extract, taken from the risk disclosures of a leading beverage company:

Obesity and other health concerns may reduce demand for some of our products.

Consumers, public health officials, and government officials are becoming increasingly concerned about the public health consequences associated with obesity, particularly among young people. In addition, some researchers, health advocates, and dietary guidelines are encouraging consumers to reduce consumption of sugar-sweetened beverages, including those sweetened with HFCS or other nutritive sweeteners. Increasing public concern about these issues; possible new taxes and governmental regulations concerning the marketing, labeling, or availability of our beverages; and negative publicity resulting from actual or threatened legal actions against us or other companies in our industry relating to the marketing, labeling, or sale of sugar-sweetened beverages may reduce demand for our beverages, which could affect our profitability.

(continued)

(continued)

In examining this one paragraph in the company's risk disclosure, several different sources of risk can be identified, some strategic and some operational. Some of the phrases in the risk disclosure paragraph have been selected and mapped to their risk source in Table 7.1.

TABLE 7.1 Risk Disclosure Paragraph Mapped to Its Risk Sources

Phrase or Sentence	Risk Category	Risk Subcategory	Risk
"Consumers . . . increasingly concerned" and "Increasing public concern"	Strategic	External relations	Consumer relations
"possible new taxes and governmental regulations concerning the marketing, labeling, or availability of our beverages"	Strategic	Legislative/ Regulatory	Product/services-related
"negative publicity resulting from actual or threatened legal actions"	Operational	Litigation	Litigation risks

Each of these risk sources would be better discussed and considered separately. Their qualitative risk assessment would benefit from a clear segregation of risks by their distinct sources; the risk scenario development interviews would flow better by starting with each individual risk source and following the downstream impacts; and risk mitigation must be addressed separately for each source of risk.

In contrast, a value-based ERM approach stresses the importance of categorizing and defining risks by their source. This is important for the risk identification, risk quantification, and risk decision making ERM process steps. However, it is also important for the risk disclosure ERM process step as well. Discussing each risk source separately provides far more clarity in a company's risk communications versus its competitors. This clarity of communications signifies a more sophisticated level of understanding of the risks by management.

2. **List risks in priority order.** Traditional ERM programs do not provide management with the capability of listing the risks in the priority order indicated by a shareholder perspective. As a result, most disclosures of risk factors include a laundry list of items not listed in priority order in the way shareholders might expect. As discussed in Chapter 2 (see "Criterion 8: Appropriate Risk Disclosures"), the improper disclosure of risk factors is the single most overlooked risk for companies in all sectors.

   In contrast, a value-based ERM approach provides management an ability to list the key risks in decreasing rank order corresponding to the perspective of shareholders. This elegant facility sends a message to shareholders that management has an ability that most of its competitors do not: an ability to quantify risk in terms of its potential impact on company value. In addition, it supports compliance with the risk disclosure requirements. Finally, this provides the board of directors and the executives with a level of comfort that the risk management program is identifying and addressing the biggest shareholder threats.

   The priority ranking should be determined by incorporating both likelihood and severity information corresponding to the individual risk scenarios. However, due to the sensitive nature of the information, as well as the uncertainty of any individual data point, it is inappropriate to reveal the likelihood or severity data. Instead, this information should merely be used internally to inform the way in which the risk disclosures convey the relative importance of the risks. This is done by listing the risks in decreasing order of importance, by providing more discussion for the more important risks, and by the relative tone used to describe management's concern about the risks.

3. **Discuss most impactful component drivers.** Most traditional ERM programs do not highlight the most important individual component drivers of the key risks, because they don't measure this properly. This is somewhat visible in the risk disclosures of these companies, in that management will talk in generalities about the risks. Value-based ERM programs, on the other hand, identify the most impactful component drivers by quantifying them in terms of the potential impact on company value, using an attribution calculation. Sharing these insights in the risk disclosures conveys a deeper understanding of the risks.

Disclosure of Risk Governance   The SEC requires annual risk disclosures of the board's role in risk oversight.[4] The requirement is written vaguely, and is intended to provide companies an opportunity to discuss the following:

- Whether primary risk oversight responsibility resides with the full board or with a board committee, such as a risk committee or the audit committee
- How risk oversight is conducted, which includes what information is monitored (key risk exposures, key ERM decisions, etc.), who provides it, and how often it is provided
- Whether primary responsibility for ERM resides with the full board or with a board committee or with management (e.g., the ERM committee)
- Whether the person with day-to-day ERM responsibilities reports directly to the full board, to a board committee, or to management

Disclosure of Risky Incentive Compensation Programs   The SEC requires annual risk disclosures of risky incentive compensation programs.[5] If a company's incentive compensation policies and practices (for any employee, not just executives) create risks that are "reasonably likely to have a material adverse effect" on the company, then the company must include discussion and analysis of the compensation program giving rise to such risks. The "material adverse effect" requirement relates to net (or post-mitigation) risk exposure, as opposed to gross (or pre-mitigation) risk exposure.

To ensure compliance with this disclosure requirement, management must be able to do the following:

1. Measure the risks taken by employees in terms of impact on value[6]
2. Define "material adverse effect" in terms of impact on value[7]
3. Integrate both of the above into the incentive compensation formula

A value-based ERM approach provides all of these capabilities. It allows the measuring of risk exposures, in terms of the potential impact on company value, from enterprise level all the way down to the individual employee level. In addition, it provides a rigorous definition of "material adverse effect" through the quantitative definition of risk appetite. Finally, it provides an ability to integrate both of these metrics into incentive compensation: Both metrics are available and are updated with a frequency that supports incentive compensation calculations and payments.

If management finds that its compensation policies and practices *do* create risks "reasonably likely to have a material adverse effect," or if management cannot confirm that they *do not* do so, then the company must disclose a discussion and analysis of the relevant portion of the compensation program. Some of the more interesting aspects of the discussion and analysis disclosure include the following four elements:

1. The reasoning behind the compensation policies and practices, in terms of its impact on employee risk taking
2. The risk assessment, if any, relied on in developing the compensation policies and practices
3. The ability to modify compensation after a risk event occurs (e.g., clawbacks)
4. Changes to compensation policies and practices made pursuant to changes in the company's risk profile (i.e., enterprise risk exposure)

Communications with Stock Analysts

A value-based ERM approach is especially helpful in communications with stock analysts. There are two key advantages provided by the value-based approach that can demonstrate management's advanced capabilities in ERM versus its competitors. First, the value-based approach to risk scenario development uses the FMEA interview technique to extract knowledge from internal subject matter experts in developing discrete deterministic key risk scenarios. The resulting risk scenarios are well thought out in terms of how the event would unfold, how it would initially impact the company, any secondary or tertiary impacts, and management's likely actions, including existing post-event mitigation plans (such as business continuity plans). Second, the value-based approach to quantification provides a dynamic internal valuation model for calculating company value, which is more accurate than the external valuation models used by stock analysts, as discussed in Chapter 5 (see "Calculate Baseline Company Value").

These two advantages come into play with stock analysts when a risk event occurs in the industry sector and analysts are querying management about the impact it may have on the company. Management using a value-based ERM approach is in a position to respond with something like the following:

Although we do agree generally with your estimate of the potential impact of this risk event on other companies in our sector, we believe you are overstating its impact on our firm. We have already thought through this eventuality in some detail. We have this risk event as one of our key risks, and we have constructed several "what-if" risk scenarios, through interviews with our subject matter experts, that include the potential financial impact on our business. Though the scenario currently unfolding does not precisely match one of our risk scenarios, it is midway in severity between two that we *did* consider, and it's playing out reasonably close to what we would expect. Two years ago, we put the following mitigation in place [details provided] as a result of our ERM program highlighting this risk and quantifying these mitigation actions as valid risk–reward trade-offs. In addition, since the event, we have already put in motion the following post-event mitigation plan [details provided].

Further, we use an internal valuation model, based on discounted distributable cash flows consistent with our strategic business plan projection, to determine the potential impact of such events on our company value. We feel you are overstating how much this will impact us in the following business segments, for the following reasons [details provided].

Such a conversation would clearly demonstrate to stock analysts that management at this firm has a far better grasp on ERM than the vast majority of their competition. Most of the competitors are unlikely, during early onset of a risk event, to yet have a sense of how, where, and to what extent the risk event will impact their company. Over a sustained period of time, similar risk messaging with stock analysts should serve as a powerful differentiator that can eventually lead to a higher multiple on the valuation of the company's stock.

Communications with Rating Agencies

Each major rating agency has its own unique perspective on, and understanding of, ERM. As a result, rating agencies each have their own set of expectations of what they would like to see from companies. This not only varies by rating agency, but also by industry sector, geography, and, often, from analyst to analyst at some rating agencies. To conduct effective risk messaging with rating agencies, management must take the following steps:

1. Understand formal positions
2. Understand variations by analyst
3. Draft risk message from company perspective
4. Customize risk message to rating agency and analyst perspectives

Understand Formal Positions

The first step in crafting an effective risk message for a rating agency is to gain a thorough understanding of their formal position on enterprise risk management. Depending on the rating agency and the industry sector, there may or may not be dedicated publications on ERM. These documents often convey the major themes of focus for the rating agency. However, some of the key points can only be obtained by reading between the lines. Rating agency documents are often championed by one or two main authors, but also reflect the input of an assortment of other associates, which can cloud some key elements.

The formal rating agency position papers on ERM are periodically updated; therefore, we will not discuss the particulars of any specific documents. However, there are two documents worth noting. As discussed in Chapter 1, in October 2005, Standard & Poor's (S&P) introduced an ERM evaluation in the insurance sector, resulting in an additional distinct ratings component, which contributed to advancing the practice of ERM. In December 2007, S&P published a monograph that includes nine separate ERM documents, including their guidance on the insurance ERM evaluation. This monograph is important because of the leadership role S&P has played in rating agency ERM evaluations. The monograph is titled "Enterprise Risk Management for Financial Institutions: Rating Criteria and Best Practices." This monograph may be periodically updated; care should always be taken to obtain the latest versions of rating agency position papers.

Another document worth noting was published by Moody's in March 2007, titled "Risk Management Assessment: Non-life Insurance Companies." This document is no longer actively part of Moody's ratings evaluation. However, I reference it here because it has some advanced thinking and offers some excellent perspectives and best practices.

Understand Variations by Analyst

Not all analysts at a rating agency share the same interpretation of the formal ERM-related position papers published by their organization. It is prudent to become familiar with the differing interpretations of the individual analyst or analysts that will be evaluating the company. Management can meet with these analysts and solicit their perspectives directly. This is helpful to an extent. Even more helpful is to gather information from others in the industry sector that have had direct experience with these analysts.

Draft Risk Message from Company Perspective

There are two types of risk messaging that can be used for communications to rating agencies:

1. Routine presentations
2. Dedicated ERM presentations

Routine Presentations Rating agencies seek to evaluate the strength of the company and evaluate how likely they are to fail. Most of the information rating agencies receive is historical, yet they must think prospectively, in an attempt to predict the likelihood of the company's failure in the future. ERM can play a big role in this regard. It offers robust information about future scenarios and characterizes the company's shock resistance to its key threats.

Management should review their routine presentations to rating agencies to identify opportunities to embed ERM information. A major example is discussions of the company's strategy and management's confidence in their ability to successfully execute it. Having a value-based ERM approach provides much fodder for inclusion in such a discussion. It strengthens the strategic planning process. It identifies the key risks. It quantifies the key risks, as well as combinations of them, in terms of how much they may damage the strategic plan, as expressed by shortfalls from the strategic plan financial projection of future distributable cash flows. It helps management select the best portfolio of risk mitigation to ensure that the strategic plan is achieved. It also provides a measure of how likely management is to meet or exceed the strategic plan goals, as well as a measure of how likely the company is to fail (using various definitions of failure), and how these change under alternate strategies and tactics. Finally, it facilitates an ability to tie a balanced risk–return profile to incentive compensation, providing another level of confidence in achieving the strategic plan due to better alignment of management and shareholder goals.

For financial services companies, another major example of an opportunity to embed ERM information in routine discussions is in discussions involving required capital calculations. Although required capital calculations should be part of their ERM program, they often pre-date the introduction of ERM. Demonstrating how the required capital calculations, such as economic capital, are effectively integrated with the ERM program offers evidence of its wider adoption and use in business decision making, significantly adding to its credibility.

Dedicated ERM Presentations   For some rating agencies in some sectors, a separate conversation about ERM is involved. One example is S&P's insurance sector, which has ERM as a distinct component of the rating. In these cases, a straightforward presentation of the ERM program is warranted.

It is important, at this point, to craft these from the perspective of the company as opposed to the perspective of the rating agency (which is the next step). Whereas the primary stakeholder for rating agencies is the bondholder, management's primary fiduciary responsibility is to the shareholders. Rating agency analysts understand that a company that is well run, that is more likely to achieve their strategic plan, and that is growing company value is also more likely not to default on its commitments to bondholders. In addition, rating agencies prefer that management present ERM information in a manner that is consistent with how it is used within the company, representing actual business practice. Presenting ERM information only in the format that management thinks the rating agency wants to hear—essentially holding up an ERM mirror—is inappropriate. The rating agencies want to hear, "We know you (the rating agency) look at ERM a bit differently, and we will later explain how we satisfy your ERM criteria, but this is how we define ERM, this is what we believe about ERM and why we believe it, and this is how we use ERM to help us make better decisions and deliver on our strategic plan."

One of the keys to these presentations is credibility. Rating agency analysts routinely tell me of how apparent it is when companies are merely presenting ERM theory as opposed to ERM practice. Rating agencies look for signs that the ERM program is real. That it is embraced by management. That it is actually used in decision making. That risk appetite—an enterprise-level calculation—is actually defined in quantitative terms. That ERM is used in risk governance, and that exposures are actually managed to within risk appetite. Providing real-life case studies goes a long way toward establishing credibility for the ERM program. Some types of case study examples that are suitable for these presentations include the following:

- Risks escalated in priority due to ERM activities
- Risk exposures reduced through mitigation, to keep them below their risk limits
- Enhancements made to the strategic planning process using ERM tools and techniques
- Decisions made differently using better risk–return trade-off information
- Disclosures improved using risk quantification information

Customize Risk Message to Rating Agency and Analyst Perspectives

After the company has presented the ERM program and its integration into key company processes from its own point of view, it is important to customize the risk message to the perspectives of the rating agency and the specific analyst(s) performing the review. The risk message must be translated into the terminology of the audience. This is critical for ERM, because even among ERM experts there is a plethora of competing definitions and terms.

In addition, a clear mapping must be provided to illustrate that the rating agency's key ERM criteria are satisfied, as well as any variations of interpretations held by the analyst(s). An effective mapping includes a list of the key ERM criteria from the rating agency and analyst perspectives, using their terminology, where each item in the list is mapped to one or more company ERM activities, using the company's terminology. This helps the analyst(s) gain a clear understanding of what the company has achieved with their ERM program. Skipping this step can result in a lack of appreciation of the company's ERM efforts by the rating agency, purely based on an erroneous belief that the company is missing something.

Communications to Regulators

At the time of the writing of this book, it is unclear what risk information will ultimately be required by U.S. regulators as a result of the Dodd-Frank bill, which became effective July 21, 2010. The Dodd-Frank bill, intended to prevent a recurrence of the global financial crisis that began in the United States in 2007, may end up requiring some risk data primarily from the largest banks. This regulation appears to have missed an opportunity to gather a broader data set which could have provided a better picture of the risks to the U.S. economy. A concentration of risk exposure that can threaten the U.S. economy exists not just at banks, but at every large company, in all sectors, particularly those that would be in the category of "too big to fail."

 SUMMARY

The fourth and final step in the ERM process cycle, risk messaging, offers numerous advantages. *Internal* risk messaging enhances performance measurement and management. If the integration of ERM into strategic planning and business decision making is the heart of risk culture, then internal risk messaging is the electrical stimulus that makes it beat. The integration of

ERM into business performance analysis and incentive compensation sends a clear signal internally that both risk and return must be managed together. This is what *drives* risk culture. In addition, the integration of value-based ERM into business performance analysis corrects the flaws in the balanced scorecard approach, and provides an ability to capture management's full contribution to company value during the year. Finally, the value-based approach better aligns management and shareholder interests by enhancing incentive compensation.

External risk messaging offers significant benefits as well. The value-based ERM approach supports complying with mandatory risk disclosures as well as using voluntary risk disclosures to signal the market regarding the company's competitive advantage in ERM. With a more advanced version of a stock analyst's own valuation tools, and other advanced ERM techniques, the value-based approach puts senior management in a stronger position when communicating with stock analysts, which can lead to better valuations. Finally, the value-based ERM approach supports rating agency communications, which can lead to strengthened ratings.

Now that we have completed our discussions of the basic ERM infra-structure in Part I (Chapters 1–3), and the ERM process cycle in Part II (Chapters 4–7), in the next chapter we move on to the final dimension of ERM infrastructure: the hierarchical structure, which is risk governance.

 NOTES

1. This refers to traditional economic capital models.
2. One argument in favor of using rating agency capital as a measure of the investment is that, for many financial services companies, this is larger than either regulatory capital or economic capital, and so, by default, the company must hold that amount, regardless of the true underlying risk, or it will lose its ratings. This has some merit. However, even in those situations, companies often choose to measure business segments on the basis of a truer measure of the actual risk, such as economic capital, and allocate the remainder to the corporate segment.
3. Code of Federal Regulations, Title 17 (Commodity and Security Exchanges), Chapter II (Security and Exchange Commission), Part 229 (Regulation S-K), Item 503(c).
4. Code of Federal Regulations, Title 17 (Commodity and Security Exchanges), Chapter II (Security and Exchange Commission), Part 229 (Regulation S-K), Item 407(h), effective February 28, 2010.

5. Code of Federal Regulations, Title 17 (Commodity and Security Exchanges), Chapter II (Security and Exchange Commission), Part 229 (Regulation S-K), Item 402(s), effective February 28, 2010.
6. This must be measured in terms of the impact on value, because the perspective of the disclosure is that of the shareholder.
7. Ibid.

PART THREE

Risk Governance
and Other Topics

CHAPTER EIGHT

Risk Governance

Constitutions should consist only of general provisions; the reason is that they must necessarily be permanent, and that they cannot calculate for the possible change of things.

Alexander Hamilton

ISK GOVERNANCE AND the ERM framework constitute the two elements of ERM infrastructure. The ERM framework provides the functional structure, which is part of the basic ERM infrastructure and must be in place before implementing the four ERM process cycle steps. Risk governance provides the hierarchical structure, which includes the way in which the ERM roles and responsibilities are divided up among individuals and groups; the organizational structure, including reporting relationships and authorities involved in ERM; and the policy and procedure documents that instruct key elements of the ERM process. Until the company completes one full ERM process cycle, only the most basic risk governance structure is warranted. The way ERM evolves, is adopted, and becomes integrated into a company's key processes differs from company to company. Until it is clear what the ERM activities will actually look like, the comprehensive risk governance structure required to support them cannot easily be determined. Now that we have completed our discussions of the ERM framework and the ERM process cycle, we are ready to discuss risk governance.

FOCUSING ON COMMON THEMES

The risk governance structure must be customized for each organization. There are two reasons for this. First, the way ERM takes shape can be different at each organization. Each organization adopts the ERM activities to a different extent, expanding some aspects more than others, and the risk governance structure must be defined around the ERM activities adopted. Second, risk governance should be conducted, to the extent possible, through the normal governance pathways already in place in the company. There are some components of ERM that are new to the organization, are truly unique, and require distinct elements in the governance process. However, ERM, to a great extent, should be integrated into the company culture: integrated into key company processes including decision making and performance measurement and management. As a result, much of risk governance will be covered by the existing governance structure over these existing company processes, which varies from company to company. However, there are some risk governance themes that are common to all companies, and these will be the focus of this chapter.

COMPONENTS OF RISK GOVERNANCE

In this chapter, we will discuss the three components of risk governance:

1. Roles and responsibilities
2. Organizational structure
3. Policies and procedures

ROLES AND RESPONSIBILITIES

We will discuss the ERM roles and responsibilities of each of the following individuals or groups:

- Corporate ERM
- ERM committee

- Risk experts
- Business segments
- Board of directors
- Internal audit

Corporate ERM

Corporate ERM, or the ERM team, includes the chief risk officer (CRO), or equivalent head of the ERM program, and the supporting members of the corporate ERM team. Corporate ERM has six major types of roles and responsibilities:

1. Build, maintain, and enhance infrastructure
2. Build buy-in
3. Ensure consistency
4. Act as central clearing house
5. Monitor exposures
6. Inform the board

Build, Maintain, and Enhance Infrastructure

The ERM team is responsible to lead the development of new ERM capabilities, to maintain existing ERM infrastructure, and to introduce enhancements over time. Below is a list of fundamental ERM program infrastructure elements that the ERM team builds, maintains, or enhances:

Build The ERM team must build the following ERM program elements:

- Setup
  - Construct the ERM framework, including details for major ERM process steps
  - Develop an ERM program implementation plan
  - Outline an initial basic risk governance structure
  - Develop a comprehensive risk governance structure after at least one pass through the ERM process cycle
- Risk identification
  - Develop the risk categorization and definition (RCD) tool
  - Design the process, tools, and materials for the qualitative risk assessment
  - Lead the development of the key risk list by conducting the qualitative risk assessment

- Develop the risk event database, which is developed during risk identification but used during risk quantification
- Develop the emerging risk identification tools and processes
- Risk quantification
  - Build the value-based ERM model
  - Calculate baseline company value
  - Design the risk scenario development process and techniques
  - Facilitate development of the key risk scenarios by conducting the risk scenario development process, such as FMEA interviews
  - Calculate the individual risk exposures
  - Facilitate the development of the key risk scenario correlation assumptions
  - Calculate enterprise risk exposure in the graph form
  - Facilitate the development of initial pain points, and produce enterprise risk exposure in the table form
- Risk decision making
  - Facilitate the definition of risk appetite and risk limits by conducting the risk appetite consensus meeting
  - Develop the methodology for the top-down allocation of risk appetite to risk limits
  - Develop the protocol for the integration of ERM information into decision making
  - Monitor risk exposures to ensure they are maintained to within risk tolerance limits
  - Facilitate the integration of ERM into strategic planning and business decision making
- Risk messaging
  - Facilitate the integration of ERM into business performance analysis and incentive compensation
  - Develop risk communications for shareholders, rating agencies, and regulators

Maintain or Enhance Over time, the ERM team must maintain or enhance the following ERM program elements:

- Risk identification
  - Maintain the risk categorization and definition (RCD) tool, such as occasionally adding risk subcategories

- Conduct qualitative risk assessments periodically, sometimes annually, often at least every two years, or whenever warranted by significant changes in the internal or external environment; periodically identify or develop supplemental information to assist survey participants, such as a comparative analysis of competitors' disclosed risks
- Update the key risk list after each qualitative risk assessment or for significant changes in decisions or in the internal or external environment
- Update the risk event database for risk events occurring in the company
- Coordinate continual emerging risk identification activities, including monitoring known risks and environmental scanning for unknown risks; periodically identify new techniques to supplement existing activities
- Risk quantification
  - Maintain, update, and provide appropriate access to the value-based ERM model; over time, modify and adapt the model for new applications
  - Recalculate baseline company value with at least the same frequency as the strategic planning process
  - Update the key risk scenarios impacted by significant changes in decisions or in the internal or external environment by re-conducting the risk scenario development process, such as the FMEA interviews
  - Recalculate the individual risk exposures with the same frequency as the strategic planning process, or whenever the key risk scenarios are updated
  - Update the key risk scenario correlations when there are significant changes in decisions or in the internal or external environment
  - Recalculate enterprise risk exposure with the same frequency as the strategic planning process, or whenever the key risk scenarios or key risk scenario correlations are updated
- Risk decision making
  - Update the definition of risk appetite, but only infrequently, with significant changes in the strategy or the internal or external environment, by facilitating another risk appetite consensus meeting
  - Update the definition of risk limits, but only infrequently; for example, with changes in risk appetite or a reorganization, by facilitating another risk appetite consensus meeting
  - Monitor risk exposures against risk tolerance limits, and ensure appropriate risk-priority actions are taken by decision makers

- Update ERM information supporting strategic planning and business decision making for changes in the business
- Over time, facilitate the expansion of applications for the integration of ERM into business decision making
■ Risk messaging
  - Over time, facilitate the expansion of applications for the integration of ERM into business performance analysis
  - Over time, facilitate the evolution of the integration of ERM into incentive compensation
  - Update communications to shareholders with the same frequency as its venue, such as annually for 10-K risk disclosures; over time, modify communications for changes in regulatory disclosures as well as changes in industry sector conventions regarding disclosures
  - Lead the routine development of rating agency communications and conduct the dedicated ERM presentations to rating agency analysts; update communications for changes in rating agency ERM criteria
  - Update communications to regulators for changes in regulations

Build Buy-in

As the champion for the ERM program, the CRO has primary responsibility to build sufficient buy-in for its adoption. With traditional ERM programs, this is often the most challenging task. Any change in the way a company does business involves some resistance and triggers the need for change management efforts. However, the reason this is so difficult is that traditional ERM programs use an approach that has many shortcomings, which are discussed throughout this book. Traditional ERM programs typically generate concern in the business segments that Corporate may impose another layer of red tape and restrictions that may impinge on their freedom to pursue business opportunities.

A value-based ERM approach is refreshingly different. One of its chief advantages is the relative ease with which the CRO can gain buy-in. At the heart of this is the fact that ERM is integrated into the business in a way that makes a business case for ERM itself, and enhances the rigor in the business case for all decision making by providing the ability to effectively manage risk and return together. This is well received by the business segments.

There are several aspects of the value-based ERM approach that build buy-in for the ERM program. We will discuss some examples of this by walking through the experience of implementing a value-based ERM program for the first time.[1]

Setup The very first steps to setting up a value-based ERM program are all fairly low key. With a value-based ERM approach, the ERM team can be kept to a small group, typically the CRO plus a handful of team members for support. In addition, the ERM implementation plan can be largely drafted by the ERM team themselves, requiring only minimal intrusion to gather input from key internal stakeholders. Finally, very little risk governance structure is needed at the outset; a more formal risk governance structure is developed later, after completing the ERM process cycle at least once. The risk governance can be mainly limited to defining the roles and responsibilities, as well as the reporting relationship, of the CRO, and letting the rest evolve informally as the ERM activities take place, until such time as a more formal risk governance structure is needed. This lighter touch, particularly at the start, means that very little political capital, as well as actual capital, has been spent.

Risk Identification The next step is the first step in the ERM process cycle: risk identification. The ERM team can produce the RCD tool mostly on their own; they do leverage data on risks from internal audit, but this is readily available and therefore not a burden. The ERM team identifies the qualitative risk assessment survey participants, produces the advance communication, and sends it to the participants.

Although survey participants are being asked to give of their time, what is traditionally a negative first impression for the ERM program actually becomes a positive experience and a good first step in building relationships, good will, and buy-in for the ERM program. This is particularly important because this first exercise involves interactions with powerful stakeholders from all key areas of the enterprise. The qualitative risk assessment in a value-based ERM program has four areas of advantage over that conducted in a traditional ERM program, in terms of building buy-in:

1. **Limited data request.** The value-based ERM approach keeps the data request limited to only what is needed at the time (see "Key #4: Gather Data Appropriately" in Chapter 4). Traditional qualitative risk assessment surveys include some data that is *never* needed, and other data that should not be requested until the risk quantification stage, at which point it is only needed for a much smaller number of risks. This is because traditional ERM

approaches usually do not even *have* a risk quantification stage for most risks. However, the value-based approach only needs to use the risk identification stage to narrow down the larger list of risks to those key risks which will then be quantified.

2. **One-on-one interviews.** Unlike the traditional approach of using templates, the one-on-one interviews used in the value-based ERM approach have five key features that help build buy-in:

   1. **Personal.** The interviews avoid the impersonal intrusion of an e-mail bearing a task which participants feel they are left to figure out on their own; instead, the participants will be individually guided through an interview by one of the ERM team members. This is a highly personal touch that builds goodwill and offers an excellent first impression of the ERM effort. In addition, the face-to-face (or voice-to-voice) communications start to build key relationships between the ERM team and internal stakeholders.

   2. **Collaborative.** Rather than requiring survey participants to fill in a complicated template, the ERM team member takes notes during the interview, documents the minutes, and gives participants an opportunity to correct them. This generates an atmosphere of collaboration.

   3. **Respectful.** Although the survey participants are being asked to spend their own time and energy, an ERM team member is matching this level of effort by being present and conducting the interview. This shows respect for survey participants' time.

   4. **Concise.** Using interviews, rather than templates, further limits the data request to only the need-to-have data, because any additional data collected would require more work of the ERM team as well.

   5. **Confidential.** The interviews may give survey participants more confidence in the ability to maintain confidentiality, which makes participants more comfortable and also builds trust.

3. **Consensus meeting.** A third area of advantage is the qualitative risk assessment consensus meeting. Getting the survey participants together as a group, whether in person or Web facilitated, and having conversations about the key risks and risk in general, starts to build a sense of teamwork in connection with the ERM program. In addition, as a group, participants have selected the key risks, which will be advanced to the risk quantification ERM process step. This act gives survey participants a sense of ownership over this key step in the ERM process, and people tend to support efforts to which they attach a sense of ownership, and in which they have had input in creating.

4. **Value added to internal audit.** A fourth area of advantage is that the first deliverable produced—a qualitative risk assessment that is based on the potential impact to company value—offers significant value to the internal audit team, which builds their level of buy-in. The internal audit team can use this information to align their efforts to the ERM program. In addition, the audit team can use this to better prioritize their audit plan to focus on risks more impactful to the value of the enterprise. Finally, this helps internal audit connect themselves to more of the strategic items on the corporate agenda.

Risk Quantification   We will discuss three items in the risk quantification ERM process step that help build buy-in:

1. Calculating baseline company value
2. Developing key risk scenarios
3. Quantifying individual risk exposures

Calculating Baseline Company Value   The first step in the risk quantification ERM process step is constructing a baseline valuation model. The ERM team can build the baseline valuation model mostly themselves, along with key input from the person responsible for the strategic plan financial projection. So, again, this involves a minimal footprint early on, which avoids stirring up any negative sentiment that can inhibit buy-in.

In addition, once the baseline company value is calculated, the ERM team has its second early deliverable: a more accurate, detailed, and dynamic valuation of the enterprise. This offers several benefits, all of which serve as positive advertising for the ERM program, building more buy-in. It helps identify opportunities for stock issuance or buyback. It also enhances communications with stock analysts. In addition, it provides an attribution of the company value by business segment, which yields various insights.[2] Finally, it offers a dynamic "what-if" model with which to evaluate decisions or changes in the environment in terms of their potential impact on the baseline company value.

Developing Key Risk Scenarios   The development of key risk scenarios is one of the most significant sources of building buy-in. There are three main aspects to this technique that generate such a high level of buy-in:

1. **Respects expertise in business segments.** Most traditional ERM programs rely too heavily on the ERM team to develop key risk scenarios, and

then build an ERM model based on these assumptions which is then unleashed on the business segments. This does not tend to gain credibility with the business segments. Those closest to the risks—largely those in the business segments—must be heavily involved.

The value-based ERM approach uses the FMEA process, which respects the expertise of the subject matter experts, who mostly reside in the business segments. The subject matter experts are being acknowledged for their expertise, and are asked to provide virtually all of the inputs needed to develop the key risk scenario. This produces a credible set of key risk scenarios. In addition, because the business segments participated in the development of the key risk scenarios, they tend to support the effort behind it.

2. **Addresses "black box" concerns.** Whenever a financial projection model is involved, there is some natural, unavoidable concern about it being a "black box" calculation, which means that its inner workings are somewhat opaque. However, the value-based ERM model is based on fundamental valuation techniques, using a simple projection and discounting of distributable cash flows. This is a bit more transparent due to its simple structure. In addition, as part of the FMEA process, the subject matter experts gain some additional comfort by providing inputs, seeing the outputs from the calculation, verifying that results are reasonable, and performing iterations if necessary.

3. **Offers help.** The FMEA interview provides a forum for the ERM team member performing the interview to offer help to the subject matter expert. At the end of the meeting, the expert from the business segment is asked, "Is there any mitigation that you feel is needed, or is there any project you had planned to do that is related to this risk scenario?" Often the answer is, "Yeah, we know we need such and such, but we just couldn't make the business case for it and Corporate did not approve it." The ERM team member is then able to respond, "Well, maybe we can help you. The ERM model is written in the language of changes in company value, which is the strongest business case possible. We can help you model the proposed initiative and show you what revenues or cost savings are needed to make it viable." This shifts the level of buy-in into high gear.

Quantifying Individual Risk Exposures The first quantification of risk comes fairly quickly, in the form of the individual risk quantification, and builds buy-in in four ways:

1. **Transparent scenarios.** The individual risk quantification results are based on transparent risk scenarios. Most traditional ERM programs use stochastic risk scenarios, which are inaccessible to management. Stochastic scenarios involve formulae and mathematics that are not intuitive to non-financial personnel. However, the value-based ERM approach uses deterministic risk scenarios which are fully transparent. Each specific individual risk scenario, along with its assumptions, is clearly laid out in easy-to-read, concise documentation. The scenarios are tangible and resonate with management. This engenders trust and a higher level of comfort in using the information.

2. **Stable results.** Traditional risk quantification is based on stochastic risk scenarios, which change every time the ERM model is run. This causes unease on the part of management. However, the value-based approach to individual risk quantification uses deterministic scenarios, which have stability. They tend to remain unchanged, unless there is a change to the risks, the business, or the external environment. This gives management the comfort they need to incorporate the information into decision making.

3. **Value-based results.** The value-based ERM approach quantifies individual risks in terms of their potential impact on company value, which gains buy-in from management. Rather than treating risk separately from return, the two are integrated together. This makes sense to management. They respond to this. They tend to act on information immediately when it is expressed in their language, which is the language of all decision-makers: the language of value.

4. **Attribution by risk driver.** The value-based ERM approach also generates support among businesspeople because it provides actionable information that directs priorities for mitigation decisions. The individual risk quantification includes an attribution of the impact by component risk driver. This helps management prioritize and focus mitigation efforts on the most important components of the risks. Actionable information, which includes clear decision-making priorities, is much appreciated by management.

Risk Decision Making By the time the third step of the ERM process cycle, risk decision making, comes around, the ERM program has already achieved a good level of buy-in from both Corporate and the business segments. However, this brings us to the main attraction in terms of gaining acceptance of the ERM program. It is the general ability of the value-based ERM approach to be integrated into the routine business decision-making processes that gains the deepest level of buy-in. Rather than a separate risk management process, value-based ERM becomes embedded in strategic planning as well as day-to-day business decisions, including strategic decisions, tactical decisions, and transactions such as mergers and acquisitions. This enhances the decision-making process by providing information on both risk and return, in the same venue, expressed in terms of changes in the baseline company value and the likelihood of achieving it. Rather than hinder business, the value-based ERM approach supports it.

Risk Messaging   External risk messaging also helps build internal buy-in, particularly by helping senior management in one of their key responsibilities.[3] Part of senior management's job is effectively managing the relationship with stock analysts and rating agencies to obtain a favorable stock valuation and to maintain the desired rating, respectively. External risk messaging improves communications with both of these key external stakeholders, supporting both of these key goals. The internal baseline enterprise valuation, along with other aspects of the ERM program, significantly enhances the quality of discussions with stock analysts. These discussions demonstrate management's superior ability to manage risk and return. In addition, rating agencies tend to react quite favorably to the adoption of value-based ERM programs. Rating agencies must project the future solvency of the company, and the value-based ERM program provides a large amount of credible prospective information on the company's shock resistance.

Ensure Consistency

The ERM team must ensure consistency of the ERM program throughout the enterprise. Consistency is one of the main advantages offered by an ERM program. It takes the different risk management activities previously existing in silo form and brings them together into a consistent program. The ERM team must ensure a high level of consistency in various aspects of the ERM program. Some examples include the following:

- Definitions, concepts, and terminology:
  - Create a common lexicon for ERM terms and concepts
  - Provide training on ERM to key stakeholders in the process
  - Ensure that risks are consistently defined by source and at the appropriate level

- Align understanding of the baseline strategic plan in terms of its financial projection (this is critical, because risk is defined as deviations from the baseline strategic plan)
- Tools and techniques, including their usage:
  - Deploy a single ERM framework enterprise-wide
  - Use a single repository (such as the RCD tool) for risk identification, emerging risk identification, and risk monitoring (risk event database)
  - Conduct qualitative risk assessment surveys in a uniform manner, in part to ensure a common understanding of the risk scenarios among survey participants
  - Use a consistent risk scenario development technique (such as FMEA interviews), and conduct it in a uniform manner
  - Provide a single ERM model accessible to all stakeholders
- Assumptions:
  - Offer input on assumptions developed for risk scenarios, when necessary, to ensure consistency
  - Review and approve risk scenario correlation assumptions, many of which cross multiple business segments
  - Ensure that a consistent standard is used to decide when ERM assumptions may be changed
- Metrics:
  - Provide a single set of metrics that can be used to:
    - Quantify all types of risk—strategic, operational, or financial—for individual risk quantification
    - Produce the aggregate metrics: enterprise risk exposure and risk appetite
- Decision making:
  - Establish a consistent process to manage risk exposures to within risk appetite and risk limits
  - Establish a consistent process for evaluating business decisions, whether risk-priority or return-priority decisions
- Risk messaging:
  - Use a uniform set of reporting templates internally
  - Ensure a consistent message is provided to shareholders through both mandatory and voluntary risk disclosures, and that this is consistent with the internal ERM program
  - Ensure that a consistent ERM message is communicated to rating agencies in dedicated and non-dedicated ERM presentations, as well as in conversations with management

Act as Central Clearing House

The ERM team serves as a central clearing house for ERM information and actions. Information must be centrally gathered, maintained, aggregated, and reported (internally and externally). It is critical to perform this centrally, not only to aggregate metrics to the enterprise level, but also to determine the net integrated impact of cross-department risks interacting to offset or exacerbate each other. In addition, the ERM team coordinates and sorts out disputes involving competing cross-department requests for increases in risk budgeting. The ERM team also must coordinate risk-priority mitigation decisions enterprise-wide. Finally, the ERM team helps coordinate responses to risk events as well as inquiries by external stakeholders, facilitating communications and actions among the board, senior management, executive risk owners, subject matter experts, and external stakeholders.

Monitor Exposures

One of the most important roles of the CRO is to effectively monitor exposures. The ERM team must monitor exposures and ensure they are maintained within risk appetite and risk limits.[4] The ERM team may not be the ones that, in isolation, make the decisions regarding what appropriate actions to take, when exposures threaten to, or actually do, exceed risk tolerance levels. In addition, the ERM team may not be the ones deciding on, or executing, the specific mitigation plans. However, their responsibility is to set up a general process by which the ERM committee can determine what the exposures are and what the appropriate risk tolerance levels should be, and provide reasonable notice to all relevant stakeholders in advance of violations or an increase in the likelihood of violations, pursuant to a predefined protocol.

Inform the Board

The CRO has a responsibility to keep the board of directors apprised of key ERM information. Items that are suitable for inclusion in the CRO report to the board include the following:

- Key risk exposures and their position relative to risk appetite and risk limits
  - Individual risk exposures
  - Enterprise risk exposure

- Future changes in risk exposures, either expected, somewhat likely, or representing significant threats (along with their corresponding contingency response plans), particularly in the near term
- Key decisions (recent and upcoming) relating to, or impacting, ERM
  - Risk-priority decisions changing exposures
  - Return-priority decisions changing exposures
- Key ERM program activities, such as enhancements
- Any recent significant risk event, and ERM lessons learned

ERM Committee

The ERM committee (which may be called by various names, including the risk committee) has a primary role of defining risk appetite and risk limits, and managing enterprise risk exposure to within these tolerance limits. The ERM committee has the following major responsibilities:

- Setup:
  - Review and approve ERM framework (including details for major ERM process steps)
  - Review and approve ERM program implementation plan
  - Review and approve initial basic risk governance structure
  - Review and approve comprehensive risk governance structure (after at least one pass through the ERM process cycle)
- Risk identification:
  - Review risk categorization and definition (RCD) tool
  - Review emerging risk identification process
- Risk decision making:
  - Define risk appetite (during risk appetite consensus meeting)
  - Define risk limits, including method of top-down allocation of risk appetite using an attribution
  - Review and approve method of integration of ERM information into decision-making protocols
  - Management of enterprise risk exposure to within risk appetite (co-responsibility with corporate ERM)
  - Review and approve integration of ERM into strategic planning and business decision making
- Risk messaging
  - Review and approve integration of ERM into business performance analysis and incentive compensation

- Review and approve communications to shareholders, rating agencies, and regulators

Risk Experts

There are many people throughout the enterprise that provide information in support of one or more ERM process steps. One example is the qualitative risk assessment survey participants. They help identify the key risks by providing individual opinions on potential key risks, their likelihood, severity, and credible worst-case scenarios. However, most of them are more experts in managing the business than they are experts in risk, per se. What we will refer to as risk experts are those who are designated as risk experts in a particular source of risk and have a routine involvement with the ERM program. These are the executive risk owners (EROs) and the subject matter experts (SMEs).

Executive risk owners are executives formally designated as such by the CRO. An ERO's role is to be the point person for coordinating efforts across the enterprise regarding one particular risk, and to help provide the required information to the ERM team. Each ERO is responsible for putting together a team of subject matter experts and managing them in support of a range of ERM activities. Not all EROs have preexisting expertise in their designated risk, at least not enterprise-wide; for example, an executive in the business segment most vulnerable to regulatory risk may be chosen as the regulatory risk ERO. In contrast, the SMEs are the leading recognized internal experts for their risk. Most SMEs are middle management, although some are executives, depending on the risk.

The risk experts—both EROs and SMEs—have the following major responsibilities:

- Risk identification:
  - Provide risk event information to the ERM team for populating the risk event database
  - Monitor known risks and scan the environment for unknown risks in support of emerging risk identification
- Risk quantification:
  - Develop key risk scenarios by participating as subject matter experts in the FMEA interview process
  - Provide input on key risk scenario correlations

- For some risks (e.g., financial or insurance), conduct the detailed modeling whose outputs are used as inputs into the ERM model, in support of risk scenario development or decision making
- Risk decision making:
  - Support management of enterprise risk exposure to within risk appetite by identifying mitigation options and helping to evaluate them by providing modified key risk scenarios
  - Make risk-priority decisions either in isolation, or for decisions requiring escalation, in concert with the ERM committee
- Risk messaging
  - Support communications to shareholders by providing information to the ERM team
  - Support communications with rating agencies by providing information to the ERM team, and attending a portion of the meetings with rating agency analysts
  - Support communications with regulators by providing information to the ERM team

Business Segments

The primary role of the business segments is to do the risk *taking*. This is just a normal part of doing business, although ERM information is integrated into the decision-making processes. In addition, the business segments provide most of the EROs and SMEs, whose contribution was separately discussed earlier. Finally, they provide many of the qualitative risk assessment survey participants.

The major ERM roles played by the business segments are as follows:

- Risk identification:
  - Qualitative risk assessment (to the extent that business segments provide survey participants)
- Risk quantification:
  - Support baseline company value calculation by providing business segment projections used in support of strategic plan financial projections
- Risk decision making:
  - Help define risk appetite and risk limits (to the extent that business segments are represented on the ERM committee)

- Manage business segment risk exposure to within risk limits (to the extent that risk limits are established by business segment)
- Support management of enterprise risk exposure to within risk appetite by providing information to the ERM team regarding unexpected business decisions or changes in the environment that change the level of risk
- Perform strategic planning using ERM information and protocols
- Perform business decision making—including strategic decisions, tactical decisions, and transactions (such as mergers and acquisitions) using ERM information and protocols
- Risk messaging
  - Conduct business performance analysis and design incentive compensation using ERM information and protocols[5]
  - Support communications to shareholders by providing information to the ERM team and reviewing risk disclosures
  - Support communications with rating agencies by providing information to the ERM team, incorporating ERM information into routine rating agency presentations, and possibly attending a portion of the meetings with rating agency analysts
  - Support communications with regulators by providing information to the ERM team

Board of Directors

A list of ERM information that is appropriate for the board to review was provided earlier (see "Inform the Board"). This information is used to perform the board of directors' four major roles in ERM:

1. Awareness of key risk exposures and risk decisions
2. Familiarity with ERM program
3. Evaluation of ERM program effectiveness
4. Involvement with defining risk appetite

Awareness of Key Risk Exposures and Risk Decisions

The board should be aware of the company's major risk exposures. Being aware of key threats to the company is not a new role for directors. In the United States, federal regulations require boards to be aware of key risk exposures and mitigating actions:

The audit committee should discuss the company's major financial risk exposures and the steps management has taken to monitor and control such exposures.

Code of Federal Regulations, Title 17 (Commodity and Security Exchanges), Chapter II (Security and Exchange Commission), Part 229 (Regulation S-K),Item 303A.07(c)(iii)(D)

However, the presence of an ERM program changes the format in which the board sees the information, improving its quality and clarifying the appropriate tolerance limits. The board must be up to date on current key risk exposures, particularly in comparison to the risk appetite and risk limits. In addition, the board should be informed, in a timely way, about significant imminent or emerging threats and corresponding ERM mitigation activities. Finally, the board should be aware of major ERM decisions impacting exposures (such as risk-priority decisions to manage enterprise risk exposure to within risk appetite).

Familiarity with ERM Program

The board should be generally aware of the ERM program design and activities. They should understand the ERM framework, including the major elements of each ERM process step. In the United States, federal regulations require this:

> . . . the audit committee must discuss guidelines and policies to govern the process by which [assessing and managing the company's exposure to risk] is handled. (commentary in brackets)

Code of Federal Regulations, Title 17 (Commodity and Security Exchanges), Chapter II (Security and Exchange Commission), Part 229 (Regulation S-K), Item 303A.07(c)(iii)(D)

Evaluation of ERM Program Effectiveness

The board has a responsibility to judge the effectiveness of the ERM program. In the United States, federal regulations require the audit committee to, at a minimum, share responsibility for an effective ERM process and to perform a general review of ERM:

The audit committee is not required to be the sole body responsible for risk assessment and management . . . Many companies . . . manage and assess their risk through mechanisms other than the audit committee. The processes these companies have in place should be reviewed in a general manner by the audit committee, but they need not be replaced by the audit committee.

Code of Federal Regulations, Title 17 (Commodity and Security Exchanges),
Chapter II (Security and Exchange Commission),
Part 229 (Regulation S-K), Item 303A.07(c)(iii)(D).

The board should determine the effectiveness of the ERM program design by comparing it to the 10 key ERM criteria defined in Chapter 2. In addition, the board must evaluate the effectiveness of the ERM program execution, primarily in terms of its most important goal: managing enterprise risk exposure to within risk appetite.

Involvement with Defining Risk Appetite

Defining risk appetite is a difficult task with sweeping implications. In defining risk appetite, the ERM committee is attempting to divine the wishes of the collective shareholders—which are often a highly diverse group with different perspectives, expectations, and investment needs—in terms of the optimal and maximum levels of risk they expect the company to be taking. It is prudent to get board input on such a decision. The level of board involvement varies, though there has been a trend toward boards *approving* the company's risk appetite, as defined by the ERM committee.

Internal Audit

We will discuss four aspects of internal audit's involvement with the ERM program:

1. Independent verification
2. Broader roles
3. Information for the ERM team
4. Alignment of internal audit plan with ERM priorities

Independent Verification

Internal audit should remain largely independent of ERM program activities. This is necessary for internal audit to perform their primary ERM function, which is independent verification that ERM program policies and procedures are being carried out.

Some of the items that internal audit must verify include the following:

- Risk identification:
  - Qualitative risk assessment
    - Performed with the required frequency
    - Data integrity is maintained from data collection through documentation
    - Qualitative risk assessment consensus meeting results are documented
  - Risk event database
    - Updated for risk events occurring in the company
    - Used as input to risk scenario development
  - Emerging risk identification process
    - Activities are taking place with the required frequency
- Risk quantification:
  - Value-based ERM model
    - Data integrity is maintained from data collection through incorporation into the model
    - Calculations, including baseline company value, individual risk exposures, and enterprise risk exposure are functioning as intended
    - Data integrity is maintained from calculated results through dissemination of communications
  - Key risk scenarios and their correlations
    - Updated properly
- Risk decision making:
  - Risk limits
    - Integrity of attribution calculation is maintained
  - Management of enterprise risk exposure to within risk appetite and risk limits
    - Exposures are kept within tolerance limits
    - Required protocols are followed (such as when soft limits are temporarily violated)
  - ERM information supporting strategic planning and business decision making
    - Data integrity is maintained from calculated results through information provided
    - Information is incorporated appropriately

- Risk messaging
  - Communications to shareholders, rating agencies, and regulators
    - Data integrity is maintained between internal ERM information and external communications

Broader Roles

Some companies are asking internal audit to take the lead in implementing their ERM program. In these cases, internal audit is serving as the ERM team. This prevents internal audit from performing an independent verification of ERM program policies and procedures. This might be temporarily justifiable for companies with minimal resources who, without an ability to leverage internal audit in this way, would not otherwise be able to launch an ERM program at all. However, even in such situations, once the ERM program matures, the ERM team should be made independent from internal audit.

Information for the ERM Team

Internal audit can offer various risk insights that are helpful to the ERM program. Internal audit provides the following information, all of which is related to the risk identification ERM process step, to the ERM team:

- Risk assessments that support the development of the risk categorization and definition (RCD) tool
- Historical data on risk event occurrences in the company, which supports the development of the risk event database
- Various input in support of the emerging risk identification process

Alignment of Internal Audit Plan with ERM Priorities

The ERM program can offer valuable information on risk to internal audit. The ERM team provides internal audit with the results of the qualitative risk assessment and the individual risk scenario quantification. Internal audit uses this information to prioritize the internal audit plan in alignment with ERM program priorities. This is of great value to internal audit, because this provides a venue for them to address more strategic items of concern to the company. Aligning the audit plan with a value-based ERM program produces a value-based audit plan focused on the items that present the greatest threats to company value.

ORGANIZATIONAL STRUCTURE

The second aspect of risk governance is the organizational structure. There are not as many common themes to discuss here as compared to the roles and responsibilities, nor should there be. A successful ERM program will have the bulk of its inner workings subsumed into the normal pathways of doing business, rather than being relegated to a separate, disconnected function. For that reason, the risk governance organizational structure should leverage, as much as possible, the existing governance organizational structure. However, there are some unique elements required, and this will be the focus of our discussion here.

We will discuss four elements of the risk governance organizational structure:

1. CRO
2. ERM committee
3. Key risk committees
4. Board of directors

CRO

We will discuss five criteria that represent best practices for the CRO position:

1. **One leader.** It is crucial to designate one person as the sole head of the ERM program. Like any change in the way of doing business, introducing an ERM program requires change management, and building buy-in is critical. It is a lot easier to build buy-in through a dedicated champion who advocates for the ERM program. In addition, the ERM program requires communicating with the board and various levels of management, liaising between constituencies across the enterprise and building consensus on issues where multiple interpretations can exist. Again, it is much simpler for one individual to manage these activities. Finally, a key ERM theme is integration. ERM seeks to take disparate risk processes and integrate them into a single coherent process. Splitting the CRO function among more than one person sends an inconsistent message about integration. More importantly, a split CRO function is unlikely to achieve a fully integrated ERM program.
2. **Dedicated function.** The CRO role should be a full-time position. As discussed earlier, there is much work to do, both upon initial ERM program

implementation, as well as on an ongoing basis. Some companies begin their ERM program with a part-time CRO position, just as a temporary measure, and later elevate the position to full time.

3. **Executive position.** It is advisable to appoint the CRO as a senior executive (see "Top Eight Traits of an Executive CRO"). The ERM program is difficult to implement without indications of strong support by company leadership. If the CRO position is not afforded a high level of authority, this can send the wrong signal enterprise-wide, making it far more difficult for the CRO to achieve success. In addition, the level of responsibility is naturally commensurate with a senior executive position.

TOP **EIGHT TRAITS OF AN EXECUTIVE CRO**

A CRO must have strong executive qualities in addition to the requisite expertise in ERM and knowledge of finance. The appropriate characteristics for a CRO depend on many factors that vary by organization. However, the following is a list of the top eight traits an executive CRO should have, in priority order:

1. **ERM expertise.** Ideally the CRO should have experience successfully implementing ERM. Realistically, there are not many who have this yet. The next best thing is for the CRO to have significant conceptual knowledge of ERM.

2. **Leadership.** The CRO must have strong leadership capabilities. Leadership is getting others to share, and follow, your vision for a better direction. The CRO must develop buy-in for the ERM program throughout the enterprise.

3. **Imagination.** The ERM process requires imagining, and getting others to imagine, a range of potential risk scenarios. This requires pragmatic creativity, an ability to imagine what is possible, for both upside and downside risk events.

4. **Communication.** A large part of the CRO's role involves communicating with a disparate range of internal and external stakeholders. The CRO must effectively tailor both oral and written communications to each audience.

5. **Executive presence.** The CRO must be able to effectively interact at the highest levels, both internally and externally.

6. **Management.** The ERM program is wide ranging and requires coordination of contributors to, and stakeholders in, the ERM program, across all business segments and levels of the organization.

7. **Diplomacy.** The CRO role requires an ability to balance the need for independence—to ensure an objective and consistent ERM process and to enforce risk tolerance limits—with the need to partner effectively with ERM contributors throughout the organization. This requires a deft diplomatic touch.

8. **Finance.** The CRO should have a strong knowledge of finance to understand and convey the quantitative ERM information.

4. **Independence.** The CRO position requires a high level of independence. The CRO, as well as the rest of the ERM team, is responsible to lead numerous efforts related to key risks that span the entire enterprise. An appropriate level of independence will help minimize conflicts of interest where the CRO is under the auspices of an individual who is the source of one or more key risks. In addition, the CRO functions in several capacities—such as ensuring consistency enterprise-wide and acting as a central clearing house—which would be well served by a proper level of independence, which would ensure, as well as convey, that the CRO is an unbiased actor.

It is best for the CRO, and the ERM team, to have a reporting line directly to the board of directors, a board committee, or the chief executive officer (CEO). This may reduce the number of potential conflicts of interest. However, it is impossible to completely avoid such conflicts, because even directors and the CEO are potential sources of risk. Many companies, especially in financial services, have the CRO report to the chief financial officer (CFO), which is the next best choice for some companies.[6]

In addition, the CRO's level of independence should be underscored by regular access to the board. This is important for fulfilling the CRO's routine role of informing the board as well as satisfying the board's requirements (receive ERM information, evaluate the ERM program, etc.). In addition, the CRO should be able to contact the board of directors directly, on an ad-hoc basis, to alert them of issues needing their urgent attention.

5. **Appropriate support.** Companies using a value-based ERM approach usually require only a small dedicated ERM team, such as three to five

people, including the CRO, or head of the ERM program, and supporting staff (see "The Supporting Cast"). This is a reasonable level of resources, given the roles and responsibilities that include an initial push to launch the ERM program as well as ongoing efforts. This is also consistent with the basic principle that ERM should be largely embedded in key company processes, rather than a separate department unto itself.

However, companies using *traditional* ERM approaches have ERM teams whose sizes vary widely. Some of these companies choose to use the ERM team as a much broader umbrella, covering a wide range of personnel involved in some ERM activities; this is usually based on their historical approach to risk management which pre-dates ERM. Although this can work, depending on the company culture, it is inadvisable, because this makes it more difficult to embed ERM into key company processes, particularly decision making, which largely resides in the business segments.

THE **SUPPORTING CAST**

The CRO only needs a few supporting staff on the ERM team to effectively implement a value-based ERM program. However, they must have the appropriate balance of skills to perform the broad and diverse range of their ERM roles and responsibilities.

The staff person that takes the lead for the ERM model should have excellent quantitative skills:

1. A basic knowledge of financial statement accounting is needed to work with the strategic plan financial projection and convert it into a calcula-tion of the baseline company value.

2. Strong spreadsheet skills are helpful to construct the dynamic elements in the ERM model for calculating the individual risk exposures.

3. Knowledge of spreadsheet programming is required to run the simula-tions necessary for the enterprise risk exposure calculation.

4. Excellent model-building skills are critical to maintain the ERM model's practicality—in the form of reliability, speed, transparency, and balance of significant digits—which is fundamental to the success of the value-based ERM approach (see the section titled "Practical Modeling" in Chapter 5).

At least one staff person, who will support the qualitative risk assessment interviews and the risk scenario development FMEA interviews, should have superior ERM knowledge and experience, as well as excellent business savvy:

1. A mastery of ERM knowledge and experience is necessary to properly guide interviewees. These are challenging interviews. For example, during the qualitative risk assessment, survey participants will proffer potential risks that are not properly defined by source or are not material enough to be key risks. Only significant experience in ERM can enable the interviewer to quickly identify and correct these problems on the fly. Another example is that during the FMEA interviews, subject matter experts will develop risk scenarios that are not properly defined by source or are not reflecting all of the financial impacts. Again, it takes years of ERM experience to immediately identify and correct these issues. For this reason, these interviews are usually led, at least the first time through the process, by ERM consultants.

2. Strong listening skills are critical to hear, understand, and properly record the information provided during these interviews.

3. Good interviewing skills are required to conduct the interviews on a consistent basis, and to effectively solicit the required information from the interviewees.

4. Excellent written communication skills are helpful in crafting the advance communication for the qualitative risk assessment interviews.

5. An ability to interact with the most senior executives, as well as board members, is necessary to conduct the qualitative risk assessment interviews and consensus meeting.

It is also helpful if some ERM team members have long-standing relationships with a variety of associates in the firm. A strong network is helpful, especially initially, when building buy-in for the ERM program is paramount.

It is best practice for the CRO to be a single leader in a full-time ERM role, with the authority of an executive position, ample independence, and an appropriate level of dedicated support. However, these best practice criteria are neither necessary nor sufficient conditions. Following these best practices does not guarantee success. There are some companies where the CRO enjoys the presence of all of these criteria, yet the ERM program has still achieved very little. In addition, ignoring these best practices does not guarantee failure, either. One of the most advanced ERM programs I have seen was achieved by a part-time CRO who was non-executive management, without significant independence, and with a bare minimum of part-time support (although the CRO did have the sole responsibility to lead the ERM program).

ERM Committee

The appropriate makeup of the ERM committee (which may be called by various names, including the risk committee) varies by organization. It is usually an executive-level committee comprised of the following individuals, at a minimum:

- Chief executive officer (CEO)
- Chief risk officer (CRO)
- Chief financial officer (CFO)
- Heads of major business segments or their lieutenants
- Chief legal counsel
- Head of compliance (nonvoting)
- Head of internal audit (nonvoting)

Risk experts—executive risk owners (EROs) and subject matter experts (SMEs)—and other business experts are occasionally invited to join committee meetings in support of discussions of key risks related to the expertise required. The ERM committee is often chaired by either the CEO or the CRO.

Key Risk Committees

The executive risk owners (EROs) and their subject matter experts (SMEs) often form key risk committees bearing the name of the key risk(s) under their purview. Some of these committees pre-date ERM, representing a silo form of risk management (such as a credit risk committee), and are appropriately leveraged into service in the ERM risk governance organizational structure. These committees are organized to help the risk experts (EROs and SMEs) perform their ERM roles and responsibilities, and also to share information (including the basic required ERM information, as well as tools and techniques, issues of concern, best practices, etc.) more effectively within committees, between committees, and upstream to the CRO and the ERM committee. The EROs have "dotted-line" reporting relationships to the CRO or to the ERM committee, indicating an informal, or less formal, organizational structure. The

SMEs have dotted-line reporting relationships to their EROs, though many of them may already be direct reports of their ERO. The ERO and SME roles are not usually full-time roles in and of themselves.

Board of Directors

The majority of companies do not set up a separate board-level committee to take the lead in fulfilling the board's ERM roles and responsibilities listed earlier, but instead either assign the tasks to the entire board or to the audit committee. If this is assigned to the audit committee, the full board should receive complete reports from the audit committee to satisfy two of their roles: awareness of key risk exposures and risk decisions, and familiarity with the ERM program. In addition, the full board should receive summary reports on the evaluation of the ERM program effectiveness. Finally, only the full board should fulfill the role of involvement with defining risk appetite.

POLICIES AND PROCEDURES

The third aspect of risk governance is the codification and communication of policies and procedures. This should evolve along with the ERM program. Detailed policies and procedures should not be written far in advance of completing the ERM process cycle at least once. It is impossible to draft effective ERM policies and procedures until management can see, for example, the enterprise risk exposure calculation, the risk appetite definition, and how the ERM program will integrate into key company processes, particularly decision making.

We will discuss two of the key ERM policy and procedure documents:

1. ERM program summary document
2. Risk appetite document

ERM Program Summary Document

The ERM program summary document contains a summary and description of the following items:

■ ERM program origins, historical development, current status, and enhancement plans

- ERM framework, including detail on each of the ERM process steps and activities
- Risk governance structure, including roles and responsibilities and organizational structure

The ERM program summary document is often accompanied by exhibits such as the following:

- Risk categorization and definition (RCD) tool, in each of its various incarnations, such as:
  - Results of qualitative risk assessment
  - Comparative analysis
  - Risk event database
- Individual risk scenario exposures
- Enterprise risk exposure
- Summary of risk appetite definition
- Summary of major risk decisions, both risk-priority and return-priority
- Description of integration of ERM into decision making, business performance analysis, and incentive compensation
- Recent ERM communications to rating agencies

The ERM program summary document is used for the following purposes:

- Documentation
- Training
- Repository for internal reporting and external risk messaging

Risk Appetite Document

The risk appetite document contains the following information:

- Definition of risk appetite, including hard and soft limits
- Definition of risk limits, including hard and soft limits, as well as the allocation methodology
- Enterprise risk exposure compared to risk appetite (both current and historical)
- Risk exposures below enterprise level compared to their corresponding risk limits (both current and historical)

■ Delegation of authority for increasing risk exposures, including escalating actions and authorities required when exposures cross soft-limit or hard-limit thresholds

SUMMARY

There are three main aspects to effectively governing risks: having the key ERM contributors knowing and performing their roles and responsibilities; establishing the organizational structure that supports the execution of these roles and responsibilities; and codifying policies and procedures. The CRO and his or her ERM team play a large role in ERM: building, maintaining, and enhancing the ERM program; building buy-in for the program; and many other critical functions. However, there are several other key contributors across the enterprise—executives on the ERM committee, risk experts, business segment personnel, the board, and internal audit—that play critical roles in a successful ERM program.

This chapter concludes our discussions on implementing a successful ERM program using a value-based ERM approach. In the next chapter, we examine a case study on the global financial crisis that began in the United States in 2007 as it relates to ERM and bank risk management practices.

NOTES

1. This discussion offers a brief summary of points made elsewhere, primarily in Chapters 4 through 7, but from Chapter 3 as well. For a more thorough explanation of each of these points, please revisit those chapters.
2. This offers valuable insights, although political care must be taken, because this may indicate a change in the relative power of the business segments.
3. The first time through the ERM process cycle, risk messaging may be limited only to *external* risk messaging. Going through the first three ERM process steps a second time irons out all the wrinkles, which is prudent prior to integrating ERM into business performance evaluation and, especially, incentive compensation.
4. Internal audit is responsible for all assurance regarding compliance with ERM policies and procedures. However, a primary role for the ERM team is to sound the alarm and take action when exposures threaten to exceed tolerance limits.
5. Business segments are defined here to include Corporate (not to be confused here with corporate ERM). Corporate is primarily responsible for these tasks,

which are usually consistently applied enterprise-wide. However, to the extent that the non-corporate business segments conduct their own internal business performance reviews, or to the extent that there are business segment–specific incentives, then these tasks are performed by non-corporate business segments as well.

6. This is more common at insurance companies than at banks. Initially, the majority of bank CROs reported to the CFO, but now the majority report to the CEO, the board, or a board committee.

CHAPTER NINE

Financial Crisis Case Study

> I am a firm believer in the people. If given the truth,
> they can be depended upon to meet any national
> crisis. The great point is to bring them the real facts.
>
> *Abraham Lincoln*

THE GLOBAL FINANCIAL crisis that began in the United States in 2007 is a complex and challenging case study. In the United States, this has been described as the most damaging economic event since the Great Depression, which followed the stock market crash of 1929. Economists still debate the facts of the 1929 crash—the relative importance of the events that caused it, the interacting factors that deepened it, and the effectiveness of the government actions to mitigate it. Certainly, the financial crisis, from which we still have not recovered at the time of the writing of this book, will be similarly debated for decades.

We will not claim to present here a definitive, or even nearly complete, discussion of this event. However, what we will do is analyze the financial crisis from an ERM perspective. During 2008, the first full year of the financial crisis, many in the ERM field were being asked the following question:

Banks have been claiming primacy in risk management for a long time. ERM is the latest incarnation of risk management, so banks must have been doing ERM, right? Yet the banks just blew up the entire global economy. So, if ERM didn't prevent this financial crisis, how can ERM be any good?

This chapter is in response to this question. We will examine whether the bank[1] risk management practices that contributed to the financial crisis were a failure of ERM theory or a failure of banks to actually follow ERM practices. We will begin with a brief summary of the financial crisis.

SUMMARY OF THE FINANCIAL CRISIS

We will only discuss here a high-level summary of the financial crisis, to introduce our topic. Our focus in this chapter is on bank risk management practices, for which we will provide more details throughout our discussion, and therefore, this brief summary will be sufficient for our purposes.

The Causes

An increase in risky mortgages—those more likely to result in foreclosure—was fueled by the unrealistic expectation by both mortgage issuers and homeowners that housing prices would continue to rise and that interest rates would continue to fall or remain low, even as housing prices peaked at an unsustainable level, referred to as a "housing bubble," and interest rates were about to rise from unsustainably low levels. The unrealistic expectation of the mortgage issuers were mainly fueled by an investment supply–demand imbalance due to an excess of foreign capital seeking investments.[2]

Banks Made It Worse

The risks already inherent in this situation were exacerbated by banks in two ways:

1. Soliciting more and riskier home buyers
2. Selling more and riskier investments

Soliciting More and Riskier Home Buyers

Banks solicited more home buyers by creating mortgages that were easier to get into but harder to maintain, and that involved risks that most consumers were not aware of, or did not fully understand. Some of these riskier mortgages even had loan amounts that *increased* over time, because the early interest payments were not covering the interest charges. In addition, banks further increased the risks inherent in the mortgage investment supply chain by growing the subprime mortgage market: home buyers with higher-than-usual likelihoods of default.

Selling More and Riskier Investments

Banks solicited more mortgage investors through complex innovative mortgage investment products that made it easier to invest in the mortgage market, and where the risks to investors were even less transparent than usual (due to multifaceted packaging of mortgages and multiple handoffs) and magnified in exposure (through leverage). Two such products were collateralized debt obligations (CDOs) and credit default swaps (CDSs).

CDOs led to less transparency. A CDO is a bond with payments based on cash flows from a package of mortgage products, such as mortgage-backed securities (MBSs) and collateralized mortgage obligations (CMOs). Different CDOs have different levels of risk, called tranches, based on how the CDO defines the way in which cash flows will be divided up. Some tranches were considered highly secure (triple-A credit rating). The multifaceted packaging of mortgages made the risk behind the investment murkier. However, further reducing transparency were CDOs of CDOs, called CDO-Squareds, which involve reselling more detailed tranches of existing CDO tranches. These multiple handoffs made investors yet another entity removed from understanding the risk.

CDSs magnified the risks. A CDS is essentially an insurance policy against the failure of a given entity. The issuer of the CDS receives steady cash inflows but suffers a large loss if the entity fails. CDSs issued on CDOs or other mortgage instruments allowed the magnification of bets on the mortgage market, through leverage, because the number of CDSs was not limited to the number of mortgages, or CDOs, on which they were based.

The Crisis

When interest rates rose, and the investment supply–demand imbalance ended, removing excess foreign capital, housing prices fell at the same time as mortgage payments rose, and foreclosures dramatically increased as a result. Banks began to fail, a credit and liquidity crisis ensued, and a threat of cascading failures leading to a vicious cycle—banks fail, companies needing credit from banks fail or cut employees, unemployed homeowners default on more mortgages, and so on—prompted governments to bail out banks and other "too-big-to-fail" entities in an attempt to stabilize the financial system.

 ## EVALUATING BANK RISK MANAGEMENT PRACTICES

We will evaluate the extent to which banks were, or were not following ERM practices, by benchmarking their risk management practices against the 10 key ERM criteria, primarily discussed in Chapters 2 and 3.

Benchmarking against 10 Key ERM Criteria

The 10 key ERM criteria are:

1. Enterprise-wide scope
2. All risk categories included
3. Key risk focus
4. Integrated across risk types
5. Aggregated metrics
6. Includes decision making
7. Balances risk and return management
8. Appropriate risk disclosures
9. Measures value impacts
10. Primary stakeholder focus

These criteria are the critical defining elements of a robust ERM program, and are a good benchmark to use in evaluating ERM programs. In Chapter 3, we discussed how a value-based ERM approach fully satisfies these 10 key ERM criteria. We will now begin evaluating bank risk management practices against this benchmark.

Criterion 1: Enterprise-Wide Scope

The ERM program must be equally applied across the enterprise. In Chapter 2, we discussed five reasons why companies may fail to satisfy this condition. The first of these was the presence of a "golden boy unit." This is a business unit that is exempt from certain activities, such as ERM, as a result of their generating large revenue growth and/or profits. This leads to a lack of understanding, or willful ignorance, of the risks involved in the business.

Many banks that contributed to the financial crisis fell into this situation. The business units issuing mortgage products were experiencing a high level of growth. Management did not want to miss out on the growth opportunity in which many of their competitors were participating. The pressure for growth, as well as the seduction of easy and rapid growth, either influenced management to consciously avoid a full level of ERM scrutiny, or unconsciously use a light touch that avoided fully looking at the risks.

Criterion 2: All Risk Categories Included

All risk categories must be included in the ERM program. Risk categories include the following:

- Financial risk, which includes market, credit, and liquidity risks.
- Strategic risk, which includes risks related to strategy, execution of strategy, governance, competitors, suppliers, external relations, regulatory changes, and so on.
- Operational risk, which includes risks related to human resources, technology, litigation, compliance, fraud, disasters, and so on.
- Insurance risk, which involves risks that generally apply only to insurance companies, and includes pricing risk, underwriting risk, and reserving risk; this risk category also applies to non-insurance companies issuing contracts that cover contingencies analogous to insurance contracts, such as CDSs.

In Chapter 2, we discussed three reasons why companies may fail to satisfy this condition. Two of these apply here:

1. **Inability to quantify strategic and operational risks.** The inability of banks to quantify strategic and operational risks was explored in depth in Chapter 3 (see "Risk Capital"), where we explained that banks use one of two alternative capital-based approaches to risk quantification. Both alternative approaches ignore strategic risks altogether. The majority of banks use Alternative 1, which poorly measures operational risks in that it is not a risk-based approach and is sometimes not even *directionally* correct. Those banks using Alternative 2 are unable to fully quantify operational risks because they ignore impacts to future revenues and expenses.

This is the first of the three core challenges to ERM identified in Chapter 3.

2. **Financial analyst bias.** In Chapter 2, we explained that financial analyst bias (an excessive focus on financial risk) stems from the fact that the financial modelers' education, training, certification, experience, and department are all focused solely on financial risk, and that their techniques only work well for these risks. Bank financial modelers definitely suffer from such bias.

This bias leads to management receiving information on enterprise risk exposure that appears complete, but is not. In fact, as discussed, research shows that financial risk only represents a fraction of the bank's overall exposure, once strategic and operational risks are properly factored in. Deepening this false impression is the level of precision with which the financial risk exposures are presented. The level of precision is implied by the significant digits in the exposure data provided to management.

We will now discuss some examples of non-financial risks not addressed by bank financial modelers, which contributed to the crisis. These examples involve human resources risks, which are a type of operational risk.

Some claim that the financial crisis was a "perfect storm" where an unforeseeable combination of rare events suddenly came together. Others contend that many bank personnel were aware of the exposures or should have been aware, but this information did not become available to their boards of directors, executives, or management. If so, why not? What went wrong? The answer to that question leads us to three non-financial sources of risk that contributed to the financial crisis:

1. Agency risk
2. Process risk
3. Errors

Agency Risk   Banks have agency risk, in terms of a misalignment of the interests of management with that of the shareholders, as well as with that of the taxpayers.

The agency risk due to misalignment with *shareholders* comes in the form of incentive compensation programs that reward management for generating high revenues and profits without properly adjusting for the corresponding increase in risk exposure. There are three features needed in an ERM program to prevent this:

1. Measure risk exposures on the basis of impact on value
2. Integrate information on risk exposures into business performance evaluation, including an attribution at the individual level
3. Integrate information on risk exposures into incentive compensation

The first feature, measuring risk in terms of value impacts, is critical to aligning management's interests with that of the shareholders, because the shareholders' primary metric is company value. However, bank risk management programs do not have this feature, because they measure risk in terms of the balance sheet, as impacts on capital or required capital.

Bank risk management programs also do not have the second and third features. Though banks do have risk exposure metrics in their business performance analysis, they are flawed. Banks typically use the Value-at-Risk (VaR) metric. VaR is often defined as the maximum amount of capital that can be lost in a single day, within a given small predefined likelihood. A key weakness of this metric is that bank associates can add large amounts of risk without accountability, by creating it, or defining it, as just beyond the likelihood threshold, so that it is not captured in the VaR metric. In addition, banks generally do not produce attributions of the risk exposure metrics at the individual level. Without knowing the level to which an individual increased risk exposure, it is impossible to build this into incentive compensation.

The presence of the agency risk causing misalignment with shareholders contributed to bank management's taking on excessively high levels of risk. Doing so increased the chances of massive bonuses. Indeed, bank management did receive massive paydays during the mortgage boom. In fact, bank management even received massive bonuses *after* it became clear that their actions contributed to the financial crisis as well as to the failure of their own firms, some of which had to be bailed out by the government.

The agency risk due to misalignment with *taxpayers* comes from the moral hazard of bank management believing that the government will not allow them to fail, but will instead bail them out, if large losses ensue from any of their excessive risk taking. This has also been eloquently referred to as the problem of "privatizing profits and socializing losses."

The presence of the agency risk causing misalignment with taxpayers encouraged banks to take on excessively high levels of risk. Banks felt even more emboldened by the fact that so many of their peers were taking the same high-risk bets, which made it even more likely that the government would need to step in, because if trouble ensued, it would cause major systemwide problems. This kind of thinking was confirmed and reinforced by government bailouts of many banks, particularly the largest ones. The Dodd-Frank legislation was intended to address this moral hazard by making future bailouts more difficult. However, many are skeptical, because the banking system is still just as vulnerable, if not more so, to another financial crisis, and when one occurs, the same political pressures for bailouts will reemerge, and a temporary emergency measure could easily be passed to empower another government bailout, notwithstanding the Dodd-Frank bill.

Process Risk   Banks have process risk in that the risk management program is not designed properly and therefore not performing as expected. This is the subject of much of this chapter, and will not be repeated here. However, there is one additional failure in the process design of bank risk management programs that is worth mentioning. See "Is It Gross or Net?"

IS **IT GROSS OR NET?**

As discussed in Chapter 3, during discussions of the ERM framework, it is important to measure, and internally report, risk exposures on both a gross (pre-mitigation) and net (post-mitigation) risk exposure basis. Most banks did not do this. Instead, they only calculated and reported these risks on a net risk exposure basis. They were issuing huge volumes of risky mortgage products that, even if some bank associates *were* aware of the excessive exposure, they didn't feel as worried, because they had what they believed to be effective mitigation, and the post-mitigation, or net, risk exposures looked acceptable to them. One example of this mitigation was the ability to offload the bulk of this risk to "suppliers" in the form of other banks or investors buying the bank CDOs comprised of these mortgages or mortgage packages. Another example of this mitigation was having a monoline insurer wrap the bank CDOs with their Triple-A rating.[3]

One of the reasons to calculate and internally report risk exposures on a *pre*-mitigation risk exposure basis is because mitigation does not always work as expected. In the context of our discussion, this is precisely what occurred in the financial crisis. Both examples of the mitigation disappeared. The bank was suddenly no longer able to offload the bulk of the risk to its suppliers, as the market dried up and these suppliers suffered huge losses. In addition, some banks had their monoline insurance company collapse, and the CDO rating immediately fell to the level of the monoline, which was downgraded.

Had these banks calculated, and internally reported, risk exposures on a pre-mitigation, or gross, risk exposure basis, the financial crisis might have been averted, or at least mitigated. Had the pre-mitigation risk exposures been reported up to executives and to the boards of directors, they would have seen a huge surge in exposures in this one area. Seeing the magnitude of the risk on the basis of "what if our mitigation disappears" might have triggered additional scrutiny and some caution that could have diminished, or even prevented, the financial crisis.

Errors   Banks have significant risk exposure to errors by financial analysts doing the modeling work to evaluate the risks inherent in bank products.[4] Bank management relies heavily on financial modelers. In fact, the banks did experience such risk events, which contributed to the financial crisis. We will discuss two examples. One was mispricing the default risk of CDOs.[5] Another was mispricing the insurance risk of CDSs.

Financial modelers significantly mispriced the default risk of CDOs by taking a disastrous shortcut. They did not do the hard work to develop individual risk scenarios from historical data, understand the structure of each CDO and how its underlying assets behave, quantify the CDO's default risk by the impacts on the future distributable cash flows of each CDO, and, further, measure the correlation between CDOs using the exposure data developed. Instead, they used a shortcut that involved a formula called a copula, which inferred the default risk of a CDO, and correlations between CDOs, from that implied by the historical market prices for the CDS on the CDO. In other words, because the CDS is an insurance contract on the risk that the CDO will default, the price changes reflect the level of default risk of a CDO, and the relationship between price changes reveals the correlations between CDOs. The market prices of CDSs on CDOs were available because CDSs were tradable securities.

This shortcut did not capture enough detail to make it appropriate for use. It assumed that correlations are constant, when in fact they are unstable. In addition, the historical data on CDSs, upon which the assumptions were based, was not appropriate for developing long-term assumptions. The historical data period was less than 10 years (because CDSs had not existed before that), which is too short. This only included a housing boom period, and certainly did not include a national downturn in housing prices, which occurs periodically. When the housing bubble burst and defaults exploded, banks relying on this inappropriate shortcut for their pricing of CDO default risk and correlation suffered huge losses.

Financial modelers also significantly mispriced the insurance risk of CDSs. Most insurance products must, by law, only be issued by insurance companies. There is a good reason for this. Insurance policies require a high level of security. They provide great social value in the form of extremely long-term guarantees upon which people rely for their future financial security. Insurance companies provide this security.[6] They are heavily regulated. In addition, insurance companies use actuaries to understand the complex insurance products, price the risks, set up appropriate reserves to pay future obligations (where the reserves have additional margins of safety for errors), set up appropriate levels of state-required capital (which provides another layer of protection), and set aside additional capital (yet another layer of protection).

However, CDSs are a type of insurance contract which can be issued by *non*-insurance companies, such as banks. The banks generally did not use actuaries as their financial modelers to understand and price the risks of CDSs, nor did banks set aside appropriate reserves or capital. This is part of what led to the excessive growth of CDSs and what made them appear so profitable (before they suffered enormous losses). The banks did not understand the risk exposures and they were essentially ignoring a large part of the cost of being in the insurance business: setting up reserves and capital. When these products suffered huge losses, the taxpayers picked up the tab for these ignored costs and more, through the government bailouts of these banks.

Criterion 3: Key Risk Focus

Most banks have risk management programs that are indeed properly focused on prioritizing risks and focusing on the most significant threats. They rank their risks and focus more efforts on the largest exposures for the enterprise as a whole.

Criterion 4: Integrated across Risk Types

Most banks do not use an integrated approach to risk management. Each department tends to manage risk separately from the other. In addition, they also measure risks one at a time, in silo form, and then attempt to use correlation adjustments to reflect risk interactions. As discussed in Chapter 5 (see "Capturing Interactions"), this fails to capture the bulk of the interactivity. As discussed in Chapter 2, silo risk management has several disadvantages, including incompleteness, inefficiency, and internal inconsistency. One of the disadvantages of incompleteness is most relevant for our topic: it omits multiple simultaneous risk events, which can lead to the largest losses. The financial crisis was such an event: There were multiple risk events occurring together, including an increase in interest rates and an ending of the investment supply–demand imbalance which removed excess foreign capital, both of which exacerbated the separate impacts of either event, in terms of their impact on housing prices, due to the triggering of the financial crisis and its downward spiraling events. In addition, as discussed earlier, there were non-financial risks that also contributed to the financial crisis.

Criterion 5: Aggregated Metrics

Banks generally do not have either of the two aggregated ERM metrics. They cannot calculate a proper enterprise risk exposure, because they do not have a single metric that can fully quantify all risks. Most banks measure the impact of risk only on the current balance sheet—in terms of change in capital or required capital—rather than on company value. As a result, businesses within the organization that do not have capital requirements cannot be so measured. In addition, strategic and operational risks cannot be fully quantified using capital-based metrics, because the majority of their impact comes from changes to future revenues and expenses.

In addition, most banks cannot clearly define their risk appetite. This is the second of the three core challenges to ERM identified in Chapter 3. This is directly related to their inability to calculate enterprise risk exposure, because it is the basis for defining risk appetite. In addition, the lack of a clear, quantitative definition of risk appetite means that these banks also do not have a top-down allocation of risk appetite to risk limits.

Because most banks do not have an aggregated enterprise-level understanding of what their risk exposure is, or what it should be, it is easier to understand why they fail so frequently, and how they were able to create such a high level of exposure that led to the financial crisis.

Criterion 6: Includes Decision Making

Most banks do not effectively integrate their risk information into decision making. This is the last of the three core challenges to ERM identified in Chapter 3. They do use risk information for mitigation decisions, but their approach is lacking. We will discuss each of the three critical elements that must be in place for effectively integrating ERM into decision making:

1. ERM metrics that support decision making
2. Practical ERM models
3. Consensus buy-in from business segments

First, the metrics most banks use do not support all decision making, because they only have robust risk quantification methods for financial risks (this was discussed earlier). In addition, the metrics that they use only provide the risk (capital) side of the equation and not the return (value) side, both of which are needed to support effective decision making.

Second, the risk models are not practical. Although the models generally have reasonably fast run times, they tend to be lacking in reliability, they use an inappropriately high number of significant digits, and they are particularly poor in terms of transparency.

Most banks do have buy-in from the business segments, but they have the reverse problem: *Too much* buy-in regarding the risk models. In the context of our discussion, this is one of the factors that contributed to the financial crisis. Most banks failed to scrutinize risk-modeling assumptions or question their validity with enough skepticism.

Criterion 7: Balances Risk and Return Management

Most banks do use risk information for both upside and downside opportunities. However, they do not do this optimally, because they only measure risk in terms of its impact on the current balance sheet, rather than on company value. Without fully integrating risk and return information, banks will continue to make suboptimal business decisions.

Criterion 8: Appropriate Risk Disclosures

Most banks do not appear to have risk disclosures that adequately incorporate the appropriate information from their risk management programs. Neither the voluntary nor the mandatory risk disclosures seem to include the information recommended in Chapter 7. As one important example, most banks do not appear to prioritize their key risks, in terms of their potential impact on company value, which would match shareholder priorities. In the context of our discussion, some banks were unable to properly disclose the financial impact of the crisis until multiple quarters *after* it took hold.

Criterion 9: Measures Value Impacts

Once again, most banks do not measure risk on the basis of its potential impact on company value. Instead, they measure it in terms of impacts to the current balance sheet capital or required capital.

Criterion 10: Primary Stakeholder Focus

Most bank risk management programs cannot support a primary focus on the shareholders because they don't use company value as the risk metric. In addition, the use of the capital-based risk metric is indicative of their focus on goals related to secondary stakeholders: maintenance of a satisfactory rating (rating agency focus) and maintaining adequate mandatory capital levels (bank regulators).

Conclusion: Bank ERM Scorecard

Table 9.1 summarizes the results of benchmarking bank risk management practices against the 10 key ERM criteria. The results clearly indicate that most banks were not actually employing ERM practices. As some of the examples in our discussion point out, the failure to follow ERM practices contributed to the financial crisis, and if banks had followed ERM practices it might have prevented the financial crisis. (Caveats: The scorecard reflects the risk management practices at *most* banks. Only a Pass/Fail score is used.)

TABLE 9.1 Bank Scorecard on ERM: Results of Benchmarking against 10 Key ERM Criteria

Criterion	Score	Main Reason(s) for Failure
1. Enterprise-wide scope	Fail	▪ "Golden boy" units lacked sufficient scrutiny
2. All risk categories included	Fail	▪ Inability to quantify strategic and operational risks ▪ Financial analyst bias ▪ Failing to address critical human resources risks, such as agency risk, process risk, and errors
3. Key risk focus	Pass	
4. Integrated across risk types	Fail	▪ Only use correlation adjustments, which do not capture all interactions
5. Aggregated metrics	Fail	▪ Do not calculate enterprise risk exposure ▪ Do not clearly define risk appetite
6. Includes decision making	Fail	▪ Risk metrics do not support decision making ▪ Risk models are not practical, particularly in their lack of transparency ▪ Not enough scrutiny of risk modeling assumptions
7. Balances risk and return management	Fail	▪ Capital-based metrics do not provide both risk and return information
8. Appropriate risk disclosures	Fail	▪ Lack of robust ERM information embedded in mandatory and voluntary risk disclosures
9. Measures value impacts	Fail	▪ Lack of company value metric
10. Primary stakeholder focus	Fail	▪ Risk management program focus is on rating agencies and regulators

SUMMARY

In this chapter, we responded to the aspersions cast on ERM by the fact that banks were the primary cause of the global financial crisis and the fallacy that banks were actually following ERM practices. We revealed that, contrary to popular claims, banks generally did not follow ERM practices, in that they fail to meet nine of the 10 key ERM criteria. In addition, we clear up another popular misconception, which is that the financial crisis was caused exclusively by financial sources of risks. We discussed three examples of non-financial risks at banks that helped cause the financial crisis:

1. Agency risk: The interests of bank management are often misaligned with the interests of shareholders and taxpayers.
2. Process risk: Most bank risk management practices are flawed, as evidenced by their failing to satisfy nine of the 10 key ERM criteria. In addition, most banks were not calculating and reporting risk exposures on a pre-mitigation, or gross, basis. Had this been done, the financial crisis might have been averted, or at least mitigated.
3. Errors: Many bank financial modelers significantly mispriced the default risk of CDOs and the insurance risk of CDSs.

Worrisome is the fact that society is still fully exposed to the first two of these risks, as well as to the broader category of the third risk. As a result, the global financial system remains vulnerable to the next financial crisis.

In the next and final chapter of this book, we move on to a more upbeat topic: a look at how to apply ERM to non-corporate entities, such as non-profit organizations, government bodies, and individuals.

 ## NOTES

1. In this chapter, we will generically define *banks* as any financial entity which is not an insurance company. This is imprecise, but sufficient for the context of our discussion.
2. In addition to banks and homeowners, there are many others that have received blame, including regulators, legislators, quasi-governmental agencies, monoline insurers, rating agencies, and others. In our discussion, we are only focusing on the prime culprits.
3. The monoline insurer is standing behind the CDO with their guarantee, based on their own triple-A rating.
4. This is different from process risk, discussed earlier; a perfect process can still be thwarted by individual errors.
5. This portion of the discussion references a *Wired* magazine article titled "Recipe for Disaster: The Formula That Killed Wall Street," written by Felix Salmon, dated February 23, 2009.
6. Historically, insurance companies are far less likely to fail than banks. The notable failure of AIG during the financial crisis was caused by their Financial Products division, which was not part of AIG's insurance entities.

CHAPTER TEN

ERM for Non-Corporate Entities

Only those who dare to fail greatly can ever achieve greatly.

Robert F. Kennedy

U P TO THIS point, we have discussed ERM in the context of applying it to corporate entities that operate for profit. In this chapter, we will discuss how to apply ERM to other entities. For convenience, we will refer to for-profit companies as corporate entities and all other entities as non-corporate entities, or NCEs. We will discuss how to apply ERM to such NCEs as non-profit organizations, government bodies, and individuals. To do this, we must first generalize the value-based ERM approach discussed throughout this book.

GENERALIZING THE VALUE-BASED ERM APPROACH

The value-based ERM approach can be generalized and applied to any entity. We will discuss five aspects of generalizing the value-based ERM approach:

1. Terminology
2. Objectives
3. Key metrics
4. Risk categorization
5. Framework

Terminology

We will generalize the term *value-based ERM* in two ways. First, we will change *enterprise* risk management to *entity* risk management.[1] Second, we will change *value*-based to *objectives*-based. Value-based implies a primary objective of increasing company value, which is appropriate for corporate entities, but non-corporate entities (NCEs) usually have other objectives. With this generalized terminology, value-based enterprise risk management becomes a special case of objectives-based entity risk management.

Objectives

With corporate entities, there is a single objective: increasing value. However, NCEs often have multiple objectives. There are two steps to clearly defining objectives for NCEs:

1. Identifying stakeholders
2. Defining objectives for each stakeholder

Identifying Stakeholders

Corporate entities have a single primary stakeholder: the shareholder. However, NCEs often have multiple stakeholders that must be equally served. For example, a charitable organization may have a mission to provide assistance to poor children and to poor elderly people.

Defining Objectives for Each Stakeholder

Corporate entities have a single objective for their primary stakeholder: increase value. However, NCEs often have more than one objective for each stakeholder. Each distinct objective must be separately defined for each stakeholder. Continuing our earlier example, a charitable organization that serves both poor children and poor elderly people may have two objectives for each of these stakeholders:

- Poor children:
    - Improve education (objective #1)
    - Improve health (objective #2)
- Poor elderly people:
    - Improve access to medication (objective #3)
    - Provide visiting nurse services (objective #4)

Key Metrics

With corporate entities, there is a single primary stakeholder—the shareholder—and a single objective for this primary stakeholder—increasing value—which leads to a single dominant key metric: company value. There are other key metrics, but company value is the primary metric. However, this is generally not the case for NCEs. The tendency of NCEs to have multiple stakeholders, and multiple objectives for each of these stakeholders, automatically results in multiple key metrics of equal or similar importance—even if there is only one key metric needed for each objective. However, there are three factors that drive the need for even more key metrics:

1. Multiple key metrics per objective
2. Time
3. Money

Multiple Key Metrics per Objective

Corporate entities only need a single dominant metric—company value—for their single objective of increasing value. This is possible because money is easy to measure. In contrast, NCEs—such as non-profit organizations, government bodies, and individuals—often require multiple metrics for each of their objectives. Rather than generating distributable cash flows for shareholders, like corporate entities, NCEs often have objectives related to serving other people. Measuring these services is more complex, and often requires multiple metrics.

Consider our earlier charitable organization example, which has two objectives related to services for poor children: improving education and improving health. For each objective, they use multiple key metrics to gauge their success. Each key metric, along with its projected result, is included in the baseline strategic plan projection.

The charitable organization in our example uses three such key metrics for the education objective:

1. Standardized test scores
2. Graduation rates
3. Percentage of high school graduates entering college

For the objective of improving health, the charitable organization also uses three key metrics:

1. Percentage of children with access to a pediatrician
2. Incidence rates of leading illnesses
3. Life expectancy

As with the value-based ERM approach, the objectives-based ERM approach quantifies risk in terms of its potential impact on baseline expectations. Therefore, these key metrics, whose results are in the baseline strategic plan projection, are also used as the ERM key metrics to measure the impact of risks.

Time

With the value-based ERM approach, time is not a complicating factor in measuring the impact of risks. The value of a dollar lost next year, or 10 years from now, is easily evaluated in terms of a dollar lost today, through the discounting of distributable cash flows using the discount rate. However, with the objectives-based ERM approach, time *is* a complicating factor that increases the number of required key metrics. Most of the key metrics are not monetary items, and cannot be discounted. NCEs often have strategic plans for expected improvements in a given key metric over the coming years. Some risks may impact a key metric in the near term, though other risks may impact the key metric further down the timeline. As a result, some key metrics need to be tracked for more than one point in time.

Continuing our example of the charitable organization, they may have a strategic goal to improve graduation rates by one percent next year and by five percent by year three. Some risks may impact the coming year's graduation rates—for example, a teacher's strike—though other risks may impact graduation rates in multiple future years—for example, a gradual erosion of the local tax base resulting in less funding for education.

Money

Money is virtually always a factor and an additional key metric for NCEs. However, NCEs tend to look at money from a different perspective than corporate entities, particularly regarding cash inflows and cash outflows.

An increase in cash *inflows* is generally viewed favorably, because more money translates into more services provided to stakeholders (i.e., more objectives achieved). However, this is not always the case, and depends on the source of the funds. Consider the federal government as the NCE. An increase in government revenues would be favorable, for example, if the source is an unexpected repayment of foreign debt. However, if the source is a tax increase, then this would generally be viewed unfavorably by taxpayers, who are a key stakeholder.

Similarly, the way in which an increase in cash *outflows* is viewed depends on its use. If the use of the increase is to pay expenses, such as an increase in vendor charges for services provided to the NCE, then this would be viewed unfavorably. However, if the use is for an increase in services provided to stakeholders, then this would be viewed favorably.

Rather than calculate company value, as do corporate entities, NCEs have different key metrics related to cash flows. These metrics often focus on the efficiencies of operating costs, the level of funding of initiatives, liquidity, and other key metrics which recognize the different attitudes toward cash flows and their sources and uses.

Risk Categorization

For NCEs, we will generalize the categorization of risks used in the risk categorization and definition (RCD) tool. Rather than limit the risk categories to strategic, operational, financial, and insurance, we will keep them open, like a blank slate, to include any categories of risk that may be relevant to the entity. It is not critical for risk nomenclature to conform to any standard, but it should be clearly defined, consistently used throughout the entity, and should match internal terminology. The value-based ERM risk categories (strategic, operational, financial, and insurance) may still wind up being the best choice for many NCEs as well, but not for all.

Framework

The generalization of the value-based ERM approach into an objectives-based ERM approach can be represented by changes to the value-based ERM framework, shown in Figure 3.1, resulting in the objectives-based ERM framework, shown in Figure 10.1, which depicts a more generic treatment of terminology, key metrics, and risk categorization.

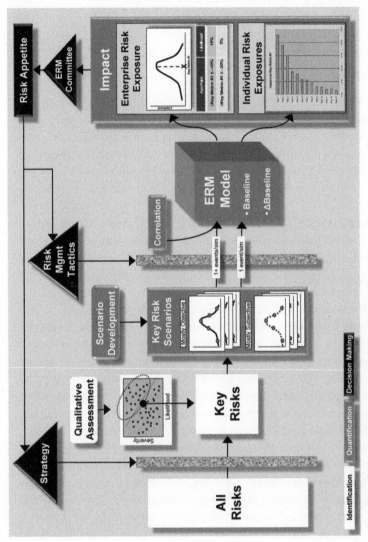

FIGURE 10.1 Objectives-Based ERM Framework

COMPLEXITIES OF OBJECTIVES-BASED ERM

There are two main characteristics of NCEs that result in adding complexity to the implementation of an objectives-based ERM program:

1. Multiple key metrics
2. Non-corporate culture

Multiple Key Metrics

In the value-based ERM approach for corporate entities, the presence of a single dominant metric was a key to elegantly performing several ERM activities. However, the objectives-based ERM approach for NCEs requires multiple key metrics. This adds complexity to the ERM process. There are five main ERM activities whose complexity is increased by the need for multiple key metrics:

1. **Selecting key risks.** The selection of key risks is more complex in an objectives-based ERM approach. It requires qualitative survey participants to score severity for each potential key risk on multiple bases. In addition, weights must be assigned, either implicitly or explicitly, to translate the multiple severity scores, one for each key metric, into a single severity ranking for each risk, to enable the selection of the key risks.

2. **Quantifying key risk scenarios.** Quantifying key risk scenarios is more complex as well. The value-based ERM model only has to project distributable cash flow items. Cash flow items are used to measure both the net *costs* of running the businesses and the *results* of the businesses. The objectives-based ERM model projects cash flow items to measure net costs, but to measure results, it instead must project values for several key metrics. In addition, weights must be assigned, either implicitly or explicitly, to translate the multiple quantified impacts, one for each key metric, into a single quantitative score for ranking each key risk scenario.

3. **Focusing mitigation efforts.** Focusing mitigation efforts also becomes more complicated. Quantifying the component drivers for a particular key risk scenario has the same complexity as quantifying key risk scenarios, and for the same reasons. The objectives-based ERM model is used to perform an attribution of the impact for each component driver, for each key metric, and then weights must be assigned, either implicitly or explicitly, to translate the multiple quantified impacts into a single attribution, to focus prioritization of mitigation efforts.

4. **Determining risk appetite and risk limits.** Aggregating metrics to the enterprise level by calculating the enterprise risk exposure is more complicated in an objectives-based ERM approach. Enterprise risk exposure must be calculated on the basis of multiple metrics, just as with the value-based approach. However, the number of key metrics is much larger. In addition, because there is no dominant metric to serve as arbiter for the competing multiple metrics, the definition of risk appetite must also be expressed in terms of a much larger array of key metrics. Analogously, this adds complexity to the risk limit setting process as well.

5. **Decision making.** Because risk and return are not both measured on the basis of a single consistent metric such as company value, decision making in the objectives-based ERM approach is more complex. This is true for both risk-priority and return-priority decisions. For example, if one risk-priority decision reduces risk exposure in terms of one key metric by a given amount, and another risk-priority decision reduces the risk exposure in terms of a different key metric by the same amount, are they equivalent? Once again, weights must be assigned, either implicitly or explicitly, to answer this question.

Non-Corporate Culture

An ERM program can be applied to any entity, as long as they can clearly define their strategic objectives. Risk is defined as a deviation from expected results as expressed in the baseline strategic plan projection. Most corporate entities have some form of strategic plan projection, including supporting detail by business segment, which is reproduced with each annual planning cycle. This is a critical starting point for a value-based ERM program.

However, NCEs do not have shareholders. Their stakeholders do not look at them as an investment. As a result, they do not have a corporate culture, and therefore they often have a less rigorous strategic planning process and resulting strategic plan projection. This complicates the objectives-based ERM approach, because without a clear vision of expected results, risk cannot be clearly defined. With NCEs, the development of a baseline strategic plan projection is more involved, because it requires additional work.

 ## EXAMPLES OF NCEs

The discussion in this chapter up to this point—generalizing the value-based ERM approach into an objectives-based ERM approach, and discussion of the added complexity this brings—along with Chapters 2 through 8, provide a foundation for understanding how to implement ERM for an NCE. In the remainder of this chapter, we will discuss some examples of NCEs, and share some additional thoughts on ERM as it relates to these entities. We will discuss the following three examples of NCEs:

1. Non-profit organizations
2. Government bodies
3. Individuals

Non-Profit Organizations

We will discuss two examples of non-profit organizations: charitable organizations and professional associations.

Charitable Organizations

A charitable organization is a typical example of a non-profit organization. Implementing an objectives-based ERM program for a charitable organization is fairly straightforward, using the objectives-based ERM framework (see Figure 10.1), which is largely analogous to the value-based ERM approach discussed throughout this book. However, we will discuss some of the unique aspects of setting up an objectives-based ERM approach, using a hypothetical charitable organization called HelpKids as an illustration.

We will discuss four of these unique aspects:

1. Objectives
2. Key metrics
3. ERM modeling
4. Key risks

Objectives There are two steps to defining objectives for an NCE:

1. **Identifying stakeholders.** To simplify our example, HelpKids has only one stakeholder: children living below the poverty level.
2. **Defining objectives for each stakeholder.** HelpKids has two major strategic objectives:
   1. Improve the education of children living below the poverty level
   2. Improve the health of children living below the poverty level

Key Metrics HelpKids selects 15 key metrics for their ERM program which are a subset of the metrics used in their strategic planning process (as well as in their business performance analysis) and which relate to their key objectives and supporting initiatives.

Seven key metrics are selected for their education program:

1. Number of children receiving HelpKids services
2. Truancy rates
3. Dropout rates
4. Standardized test scores
5. Graduation rates
6. Percentage of high school graduates entering college
7. Donations and grants received

Eight key metrics are selected for their health program:

1. Number of children receiving HelpKids services
2. Percentage of children with access to a pediatrician
3. Incidence rates of leading illnesses
4. Life expectancy
5. Mortality rates
6. Hours of weekly physical activity
7. Percentage of children with two or more daily nutritious meals
8. Donations and grants received

ERM Modeling   The objectives-based ERM model must project values for each of these key metrics into future years in a way that is consistent with the HelpKids baseline strategic plan. The model must include the value drivers behind each of these key metrics to capture how risks, or decisions, will shock the baseline values. The value drivers are those variables which HelpKids is likely working to improve. For example, if truancy levels are related to three shortcomings in the child's environment, then HelpKids may have initiatives, supporting the strategic objective of decreasing truancy, that address each of these shortcomings.

Key Risks   Once the key metrics are defined, as well as the ERM modeling methodology, the risks are identified as those events which will result in a deviation from the baseline projection of the key metrics. A list of risks will be populated into the risk categorization and definition (RCD) tool for use in the risk identification process to identify the key risks.

Some examples of key risks for HelpKids are as follows:

- Various risks related to damaging HelpKids' reputation, where the individual sources of risk include the following:
  - Misappropriation of charitable funds
  - Any form of mistreatment of children

- ▪ Perception of inefficient use of charitable funds (overpaid CEO, excessive proportion of budget spent on fundraising, etc.)
- ▪ Competition (for charitable donations and grants)
- ▪ Economic downturn (reduces charitable donations and grants)
- ▪ Inability to recruit and retain key employees
- ▪ Economic *upturn* (makes it more difficult to recruit and retain key employees, as opportunities elsewhere increase)
- ▪ Regulatory change
- ▪ Compliance risk
- ▪ Litigation

Professional Associations

Professional associations are a non-profit organization NCE, but they have two qualities that make them similar to corporate entities in an ERM context. First, they largely serve a single primary stakeholder—members—which indicates the possibility of a single dominant key metric. Second, because the primary stakeholders are similar to "owners" of the entity, a key metric can be constructed that is a value-based metric similar to the company value metric, based on distributable cash flows. We will introduce a hypothetical professional association, and discuss these two qualities.

A hypothetical professional association called the American Association of Advanced Financial Professionals, or AAAFP, has 100,000 members nationwide and one major strategic objective: to grow the value of the AAAFP credential. Its members are those who:

- ▪ Pass the one-day AAAFP certification test annually
- ▪ Attend 10 hours of AAAFP-provided continuing education annually
- ▪ Abide by the AAAFP code of professional conduct
- ▪ Pay AAAFP dues annually

Value-Based Metric The AAAFP, even though it is an NCE, has a quality that makes it similar to a corporate entity. The primary stakeholders, or the primary beneficiaries of the entity's activities, are the members themselves.[2] A corporate entity directly produces distributable cash flow for shareholders, in return for their capital investment, by running a business. The AAAFP *indirectly* generates *additional compensation* for its *members*, in return for their *dues and fees*, by *creating a valued credential* recognized by employers.

As a result, we can construct a metric analogous to company value for AAAFP: We will define *credential value* as the present value of projected *credential cash flows.* The credential cash flow measures the net cash flows into a member's pocket due to the credential: cash inflow from additional compensation from their employer, less cash outflow for dues and fees to AAAFP. The credential cash flows for a single member are calculated as follows:

$$CCF_{member} = Add'l\ Comp_{member} - Dues_{member} - Fees_{member}$$

Where:

- CCF_{member} = credential cash flow, per member
- $Add'l\ Comp_{member}$ = the (estimated) additional compensation earned, per member, by virtue of possessing the AAAFP credential
- $Dues_{member}$ = annual membership dues, per member
- $Fees_{member}$ = annual certification and continuing education fees, per member

The credential cash flows for the entire entity AAAFP can be calculated as follows:

$$CCF_{AAAFP} = \sum_{i=1}^{N} CCF_i$$

Where:

- CCF_{AAAFP} = credential cash flow for AAAFP
- CCF_i = credential cash flow, per member i
- N = total number of AAAFP members

The credential value for AAAFP is calculated by projecting CCF_{AAAFP} into future years, and taking the present value, using a discount rate:

$$Credential\ value = \sum_{j=1}^{M} (CCF_{AAAFP:Year\ j})\ x\frac{1}{(1+d)^j}$$

Where:

- $CCF_{AAAFP:Year\ j}$ = credential cash flow for AAAFP, in projection year j
- j = year of the projection
- M = total number of years in the projection
- d = the discount rate

Other key metrics can be developed as well. In addition to the total credential value for the organization, AAAFP can estimate the average credential value per member, the average credential value per member by subgroup, and other useful metrics.

Credential value is a value-based metric analogous to company value. It can provide some of the facility afforded by the value-based ERM approach for a corporate entity and avoid some of the additional complexities usually present in an objectives-based ERM program for an NCE, as discussed earlier.

However, the credential value metric is not exactly the same as the company value metric. The credential value metric has one major short-coming. The credential value metric equates losses in growth of numbers of members with losses in compensation, and these are not necessarily viewed equally by members. Consider the following example of two key risk events, along with their potential impacts on credential value:

1. Immediate and permanent 5 percent decrease in $Add'l\ Comp_{member}$ (the additional compensation earned, per member, by virtue of possessing the AAAFP credential), decreasing credential value by 5 percent
2. Recruiting produces fewer new members than expected over time, de-creasing credential value by 5 percent

The impacts of these two key risk events on credential value are identical. However, although shareholders are indifferent between two equivalent de-creases in company value, the same is not true for member attitudes toward all equivalent decreases in credential value. Members are likely to prefer the second key risk event—the loss, versus expectations, of some future new members—rather than the first key risk event—the immediate and permanent loss of some of their own compensation.

Single Dominant Key Metric The AAAFP appears to be similar to a corporate entity in that it seems to have a single primary stakeholder, which implies the possibility of a single dominant metric and all its corresponding advantages, as with the company value metric. Unfortunately, this is often not precisely the case. Professional associations often have sub-constituencies which must be identified and served individually. For example, it may be necessary to separate the AAAFP members into subgroups, because some key risks may impact one subgroup more than others. Some examples of necessary subgroups may include:

- Experience level (such as number of years in the industry)
- Geographical differences (such as different regions of the country)

- Industry sector (energy, manufacturing, banking, insurance, etc.)
- Practice area (accounting, financial projections, ERM, etc.)

In other words, once again, not all impacts on credential value are equivalent. Consider the following example of two key risk events, along with their potential impacts on credential value:

1. California passes a regulation resulting in the elimination of all 1,000 jobs in the state for AAAFP professionals, decreasing credential value by 1 percent
2. A federal regulation passes decreasing $Add'l\ Comp_{member}$ by 1 percent

The impacts of these two key risk events on credential value are identical. However, members are likely to prefer the second key risk event—the relatively palatable loss of 1 percent of the additional compensation earned from having the credential—rather than the first key risk event—the total loss of compensation (not just the loss of 100 percent of the additional portion attributable to the credential) of 1,000 of their AAAFP brothers and sisters.

Government Bodies

Government bodies, particularly at the federal level, present special challenges for ERM. They have a large number of stakeholders and strategic objectives, both of which are not only difficult to clearly define, but which also shift in relative importance, sometimes dramatically, based on fickle internal political winds and highly dynamic external factors. In addition, politics will often trump funding allocation recommendations based on need. The easiest governmental bodies at which to implement an ERM program are sub-entities, which often have clear, ongoing tasks with a fairly certain budget, and which can benefit from ERM's superior identification of risk–reward trade-offs to better prioritize efforts within the given budget.

The Need for ERM at the Federal Level

Despite the difficulty involved, it is worthwhile to consider applying ERM at the federal level. This is the level at which the largest opportunity for a positive impact exists. The primary role of the federal government is to protect people. Countries face a large number of threats from a wide variety of sources, yet the risks are usually managed in silos, by department, without much integration. Let's take the United States as an example.

After the September 11th attacks, the U.S. federal government recognized the need for a better approach to manage terrorist threats, including broader sharing of information for risk identification and better coordination of risk assessment, prioritization, and response. There were two major changes that led to improvement: consolidation of agencies and centralization of responsibility.

The first change was to consolidate some agencies under a new umbrella: the Department of Homeland Security (DHS). DHS contains several agencies related to securing the border (such as the Coast Guard, the Transportation Security Administration [TSA], and immigration-related agencies), Federal Emergency Management Agency (FEMA), and the Secret Service. This was not a complete consolidation, because the Federal Bureau of Investigation (FBI) and the Central Intelligence Agency (CIA) remained separate.

The second change was to centralize responsibility. The federal government established a central point for coordination and integration of all activities related to terrorist threats, creating the Office of the Director of National Intelligence (ODNI). The Director of National Intelligence (DNI) is the single point person responsible to coordinate and integrate the approach to defending against terrorist threats. According to the ODNI Web site, the DNI is "overseeing and directing the implementation of the National Intelligence Program and acting as the principal advisor to the President, the National Security Council, and the Homeland Security Council for intelligence matters related to the national security." In addition, " . . . the DNI's goal is to effectively integrate foreign, military, and domestic intelligence in defense of the homeland and of United States interests abroad."[3]

However, the federal government did not integrate the approach for managing risks from other sources. Table 10.1 shows a partial list of U.S. federal agencies along with an example of the risks for which they are responsible. This is a silo approach to risk management, whose disadvantages were enumerated in Chapter 2.

What is needed is not so much a consolidation of these federal agencies; rather, what is needed is leadership in coordinating and integrating these risk management efforts. Without a leader to implement an ERM program at the federal level, it is undoubtedly the case that resources are wasted on risks that should be lower priority, but, far more worrisome, that some of the largest threats are not receiving the priority they need. Whereas the DNI is intended to be such a coordinating leader for terrorism-related threats, what is needed is an equivalent leader for coverage over *all* sources of risk, such as a *Director of National Risk Management*, or DNRM. The DNRM would lead the implementation of an ERM approach at the federal level.

TABLE 10.1 Federal Agencies Responsible for Managing Risks (Partial List)

U.S. Federal Agency	Examples of Risk Source Managed
Army Corps of Engineers	Disasters
Board of Governors of the Federal Reserve System (the Fed)	Economic instability
Centers for Disease Control and Prevention (CDC)	Disease
Central Intelligence Agency (CIA)	Foreign threats
Department of Defense (DoD)	Military attacks
Environmental Protection Agency (EPA)	Damage to the environment
Federal Aviation Administration (FAA)	Airplane crashes
Federal Bureau of Investigation (FBI)	Organized crime
	Terrorism on U.S. soil
Food and Drug Administration (FDA)	Food poisoning
Department of Homeland Security (DHS)	Terrorist attack
National Highway Traffic Safety Administration (NHTSA)	Automobile accidents
Securities and Exchange Commission (SEC)	Defrauding investors

There is much to be gained, at the federal level, in using an ERM approach. Some of the more important benefits include the following:

- Clear identification of overlaps and gaps in the responsibilities for key threats, using a consistent approach to identifying risks by source
- Uniform approach to identifying all types of emerging risks
- Better prioritization: Identifying key risks through qualitative risk assessments and ranking their key risk scenarios by quantifying their potential impact on key metrics; see "Threats to the Financial Stability of the Country"
- More efficient allocation of limited resources by focusing mitigation on the most impactful component drivers of key risk scenarios, through quantitative attribution analysis
- Better decision making based on quantifying the relative impact of alternative options, using an objectives-based ERM model
- Simpler method of sharing risk information across all federal agencies, using a standardized terminology for risk

THREATS **TO THE FINANCIAL STABILITY OF THE COUNTRY**

O ne specific application of ERM that is worth highlighting further is the ability to rank key risk scenarios by quantifying their potential impact on key metrics. This can be used for an issue of vital importance to the U.S. economy. The Financial Stability Oversight Council, established by the Dodd-Frank bill passed in response to the global financial crisis that began in the United States in 2007, is charged with taking three actions related to large and complex financial institutions:

1. Establish regulatory authority over non-bank financial companies that "pose a risk to the financial stability of the U.S."
2. Put restrictions on financial companies that "pose risks to the financial system"
3. Break up financial companies that "pose a grave threat to the financial stability of the U.S."

The ability to rank key risk scenarios by quantifying their potential impact on key metrics can be used to identify and rank the entities that present these threats to the economy if they were to fail. Scenarios can be developed for the failure of firms that potentially represent this level of risk to the economy, and the impacts can be evaluated on a consistent basis and compared to identify the largest threats. In addition, an objectives-based ERM approach can also provide an ability to evaluate mitigation options to reduce the level of riskiness (e.g., the level to which firms may need to be broken up).

Implementing ERM at the Federal Level

We will begin the discussion on how to implement ERM at the federal government level to illustrate the different approach needed for government entities; however, we will not complete it. A comprehensive discussion on this topic would require its own book.

Imagine that the U.S. federal government establishes a new position of Director of National Risk Management (DNRM). Unlike the DNI, the DNRM's purview is over all sources of risk for the country. Now, imagine that the DNRM asks us to assist in establishing an ERM program at the federal level. How would we begin? How would we set the priorities?

We will recommend an objectives-based ERM approach. The following discussion is just a beginning on how to think through some of the unique aspects of implementing an objectives-based ERM program for the federal government. We will discuss three of these unique aspects:

1. Objectives
2. Key metrics
3. Decision making

Objectives   There are two steps to defining objectives for an NCE:

1. **Identifying stakeholders.** The federal government is an NCE with a single primary stakeholder: citizens. However, there are many other stakeholders, or entities that receive government services. One example is legal aliens residing in the country on their way to citizenship. Another example is visitors to the country.

   Two additional examples of noncitizen stakeholders relate to entities outside the United States. Each of these examples serves to illustrate the complex nature of government NCEs. One example is U.S. allies. The United States, as do all countries, provides assistance to its allies. Some of this assistance is provided in the indirect service of achieving objectives for U.S. citizens; for example, providing intelligence services in exchange for similar assistance in return, which protects U.S. citizens. However, other assistance is provided altruistically, where the government is acting more like a charitable organization, with little or no expected benefit to its citizens in return; for example, gifts to poverty-stricken nations.

   A second, though rare, example of stakeholders outside the country, is U.S. adversaries. When a major disaster strikes adversaries, the United States tends to offer assistance in the form of relief efforts; for example, the United States sent aid to Iran in response to a December 26, 2003, earthquake measuring 6.6 on the Richter scale.[4]

2. **Defining objectives for each stakeholder.** To simplify our discussion, we will only address the citizen stakeholder from here onward. Now we must define all of the federal government objectives related to serving the citizen stakeholder. The U.S. federal government has numerous such objectives. We will simplify the discussion by selecting only one objective: protecting the lives of citizens. This is the first of the three "unalienable rights" listed in the U.S. Declaration of Independence, as "life, liberty, and the pursuit of happiness."

Key Metrics   What should be the key metric, or metrics, for protecting the lives of citizens? Should it be the number of lives? For example, do we want to quantify key risks in terms of their potential impact on the number of lives lost? To see why this is not a sufficient metric, consider that two people are about to fall off of a cliff, and you can only reach out and save one of them. The number of lives lost in either case is one. However, one person is 90 years old and the other is 10 years old. Which one do you save? Most people would say the 10-year-old. Why? Because the child has many more future expected life-years to live. Now we have just moved beyond the "number of lives lost" metric, and into the realm of the "life-years lost" metric, which is better.

But is it that simple? Does the life-years lost metric capture all of society's values toward protecting life? Not exactly. Society does sometimes send its young women and men to fight and die to allow the rest of society to live in freedom.[5] Now, we have just moved beyond the life-years lost metric, and, adding a multiplier representing the quality of life, into the realm of the "quality-life-years lost" metric. Life by itself is not enough, because our societal values reveal that we put living in freedom above that, at times. There are many other factors that can be included in a quality-of-life multiplier.

But is it even *that* simple? Which of the following two threats would you rank as a higher priority, in terms of the quality-life-years lost metric, assuming that they are both equally likely to occur?

1. A terrorist attack that kills 10 people
2. A terrorist attack that makes 10,000 people ill, causing each of them to lose one-tenth of one year (0.1 years) off of their life expectancy

Let's assume there is no quality of life issue, and that our key metric is reduced to a life-years lost metric. Further, let's assume that each of the people involved at the time of the attack has 50 more expected life-years. Each threat has the following impact on the life-years lost metric:

1. 500 life-years lost (10 people × 50 years)
2. 1,000 life-years lost (10,000 people × 0.1 years)

By the numbers, the second threat is twice as large. But would this be a higher priority to you? Wouldn't 1,000 people each give up just a little over one month of their life expectancy to collectively help save 10 people's lives? Different people may answer differently, but there is not a clear answer. As a result, a more sophisticated metric may be warranted. Refinements needed may depend on the context in which the metric is used.

This illustrates the complexity involved in trying to measure something even as simple as the goal of protecting life. This is not an academic discussion. There are metrics in use by governments and other organizations that attempt to capture life-years, including a quality of life adjustment. For example, the World Health Organization (WHO) uses a years of life lost (YLL) metric analogous to our life-years lost metric. The WHO also uses a disability-adjusted life years (DALY) metric, which is a form of a quality-of-life adjustment to life years, related to our quality-life-years lost metric.[6] Another example is the United Nations' Human Development Index (HDI), which attempts to capture the level of well-being of a country's citizens. The HDI combines many factors, such as life expectancy and standard of living.[7]

Decision Making Assume now that we have mapped out the major federal government stakeholders, the objectives related to each stakeholder, and the key metrics for each of the objectives. Decision making at the federal government level is complex, and any one decision may negatively impact one or more key metrics while simultaneously positively impacting one or more other key metrics. One example is highway speed limits. We know with certainty that if we legislate and enforce lower speed limits on highways, it will save a significant number of lives. However, our choice to keep speed limits at their current level reflects our relative weights for competing key metrics, where one is "protecting lives" and let's say, for simplicity sake, that the other may be represented as "economic prosperity," because rapid transit by automobile is a contributor to economic growth.[8] However, these weights are assigned implicitly, not explicitly, and a more explicit treatment, which is facilitated by an ERM program, may lead to better decision making.

An example of a related project that has some of the integrated characteristics of an objectives-based ERM approach is a traffic model called the Balanced Transportation Analyzer, designed by traffic expert Charles Komanoff. The Komanoff traffic model is designed to help government entities make more-informed trade-off decisions between traffic fees and tolls and the resulting integrated economic impact on citizens. The model factors in the explicit impacts of new fees and tolls, as well as the implicit impact of congestion on productivity, and has a holistic scope, recognizing time of day, whether citizens live in the city or the suburbs, and even delays caused by passengers digging for change in their pockets before boarding a city bus.[9]

Individuals

Not only can ERM be applied to corporate entities and non-profit organizations, but, as we have just discussed, it can be applied at a higher level of abstraction—at the government (or country) level. However, ERM can also be applied at a *lower* level of abstraction—at the individual level.

The Need for ERM at the Individual Level

We each, as individuals, are prime candidates for the application of an objectives-based ERM approach. We face a variety of risks. We lack a holistic approach to identifying, prioritizing, and mitigating the risks particular to our individual situation. As a result, we make suboptimal decisions, based on a silo risk management approach, to allocate mitigation funds. This leads to a higher likelihood of failing to achieve our individual goals.

We face a variety of risks. A partial list of such risks includes the following:

■ Dying too soon
■ Living too long (outliving our assets)
■ Accidental injury (such as an automobile accident)
■ Medical illness
■ Disability
■ Unemployment
■ Disaster (such as a fire or flood that causes property damage)
■ Investment risk
■ Divorce
■ Litigation
■ Theft

There is no one place where we can get an objective qualitative ranking of all of the risks specific to our situation, to allow us to identify our key risks. It is rare to find an unbiased advisor who is qualified to help us identify and prioritize all the risks we personally face, for our particular situation. Some people use fee-based financial planners for this, but their expertise is usually limited to investment risk and they do not use ERM-like tools and techniques; see "Risk Appetite in Five Questions?"

Without a holistic view on the relative importance (or even existence) of each of the key risks we should be mitigating, we typically go to a variety of places for advice as well as mitigation, for one risk at a time. For example, we may go to an insurance salesperson to figure out how much life insurance

RISK **APPETITE IN FIVE QUESTIONS?**

An important part of an ERM process is the definition of risk appetite, or what some refer to as risk tolerance. For corporate entities, this involves inferring the will of the shareholders in terms of the level of risk they want the company to take. For individuals, this involves understanding their personal tolerance for failing to achieve their goals.

Financial planners typically attempt to capture an individual's risk appetite by having them answer about five questions, sometimes more. The questions usually relate to the individual's feelings about the desired investment time horizon, expected returns, and tolerance for volatility and losses. These answers are used to map the individual into one of usually five categories, sometimes more, ranging from *conservative* to *aggressive*, or something similar. The category is then mapped to a recommended allocation for investing assets among stocks, bonds, and cash investments.

This is a crude approach, for three main reasons:

1. **Incomplete sources of risk.** The financial planning approach only looks at sources of risk related to invested asset fluctuation. This ignores the vast majority of an individual's key risks, such as illness, early death, unemployment, divorce, and so on.

2. **Poor risk measure.** The financial planning approach expresses risk in terms of the volatility of invested assets. Instead, risk must be expressed in terms of a failure to achieve the individual's goals. For example, an individual is shown that a given portfolio allocation will result in only a 35 percent chance of meeting all of his or her goals.

3. **Incomplete portfolio.** The financial planning approach only addresses the individual's portfolio in terms of stocks, bonds, and cash investments. What is needed is a holistic look at the entire portfolio of holdings, including stocks, bonds, cash, life insurance, medical insurance, disability insurance, unemployment insurance, immediate annuities, deferred annuities, and so on. All of the financial instruments can be reduced to their basic cash flows, integrated into a single projection model, and evaluated in terms of how they mitigate key risk scenarios by dampening their cash flow impacts.

In contrast, an ERM approach resolves all of the shortcomings in the financial planning approach to determining risk appetite. The ERM approach includes all sources of risk, expresses risk in terms of the impact on the ability to achieve the individual's goals, and examines a complete portfolio of financial products.

to buy, we may get information from our employer on health insurance coverage options, we may go to an investment broker for advice on investment portfolio allocations (e.g., mix of stocks, bonds, and cash), and so forth.

This is a silo approach, which is suboptimal. We lack an objective recommendation on how to most effectively allocate our resources to mitigate the entire portfolio of risks that we personally face. As a result, we are not necessarily making the best risk–reward decisions regarding our lives. Even if each advisor was completely unbiased, a silo approach can result in over-mitigating risks that are relatively unimportant for our situation, while ignoring, or under-mitigating, some of our biggest threats.

We need a holistic approach—one that includes all potential sources or risk. We don't care *which* source of risk causes us to go bankrupt . . . we just don't want to go bankrupt. A holistic approach to understanding our risks can lead to a re-allocation of funds that makes us more likely to achieve our individual goals.

Implementing ERM at the Individual Level

We will discuss three aspects of applying an objectives-based ERM approach to individuals:

1. Objectives
2. Key metrics
3. ERM modeling

Objectives   There are two steps to defining objectives for an NCE:

1. Identifying stakeholders
2. Defining objectives for each stakeholder

Individuals serve multiple objectives, such as providing cash flows—to themselves, dependents, and charities—as well as intangible items. For our discussion, we will focus only on the objective of providing cash flows.

1. **Identifying stakeholders.** For simplicity, we will use an example of an individual with the following situation:
   - Married
   - Two children dependents
   - Two living parents, one from each spouse
   - Core value of donating money to charity each year

The stakeholders for individuals typically change over their lifetimes. Let's assume we are interested in an objectives-based ERM program whose time horizon is the length of the individual's lifetime, or that of the spouse's, whichever is longer. In this case, we must consider current stakeholders and likely future stakeholders. The current stakeholders include the individual, the spouse, their two children, and the charity to which they donate. Depending on the health and financial situation of the two living parents, as well as other factors, the parents may become stakeholders in the future. Each stakeholder has a different level of importance, and this will factor into trade-off decisions; for example, most individuals in this situation place the highest level of priority on their two children.

2. **Defining objectives for each stakeholder.** Each individual has different goals, and the objectives-based ERM approach must be customized to each person. However, we will use a simplified objective by assuming that this individual, jointly with his or her spouse, has only the following goals, in priority order:

   ■ Maintain their current standard of living
   ■ Fund their children's education costs through college
   ■ Fund long-term care costs for their parents
   ■ Fund their children's wedding costs
   ■ Donate to charity each year
   ■ No specific goal for leaving an inheritance, but wishing to leave no debt

   All of these goals can be summarized in a single objective of "having sufficient funding for these goals, with no debt remaining after the death of both the individual and his or her spouse."

Key Metrics In an objectives-based ERM approach for this individual, it may initially appear that we only need a yes/no indicator for whether or not the single objective is met over the entire projection period. For example, the impact of any individual risk scenario may be quantified in terms of whether there was a failure to meet the objective at any time over the projection period.

However, this is too simple for two reasons. The first reason is that not all failures are equal. For example, if one risk scenario results in the individual coming up one dollar short of funding the goals in the last year of the projection (i.e., leaving one dollar of debt to their heirs), this is not the same as massive debt resulting in bankruptcy in the 10th year of the projection.

Both the severity and the timing of any shortfall are meaningful factors and they must also be captured. The second reason a yes/no failure indicator is too simple is that an ERM metric should capture the upside as well. Those risk scenarios that succeed in meeting the goals must be differentiated by the size of their positive impacts.

There are a variety of ways to define key metrics to adequately quantify the risks for this individual. One example involves two key metrics. The first key metric measures the failures, capturing the severity of the shortfall and its timing. This key metric is the present value of the largest shortfall over the projection period. The second key metric measures the successes, capturing the magnitude of the upside. This key metric is the amount of the inheritance, or, the accumulated net worth, equal to assets less liabilities, upon the death of the remaining spouse. Although this individual did not have a *specific* goal for the size of an inheritance, more is assumed to be better, and this is a good way to capture the accumulated positive impacts of any risk scenario.

ERM Modeling   The objectives-based ERM model must include a baseline cash flow projection, supported by an income statement and balance sheet. The income must reflect all sources, such as salary, bonus, investment income, and so on, expected from both spouses. The expenses must reflect all expected expenses, such as mortgage payments, food, insurance for current dependents, and so on, as well as the funds needed to meet each of the individual goals in the objective, such as vacations, entertainment, payments to the college fund, and so on. The balance sheet must reflect all invested assets, such as stocks, bonds, cash, insurance policy cash surrender values, home equity, and so on, as well as liabilities, such as mortgage and other outstanding loans.

The ERM model must also reflect the entire current portfolio of products—both investment (stocks, bonds, and cash) and insurance (life, health, annuities, etc.)—in terms of how they act as mitigation, protecting the baseline projected cash flows from a variety of risks. In addition, the ERM model must be able to incorporate additional purchases (or sales) of these products, in support of decision making. This provides a powerful ability to the individual: to find the best allocation of limited funds, across all types of financial products, that will best protect the individual against all of their specific key risks, over a lifetime, giving the individual the best chance of achieving his or her goals.

SUMMARY

We can generalize the value-based enterprise risk management approach for corporate entities into an *objectives*-based *entity* risk management approach for all types of non-corporate entities (NCEs). NCEs present additional challenges for ERM, mostly due to the absence of a single dominant metric, but the payoffs are worthwhile. An objectives-based ERM program can help NCEs do more with less, and increase the likelihood of achieving their multiple objectives. For professional association non-profits supplying credentials to their members, an objectives-based ERM approach has the added advantage of being able to calculate *credential value*, the dollar value of the credential to each member and to the association as a whole. There is much to gain by applying ERM to federal governments, because they are large, silo-based, and impact the health, welfare, and security of all their citizens. Finally, individuals like me and you need ERM as well. We have a wide variety of risks facing us and no single place to go to for advice, whether to identify our biggest threats, to measure them, or to mitigate them. An objectives-based ERM approach can help individuals like us achieve an integrated view for diversifying across investment, insurance, and other financial products, in a manner tailored to our personal goals, the risks we face, and our tolerance for risk.

CONCLUSION

This concludes our discussions of ERM . . . at least for now. I hope you found this enjoyable as well as useful. Thank you for your time and attention.

I would be pleased to continue our discussion anytime. Please feel free to do any or all of the following:

- E-mail me directly: sim@simergy.com
- Visit my Web page with additional resources related to this book: www.simergy.com/ermbookresources
- Visit my Web site with additional resources related to ERM: www.simergy.com

NOTES

1. We will use ERM as an acronym for both enterprise risk management and entity risk management.

2. Technically, future members are also stakeholders, because the goal is to grow the value of the credential, and part of that is growth in membership; however, they are secondary to current members. In addition, the general public is also a stakeholder, but serving the general public is understood, and is also secondary to, and subsumed in, the goals of the members, because (a) the AAAFP entity would not exist without the members, and (b) if the public interest is violated, this will damage the credential and thereby the members.
3. Although national security is a much broader responsibility than terrorist threats, it is the latter that was the primary reason for establishing a DNI role.
4. "Assistance for Iranian Earthquake Victims." Available at www.usaid.gov/iran/
5. This relates to the second of the unalienable rights mentioned earlier: liberty.
6. "Distribution of years of life lost by broader causes (percentage of total)." Available at www.who.int/whosis/indicators/compendium/2008/1llr/en/index.html
7. UN Human Development Index - Definition. Available at www.wordiq.com/definition/UN_Human_Development_Index
8. This relates to the third of the unalienable rights mentioned earlier: pursuit of happiness.
9. Felix Salmon, "The Man Who Could Unsnarl Manhattan Traffic," *Wired*, May 24, 2010.

Glossary

10 Key ERM Criteria Ten critical characteristics that define an ERM program, and which can be used as a benchmark to evaluate the robustness of any ERM program.

Agency risk A misalignment of interests between management and the primary stakeholders.

Aggregated metrics Two ERM metrics at the enterprise level: enterprise risk exposure and risk appetite.

Balanced scorecards A tool for performance measurement and management that includes financial goals and non-financial goals.

Basel Accords Guidelines developed by a group of global banking regulators in an attempt to improve risk management practices. Basel II, an international guideline for risk management, influenced the advancement of ERM practices in the financial services sector.

Baseline company value Management's calculation of company value based on distributable cash flow projections consistent with the strategic plan baseline financial projection. This is management's estimate of shareholder value, contrasted with market capitalization, which is the market's estimate of shareholder value. The baseline company value is the value investors would pay today, if they believed that management will be able to perfectly execute the strategic plan and that everything will go the way the company expects. This is the baseline from which any deviation constitutes a risk in the value-based ERM approach.

Baseline risk scenario The risk scenario which is neither upside nor downside but where the risk event occurs precisely as expected in the baseline strategic plan financial projection. Technically, this is not a risk, but it is tracked as one for ERM modeling purposes.

Basis points An expression of percentages in unit terms, where 1.00 percent is expressed as 100 basis points.

C-Suite   Chief executives, such as chief executive officer (CEO), chief financial officer (CFO), and chief risk officer (CRO).

CAGR   See **Compound annual growth rate**.

Capital requirements   Requirements by external stakeholders, such as regulators or rating agencies, to hold a certain amount of capital as a buffer against existing liabilities.

Cash flow   The cash generated by the business.

CDO   See **Collateralized debt obligation**.

CDS   See **Credit default swap**.

Chief risk officer (CRO)   Head of the ERM team, an executive who champions the ERM program development, maintenance, and enhancement.

Collateralized debt obligation (CDO)   A bond with payments based on cash flows from a package of mortgage products, such as mortgage-backed securities (MBSs) and collateralized mortgage obligations (CMOs), with different levels of risk, called tranches, based on how the cash flows will be divided up.

Company value   An internal valuation, performed by management, which calculates the value of the company from the perspective of the shareholders as the present value of distributable cash flows. See **Baseline company value**.

Technically, company value also includes distributable equity capital at time zero, which is calculated differently for different types of companies. For non-financial services companies, it is adjusted shareholder equity. For financial services companies, it is available capital (adjusted shareholder equity minus required capital). To simplify our discussions and illustrations in this book, we omit this.

Competitor risk   Unexpected change in competitive landscape, such as new entrants, aggressive competitor actions against the company, and price wars.

Compliance risk   Level of compliance not matching expectations, such as financial reports are not as accurate as expected.

Component risk driver   One of the driving factors in the financial impact of a risk scenario, and whose marginal impact is quantified with an attribution calculation, which is used to focus mitigation efforts.

Compound annual growth rate (CAGR)   The growth over a period of years reduced to an annualized rate.

Concentration risk Definition 1: A misnomer, because this is not a source of risk. Concentration risk refers to a high level of risk exposure from one particular risk source or group of sources.
Definition 2: A concentration of power, such as in the form of a rainmaker, a mastermind, a critical supplier, a large customer, or a large distributor.

Conduct risk Unexpected conduct by management, staff, board member, or other person identified with the company. Some examples include unseemly public behavior, criminal conduct, and fraud.

Corporate ERM See **ERM team**.

Correlation See **Risk correlation**.

COSO An internal control framework, developed in the early 1990s, intended as a process to help achieve effectiveness and efficiency of operations, reliability of financial reporting, and compliance.

Cost of capital The cost of company funds, including equity from shareholders and debt from bondholders.

Cost of equity capital The required returns from shareholders for their investment.

Credential cash flow (CCF) The net cash flows into a professional association member's pocket due to the credential, such as cash inflow from additional compensation, less cash outflow for dues and fees.

Credential value The collective value of a professional association's credential, calculated as the present value of projected credential cash flows (CCFs) for all members.

Credible worst-case scenario A scenario whose likelihood of occurrence is remote, but not out of the realm of possibility, and where the severity of impact would be significant. This is used in the qualitative risk assessment scoring and in the risk scenario development FMEA interviews.

Credit default swap (CDS) Insurance against the failure of a given entity, with regular premium payments made *to* the issuer and a large payment made *by* the issuer if the entity fails.

Credit risk Unexpected changes in credit markets (availability), prices (credit spreads), or creditworthiness of issuers, related to (a) general credit market movements (although the source for this is often economic risk) or (b) a specific issuer of a fixed income security on the company's balance sheet or (c) a counterparty to whom the company has extended credit.

CRO See **Chief risk officer**.

Deterministic risk scenarios　Individual risk scenarios, selected using human judgment, and which remain static with each run of the ERM model.

Director of National Intelligence　In the United States, the single point person responsible to coordinate and integrate the approach to defending against terrorist threats.

Disaster risk　Unexpected natural or man-made disasters, such as weather-related (for example, hurricane, flood, tornado, earthquake, and drought), health-related (such as pandemic), accidental (such as fire), general acts of destruction (such as war, terrorism, and rioting), and specific acts of destruction against the company (such as product tampering, attack on employees, and sabotage). This also includes unexpected man-made disasters caused by company employees or agents, such as environment damage.

Discount rate　The interest rate used to discount cash flows in a present value calculation. The appropriate discount rate depends on the perspective of the entity valuing the cash flows. For example, a discount rate equal to the cost of equity capital is used in a company value calculation involving the present value of distributable cash flows to shareholders.

Dispersion analysis　An analysis performed on both the likelihood and severity scores in the qualitative risk assessment to identify any scores for which there is not a clear initial consensus.

Distributable cash flow　Cash flow available to be distributed to shareholders, generally calculated as net income, plus depreciation and amortization, minus increase in working capital, minus capital expenditures. For financial services companies, it is calculated as net income, plus depreciation and amortization, minus increase in working capital, minus capital expenditures, minus increase in required capital. Technically, distributable cash flow also includes changes in the level of debt, which includes repayment of principal to bondholders as well as issuance of new debt; to simplify our discussions and illustrations in this book, we omit this.

Distribution　A range of potential outcomes and their likelihood. An example is enterprise risk exposure in graph form, where the vertical axis is likelihood of occurrence and the horizontal axis is severity of outcome.

DNI　See **Director of National Intelligence**.

Dodd-Frank legislation　U.S. legislation, effective July 2010, formally named the Dodd-Frank Wall Street Reform and Consumer Protection

Act, commonly named for its sponsors in the Senate and House of Representatives, and intended as a response to the global financial crisis.

Downside risk event   The occurrence of a risk scenario where results are below expected, or baseline projections.

Downside risk scenario   A risk scenario where results are below expected, or baseline projections.

Downside standard deviation (DSD)   A measure of dispersion below baseline expectation, downside standard deviation, or $\sigma_{downside}$, is calculated as $\sqrt{\dfrac{1}{m}\sum_{y=1}^{m}(y-\bar{\bar{x}})^2}$, where m is the number of data points in the distribution that correspond to a result below baseline expectations, y is a single data point that corresponds to a result below baseline expectations, and $\bar{\bar{x}}$ is the baseline expectation.

Downside volatility   A general reference to the level of downside risk, or the range of likelihoods corresponding to results being below baseline projections.

Economic capital (EC)   A measurement, commonly used in the insurance sector, of the amount of capital needed on hand today to limit the probability of ruin, over a given time horizon, to within a given small predefined likelihood.

Economic risk   Unexpected changes in the economy. This is often the source of risk that triggers multiple simultaneous unexpected changes in other items, such as consumer disposable income (impacting demand for the company's products or services), employment markets (impacting the company's fixed expenses), inflation/deflation (impacting the company's variable costs), items related to market risk, and items related to credit risk.

Embedded value (EV)   At an insurance company, embedded value is the portion of the insurer's value attributable solely to the "inforce" business, which is a run-out of the insurance policies already on the books, and excludes new business expected to be sold in the future.

Emerging risk identification   The third component of the risk identification ERM process step, this is a process to (a) monitor known non-key risks for any changes that might increase their ranking enough to become key risks; and (b) to scan the environment for unknown risks.

Enterprise risk exposure   A calculation that reflects the current aggregate enterprise-level risk exposure, in the form of a distribution representing the full range of possible combinations of individual risk scenarios. The graph form depicts the entire distribution. The table form expresses select "pain points" in terms of their likelihood of occurrence and severity of impact.

Enterprise risk management (ERM)   Definition 1: The process by which companies identify, measure, manage, and disclose all key risks to increase value to stakeholders.
Definition 2: A business process that satisfies the 10 key ERM criteria.
See **Value-based enterprise risk management** and **Entity risk management**.

Entity risk management (ERM)   A generalized version of enterprise risk management used for non-corporate entities (NCEs) such as non-profit organizations, government bodies, and individuals. See **Objectives-based entity risk management** and **Enterprise risk management**.

ERM   See **Enterprise risk management** or **Entity risk management**.

ERM committee   An executive-level committee, often chaired by either the CEO or the CRO, which has a primary role of defining risk appetite and risk limits and managing enterprise risk exposure to within these tolerance limits.

ERM framework   The functional structure of ERM, describing what activities take place, in what order they take place, and how they interact.

ERM model   A financial model, which, in a value-based ERM approach, is in the form of a spreadsheet-based tool that calculates the baseline company value, as well as changes in the baseline company value resulting from one or more individual key risk scenarios occurring at a time.

ERM process cycle   The continuous, evolving, and integrated process cycle involving four ERM process steps, including risk identification, risk quantification, risk decision making, and risk messaging.

ERM program summary document   A document that contains a summary and description of ERM program origins, the ERM framework, the risk governance structure, and supporting exhibits, such as the RCD tool.

ERM team   The chief risk officer (CRO), or equivalent head of the ERM program, and supporting team members.

ERO   See **Executive risk owner**.

Execution risk   Strategy is not implemented as expected. This is highly variable by company and must be customized.

Executive risk owner (ERO)   An executive formally designated by the CRO to be the point person for coordinating efforts across the enterprise with regard to one particular risk.

External fraud risk   Unexpected change in the amount of fraud by external parties.

External relations risk   Unexpected changes in the company's relationship with external stakeholders with public voices, such as the media, consumer advocates, equity analysts, rating agencies, regulators, and politicians.

Failure modes and effects analysis (FMEA)   A technique adapted from the manufacturing sector used to develop risk scenarios in the risk quantification ERM process step by interviewing subject matter experts.

Financial analyst   In this book, this is defined as those financial personnel building, maintaining, and enhancing the risk models or ERM model. They are also referred to herein as *financial modelers* or *modelers*.

Financial crisis   The global financial crisis that began in the United States in 2007 when subprime mortgages began to default in large numbers.

Financial modeler   See **Financial analyst**.

Financial risk   A category of risks related to unexpected changes in external markets, prices, rates, and liquidity supply and demand. Examples include market risk, credit risk, and liquidity risk.

FMEA   See **Failure modes and effects analysis**.

Golden boy unit   A business unit that is able to avoid internal scrutiny, such as risk governance, because they have been generating large revenue growth and/or profits.

Governance, risk, and compliance (GRC)   A repackaging by audit firms of three service offerings: corporate governance; an expanded version of SOX activities (erroneously relabeled as ERM); and compliance.

Governance risk   Governance is not functioning as expected.

GRC   See **Governance, risk, and compliance**.

Gross risk exposure   The amount of exposure before mitigation is taken into account. This is also called inherent risk or pre-mitigation risk exposure.

Hard limits   Part of the risk appetite and risk limit definition, hard limits are the maximum limits which risk exposures should rarely, if ever, exceed.

Heat map   A type of risk status report, often used for senior management or the board of directors, which involves a simple chart listing key risks and scoring them at a high level, usually with color coding (such as red, yellow, and green).

Hedge A position that offsets an existing risk exposure. This is a common form of risk mitigation.

Human resources risk Human resources (i.e., people) are not performing as expected, such as unexpected changes in talent management, performance, productivity, and conduct.

I/T risk See **Technology risk**.

Individual risk exposures The potential financial impacts on key metrics, and the corresponding likelihood, related to individual risk scenarios occurring one at a time.

Industry practices risk Widespread abusive practices unexpectedly discovered in the company's industry sector.

Inherent risk exposure See **Gross risk exposure**.

Insurance risk A category of risks involving poor performance of the pricing, underwriting, reserving, or setting of required capital for insurance products.

International risk Unexpected changes in the business environment of foreign countries in which the company operates, such as unexpected changes in the government's stability, attitude towards foreign companies, and tariffs.

Key metrics The metrics used to quantify the impact of risk events.

Key risk committee A committee formed by the key risk executive risk owner (ERO) and his or her subject matter experts (SMEs) to help them perform their ERM roles and responsibilities, and to share information more effectively within committees, between committees, and upstream to the CRO and the ERM committee.

Key risk indicator (KRI) A leading indicator which is highly correlated with a risk's exposure metric, and serves as an advance warning to management about a likely impending change in the level of exposure.

Key risks The approximately 20 to 30 risks representing the most significant threats to the organization, initially based on the qualitative risk assessment, and later replaced by the quantification of key risk scenarios, in terms of their potential impact on key metrics.

KRI See **Key risk indicator**.

Legislative/regulatory risk   Unexpected changes in laws or regulations.

Likelihood of occurrence   The probability, or chances, that a risk event involving one or more individual risk scenarios will occur.

Liquidity risk   Unexpected changes in liquidity supply or demand, related to three different levels of impact on the company: (a) untimely asset sales; (b) inability to meet contractual demands; or (c) default. A change in liquidity supply involves an unexpected change in the ability to sell assets as expected in the market, in terms of price, volume, or timeliness. A change in liquidity demand involves an unexpected change in demand for liquidity by option-holders, such as bondholders exercising early put options or "run-on-the-bank" situations for financial services companies, where account-holders suddenly request the withdrawal of funds from their accounts, en masse.

Litigation risk   Unexpected civil suits or judgments against the company.

Mandatory risk disclosures   Public risk disclosures required by law or regulation.

Market capitalization   The market's estimate of shareholder value, calculated as the stock price multiplied by the number of outstanding shares.

Market risk   Unexpected changes in external markets (such as stock markets), prices (such as commodity prices), or rates (such as interest rates), related to (a) general market movements (although the source for this is often economic risk) or (b) a specific asset on the company's balance sheet. Some examples include equity market risk, interest rate risk, and currency risk.

Mitigation   See **Risk mitigation**.

Mitigation in place   Mitigation already present in the organization, such as the compliance department or insurance coverage.

Modeler   See **Financial analyst**.

NCEs   See **Non-corporate entities**.

Net risk exposure   The amount of exposure after mitigation is taken into account. This is also called residual risk or post-mitigation risk exposure.

Non-corporate entities (NCEs)   Entities other than corporations, such as non-profit organizations, government bodies, and individuals.

Objectives-based entity risk management   A generalized version of value-based enterprise risk management used for non-corporate entities

(NCEs), such as non-profit organizations, government bodies, and individuals. See **Value-based enterprise risk management**.

Operational risk   A category of risks related to unexpected changes in elements related to operations, such as human resources, technology, processes, and disasters.

Pain points   Risk tolerance thresholds, for which management wants the likelihood of crossing them to be quite small, used to convert the graph form of enterprise risk exposure into the table form, and to define risk appetite.

Performance risk   Management or staff not performing their function as expected, such as related to research and development or the finance department activities (including accuracy of financial reporting).

Phantom stock   An internal calculation of the company's stock price based on a calculation of company value.

Post-mitigation risk exposure   See **Net risk exposure**.

Pre-mitigation risk exposure   See **Gross risk exposure**.

Present value   A calculation that reduces a series of future cash flows to a single equivalent value at the present time, adjusting for the time value of money.

Probability   The chances, or odds, of something occurring. See **Likelihood of occurrence**.

Process risk   Company processes not functioning as expected.

Productivity risk   Management, staff, or non-employees upon whom the company depends, not performing at the level of productivity expected.

Qualitative risk assessment   The second component of the risk identification ERM process step, the qualitative risk assessment involves prioritizing the list of potential risks and narrowing them down to the list of key risks. This involves soliciting input from internal personnel regarding the organization's key risks, and a high-level qualitative scoring of each potential key risk's likelihood of occurrence and severity of impact.

Qualitative risk assessment consensus meeting   A meeting where qualitative risk assessment survey participants arrive at a consensus regarding the scoring of potential key risks, and finalize the selection of the key risks.

Rating   A creditworthiness score assigned by a rating agency, which largely determines the company's cost of debt capital.

Rating agency capital   See **Required capital**.

RCD tool   See **Risk categorization and definition tool**.

Regulatory capital   See **Required capital**.

Regulatory risk   See **Legislative/regulatory risk**.

Required capital   For financial services companies, this is the amount of capital that is required to remain on the balance sheet in support of existing business on the books, and cannot be used to support future growth. This can refer to required capital defined by management, by rating agencies, or by regulators.

Reputational risk   A misnomer, since this is not a source of risk, this refers to the intermediate impact of reputation damage, which can be caused by multiple sources of risk, and which may, or may not, trigger financial impacts.

Residual risk exposure   See **Net risk exposure**.

Return-priority decisions   Decisions whose primary goal is related to increasing enterprise value, such as strategic planning.

Risk   Uncertainty which can cause a deviation, either upside or downside, from expected results.

Risk appetite   A management-defined quantitative expression of the level of enterprise risk exposure that is acceptable, at the limit. Also sometimes referred to as risk tolerance. See **Hard limits** and **Soft limits**.

Risk appetite consensus meeting   Meeting at which the ERM committee comes to a consensus definition of risk appetite and risk limits.

Risk appetite document   A document that contains the definitions of risk appetite and risk limits, a comparison of current and historical risk exposures to risk tolerance thresholds at the enterprise level (risk appetite) as well as below enterprise level (risk limits), and the delegation of authority for increasing risk exposures.

Risk capital   See **Required capital**.

Risk categorization and definition   The first component of the risk identification ERM process step, which produces the risk categorization and definition (RCD) tool.

Risk categorization and definition (RCD) tool   A tool with several applications in the ERM process, the RCD tool includes a risk categorization hierarchy (such as risk categories, risk subcategories, and risk divisions), the risks themselves, and a definition of the risk.

Risk correlation The tendency of two risk scenarios to occur together. Some risk scenario pairs are more likely to occur together (positively correlated) than the multiplication of their probabilities would otherwise indicate, some are less likely to occur together (negatively correlated), and some are independent of each other.

Risk culture The extent to which ERM is integrated into decision making (including strategic planning, strategic decisions, tactical decisions, and transactions), business performance analysis, and incentive compensation.

Risk decision making The third step in the ERM process cycle, this involves defining risk appetite and risk limits, managing risk exposure levels to within these tolerance limits, and integrating ERM into strategic planning and other business decision making.

Risk disclosures Communications with external stakeholders, such as shareholders, rating agencies, and regulators, involving ERM information.

Risk event database A database about risk events that have occurred in the company, capturing information such as the originating source of the risk, how the event emerged and unfolded, management actions, and the ultimate financial impacts. This information can be used to enhance the development of risk scenarios, and enhance the entire ERM program through what is often referred to as *risk learnings*.

Risk experts Those who are designated or recognized as risk experts in a particular source of risk and have a routine involvement with the ERM program. These are the executive risk owners (EROs) and the subject matter experts (SMEs).

Risk exploitation Risk exploitation is no different from any routine business decision that simply involves taking on more risk. However, in an ERM context, risk exploitation refers to the conscious decision to take on additional risk exposure, as part of a risk-priority decision either to increase the overall enterprise risk exposure of the firm (closer to the soft limit of risk appetite, for a better overall risk-return profile) or to increase the individual risk exposure (closer to its risk limit) of a specific risk, where the company has a competitive advantage in taking such exposure and expects a profitable risk-return trade-off.

Risk exposure An expression of the amount of risk to which the company is currently exposed, in terms of the likelihood of occurrence and severity of impact.

Risk governance The hierarchical structure of ERM, including the roles and responsibilities, organizational procedures, and policies and procedures that govern the ERM program.

Risk identification The first step in the ERM process cycle, this involves determining the key risks, which represent the biggest potential threats to the company. Risk identification includes risk categorization and definition; qualitative risk assessment; and emerging risk identification.

Risk interactivity The level to which two or more risks scenarios occurring simultaneously impact each other. In the value-based ERM approach, this is captured in three ways: risk scenarios (such as including within one risk scenario the triggering of a separate risk scenario); impact calculations (directly calculating the extent to which the financial impacts exacerbate or offset each other); and correlation adjustments to the likelihood of occurrence. See "Capturing Interactions" in Chapter 5.

Risk learnings Lessons learned from past risk events occurring at the company.

Risk limits A management-defined quantitative expression of the level of risk exposure that is acceptable, at the limit, for exposure concentrations below enterprise level.

Risk management See **Silo risk management**.

Risk management tactics See **Risk mitigation**.

Risk messaging The fourth step in the ERM process cycle, this involves internal risk messaging, which is the integration of ERM into business performance analysis and incentive compensation, and external risk messaging, which is the integration of ERM into communications with shareholders, rating agencies, and regulators.

Risk mitigation Implicit or explicit actions that reduce the likelihood and/or severity of risk events.

Risk-priority decisions Decisions whose primary goal is related to managing the level of risk to an appropriate level (up or down), such as managing enterprise risk exposure to within risk appetite.

Risk quantification The second step in the ERM process cycle, this involves quantifying baseline company value, key risks on an individual basis (producing individual risk exposures) and key risks on an integrated basis (producing enterprise risk exposure).

Risk-ranking criteria   A rule or guideline for combining the qualitative likelihood and severity scores into a single number that is used to rank all the risks identified in the qualitative risk assessment.

Risk scenario   A potential future outcome related to a risk source, such as pessimistic (downside), optimistic (upside), or baseline (no risk occurs).

Rule of significant digits   See **Significant digits**.

Risk tolerance   See **Risk appetite** and **Risk limits**.

Sarbanes-Oxley Act (SOX)   U.S. legislation passed in 2002 in response to a wave of accounting scandals. SOX significantly increased requirements on publicly-traded companies to ensure the accuracy of their financial reports and to have executives attest to this.

Scoring criteria   Guidance provided to qualitative risk assessment survey participants for scoring the likelihood and severity metrics to ensure a consistent form of input from participants.

Seasonal weather risk   Unexpected changes in seasonal weather. This is a strategic risk for companies with products or services for which consumer demand is weather-sensitive. For example, a warm winter or cool summer reduces energy usage, and a cold or rainy summer reduces soda consumption.

SEC   Securities and Exchange Commission.

Severity of impact   The magnitude, or amount, of the deviation from expected, or baseline projections, caused by the occurrence of a risk event.

Shareholder value   A measure of the value of the company from the perspective of shareholders. Management's estimate of shareholder value is company value. The market's estimate of shareholder value is market capitalization. See **Company value** and **Market capitalization**.

Shock scenario   A risk scenario, or scenarios, which result in a deviation from expected or baseline projections.

Significant digits   The number of digits used to express a mathematical result which appropriately reflects the level of accuracy in the number.

Silo risk management   The traditional approach to risk management whereby each source of risk is managed by separate "silo" departments, and which involves a large volume of risks, the vast majority of which are not significant threats to the company.

Simulation   A single picture of future events, where one of the individual risk scenarios (including baseline) is projected to occur for each key risk.

Simulations are run with the ERM model to generate the enterprise risk exposure, which represents the distribution of possible outcomes involving one or more risk events occurring simultaneously.

SME See **Subject matter expert**.

Soft limits Part of the risk appetite and risk limit definitions, soft limits are set as triggers for escalating levels of attention to carefully monitor the risk exposures and ultimately lower them back to within their soft-limit thresholds.

SOX See **Sarbanes-Oxley Act**.

Standard deviation A measure of dispersion away from the mean, or average, value in a distribution, standard deviation, or σ, is calculated as $\sqrt{\dfrac{1}{N}\sum\limits_{i=1}^{N}(x_i - \bar{x})^2}$, where N is the number of data points in the distribution, x_i is a single data point, and $\bar{x}$ is the mean value.

Stochastic risk scenarios Individual risk scenarios, selected using automation—whose setup involves developing a formula to capture the shape of the risk distribution and a random number generator—and which are randomly changed with each run of the ERM model.

Strategic relationships risk Unexpected change in strategic relationships, such as a parent company or joint venture partner.

Strategic risk A category of risks related to unexpected changes in key elements of strategy formulation or execution. These are highly variable by company and must be customized.

Strategy risk Viability of strategy—such as choice of products, distribution channels, markets, or value proposition—does not match expectations. This is highly variable by company and must be customized.

Strengths, weaknesses, opportunities and threats (SWOT) analysis An analysis performed during strategic planning.

Stress test See **Risk scenario**.

Subject matter expert (SME) A recognized internal expert on subject matter related to a particular risk.

Supplier risk Unexpected changes in supplier environment, such as supplier capacity, supplier failure, or change in the cost of goods or services. This also includes unexpected changes in rating agency ratings or regulatory licenses.

SWOT See **Strengths, weaknesses, opportunities and threats (SWOT) analysis**.

Systemic risk The risk that failures in one part of the economic system can spread contagiously to others, resulting in a cascading set of failures threatening to crash the entire system.

Tail scenario Extremely pessimistic scenarios, which are in the "tail" portion of the distribution.

Talent management risk Unexpected change in the ability to maintain the expected level of talent, involving aspects of human resources such as recruiting and retaining employees, succession planning, maintaining critical knowledge of key employees, and labor or producer relations.

Technology risk Technology not performing as expected. Some examples include data security, data privacy, data integrity, capacity, and reliability.

Three core challenges to traditional ERM programs The three main obstacles in traditional ERM programs, which are overcome by a value-based ERM approach: (1) an inability to quantify strategic and operational risks; (2) an unclear definition of risk appetite; and (3) a lack of integration of ERM into decision making.

Uncertainty When there is less than a 100 percent chance that something will occur.

Upside risk event The occurrence of a risk scenario where results are above expected or baseline projections.

Upside risk scenario A risk scenario where results are above expected or baseline projections.

Upside volatility A general reference to the level of upside risk or the range of likelihoods corresponding to results being above baseline projections.

Value See **Company value** and **Shareholder value**.

Value-at-Risk (VaR) A measurement of risk exposure, used in the banking sector, often defined as the maximum amount of capital that can be lost in a single day, within a given small predefined likelihood.

Value-based enterprise risk management Definition 1. A synthesis of ERM and value-based management, providing the missing link between risk and return, transforming ERM into a strategic management approach that enhances strategic planning and other business decision making. Definition 2. A practical yet advanced approach to integrate both risk and return information into strategic planning, business decision making, business performance analysis, incentive compensation, and external communications.

See **Objectives-based entity risk management**.

VaR See **Value-at-Risk**.

Volatility The level to which results are likely to deviate from expected or baseline projections.

Voluntary risk disclosures ERM communications that management chooses to share publicly.

About the Author

SIM SEGAL IS PRESIDENT and founder of SimErgy Consulting, a consulting firm headquartered in Manhattan, providing ERM consulting services and executive education seminars on ERM. Segal has ERM experience with companies in a range of sectors, such as manufacturing, energy, entertainment, technology, services, telecommunications, banking, and insurance, and also with non-corporate entities, such as non-profit organizations and government agencies. Prior to SimErgy, he led ERM consulting practices at Deloitte Consulting, Aon, and Towers Watson.

Segal also serves as an adjunct professor at Columbia Business School, where he teaches an MBA/EMBA course on ERM. He has also led and co-authored ERM research studies.

Segal is often quoted in industry media, such as *Financial Week* and *Treasury & Risk*, as well as mainstream media, such as the *Wall Street Journal*. He has written frequently on the topic of ERM and has had byline articles in major publications, such as *Forbes*, *Corporate Finance Review*, and *American Banker*. Segal is a professional speaker on ERM and has made over 100 speeches on ERM and risk-related topics.

Segal is inaugural chair of the risk committee of the Society of Actuaries (SOA), the largest global actuarial association, leading the design and implementation of their ERM program. He is vice president on the SOA board of directors, and is also a member of the ERM Symposium program committee.

Segal has a B.A. in mathematics and holds two risk-related credentials: He is a Fellow of Society of Actuaries (FSA) and a Chartered Enterprise Risk Analyst (CERA). Segal is one of a select group of ERM experts globally to be awarded the CERA credential based on his "thought leadership and significant contributions to advance the practice of ERM."

Index